LIVINGSTONE'S
MISSIONARY CORRESPONDENCE
1841–1856

D1083531

DAVID LIVINGSTONE

Livingstone's
MISSIONARY
CORRESPONDENCE
1841–1856

Edited with an Introduction
By
I. SCHAPERA

1961
UNIVERSITY OF CALIFORNIA PRESS
BERKELEY AND LOS ANGELES

Published in the
United States of America
By the University of California Press of
Berkeley and Los Angeles, California

★

Published in Great Britain by
Chatto and Windus Ltd
42 William IV Street
London W.C. 2

CONTENTS

v

ILLUSTRATIONS

PLATES

IN TEXT

MAP

LIST OF LETTERS

ABBREVIATIONS, Etc.,
USED IN FOOTNOTES

BIOGRAPHERS of Livingstone are generally cited by name only, e.g. Blaikie, Campbell, Seaver; the titles of their works are given in the list of main references on page 327.

Letters written by Livingstone are cited simply by date and name of addressee, e.g. 17.iii.47 Watt means 'letter from Livingstone to Watt, 17 March 1847'.

Other abbreviations commonly used include the following:

Apprenticeship   Apprenticeship at Kuruman: journals and letters of Robert and Mary Moffat, 1820–1828; ed. Schapera

Chamberlin   *Some Letters from Livingstone*, ed. D. Chamberlin

D. L.   David Livingstone

D. N. B.   Concise Dictionary of National Biography, I. To 1900

Fam. Letters   David Livingstone: Family Letters 1841–1856; ed. Schapera

JRGS   Journal of the Royal Geographical Society

LMS   London Missionary Society

Miss. Labours   Missionary Labours and Scenes in Southern Africa, by Robert Moffat

MS. Journal   Livingstone's Journal for 1853–6 (unpublished)

Oswell   William Cotton Oswell, by W. E. Oswell

P. P. England   British Parliamentary Papers (cited by year and official reference number)

Private J.   Livingstone's Private Journals 1851–1853; ed. Schapera

Register   London Missionary Society: *A Register of Missionaries, Deputations, ets., from 1796 to 1923*; fourth ed., 1923

Report   [Annual] *Report of the Directors ... of ... The London Missionary Society*

S.A.Miss. Report   [Annual] *Report of the Missions in South Africa, and of Auxiliaries, [of] the London Missionary Society*

Travels   Missionary Travels and Researches in South Africa, by D. Livingstone

INTRODUCTION

(i)

THE letters published in this book fall into three groups. The largest consists of those written by David Livingstone (or, in one instance, on his behalf) to the Directors of the London Missionary Society while he was still in their service as a missionary in southern Africa. They were usually addressed personally to the Society's Foreign Secretary at its headquarters (Mission House, Blomfield Street, Finsbury, London). The office, during the period they cover, was at first held jointly by Revs. Arthur Tidman (1792–1868) and Joseph John Freeman (1794–1851), and from 1846 onward, when Freeman became Home Secretary, by Tidman alone. The Directors' replies, dictated and signed by the Foreign Secretary, comprise the second group; the originals sent to Livingstone do not seem to have been preserved, but copies (made by means of a copying-press) are available in the Society's letter-books. Thirdly, there are the letters written by Livingstone, with one exception in and after 1852, to Rev. William Thompson (1811–89), Agent at Cape Town since June 1850 for the South African Missions of the Society. Thompson's replies, if indeed still extant, are not in the L.M.S. archives.

This correspondence is a basic source of information about what was, or should have been, Livingstone's main activity during the period of his first residence in Africa: his work as a missionary to the heathen. For the whole of that period he was employed by the L.M.S., and like all his colleagues in the field he was under standing instructions to report periodically to its Board of Directors.

'The Directors expect that you will write to them regularly, at least twice every year, communicating all the information in your power relative to your operations, and laying before them any circumstances, or subjects, to which it may be necessary for them to devote their attention. . . . State freely and fully your trials and difficulties, as well as your encouragements and success. . . . Maintain that sacred control over your imagination and feelings which, while it shall not allow you to withhold what is due to the Directors and the friends of the Society, shall preserve you from a mode of representation adapted to mislead, by producing an impression in any respect at variance with truth and fact. . . . Consider your correspondence with the Directors as an important duty, which must neither be neglected nor performed in a careless and unbusiness-like manner. To avoid this, maintain strict regularity, and do not, unless under very urgent circumstances, put off writing till you are obliged to do it in a hurry.'[1]

Livingstone was a voluminous correspondent, who needed neither encouragement nor exhortation to write. Several hundreds of his other letters from southern Africa survive, addressed to relatives, personal friends, and a varied assortment of acquaintances. In these he often refers to his missionary experiences, hopes, and disappointments. But it is above all in what he wrote to the officers of the L.M.S. that we should expect to find the fullest account of what he was doing, the methods he employed, the progress he was making, and the obstacles he encountered; and it is in their replies, too, that we should expect to find some indication of how those by whom he was employed regarded his efforts and achievement.

Comparison of his letters to the Directors with those written by his fellow-missionaries shows that he was in many ways unique. He had received a better education than most of his colleagues, had far greater intellectual curiosity and a wide range of scientific interests, and despite his statement in *Missionary Travels* (p. 8) that he 'would rather cross the African continent again than undertake to write another book', he did while still in Bechuanaland make several ventures into authorship, usually in articles on missionary and political topics. He read extensively, spending on books and periodicals money he could ill afford; the sack of his premises at Kolobeng made him lament the destruction of 'a fine medical library, and many good works on general subjects. The former was my pride, and a great comfort.'[2] His literary bent, which apparently none of his fellows shared (beyond engaging in Biblical and other religious translations), is reflected in the character of his letters. He wrote vigorously and lucidly, and even at his lengthiest was seldom irrelevant; he avoided the pious meditations and edifying discourses so often indulged in by Moffat and others, enhanced the effect of his narratives and descriptions by judicious compression, and, as in the famous sentence, 'The end of the geographical feat is but the beginning of the missionary enterprise',[3] was obviously not afraid to risk turning a fine phrase.

It is rather in content than style, however, that his letters are most distinctive. This applies especially to his frequent comments on missionary aims and policy, comments of a kind rarely attempted by his colleagues. He was well aware that the natives among whom he worked could not be converted rapidly, or, as he himself put it, that 'Time

---

[1] *Letter of Instructions*, &c [n.d.], pp. 42–4.   [2] See below, p. 218.
[3] See below, p. 303.

seems to be an essential element in African success';[1] and in contemplating his own evident lack of success he repeatedly sought consolation in the words of Isaiah, 'He that believeth shall not make haste'. But, unlike Moffat for example, he was nevertheless not prepared to labour indefinitely at one place, and he apparently thought it strange to be asked by the Boers 'why I did not remain with the Bakwains till they were all converted'.[2] He did indeed once write to Tidman, 'If I were to follow my own inclinations, they would lead me to settle down quietly with the Bakwains or some other small tribe, and devote some of my time to my children. But', he added significantly, 'Providence seems to call me to the regions beyond.'[3] To him, the essential duty of the missionary was 'to preach the gospel to every creature'. 'We ought to give all if possible a chance', he wrote to his friend Watt, 'and not spend an age on one tribe or people', and to Freeman he remarked, 'To me those who never heard the gospel are greater objects of compassion than those who have heard it for seven years and rejected it'.[4]

It is this conception of the missionary's task ('Go ye therefore, and teach all nations') that accounts for Livingstone's repeated and outspoken criticism of L.M.S. policy in the Cape Colony, where mission stations were being maintained, often in competition with other Societies, long after local churches had been established. To him — but to few of his colleagues — such a policy seemed wasteful of both personnel and money. Once a church had got going, he contended, it should become self-governing and support its own minister, and the missionaries sent out and paid by the Society should then proceed to still heathen tribes. He would not even always concede that a missionary should stay at his post until a church had been founded. 'I am more and more convinced', he wrote to Tidman in March 1847, 'that in order to [effect] a permanent settlement of the gospel in any part, the natives must be taught to relinquish their reliance on Europe. An onward movement ought to be made, whether men will hear or whether they will forbear. I tell my Bakwains that if spared ten years I shall move on to the regions beyond them. Now is their opportunity, and if they do not learn the guilt will rest on their own heads.'[5] Two months earlier he had written to Watt: 'As soon as I can leave them under native instruction, forward I go.'[6] He had then been with the BaKwena for little more than a year.

His conviction that the 'word of God' should be spread as widely and

---

[1] Unsigned article in *Brit. Quarterly Review*, xiv, (August) 1851, p. 113.
[2] See below, p. 129.   [3] See below, p. 178.
[4] 1.xii.51 Dyke; 29.ix.51 Watt; and below, p. 150.   [5] See below, p. 108.
[6] 17.i.47 Watt.

rapidly as possible helps to explain his enthusiasm for native evangelists or 'teachers'. The smallness and uneven distribution of the population in Bechuanaland (and only he considered those facts important) made it both inadvisable and costly to employ many European missionaries. Such men were more urgently needed in other parts of the world; and the mere news that the Bechuana Mission was being reinforced from England was enough to distress him.[1] Far better was the extensive use of native teachers, to work continuously at outlying villages under the periodical supervision of a European located at some strategic centre. Such teachers were not only much cheaper to employ; in some ways they were even more effective than Europeans, since Christianity when preached by them was devoid of that 'peculiar strangeness which always clings to foreigners in every country'.[2]

During his first few years in Bechuanaland he therefore kept urging the Directors (who on this matter thought as he did) to make more provision for 'native agency'. He also appealed for help to some of his own friends in Scotland and elsewhere. But when funds did become available he discovered a lack of suitably-qualified men for the work. To remedy this he suggested to his colleagues the establishment of a training institution. Moffat and other senior missionaries effectively opposed the suggestion, but several years later, when he repeated it to the Directors, it was adopted in the form he recommended.[3]

Missionary policy generally, and native agency in particular, are topics that feature prominently in Livingstone's letters to the Directors. The views he held about both are reflected also in his own movements. He reached Kuruman from England on 31 July 1841, and it served as his base until the end of 1843. During that time he made four lengthy trips into the interior, each of roughly two to five months. From the beginning of 1844 until April 1851 he had his own mission station, first among the BaKgatla at Mabotsa (1844–5) and then among the Ba-Kwena at Chonwane (1845–7) and Kolobeng (1847–51). During that time he paid at least four visits to tribes farther East, and also went twice to Ngamiland in the distant North-West. In 1851 he made his first successful expedition to the MaKololo of what is now North-Western Rhodesia. This, in effect, marked the end of his connection with Bechuanaland. He returned south at the end of the year and proceeded to Cape Town to despatch his wife and children to England (April 1852). Then, after five months' delay at Kuruman (until December), owing to the disturbances caused farther north by the Boers, he went again to the MaKololo, explored the valley of the upper Zambesi, and

[1] See below, p. 43.   [2] 2.xii.41 Naismith.   [3] See below, pp. 100, 110.

journeyed to Luanda in search of a feasible route to the West Coast. Not finding one, he retraced his steps and continued right across the continent to Quelimane on the East Coast, which he reached in May 1856. From there he sailed back to England.

In his journeys to the MaKololo, and subsequently, he was seeking a healthy and accessible site for a new mission station beyond the borders of Bechuanaland and the reach of the Boers. But during the two and a half years that he was based on Kuruman he spent about thirteen months on excursions into the interior, and during the seven and a quarter years that he was stationed with the BaKgatla and BaKwena he was away from home for nearly a third of the time — in 1849 alone, as he informed Freeman,[1] for eight months. In both time and distance his journeys greatly exceeded those of his fellow-missionaries; and, as his letters show, this was due primarily to his belief in the value of 'extending the gospel' by means of itineracy and the placing of native agents. He did not succeed in the second objective, mainly because he offended the Boers by his speech and conduct. Edwards and Inglis, stationed inside the territory of the Boers, were less ambitious and aggressive, and for several years worked there with relatively little interference. But when the time came, they too protested vigorously at the enslavement of native children captured in war — and after a farcical trial by the Boer authorities were promptly expelled.

Because he travelled so extensively, Livingstone's letters usually contain much more information than those of his colleagues about the country and its inhabitants. He was of course writing primarily for the Directors, so that his observations on such topics as climate and topography, tribal customs and politics, local products, and the treatment of natives by Boers, were all related to problems of missionary enterprise. Even the lengthy descriptions he gives of Barotseland and Angola, notably in his letter of 12 October 1855, should be regarded essentially as intelligence reports, designed to help the Directors assess the prospects for the commencement of a new Mission. That those descriptions are also of great scientific interest and value was due only partly to their dealing with regions hitherto unknown; it was Livingstone's own remarkable ability and thoroughness that made him such an outstanding informant.

In contrast, his reports about his own stations lack much of the detail found in the letters of, say, Ross, Edwards and Inglis. Like the last two, he had indeed little to show for his efforts; but if we really want to know what he did and what went on at Mabotsa, Chonwane, and Kolobeng,

[1] See below, p. 139.

we must read what he wrote to his relatives and friends, especially Moffat, and not his letters to the Directors. Even Sechele's relapse, sorrowfully recounted at length to Moffat, is mentioned to Tidman almost by way of afterthought.[1] It is hardly surprising that Tidman on one occasion wrote back: 'Your recent references to the affairs of the Kolobeng Station have been so meagre as to afford no topic for remark.'[2]

Of Livingstone's personal affairs these letters also do not tell us much more than was relevant to his vocational activities. His remarks about his marriage, wife, and children, are for example few and mostly brief — though one would hardly have expected to find included among them the problem of 'frequent pregnancies'.[3] The repeated attacks of fever he suffered on his transcontinental journey are necessarily given some prominence, and our respect for that great achievement is heightened by his modest accounts of the many severe hardships he then suffered. His financial concerns are also mentioned from time to time, often to explain why he had overdrawn on his salary. He was certainly not extravagant, except perhaps on books and scientific equipment, but his expenses were heavy. He had to import all such goods as clothing, groceries, utensils, and medicines, from England or the Cape Colony, and, owing to the great distances involved, by the time they reached him their cost had usually been more than doubled by the price of transport. He found his salary of £100 barely sufficient for maintaining himself and his family, and his removal to Chonwane and then Kolobeng entailed extra expenditure on house-building. But the main burden was due to the cost of travel — hire of servants and guides, wear and tear of wagons, and replacements of oxen (including those fatally bitten by tsetse). Had it not been largely for very generous assistance from others, especially Oswell, he could hardly have paid his way; but, on the other hand, had he not travelled so extensively he would not have needed to spend as much as he did. Most of his fellow-missionaries were no better off than he, yet their letters do not reveal as much financial anxiety.

About his fellow-missionaries, except Moffat, he is rarely complimentary in writing to the Directors. He not only expressed contempt for their activities, he evidently also despised them as persons. He himself was highly sensitive to criticism; the very long letter in which he so minutely reviews the 'charges' (mostly trivial) made against him by Edwards reveals an astonishing touchiness.[4] But apparently it seldom occurred to him to allow for the human failings of others. He started by liking and even admiring Inglis and Edwards; he ended by declaring it

---

[1] *Fam. Letters*, ii, pp. 29–30, 41–3; and below, p. 130.
[2] See below, p. 168.   [3] See below, pp. 190, 194.   [4] See below, pp. 65–80.

'a mere waste of life to labour near them' and pointedly hinted that the Society would do well to get rid of them.[1] He was on bad terms with Ross ever since their voyage together from England, and Ashton he considered a coward. He may well have had good reason for all this, but it is difficult to believe that he alone was wholly irreproachable. Nor did he think it improper to disparage them to the Directors, and when Tidman reproved him for some remarks considered uncalled for, he reacted as if he were an injured innocent.[2] In his letters to Thompson he is similarly scornful of Bishop Gray, Dr Robertson, and others. Such adverse comments, directed chiefly against fellow-clergymen, suggest that he was apt to be offended by whoever of them did not share his own views and ideals.

Thompson was obviously not one of those clergymen. He and Livingstone were of nearly the same age, and from the time of their meeting again at Cape Town in 1852 Livingstone seems to have considered him a congenial spirit, who could be addressed much more freely than the Directors. The letters written to him are familiar in tone, occasionally even playful. They do sometimes repeat information sent to the Directors, but contain much additional matter about Livingstone's activities and plans, opinions and problems. Because of Thompson's residence and official position, they also deal fairly often with events and personalities in the Cape Colony seldom discussed with the Directors.

The Directors' replies show that they had a high opinion of Livingstone's abilities, and from the beginning encouraged his plans of pushing forward into the interior. They were gratified by his enthusiasm for native agency, valued though they did not always agree with his views on 'missionary operations', and financially treated him more generously than some of his biographers suggest. He was not as scrupulous as they might have hoped in complying with their wishes. He never did supply the information for which they asked about his own native teachers, and his blunt answer, 'I cannot promise to keep a journal',[3] was a curt rejection not only of a well-meant suggestion but of an obligation actually imposed upon him (and all other missionaries) in the printed *Letter of Instructions*. They naturally resented his implied charge of maladministration in their conduct of the South African Missions, and deplored the way in which he tended to write about his colleagues. But although they occasionally had to rebuke him, they were far more often able to express sincere appreciation of the work he was doing. He certainly could not complain that he was given neither approbation nor, if

[1] See below, p. 202.   [2] See below, p. 231.   [3] See below, p. 204.

need be, sympathy; and he could hardly have wished for a more generous tribute than Tidman paid him at the annual meeting of the Royal Geographical Society in May 1850, when receiving on behalf 'of my excellent friend' the Royal Premium awarded for the discovery of Lake Ngami: 'He is a man of great self-denial and of singular intrepidity, combined with sound discretion. His benevolent character and blameless life make him regarded by the natives as their friend and benefactor; and as a Christian Missionary, sustaining this honourable consistency, he travels without fear where the face of a white man has not been seen.'[1]

Extracts from his letters, occasionally prefaced by complimentary expressions, were often published in the Society's monthly *Chronicle*. (His colleagues in Bechuanaland did not always regard this with altruistic pleasure. As he wrote to his mother in 1845: 'Perhaps you were gratified to see my letters quoted in the Chronicle. In some minds they produced bitter envy, and if it were in my power I should prevent the publication of any in future.'[2]) So, too, even before he went to Lake Ngami his journeys into the interior were thought worthy of favourable mention in the Society's annual Reports. The discovery of the Lake received special prominence. In part, at least, this was due to the enthusiasm with which leading geographers hailed the news. Their publicly-expressed appreciation not only of Livingstone himself but of the valuable aid to exploration rendered by missionaries in general was found 'very gratifying'.[3] Undoubtedly the Directors from now on thought still more highly of him because they realized that his scientific achievements effectively advertized the sacred cause he was serving.

However, that was hardly the main reason for their gratification. As men dedicated to the diffusion of Christianity they welcomed the prospects opened up by Livingstone's discoveries for the establishment of new Missions in the interior of the dark continent. In their annual Reports they more than once referred to their hope 'that his labours may prepare the way for the introduction of the Gospel to the multitudes by whom that vast country, hitherto unknown, is inhabited.'[4] They undertook to support his wife and children in England so that he might be free to carry on his explorations 'devoid of family cares'; and, at least up to August 1855, there is no suggestion in their letters that they considered his plans as being 'connected only remotely with the spread of the Gospel'.[5] On the contrary, he was fully justified in believing, from the way they wrote to and about him, that they approved whole-

---

[1] *JRGS*, xx, 1850, p. xxxii; *Chronicle*, xiv, 1850, p. 159.
[2] *Fam. Letters*, i, p. 121.
[4] *Report*, 1854, p. 11; cf. *ibid.*, 1852, p. 15; 1853, p. 15.
[3] See below, p. 145.
[5] See below, p. 277.

heartedly of what he was doing; nor, in turn, was he being merely polite when, having decided to leave the L.M.S., he stated to Thompson: 'The Directors have always treated me well, and I shall always remember you all with affection.'[1]

(ii)

Livingstone's views on the slave trade and 'legitimate commerce', often mentioned in his later letters, have been dealt with admirably in Professor Coupland's introduction to Chamberlin.[2] His relations with the Boers, another recurrent topic, are discussed in detail elsewhere.[3] It accordingly seems needless to comment on either again. There are, however, certain other aspects of his missionary career that call for some notice here, partly because of what he himself published about them, and partly because they have been misrepresented by some of his uncritical biographers.

The first is a relatively minor point, except for what it suggests about Livingstone's character. In *Travels* he states (p. 9) that on arriving at Kuruman from England he stayed there no longer 'than was necessary to recruit the oxen, which were pretty well tired by the long journey from Algoa Bay', and then 'proceeded, in company with another missionary, to the Bakuéna or Bakwain country.' To Tidman he wrote similarly in May 1856: 'The Directors wished me to endeavour to carry the gospel to the tribes North of the Kuruman. Having remained at that station sufficient time only to recruit my oxen, I proceeded in the direction indicated.'[4]

The obvious implication is that he had already determined on the journey, and undertook it as soon as his oxen allowed him. In fact, he remained at Kuruman for over eleven weeks before starting (Oswell, in 1849, reached Kolobeng 'on the 25th or 26th of May', and within a week was on his way to Ngamiland with Livingstone[5]); nor could one deduce from the statements quoted that the journey was originally planned by Edwards, who delayed it in order to await Ross and Livingstone, and then suggested that one of them might go with him.[6] As Livingstone himself wrote to Freeman at the time (September 1841): 'I purpose accompanying Br[other] Edwards in his journey to the interior, as I am informed by the bretheren who are best able to judge it will be advantageous for me in many respects.'[7]

---

[1] See below, p. 323.
[2] Chamberlin, *Some Letters from Livingstone*, 1940, pp. xvi–xix.
[3] Schapera, 'Livingstone and the Boers', *African Affairs*, lix, 1960, pp. 144–56.
[4] See below, p. 315.   [5] *Oswell*, i, p. 195.
[6] See below, p. 3n.   [7] See below, p. 3.

The object of that journey was to visit the BaKwena; but, as Living-stone indicated in contemporary letters to friends, before proceeding to the BaKwena Edwards and he first went to the BaKgatla near Mabotsa. Subsequently, when dealing with the complaints made against him by Edwards, he told Tidman that the journey had been 'in a totally different direction' from the country of the BaKgatla.[1] He was either unusually forgetful — or unwilling to adduce anything that might entitle Edwards to share in the credit for starting the Mission at Mabotsa.

Again, in November 1852 Livingstone wrote to Tidman: 'I can scarcely believe that the Directors are totally oblivious of the fact that, for the sake of peace, I yielded up a splendid station and good prospects.'[2] The reference is to his removal from Mabotsa, and the implication (accepted at face value by all his major biographers) is that he moved away only because Edwards had quarrelled with him. It would obviously have been difficult, as the Directors themselves conceded, for him and Edwards to remain together at Mabotsa thereafter, and Edwards's out-burst may well have precipitated his action. But it was not the initial cause of that action. The quarrel took place about the end of May 1845, immediately after Livingstone's return from a long visit to Kuruman (where he had gone to be married). Yet in January he had written (from Kuruman) to a friend in England: 'At Mabotsa matters go on pretty well. But I don't expect to remain there long. The sphere is too small for two missionaries. As I am the younger I purpose to go on to the Bakwains of either Bubi or Sechele.'[3] And to Tidman he reports having mentioned at a meeting of the District Committee in February (which Edwards did not attend) his desire 'to extend missionary labour to another tribe'.[4] But, although frankness was a quality he claimed to admire, he had not told Edwards of what he was thinking; and Edwards, whatever his shortcomings, can hardly be considered impudent ('cool' is Livingstone's adjective) for remarking 'that had he only known of my *previous intentions*[5] he might have waived all matters of difference between us.'[6]

Livingstone's propensity to recall events differently from the way in which they occurred is seen also in the reasons he gives for abandoning his mission among the BaKwena. To Thompson he wrote in September 1855 that 'the principal one was determined hostility to the require-ments of the gospel'.[7] Three years earlier, soon after the Boer attack on

---

[1] See below, p. 76.
[2] See below, p. 231.
[3] 28.i.45 Pyne (quoted below, p. 68).
[4] See below, p. 68.
[5] My italics.
[6] See below, p. 79.
[7] See below, p. 286.

Dimawê, he had similarly written to Tidman: 'The Bakwains, Wanketse and Bakhatla have wilfully rejected the gospel, and have brought
on themselves the just judgements of God by their unbelief.'[1]

While still among the BaKwena, he said nothing about wilful rejection or determined hostility. On the contrary, the people were 'uniformly kind and respectful' towards himself, 'attended . . . perseveringly
on our instructions', 'have increased in knowledge since our residence
among them', and were even observing the Sabbath as a day of rest. 'I
do not believe', he wrote in September 1849, 'there is in the present or
past state of the people the least cause for despondency.'[2]

'The failure of the mission' (his own words) he immediately after
leaving the BaKwena ascribed primarily to the combined effects of continuous famine and recurrent threats of Boer aggression. 'The Bakwains
promised fairly', he wrote in October 1851, 'and I by no means give up
the hope that they will recieve the gospel; but they have been so pinched
by hunger and badgered by the Boers they could not or rather they had
too good an excuse for not attending to instruction.'[3] In *Travels*, as in
his Cambridge lectures, he suggests that the hostility of the Boers, to
himself as well as the BaKwena, was what finally made him resolve 'to
go into the country beyond'.[4] In his letters and journal two different
reasons are given: the decision of the BaKwena to move from Kolobeng
'to some other part of their country, . . . where native corn may be
raised', and his own desire to work in the densely-populated regions he
had discovered beyond Lake Ngami. His first expedition to the Lake,
incidentally, had already been mooted to Oswell in April 1848,[5] eight
months before his clash with the Boer leaders and their subsequent
threat to expel him from Kolobeng.

It is at least certain that the 'wilful' refusal of the BaKwena to embrace Christianity was not originally the 'principal' or even a significant
motive for his leaving them. And to describe the results of the Boer
attack upon them as 'the just judgements of God' for 'their unbelief'
seems both harsh and narrow-minded. Moffat when among the Ba-
Kwena in 1854 actually told them that God 'may yet punish' them and
the BaKgatla 'more than he has done, for having rejected the Gospel.'
To this Sechele's brother Kgosidintsi retorted by asking how that could
apply to some of the tribes in the Transvaal, which although never even
offered the gospel had also been 'destroyed and enslaved' by the Boers.[6]

[1] See below, p. 233.　　[2] See below, p. 138.　　[3] See below, p. 189.
[4] *Travels*, pp. 44–5; *Lectures* (2nd ed., 1860), pp. 151, 177, 182.
[5] *Oswell*, i, p. 171. The date (10.iv.48) of Livingstone's letter is not mentioned by
Oswell; it is fixed by a reference in MacQueen, *JRGS*, 1850, p. 239.
[6] *Matabele Journals* (ed. Wallis), 1945, i, pp. 378–9.

Some of Livingstone's own colleagues were critical of his work among the BaKwena. Freeman, after visiting Kolobeng at the end of 1849, reported that 'the apparent results' of his labours 'are very limited'. Ashton condemned his abandonment of Sechele without first informing the District Committee of his intentions and 'at the same time requesting that some provision should be made for his station'. Even Moffat shared such views. 'Notwithstanding the importance of Mr Livingstone's discoveries', he wrote to Tidman in July 1852, 'we never approved of Sechele's having been abandoned, just, too, at the very time he required most the watchful eye & encouraging voice of his Missionary.' And he continued, referring to Livingstone's paper in *The British Quarterly Review* about L.M.S. policy, 'His remarks on Native teachers are exaggerated, & some very erroneous. He has had what no Missionary had, two native teachers on his station, the two best, the very pick of all. And as to anything that they have accomplished, we are of opinion he would have been better without them.'[1]

My final comment is about Livingstone's decision to leave the L.M.S. The immediate stimulus was unquestionably the Directors' letter of August 1855, in which 'I am told by Dr Tidman that it is not likely they can afford to begin a new mission in an unknown field'.[2] Livingstone had already had misgivings that this might happen, and was prepared for it. As early as September 1853, just before starting his Angolan journey, he had written to his family in Scotland that 'if the Society should object' to his plans 'I would consider it my duty to withdraw from it';[3] and in September 1855, before setting out from Dinyanti for the East Coast, he had written to Mrs Moffat: 'The contrast between the Colonial missions and the world to the North, East & West of this makes my heart sore. In the one case the people are crammed, in the other starved. If it is decided that this field be left still and I must go to the South, my missionary carreer will be ended'.[4]

His decision was therefore not made on the spur of the moment, though, as he indicated to both Tidman and Thompson, he was deeply hurt that what he had done, always with the approval of the Directors, should now be labelled 'plans connected only remotely with the spread of the Gospel'.[5] But the Directors had also said that they 'much wish to confer with me on the subject' when he reached England.[6] The outcome of the discussions then held was that the Board, on his advice,

---

[1] Letters to Tidman from Freeman, 2.ii.50; Ashton, 14.ix.52; Moffat, vii.52.
[2] 27.vi.55 Gabriel (quoted by Seaver, p. 272).
[3] *Fam. Letters*, ii, p. 228.   [4] *Fam. Letters*, ii, p. 272.
[5] See below, pp. 217, 314, 318.   [6] 27.vi.55 Gabriel (Seaver, p. 272).

agreed to start Missions among both the MaKololo and the MaTebele. They decided also, in view of their financial position, to launch a special appeal for funds to meet the cost. The appeal, for £5,000, was first published in March (1857). By the end of the year £6,400 had been contributed,[1] and plans for the two Missions were well in hand.

In the event, Livingstone did not join the 'Makololo Mission', though it represented the fulfilment of his efforts and desires of the past few years. The Board's Southern Committee had recommended (22 January) 'That . . . Mr. Moffat be invited to commence the proposed new Mission among the Matabele', and 'That a Missionary be appointed to assist Dr. Livingston in the organization of the intended Mission among the Makololo.' Dr Edwin Smith argues, from the form of the wording, that Livingstone's role in the Makololo Mission was to be limited to 'organization'; and that when on 12 January he had met and addressed the Directors (who then asked the Southern Committee 'to confer further' with him) he was already determined 'to embark upon another course'.[2] The minutes of that meeting record him as saying that, 'in his judgment', the removal of the MaKololo to 'the most healthy and eligible position for the establishment of a Mission' (viz., the Batoka Plateau) 'would be promoted by the residence of himself and Mrs. Livingston amongst them'; but, Dr Smith maintains, 'he must have been misunderstood, since at this time he had decided not to join the mission.' 'I have found nothing in the records', he concludes, 'that indicates Livingstone was to have charge of the Kololo mission.'[3]

The facts do not support that conclusion. In their annual Report, submitted to the Society's general Meeting on 14 May, the Directors included a Resolution said to have been adopted at a special meeting of Town and Country Directors on 10 February (a meeting at which Livingstone was present, and in whose recommendations 'he expressed his entire concurrence'). The opening words of the Resolution are: 'That two new Mission Stations should be opened — the one among the Makololo, north of the Zambese, *under the charge of Dr. Livingston*, assisted by another Missionary; and the other among the Matabele...'.[4]

---

[1] *Chronicle*, xxi, 1857, pp. 55, 276.

[2] E. W. Smith, *Great Lion of Bechuanaland ... Roger Price*, 1957, pp. 24, 28; LMS Archives (Board Minutes).

[3] LMS Board Minutes; Smith, *op. cit.*, p. 24, notes 5, 6.

[4] *Report*, 1857, p. 29; *Chronicle*, (June) 1857, p. 141; my italics. The minutes of the special meeting of 10 February do not in fact contain the wording of the Resolution given in *Report*, but say merely 'That in accordance with the recommendation of the Southern Committee' [quoted above] 'efforts be forthwith made with a view to the establishment of Missions upon the North and South of the river Zambesi.'

Livingstone attended the Annual General Meeting, to which he delivered a long address;[1] and nothing in what he said suggests that he did not agree with the wording of the Resolution. Together with the rest of the Report, it was 'approved and adopted' unanimously. In the Society's *Chronicle* for July, moreover, the allegedly misunderstood statement about the residence of himself and his wife among the Ma-Kololo (first published in the March number) was repeated.[2]

As late as the middle of May, therefore, and even afterwards, the members of the L.M.S., and all others who responded to its appeal for funds, must certainly have understood that Livingstone was to head the Makololo Mission. But by that time the negotiations that resulted in his appointment as British Consul in East Africa and leader of the Zambesi Expedition of 1858–63 were already well under way. An approach on his behalf, apparently initiated by Murchison, had been made at the beginning of the year to the Foreign Secretary (Lord Clarendon); on 26 January Livingstone himself submitted through Murchison a formal offer of service to Clarendon; on 15 April he wrote to Murchison: 'I have been thinking since we parted that it may be better to defer the application for an appointment till nearer the period of my departure. I fear if I got it now my friends of the Mission House will make use of the fact to damage my character in the public estimation by saying I have forsaken the Mission for higher pay. I have refused to take any more from them, and wish to do my future work in as unostentatious [a] way as possible'; and on 13 May he wrote to Maclear: 'I am not yet fairly on with the Government but am nearly quite off with the Society, though I don't mean to be a whit less a missionary than heretofore. I shall not accept the Government appointment if it trammels my operations, but Lord Clarendon does not wish to do so.'[3]

Unless we are cynical enough to believe that Livingstone's name was being deliberately though falsely used to attract contributions to the appeal, and that he himself connived at the deceit, we must assume that the Directors meant what they reported to the Annual Meeting, and had no reason to believe that he would not be in charge of the Makololo Mission. The only charitable explanation is that since the negotiations with Clarendon had by then not been concluded (the formal appointment was not made until February 1858), Livingstone did not yet feel

---

[1] *Chronicle*, (June) 1857, pp. 151–5.

[2] *Chronicle*, 1857, pp. 54 (March), 162 (July).

[3] Letters to Murchison (15.iv.57) and Maclear (13.v.57) quoted by J. P. R. Wallis, *The Zambesi Expedition of David Livingstone*, 1956, pp. xxiii, xxiv. For the negotiations with Clarendon, cf. *ibid.*, pp. xxiii–xxix; E. W. Smith, *op. cit.*, pp. 26–8; Seaver, *David Livingstone*, pp. 296–316.

free to communicate his change of plan to the Directors. The records of the L.M.S. suggest that apparently they did not become officially aware of it until as late as 27 October, when, at a meeting of the Board, Tidman read a letter from him stating that 'although he declined to receive pecuniary support from this Society, and would probably in future sustain some relation to the British Government, he would, there was every reason to believe, render the Directors his best assistance in the establishment of a Mission north of the Zambesi.'[1] The Board's reactions are not mentioned in the minutes. But Livingstone had already indicated his intention in *Travels*, where he announced that 'various reasons induce me to withdraw from pecuniary dependence on any Society.'[2] Since the book was published on 10 November, those words must have been written some time before. There is obviously need for further research into the exact time and method of his resignation from the L.M.S.; the records in the Society's archives do not provide a conclusive answer to the problem.

I have referred in some detail to these controversial matters, because a careful reading of Livingstone's correspondence indicates that the generally-accepted story of his missionary career is at times more pious than accurate. He was too great a man to need being treated in such a way; and the comments I have made are designed primarily to direct the attention of future biographers to aspects of his character and history that seem to call for re-examination.

(iii)

Of the fifty-five letters in this book written by Livingstone, eleven have never before been published, and only fourteen of the others have already appeared elsewhere in full. Extracts from the remainder occur in the L.M.S. *Chronicle*, Chamberlin's edition of Livingstone's letters, and the works of such biographers as Blaikie, Campbell, and Seaver; they are listed in the text, at the head of each letter, only if fairly substantial and taken directly from the original MS. Of the Directors' letters, nine have also never before been published, and the remaining three have appeared only in the form of extracts.

As in my other editions of Livingstone's writings,[3] all the letters are given here in full, and with the original spelling; but the punctuation has been normalized, and long paragraphs subdivided. For the reader's convenience I have also grouped the letters into eleven chapters accord-

---

[1] Board Minutes. The letter read by Tidman is not in the LMS archives.
[2] *Travels*, p. 677.
[3] *Family Letters* (1959); *Livingstone's Private Journals, 1851–1853* (1960).

ing to period or topic; the letters themselves, however, appear throughout in strictly chronological order, those from the Directors being
inserted wherever appropriate.

I am deeply grateful to the present Directors of the L.M.S. for
allowing me to undertake this work, and for free access to the rich store
of material in the Society's archives. I am indebted also to the National
Archives of Rhodesia and Nyasaland for a microfilm copy of, and permission to reproduce, Letter 63. Miss Irene Fletcher, librarian of the
L.M.S., has, as on previous occasions, been consistently most helpful
and obliging; without her invaluable cooperation I would have been
unable to explain many of Livingstone's allusions to persons and events
connected with the affairs of the Society. Mr D. H. Varley, Chief
Librarian of the South African Public Library, Cape Town, generously
sought out and procured for me copies of letters and other material in
old South African newspapers. For minor, but equally appreciated,
assistance I am indebted to Mr Robert R. Barr (Secretary of Oberlin
College, Ohio); the Director of the Trigonometrical Survey, Pretoria;
and the Secretary of the Public Records Office, London.

I

FIRST JOURNEYS AND IMPRESSIONS

1. To J. J. FREEMAN
23 September 1841

[LMS 16. Received 14 February 1842]

Kuruman
23rd Septr. 1841

Dear Sir,

That I might be able in my first communication to inform the Directors respecting my prospects of usefulness in the cause of Christ amongst the Heathen, I have delayed announcing my arrival at Kuruman for a period of nearly two months. We came hither on the 31st July,[1] and received a most cordial welcome from the bretheren Hamilton and Edwards.[2] The warmth of it awakened in my bosom feelings of fraternal affection to both, and these subsequent intercourse has tended much to increase.

As it is in accordance with my own long cherished desire, and the intentions of the Directors, that my chief energies should be directed to the evangelization of the tribes in the interior, the mode in which this can best be effected has become a topic of intense interest in many conversations we have had together. The decision of the Directors, from judgements matured by long experience, is that an extensive native agency is the most efficient mode of spreading the gospel. In this decision most of the missionaries I have seen fully concur.

The question therefore, where are these to be got for the extensive field beyond us, has become to me one of peculiar interest. Whilst in England I had formed the opinion that great things might be done by means of this Mission — that it might be formed into a sort of focus, from which might diverge in every direction the beams of Divine truth. But after having personally inspected most of the surrounding localities

---

[1] Sailing from England on 8 December 1840, D. L. had reached Cape Town on 15 March 1841, and Port Elizabeth a month later. He had then travelled overland by ox wagon to Kuruman (27° 27′ S., 23° 26′ E.), the chief LMS station (founded 1817) in Bechuanaland.

[2] Robert Hamilton (1776–1851) and Rogers Edwards (1795–1876), missionary artisans; stationed at Kuruman since 1817 and 1831 respectively (*Register*, pp. 11, 24).

in connexion with this station, I am compelled partially to relinquish the hope in so far as very extended operations are concerned. The great desideratum is a want of population. There is no want of success considering the smallness of the number who usually attend the preaching of the Word, nor can we consider even the attendance small when we remember the paucity of people actually within a reasonable distance of the church. What in England we should call a fair proportion pay respect to the gospel by their presence, and a larger proportion still give gratifying evidence of attattchment to its principles by their walk and conversation. But, the population being small, even although there is a large proportion of believers there must be but a small number qualified, if with nothing more with only the willing mind to endure hardship for the benefit of their fellow men.

I should not have called your attention to this, which appears the only unfavourable feature in the Mission, had there been any probability of an increase of population. The cause of the steady decrease instead of augmentation of inhabitants has been in operation for a great number of years. The interior is quiet. As the gospel extends its influence peace will become more permanent, and unless the Bechuanas entirely relinquish their present mode of life, hold something else in estimation as their chief riches than cattle, we cannot expect that Kuruman will ever become populous. Regard for the welfare of their cattle will always lead them to choose more healthy locations for them than what this district presents.

That the Directors may judge whether my fears are well grounded, I may mention that within a circle of 8 or 10 miles around the station there are not a thousand inhabitants. The total number of native houses (occupied & unoccupied) on the station is 185. $\frac{1}{5}$ at least should be deducted for the unoccupied or used only as sort of store rooms and sleeping apartments for the unmarried females. But if we take this number, and take as an average the highest from frequent personal inspection I should say we can possibly give, viz. 5, we have only 925 as the total number of men, women, and children. The above average exceeds by 2 that usually taken by the French missionaries in estimating the population around them.[1] There is however a much larger population about 16 miles off. Probably there are in that location 1,500 souls, amongst whom also the gospel has met with considerable success. In another direction, about 30 or 35 miles distant, there are two villages each containing from 150 to 200 inhabitants.

[1] The Paris Evangelical Missionary Society had a station at Motito, about 35 miles N.E. of Kuruman.

Although the population is small in this district, there is no want of inhabitants farther to the North and North-East. At Taons (pronounced Towns),[1] which lies about East by North of this, Mr Owen of the Church Missionary Society[2] estimated the population at 15[000] or 20,000. The bretheren itinerate thither although it is nearly 100 miles distant, and though but little positive success has attended their endeavours the prospect is cheering. The truth is working its way, and will soon prevail. Even the violent opposition manifested is encouraging, for anything is better than stupid indifference.

In view of the limited choice we are reduced to at this station, I may be allowed to suggest that we make the most of whatever agents we can find. Although desirable that they have somewhat more than decided piety, it is, I conceive, not absolutely necessary. Evils may arise from their ignorance and mistakes, but good will certainly be done, and I should hope it will abide, while the effects of their deficiencies will vanish before more efficient agents whom they themselves may now be instrumental in partially preparing. Making the most of every man under them seems to have been the reason, by the blessing of God, of the great success of the bretheren at Griqua Town.[3]

I purpose accompanying Br. Edwards in his journey to the interior,[4] as I am informed by the bretheren who are best able to judge it will be advantageous for me in many respects. I shall become better acquainted with the habits of the people [and] their language, and by exclusion from all European society for some time I hope to slip more readily into their mode of thinking, which is essentially different from ours. Mr Edwards seems intimately acquainted with native character, and there is little fear but we shall be kindly received, more especially by those who have again & again sent messages for missionaries. There is reason

---

[1] Taung, about 90 miles E. of Kuruman. The village was then situated near where the railway station now is (27° 34′ S., 24° 45′ E.).

[2] Francis Owen (1802–54) worked successively among the Zulu in Natal (1837–1838) and the BaHurutshe at Mosega, Transvaal (Dec. 1839–Sept. 1840); his Society then abandoned its mission in S. Africa.

[3] An LMS station (since 1804) at 28° 51′ S., 23° 15′ E., about 100 miles south of Kuruman. Principal settlement of the Griquas, a hybrid people composed basically of Hottentots, with much European and other alien admixture.

[4] 'In June, when about to visit the Bokuane [BaKwena] tribe, I received a letter from Dr Philip, from which it appeared evident we might daily expect to see the Brethren Ross and Livingston. Mr Hamilton therefore wished me to remain at home till then. When they arrived, I purposed that one or both go also. Mr Livingston agreed to the proposal, but the journey will not be undertaken till next month in order, among other considerations, that I might be useful to them in the language' (Edwards to Tidman, 24.ix.41).

to believe that the names of Hamilton, Edwards, & Moffat[1] are well known hundreds of miles beyond us, as the nomadic habits of the people very much favours the transmission of news. We take with us two of the best qualified of our members here, for the purpose of planting them as native teachers in some promising locality, the expense of one of whom (if I do not receive in time the concurrence of Dr Phillip[2]) I shall endeavour to defray myself. The work is urgent. Souls are perishing, and what more efficient introduction can there be for the new missionaries, which I hope will soon follow us, than the residence for some months previously of one or two native teachers?

I am exceedingly gratified to observe the confidence which has been inspired into the minds of the Bechuanas of the efficacy of our medicines, by a very successful case of treatment which happened a day or two after our arrival. The bretheren say it is altogether unprecedented, and an unsuccesfull case since has not in the least abated their confidence. I feel thankfull, and hope it will by the blessing of God enable me to win their attention to a much more important topic than the preservation of their bodies, even the salvation of their immortal souls.

Faithfully & affectionately yours,

David Livingston

2. To J. J. FREEMAN
22 December 1841

[LMS 17. Received 30 April 1842]

Kuruman

22d *Decr.* 1841

Dear Sir,

There is one measure connected with missionary operations, viz. the employment of native agency in the work of evangelizing the heathen, to which although in my last communication I did not very pointedly advert I have been most anxious to call the attention of the Directors. Formerly, when viewing the heathen world at a distance, the measure appeared one of great importance, and I resolved to give it my earliest attention. But now when I have come into close contact with it, and beheld a little of that vast extent of surface over which the population is

---

[1] Robert Moffat (1795–1883), since 1821 the senior missionary at Kuruman. His book, *Missionary Labours and Scenes in Southern Africa* (1842), describes in detail the early history of the station.

[2] John Philip (1775–1851), Superintendent since 1820 of LMS missions in S. Africa; resident in Cape Town (*Register*, pp. 19–20).

scattered in the regions before me, I powerfully feel its special, nay overwhelming, importance.

Having lately in company with Revd. R. Edwards of this Mission performed a journey (in going & returning) of about 700 miles in length,[1] the tract of country we saw seemed to me of immense extent, but when I look to the map it is a mere iota compared to what is yet to be possessed by the missionaries of the cross. But although the territory is larger than can be imagined by any one who has not seen a little of it, and though the tribes are situated at very formidable distances from each other, I see no cause for discouragement. And if at any time the prospects of success assume any other than a bright & cheering aspect, it is when I leave out of view the machinery of native agency put into vigorous operation.

In stating to the Directors my conviction that in this country this means of evangelization is specially indicated, I need scarcely advert to the great efficiency of this class of laborers. Of their warm affectionate manner of dealing with their fellow countrymen, of their capability to bring the truth itself before their minds entirely divested of that peculiar strangeness which cleaves to foreigners, and of the very eminent success of those employed by the bretheren of Griqua Town, I am persuaded they are already well aware. Their success is most encouraging, and no less so are the results which have followed the comparatively recent employment of two by this Mission. Indeed, I have no hesitation in affirming that during the short period since they have been employed these two have been as efficient in propagating both a knowledge & love of Christianity as could have been anticipated by even the warmest admirers of native agents. In their hands the work still goes on well, and every now & then our hearts are cheered by goodly accessions to the church of such as we hope that they are the 'saved in Christ Jesus'. And if the measure is allowed free operation, if we are allowed by the Directors to employ a few more, who in the judgement of the bretheren are fit for the work, we may anticipate conversions, by the Divine blessing, to increase in a compound ratio, & regions not yet explored by Europeans will soon be supplied with the bread of life.

I do most earnestly beg the sanction of the Direction for the employment of a few who are both able & willing to devote their attention to this work, and in this request I have the full concurrence of those bretheren on whose long experience greater confidence can be placed. I may also state, as a garauntee for the purity of the motives of those who

---

[1] Briefly described in *Fam. Letters*, i, pp. 45–9. Starting on 18 October, it lasted about six weeks.

are willing to devote themselves, that £10 is by no means sufficient to support a native of this country. It is consequently at a sacrifice they engage in the work of the Lord.

With respect to the points at which operations could at present be most advantageously put in operation, both the candidates and missionaries who know the country have but one opinion, and that is, that the tribes 250 miles northward are in a much more favourable state for our object than those in the surrounding localities. The adjoining tribes amongst which no regular systematic operations have been carried on are decidedly hostile to the gospel. They treat missionaries with respect, but at the same time manifest very great opposition to the doctrines we teach, and with scarcely one of them would a native teacher be allowed to live. I state this with diffidence, because it is at direct variance with the opinions expressed in my written instructions,[1] yet at the same time I indulge the hope that, when I state that the very opposite of a great desire for religious instruction prevails, my change of sentiment will not be ascribed to insufficient consideration, for conviction has been forced upon me by proofs of which, had it been possible, both my prejudices and expectations should have induced me gladly to have resisted the pressure.

The tribes within 100 miles North & North-East of this are all partially acquainted with the requirements of the gospel, but manifest the greatest hatred to them, and this is just what our knowledge of the human heart would lead us to expect. The same depravity exists everywhere, and this, although to Christians it may seem but the bare enunciation of a self-evident truth, ought to stand out prominently alongside the expectations of every young missionary. Those tribes however which lie at a greater distance, say 250 & 300 miles northward, are in quite a different condition. They know nothing of the gospel, & consequently form neither a good nor bad opinion of it. They know nothing more of missionaries than that they are a friendly race of whites who love all men, and in many respects we occupy the same position with respect to them as some of our missionaries have with the South Sea Islanders. There exists a strong impression in favour of Europeans, strongest among those not previously visited by missionaries, traders, &c, but only in a minor degree in the tribes nearer.

To account for this phenomenon, it is only necessary to remember the terrible scourging to which nearly all the Interior tribes have been in recent years subjected. They have experienced the cruelties of the, to the Bechuana, invincible marauders who overan the whole country,

[1] Not in the LMS archives.

and they have all heard of their successive repulses by mere handfuls of whites; and now the most distant are most anxious to secure the friend-ship of Europeans. The last marauder, the notorious Mosilekatsi,[1] al-though obliged by the Boors to retire to the Eastern extremity of a lake in the Interior, has recently recommenced plundering, and the whole country is in a state of alarm. Those who dread him most have the greatest anxiety to obtain alliance with Europeans, and this feeling will induce them to receive either missionaries or teachers gladly.

Now if we can while this impression lasts confer on them a decided benefit, we may hope it will continue. But if we allow this opportunity to pass unimproved, it appears to me the time is not far distant when the Interior tribes will be in the same state of indifference & opposition to those nearer. Injurious influences are now in operation to effect this. The Boors of Port Natal have advanced right into the centre of the continent & seized most of the country & the best of the fountains to-wards the North-East.[2] These on the one hand, and from this direction traders, Griqua hunters, & individuals from the tribes which hate the gospel, are every year passing in with more freedom, and in many in-stances they prove curses instead of blessings. (A Griqua has during this present year to my knowledge communicated the venereal disease to three tribes amongst whom it was unknown before. One of these has been visited by missionaries, but the other two have received one of the worst accompaniments of civilization before the missionaries came to give any of its blessings. This Griqua does not belong to any Mission station.)

May I beg an early intimation empowering us to make an effort immediately in behalf of the poor ignorant heathen in the Interior? If it is in accordance with the intentions of the Directors to form a new Mission in the Interior, I beg leave to call their attention to a tribe called the Bakhatla,[3] the location of which is the best I have seen in the Interior. A large valley with a fountain about equal to this at Kuruman,

---

[1] Mzilikazi (called 'Moselekatse' by the BaTswana) was chief, 1821–68, of the AmaNdebele (Tswana 'MaTebele'), who had seceded from the Zulu kingdom in Natal. In c. 1825 they invaded and settled in W. Transvaal, conquering many of the local tribes and periodically raiding others. In 1837 they themselves were twice defeated by the Voortrekker Boers (emigrants from Cape Colony) and retreated north into the region now known after them as Matabeleland (S. Rhodesia).

[2] Many of the Voortrekkers had originally settled in Natal, but subsequently migrated to S.W. Transvaal, already occupied (since the expulsion of the MaTebele) by some of their compatriots.

[3] BaKgatla-baMmanaana, then living near Mabotsa, about 250 miles N.E. of Kuruman. They were one of the Tswana tribes recently visited by D. L. and Edwards.

& much more land, which by reason of the great height of the point from which the water comes out could be irrigated without any expense, abundance of pasture for cattle, with several other fountains at no great distance, and a manufacture of iron from ore found in abundance in the adjoining mountains, constitute the local attachments. Being a valley, however, it may be exposed to vicissitudes of temperature unfavourable to health, but it does not contain anything like the amount of decaying vegetable K[uruman] valley does, yet this is a healthy spot. I shall in my next furnish fuller information on this topic.

David Livingston

3. To JOHN ARUNDEL[1]
22 December 1841

[LMS 18. Received 'May 1842']

Kuruman
22 *Decr.* 1841

My dear Sir,

You kindly permitted me to address you occasionally a private communication, and though I have now been away from England more than twelve months I have not yet availed myself of that privelege, but I have not delayed long. I have indeed been long from England, but I have only been but a very short time here. My time has been spent in the long long journey to this place, and recently I have returned from another pretty long journey beyond it. I undertook this latter journey by the advice and with the approbation of Mrss[2] Hamilton & Edwards, to whose counsels I was commended by the Directors before leaving home. The object of it was to ascertain the state & disposition of certain tribes living North & North-East of this. They had frequently sent messages to the bretheren requesting missionaries, and as frequently the bretheren were anxious to visit them, but Mr E. could not leave Mr Hamilton alone for so long a period as was necessary, and it was only when we arrived that the way seemed open. As the Interior is to be my field of labour, I confess I was glad of an opportunity of entering it at this time.

Our journey was, in going & returning, at least 700 miles in length, but though so long we were not at any time more than 250 directly

---

[1] Home Secretary of the LMS 1819–46; b. 1778, d. 1848.
[2] D. L. normally uses this contraction for the modern 'Messrs.'

north. This however is farther in that direction than any missionaries have yet been. In one case the people had not before seen a white face, and in some others only one, viz. that of an enterprising trader who has frequently penetrated far beyond anyone else.[1] We were however everywhere received with respect, and by those tribes situated farthest off even with kindness.

I was astonished at the difference observable near to Mission stations. Within a distance of 100 miles, the people who do not live actually on the stations are violent opponents of the gospel. They partially know the requirements of the gospel, they know they must put away their superfluous wives, &c &c, and on that account they hate it cordially. They won't listen. The chiefs to please the teachers call the people together, but the latter know the minds of the chiefs, & they refuse to come. They flock[e]d round the waggons for medicine, & would talk on any subject except that which of all others is the most important to be known, and I was pained to hear the scorn thrown on the name of Jesus when they thought I did not hear them. One chief got up a dance round Mr Hamilton lately to drown his voice while preaching.[2] This was an outrage that would not be committed by any other chief but himself, but though not openly opponents to that extent they are no less certainly unfavourable to preaching. When I say this I don't refer to those situated far beyond us. They know nothing of the gospel nor of missionaries, except that we are good people & friendly with all. But they, equally with those nearer & perhaps to a greater degree, possess an impression that Europeans are a decidedly superior race of people & it would be dangerous to provoke our enmity. In respect to their opinion of us, it must have undergone a complete revolution in the space of the last 20 years.

And to what are we to attribute this favourable change, by which any white man may travel through the length & breadth of the land without fear of molestation? It would be pleasant could we attribute it to the influence of the gospel which has so long, so affectionately & faithfully been preached to them. I expected this was the case, but when I have seen one impression over all the tribes, and this stronger in proportion as we recede from the regions where the gospel is known, I am compelled to give the credit of the change to a less lovely influence, viz.

[1] Presumably David Hume (1796–1863), whose ventures into the Interior had included a visit in 1833 to the BaNgwato. In 1838 he established a trading-store at Kuruman.

[2] This was in September 1841; cf. Hamilton's account in *Chronicle*, vi, 1842, p. 171 (letter dated 20.i.42). The offender was Motlhabani, chief of the BagaMaidi near Taung.

the successive defeat of two large bands of marauders, who had over-come & treated with great cruelty nearly all the Bechuanas, by a mere handful of Boors & Griquas.[1]

But this impression, which exists in full force in all the tribes beyond 100 miles of this, will not long remain so. They are now purchasing guns themselves rapidly. They are visited by traders every year, and also by Griquas for the same purpose with the traders, and these latter are giving them the diseases of Europeans without any of their civiliza-tion. (The venereal disease was unknown amongst them untill this same year it was taken into the Interior by a Griqua whom I know.) Persons also from the tribes adjoining us are passing in for the sake of getting game; and if a vigorous effort is not instantly made by us, I see no prospect left but that soon the tribes situated 200 & 250 miles distant will become as much opponents of the gospel as those within 100 miles of us.

Now you must not think me visionary when I say the effort could be made immediately. We don't need European missionaries to do it. They are good, but much can be done with far less expensive machinery. The whole of the tribes we visited could now be placed under effective in-structors, had we only the means to employ them. The distant tribes would all receive them, not however from a desire to be instructed, for I could not ascertain that motive was present in the mind of a single individual we visited. It is not by any means like the South Sea Islands. One wishes a teacher because it will make him of more importance in the eyes of his neighbours, another expects a lot of guns with him, &c. But it is well they are willing at all to allow teachers to come amongst them. Some of the tribes nearer would not allow so much; they say if a white teacher comes we will listen to him, but we won't have a black one. This however is just an excuse, for they won't listen to a white teacher neither. The native teachers are really most efficient agents in the dissemination of religious truth, and if we had two with each of the Interior tribes I don't hesitate to affirm that as much would by the Divine blessing be effected by them, in the way of removing prejudice & enlightening & saving the people, as would be effected by any two Europeans for the first half dozen years at least.

That you may judge whether I am right or not, I shall mention some facts which I wish I could mention to the Directors without appearing to make an invidious comparison. The facts stare me every

---

[1] Those 'marauders' were, presumably, the 'Mantatees', defeated in June 1823 by the Griquas and BaTlhaping, and the MaTebele, defeated in January and Novem-ber 1837 by the Boers.

day in the face, and were I not anxious to stand entirely aloof from
party feeling and anything like impeaching the wisdom of those who
have preceded me in the work, & who are all greatly my superiors in
prudence & piety, I should certainly make them publicly known to the
Directors. But knowing that they are fully aware of the value of native
agents, & that they need nothing from me to strengthen their conviction
on the subject, I do no more than mention them to you privately for
your own information.

It has been the policy of the Griqua Town missionaries all along to
employ native agents. The consequence has been, the believers have
increased in a compound ratio. They have many imperfections, but
God has blessed them wonderfully. On our way here we unexpectedly
came upon a village on a Sunday morning, the want of water having
compelled us to travel at that time.[1] They knew nothing of us, & we
were entirely ignorant of them. Yet we found that public worship &
school for the children were regularly kept up, although from the illness
of Mr Hughs,[2] & the distance being 60 or 80 miles from Griqua Town,
they had been visited by no missionary for 10 months previously. This
fact greatly strengthened my predilections in favour of employing as
soon as possible all who are capable of making known the way of life.
We had the best possible opportunity of observing their conduct, and
who after seeing it would not wish to have a band of such assistants to
aid on the cause of truth & holiness?

They have imperfections, but I see nothing else in the operations of
the G. Town Mission to account for its success but these very imperfect
instruments. The missionaries now can do little else than itinerate &
superintend them, and they occupy not only what may be called their
own field, but great part of ours. Am I sorry to see them stretching out
on all sides & passing us as they are now doing W. by N.? No, I rejoice
at it, & don't care though they hug us by & by in their arms & squeeze
us out towards the North. If no other motive will send us north, their
progress will. It is all the same whoever brings in sinners to Christ. It is
common cause, & I am really glad to see the work going on. But unfortunately a little rivalry other than provoking to love & good works
has got in amongst us, & those who have been longer in the work have
local associations which prevent them seeing some things in the same

---

[1] In a letter to Drummond, 4 viii.41, D. L. mentions that the inhabitants reproved
him 'for travelling on the Sabbath' (Chamberlin, p. 26). He was then on his way
from Port Elizabeth to Kuruman.

[2] Isaac Hughes (1798–1870), LMS missionary at Griquatown, 1828–45, and subsequently elsewhere (*Register*, p. 24).

light we do. They look at the subject from a different point of view, &
consequently it appears in another form to them.

But native agency has been tried here too, as well as at Griqua Town.
After Mr Moffat went to England[1] he seems to have changed a little
his opinions on that subject, for he wrote back advising the bretheren
here to make a trial of two. These were appointed, and the consequence
has been a large accession to the church. Each at his location has more
members under him than are at the station, that is, they have more than
⅔ of the church, & the chief accessions to it are always from their
ministry. Add to this they are much more consistent in their deport-
ment than those here, & so affectionate to us & to each other it is quite a
treat to visit them. And this notwithstanding Mr Edwards is an excellent Sicuana[2] scholar, & an excellent preacher in it too. Since I understand him I am quite delighted to hear him. I believe this is the case too
with the G[riquatown] Mission, for the truth seems so much more
effectual & comes home to the heart better in proportion as it is divested
of all that strangeness which attaches to foreigners in every country.

I am most anxious that more native teachers be employed, & in this
anxiety the bretheren E[dwards] & Hamilton now both cordially join.
Along with this I make an application to the Directors, and I wait with
much anxiety for an answer.

I should feel greatly obliged by a communication, however short.
Please let me know how you are in health. My sheet is filled, & I have
not said half of what I would, but I shall write you again I hope a more
connected letter.

Yours affectionately,
D. Livingston

4. To DAVID LIVINGSTON
18 February 1842

[LMS: Outgoing Letters, Africa, Box 4, pp. 374–5]

London
February 18, 1842

Dear Brother,

We cannot lose the present opportunity of acknowledging your letter
of April 24,[3] by which we received the pleasing intelligence of your safe

[1] Early in 1839. He did not get back to Kuruman until December 1843.
[2] SeTswana, the language of the BaTswana ('Bechuana').
[3] Not in the LMS archives.

arrival at Port Elizabeth after a prosperous and comfortable voyage. We were happy to find that, in consequence of the ship having touched at Cape Town, you had an opportunity of making the acquaintance of the Rev. Dr. Philip and of conversing with him on the subject of your Mission. Your hints as to the best arrangements for the conveyance of Missionaries proceeding hence to the interior of Africa are worthy of consideration, and shall certainly be borne in mind. We are, as you justly presume, very anxious to economise the expenditure of the Society under the head of passage money, so far as it can be done consistently with the comfort of our Missionaries.

Your arrival at Griqua Town has been reported to us by Mr Wright,[1] and by Mr Edwards we have been apprised of your arrival at Lattakoo,[2] the field to which the Great Head of the Church has directed your choice. It always cheers us to be informed of the actual entrance of a new Missionary on his intended sphere of action, and of his first attempt to carry out the design of his appointment. Every such event serves to strengthen our faith and animate our assurance as to the final triumph of the cause in which we are embarked. We rejoice to think you are now amongst the people to whose welfare your life is devoted, and have begun to put forth those efforts which, by the blessing of the Most High, will promote at once their social and spiritual interest. We indulge a grateful persuasion that your labors will in various ways produce a large amount of good amongst the Native tribes, and at no distant day become, through Divine grace, instrumental to the salvation of many. We entreat you to give your close and constant attention to the Native language until you acquire that knowledge of it, both for literary and colloquial purposes, which is so essential to your efficiency and success as a Missionary of the Cross. We trust you will be graciously sustained in all your endeavors to extend the kingdom and promote the glory of our Lord. May his holy service be an ever-augmenting source of joy and satisfaction to your mind, may his presence console you under every trial and invigorate you for every duty, and in his strength may you continue to the end of a long-protracted course a stedfast and successful laborer in his vineyard.

We remain, Dear Brother,

---

[1] Peter Wright (1798–1843), principal missionary at Griquatown 1827–42. His letter, dated 14.viii.41, said that D. L. and Ross had reached that station on 16 July and remained till the 26th, when they left for Kuruman (*Chronicle*, vi, 1842, p. 9).

[2] 'New Lattakoo', an early name for Kuruman, to which the Mission station had been moved in 1817 from 'Old Lattakoo' (about 45 miles N.E.). The name is a corruption of Dithakong, 'the place of stone walls'. Edwards had written on 2.viii.41 reporting the arrival of D. L. and Ross 'on Saturday last' (*Chronicle*, vi, p. 8).

On behalf of the Directors,
faithfully and affectionately yours,
Arthur Tidman ⎫
⎬Foreign Secs.
J. J. Freeman ⎭

P.S. We have just received your letter of Sept. 23, and will embrace the earliest opportunity of writing to you in reply.

5. To J. J. FREEMAN
3 July 1842

[LMS 21. Received 26 November 1842. Previous publication: *Chronicle*, vol. vii, 1843, pp. 37–8, 58–9 (edited extracts); Blaikie, pp. 47, 48 (three paragraphs); Chamberlin, pp. 32–7 (incomplete)]

Kuruman
3d July 1842

Dear Sir,

On the 10th of February last I left this station, and having proceeded into the interior of the Bechuana country remained there during the months March, April, May, and part of June. The whole of that period was characterised by the continued manifestation of the Divine goodness towards me, and now, with humble gratitude to Him whose Providential care watched over and brought me back in safety, I shall endeavour to state to you the objects for which this journey was undertaken, and the manner in which they were followed out.

The objects I had in view were the following: that I might by exclusive intercourse with the natives facilitate my labour in the acquisition of the language, that I might for a season be freed from all attention to medicine, and that, though still but imperfectly acquainted with their tongue, I might make an effort for the eternal welfare of the tribe or tribes with whom I should sojourn by means of native agents.

In order the more effectually to carry into operation the last & principal object I had in contemplation, I took with me two natives, members of the church in this place, and with two others connected with the management of the waggon we proceeded in a direction nearly North-East of Moteeto.[1] This route brought us near to none of the tribes which lie East and West of it, and consequently we saw no people save

[1] Motito (nowadays called Bothithong), 27° 04′ S., 23° 49′ E., about 35 miles N.E. of Kuruman.

14

a few of the Bakalihari[1] and Bushmen,[2] untill after twelve days' travelling we arrived in the valley of the Bakhatla. There we saw three villages, each of which may be stated to contain a population of 400 souls. The situations of these are very inviting, for the valley is both beautiful and large, not less I think than forty miles in length and from two to four in breadth, and besides abundance of iron-stone it contains no fewer than seven fountains, each of which pours out a copious supply of excellent water.

As the people, however, are the sole manufacturers of the iron and wooden utensils in use among the Bechuanas, and in trading pass among all the tribes to the Southward, I thought it probable that they may have imbibed some of the prejudices to the gospel which prevail to such a lamentable extent among these, and consequently might not be in such a favourable state for the operations of native teachers as some tribes which live still farther to the North. We therefore only remained a few days with them. Their behaviour to us was, however, as kind as we could have expected. We found no difficulty in collecting them together, and when we addressed them on salvation by Christ they listened with respectful attention. I earnestly hope the time is not far distant when they shall hear statedly and with believing hearts the glad tidings of mercy.

Nearly directly North of the Bakhatla and a little more than one hundred miles distant lives Bubi, one of the chiefs of the Bakwain (Baquane),[3] and one of the most sensible of his class I have yet seen. To him we next proceeded, and the very friendly reception Mr Edwards and I met with from both him and his people last year, the very favourable character he bears among all the tribes, and the fact that Mr E. found them entirely ignorant of the gospel, induced me to prefer making a commencement for a native teacher with them.

The beginning of the school for the children was as favourable as we could desire. The chief expressed much joy at the thought of having the foreigners as his friends, and went himself and collected the children. He supplied me with milk regularly, and when payment was offered he promptly declined. His under-chiefs continued to supply my people with

[1] BaKgalagadi, 'people of the Kalahari [Kgalagadi] Desert', a collective name applied to the earliest Tswana occupants of Bechuanaland. Most of them had by now become serfs of such later invaders as the BaKwena and BaNgwato.

[2] The aboriginal inhabitants of the country; nomadic hunters living in small bands, and differing considerably from the BaTswana in race, language, and culture.

[3] BaKwena, one of the major Tswana tribes in Bechuanaland. It consisted at that time of two hostile divisions, headed respectively by Sechele and his uncle Bubi. The latter lived at Dithubaruba (c. 24° 27′ S., 25° 21′ E.).

food during most of our stay, and although the waggon attracted crowds of visitors dailly, on no occasion did we miss a single article.

Not long after our arrival, it occurred to me that it would be advantageous if we could lead out for irrigation the fine stream which winds round the foot of the hill on which their town is built, and this because it would both furnish the teacher with an available garden and also help to convince the people that they might by a little industry render themselves independant of those impostors called 'rainmakers'. I accordingly explained to the chief and his principal men our mode of irrigation, and was glad to find that they were quite delighted with the idea. The chief said he would send as many men as it needed, if I should only shew them how to do the work. (Two of those he sent are his principal under-chiefs, & another is his own favourite doctor or rainmaker.) I had not thought of engaging in a work of this nature when I left Kuruman, & had none of the necessary implements with me. But seeing it would not do to lose the favourable season when all were eager to work, I commenced with such as I could invent. Sticks sharpened to a point served for digging a canal between four & five hundred feet in length, three in width, and in some places more than four in depth. The earth was lifted out in handfuls and carried to the dam in karosses, wooden bowls, and tortoise shells.

This information, I am quite aware, is not strictly connected with the great object for which I have been sent to the heathen. But I mention these particulars, because I am by them induced to indulge the hope that they are indicative of a better state of things among this people than what the early missionaries found among the Batlapi.[1] And if so, if all the missionaries who are sent to the Interior are allowed to devote their energies exclusively towards the amelioration of the spiritual condition of the people, may we not hope that thereby the chariot of the everlasting gospel will go on with accelerated speed, and the whole country soon be enlightened by the glory of the Lord?

The Bakwains shewed surprising industry and perseverance in this work, and such I conceive as warrants me to indulge the hope I have stated above; for although the dam was twice swept away by floods, and I was unable, in consequence of getting both legs and arms severely sunburned, to stimulate them by my example, they did not seem in any way discouraged, but laboured on to the end.

I sincerely regret to add that I have been unable to try the experi-

---

[1] BaTlhaping, the southernmost Tswana tribe, among whom the LMS had started its 'Bechuana Mission' in 1816, when they were still at 'Old Lattakoo' (Dithakong).

ment whether the favourable beginning would have continued, for in consequence of great weakness, the effect of a violent fever with which the teacher I intended to leave with them was affected, I was obliged to bring him away, and no continued efforts for the good of this interesting people are at present being made. At this period it would have given me the greatest satisfaction to have known what are the intentions of the Directors in relation to native agency and this Mission. But unfortunately no instructions have yet arrived.

Having remained with the people of Bubi for nearly a month, I proceeded Northward in order to visit the Bamangwato, Bakaa, and Makalaka, three tribes having their countries in Lat. 22° S. and stretching from 28° to 30° E. Long.[1] The last-named is the smallest of the three, but it is a section of a people of very considerable numbers and who speak a language differing very decidedly from the Sitchuana. None of the Bechuanas I had with me could understand it. But from some of the words which I caught, I am inclined to think it belongs to the same root with their tongue. Their manners, too, are somewhat different from the Southern tribes, inasmuch as they are not entirely dependant on the rude kaross for covering, but manufacture cotton cloth for shawls &c. And besides the knowledge how to manufacture iron and copper, one of the five tribes into which the Makalaka are divided, called the Mashona, fight with guns instead of the assagai. These they obtain from the Portuguese on the Eastern coast, and from some circumstances which have come to my knowledge I am inclined to believe they procure them in exchange for slaves.

By conversation with many different individuals, and these of different grades, I ascertained the existence of no fewer than 28 tribes of people hitherto unknown to Europeans. Thirteen of these are reported to have another tongue, and the remainder speak Sitchuana. But as reports cannot (however carefully examined) be absolutely depended on, I shall turn to those which I myself visited.

Our route to the Bamangwato skirted the sandy desert which flanks the Bechuana country to the Westward. And as the sand proved very fatiguing for the oxen, when within 40 or 50 miles from that people they were unable to proceed farther, and I had to leave both oxen and waggon and perform my visit on foot. But I had not the least reason to

---

[1] All three were then living in the general vicinity of the Shoshong hills (c. 22° 50′ S., 26° 27′ E.). The 'Bamangwato' (BaNgwato, an early offshoot of the BaKwena), and BaKaa (an early offshoot of the BaRolong), are of Tswana stock. 'Makalaka' is the Tswana name for the BaKalanga (western MaShona), who belong to a different division of the Bantu-speaking peoples and are found mainly in S. Rhodesia.

regret having done so, for the chief (Sekomi)[1] was evidently pleased that I had thrown myself on his bounty without the least appearance of distrust. Indeed, before I had been 10 minutes in his company, and while sitting surrounded by hundreds of his people, he began to shew his satisfaction by feeding me with the flesh of the rhinoceros and some other things which they consider dainties. He then took me to the house of his mother, presented me with a large elephant's tusk, more food, and, as we became better acquainted, he frequently and emphatically exclaimed, 'You have come to us just like rain', and 'If you had brought your waggon I should have detained you at least a month looking at you'.

Sekomi has a large number of people under him. In the town alone I numbered 600 houses, which is a number considerably larger than I have been able to count in any other Bechuana town in the country. But they are all very small, and cannot contain many individuals each. The one in which I lived was quite as large as any in the town, and three of us could not sleep in it without touching each other, unless we put out our fire.

The population is sunk into the very lowest state of both mental and moral degradation, so much so indeed it must be difficult or rather impossible for Christians at home to realize anything like an accurate notion of the grossness of the darkness which shrouds their minds. I could not ascertain that they had the least idea of a future state. And though they have some notions which seem to us to be connected with a belief in its existence, I have not met one who could put the necessary links together in the chain of reasoning so as to become possessed of the definite idea. Indeed, they all confess that they never think of anything connected with death, and do not wish the introduction of that subject. Their conceptions of Deity are of the most vague and contradictory nature, and his name conveys no more to their understanding than the idea of superiority. Hence they do not hesitate to apply the name of God to their chiefs, and I was every day shocked by being addressed by that title, and although it as often furnished me with a text from which to tell them of the only true God, and Jesus Christ whom He has sent, yet it deeply pained me, and I never felt so fully convinced of the lamentable deterioration of my species before. It is indeed a mournful truth that 'man has become like the beasts that perish'.

The country abounds with lions, and so much are they dreaded by

[1] Sekgoma I, chief of the BaNgwato 1834(?)–75 (with two breaks); died 1883. He was the father of the famous Christian chief Khama, by whom he was ousted in 1875.

the natives one man never goes out alone. The women have always some one to gaurd them when they go to their gardens, & they always go in companies to draw water, for the sake of the protection which numbers give. Nor are these precautions unnecessary. For a time I could not believe but that they were. But the earnestness with which the chief chode with me for going a few hundred yards from the town unattended, and the circumstance that he always sent an attendant if at any time he saw me going out afterwards, together with the fact that a woman was actually devoured in her garden during my visit, and that so near the town I had frequently walked far past it, fully convinced me that there are good grounds for their fears and precautions. It was most affecting to hear the cries of the orphan children of this woman. During the whole day after her death the surrounding rocks and vallies rung and re-echoed with their bitter cries.

I frequently thought, as I listened to the loud sobs painfully indica-tive of the sorrows of those who have no hope, that if some of our churches could have heard their sad wailings it would have awakened the firm resolution to do more for the Heathen than they have done. In some countries the light which the gospel once shed has gone out and darkness has succeeded. But though eighteen centuries have elapsed since life and immortality were brought to light, there is no certainty that these dark regions were ever before visited for the purpose of mak-ing known the light and liberty and peace of the glorious gospel. It would seem that the myriads who have peopled these regions have always passed away into darkness, and no ray from heaven ever beamed on their path. And with whom does the guilt rest if not with us who compose the church militant on earth?

You will, I am sure, bear with me in this digression from my narra-tive, for my mind is filled with sadness when I contemplate the pros-pects of these large masses of immortal souls. I see no hopes for them except in native agents. The more I see of the country, its large extent of surface, with its population scattered and each tribe separated by a formidable distance from almost every other, I feel the more convinced that it will be impossible if not impolitic for the church to supply them all with Europeans. Native Christians *can* make known the way of life. There are some in connection with both this and the church at Griqua Town who have done it effectually. Others too are rising up who will soon be capable of teaching, and if their energies are not brought into operation by taking up the field now open before us, I don't see where the benevolent spirit which we hope is springing up among the converts of the two Missions is to find an outlet. I conceive that even now the two Missions by cordial cooperation might at once supply with native teachers all the tribes within the range of our knowledge who are not inimical to claims of the gospel. It would not require more than six from each Mission to give two to each friendly tribe. And that this measure, or an attempt at it, would be advantageous to both churches, I need not refer you to the effects which increased benevolent exertions have on churches at home, and how often it happens that when churches have not work set before them in the cause of Christ, even more than they can actually perform, their benevolence degenerates into selfish quarreling. You will please to observe that I do not advance this proposition without diffidence, for I am sensible my sentiments, on account of want of experience, are entitled to much less deference than those of others in the same field.

I may perhaps be permitted to relate an incident which seems to indicate that even the darkest minds feel the need of a something to speak peace to their troubled thoughts. On one occasion Sekomi, having sat by me in the hut for some time in deep thought, at length addressing me by a pompous title said, 'I wish you would change my heart. Give me medicine to change it, for it is proud, proud and angry, angry always'. I lifted up the Testament & was about to tell him of the only way in which the heart can be changed, but he interrupted me by saying, 'Nay, I wish to have it changed by medicine, to drink it [and] have it changed at once, for it is always very proud and very uneasy, and continually angry with some one'. He then rose and went away. This seemed to me the more remarkable as we had not then spoken to either him or his people on the necessity of a change of heart.

Another incident which also happened amongst the Bamangwato gave me some encouragement to hope that even itinerating by native Christians may by the Divine blessing be productive of good. Late one evening, as I was asleep on one side of the hut, a young man having a most intelligent expression of countenance came in with a present of food, and said, 'I once carried the gun of Sepamore[1] (a member of the church here) when he was in this country hunting, and I asked him what he thought about God.' (Here he gave me a surprisingly correct account of the Supreme Being.) 'But', added he, 'what do you say?' Most gladly I confirmed what he had heard, and added a little more to his stock by telling him of 'Jesus and the Resurrection'. This may have been all curiosity. But it may please the Holy Spirit to operate by even these small portions of truth, and lead some though unknown to us into

---

[1] Seêpamore, a native of Kuruman, who like others from that station made periodical hunting and trading trips into the interior.

the regions of everlasting glory. And if so, our itineracies will not be in vain.

I was much gratified by the hospitality shewn by the Bamangwato to myself and the two natives who accompanied me. We came among them without anything to insure us a good reception, and after living for a fortnight entirely on the bounty of the chief, when we left he sent 30 of his people to gaurd us and carry the presents he had given to both myself and people safely to the waggon. Four of these he instructed to proceed with me to Kuruman and bring him back a faithful report of all the wonderful things I had told him. They are, an under-chief of his and three servants. I wish and pray that I may be useful to them, so that when they return they may tell not only the strange customs of the 'Makuas'[1] but also the 'wonderful works of God'.

I have finished what I had to say about the Bamangwato. But my visit to them was not accomplished in one space of time. I walked to the Bakaa, who live about 24 miles East by South of Sekomi, remained there a few days, proceeded to the Makalaka, who lie about 15 miles North by West of the Bakaa, and then returned to the Bamangwato. Thence after two days accross the sands I reached the waggon in safety.

The Bakaa live on a very high range of dark-coloured, naked basaltic rocks. These lie close upon the right nearly the whole way from the Bamangwato; and when arrived opposite where the villages are built, we turn suddenly round and begin to ascend by a narrow ravine or rather cleft in the rock, down which there rushes a mountain stream. By this path we attain an elevation of three or four hundred feet above the valley we have left, and enter a flat area covered with trees. But bare rocks rise up perpendicularly on all sides except at the narrow door-way by which we entered. Directly in front the rocks are nearly 700 feet high, and on the top of them we now perceive, perched like eagles' nests, the little huts of the Bakaa. We began to climb up towards them, and frequently looked up to see when a crowd of natives should collect to gaze at our arrival. But we were permitted to ascend in silence, and when on the top we were allowed, although near to the houses, to gaze around on the strange scene now presented to us, and no one to disturb our emotions. (Conscience was at work amongst the Bakaa. The cause I shall mention below.)

We found that the curious and deep basin from which we had ascended was but one of a great number all similarly formed. Some were

[1] *Makgowa*, the Tswana term for Europeans in general, and Englishmen in particular.

as large as Finsbury Circus,[1] others of smaller dimensions, and the rocks as a whole present the most singular appearance I ever beheld, resembling more than anything else I know the pews of a church on a gigantic scale. The rocks are rent and split in every direction, and their sides are covered by huge angular blocks which have slipped down only a short distance from the places whence they have been detached. In rolling or rather sliding downwards they have impinged on each other and the rocks below in some places where considerable rents run into the body of the rock, and thus form considerable cavities, which are used by the Bakaa as retreats in time of danger from their enemies. The one which I entered held nearly all the inhabitants of a village, and Mosilikatsi was completely foiled in all his attempts to destroy them. None of his people could enter, for the entrance has to be performed crawling on the belly, and when once in a dozen men could stand and defend the passage against the ingress of one individual, and he so situated. And their attempts to suffocate them were also in vain, for the rents are so numerous the Bakaa breathed with freedom notwithstanding the smoke.

The Bakaa have a bad name among all the other tribes, and I believe they fully deserve it, for a few years ago they destroyed by poisoning both food and water the second white man that ever visited them.[2] He was a trader, and when he with two of his people fell victims to the treachery of the Bakaa a fourth still lingered under the effects of the poison, but they put a leathern thong round his neck and finished him. They burned the waggons in order to get the ironwork of them, and devoured the oxen.

As I happened to be the first European who has visited them since this deed of darkness, their consciences loudly accused them; and when I came into their town, except the chief and two attendants the whole had fled my presence. These were in the usual place of meeting,[3] and in their faces they had evidences of perturbation such as I never saw in black countenances before. Nothing I could do in the way of appearing perfectly at ease, and squatting down beside them, could remove the almost ludicrous expression of fear untill they had got a dish of porridge cooked; and when they saw me partake of it without distrust the act

[1] An open space in the City of London, close to the LMS headquarters of that time. It is about 4½ acres in extent.

[2] As mentioned below, his name was Gibson. He had visited the BaKaa c. 1834, having been preceded by Hume. In *Travels*, p. 10, D. L. says that he died of fever, which is confirmed by contemporary evidence (summarized in Schapera, 'Notes on the History of the Kaa', 1945, pp. 11-14).

[3] The council-place (*kgotla*), usually a large circular enclosure, which is a distinctive feature of every Tswana village.

seemed to excite their confidence. But lying down to sleep, in consequence of the fatigue of the long walk, seemed to have the full effect I desired, and they soon came round me in considerable numbers. There seemed to be something horrid in the appearance of these people, but perhaps the impression on my mind may be accounted for by the fact that I saw as ornaments round their necks peices of gun locks, tin jugs, &c, and one had a peice of sail cloth round his head which I felt sure must have been taken from the waggon of the unfortunate Gibson.

They however during the few days of my stay with them treated me with kindness, and I had more than ordinary pleasure in telling these murderers of the precious 'blood which cleanseth from all sin'. And I blessed God that he has conferred on one so worthless the distinguished privelege & honour of being the first messenger of mercy that ever trode these regions. It being also the first occasion in which I had ventured to address a number of Bechuanas in their own tongue without reading it renders it to myself one of peculiar interest. I felt more freedom than I had anticipated. But I have an immense amount of labour still before me ere I can call myself a master of Sicuana. This journey discloses to me that when I have acquired the Batlapi there is another and perhaps more arduous task to be accomplished in the other dialects. But by the Divine assistance I hope I shall be enabled to conquer. When I left the Bakaa the chief sent his son with a number of his people to see me safe part of the way to the Makalaka. I shall not however say anything more respecting them untill I get better acquainted with their actual condition.

On returning to the country of Bubi, I found 16 of the people of Sebegwe (g sounded gutterally) waiting my arrival. He is chief of one half of the Wanketze tribe,[1] & lives nearly ten days directly west of Bubi. He was driven into his present position in the sandy desert by Mosilikatsi, and there he had the address to cut off many detachments of the forces of that marauder while all the other tribes fled before them. By superior generalship he managed to keep possession of his cattle. The others having lost theirs are envious, and having leauged together lately purchased a number of horses & guns in order to deprive Sebegwe of what he alone had courage to defend. In order that he might be a more easy prey to them, they have been trying for some time to induce

---

[1] BaNgwaketse, an early offshoot (and southern neighbours) of the BaKwena. Shortly before 1820, and during the reign of Makaba II, his heir Tshosa had seceded with part of the tribe. In 1824 Makaba was killed in battle, and Sebego (his son by the second-ranking wife) then became chief of the main body. (Schapera, 'Short History of the BaNgwaketse', 1942, pp. 5–6).

him to come out of his present situation to a country near to Bubi, where he can sow corn, &c. Sebegwe could not trust the tribes in this direction, for he knew that the individuals who had prepared to attack him belong to all the Southern tribes. Even his own brother Sehutsane,[1] chief of the other half of the Wanketze, murdered the ambassadors which Sebegwe had sent to conciliate him. The plundering expedition was to have left this quarter during the time I was in the Bakwain country. I therefore felt anxious to inform him of his danger, and thus by doing as I should have wished to be done by perhaps prevent much bloodshed. But I found it quite impossible to proceed into the desert. The sand and want of water are almost insuperable obstacles to the traveller in that direction.

Bubi, however, unknown to me sent off a messenger to Sebegwe to state to him my wish to see him. The result was that these people were sent to invite me to an interview, in order, as Sebegwe stated, that 'I might speak words of truth to him'. He wished to come out of his present uncomfortable situation in order that his people may grow corn &c. But the machinations of certain individuals in the tribes in this direction has hitherto prevented him. He says he would have come immediately to live with me at Bubi's had I intended to remain. But not knowing the intentions of the Directors with respect to the Interior I could not invite him to remove. So great is the impression in favour of our superior power amongst all the people in the interior, each tribe imagines if one European lived with them they would be quite safe. They think those who conquered Mosilikatsi are invincible, and don't distinguish as yet the difference between us and the Boors. I believe Sebegwe knows what missionaries are, & perhaps that was the reason he had confidence in my veracity. He has been visited by Mr Moffat when not so far north as at present.[2]

I am happy to be able to add that the Lord has turned the counsels of those who were bent upon plundering Sebegwe into foolishness. Many from the neighbouring tribes have sent for horses and guns as far as to Colesberg,[3] but all their plans have a few days ago fallen to the ground. It is also pleasant to add that through the whole, although frequently enticed, the believers to a man have stood true to their principles and

[1] Segotshane, younger brother of Tshosa (who had died in 1822). His village was at Tswaneng (Chuaning, 25° 31′ S., 24° 59′ E.). (Schapera, *op. cit.*, pp. 6–7, 9.)
[2] This was in May 1827, when Moffat was staying temporarily at Tswaing Pan (Morokweng, about 100 miles N.N.E. of Kuruman), where Sebego went specially to see him. Cf. *Miss. Labours*, pp. 469–70; *Apprenticeship*, pp. 254–7.
[3] At that time the nearest European centre in Cape Colony; situated 30° 43′ S., 25° 06′ E., about 300 miles S.E. of Kuruman.

refused to have anything to do with the counsels of the wicked. All is now peace within our borders.

With respect to the prospects for missions in the Interior, I think they are encouraging. There is no desire to have us, but there is security for both life & property with any of all the tribes we know, and scope for our labours provided we enter the field. Here on the outskirts we might remain without the probability of being disturbed, but we should not have scope so wide as in thousands of villages in England. We must I conceive go forward, and go forward far too, in order to get at the heathenism of this country.

With respect to Mosilikatsi, he is so much dreaded by the natives here that if we listen to their accounts we should expect him to come down upon Kuruman whenever he liked & carry all before him. I have only to say that if one travelled at the rate of 20 miles per day for the space of a full month in a north-east direction he might expect to find him, but not sooner. When I went to the Bakwains, the natives here positively assured me that he was a little way only to the north of them. But I found from the Bamangwato that he is at least 14 days North-East of them, & on the banks of a collection of water called Mokhoro[1] or the Lake of the Botletli, and he has been completely humbled by the Boors. This latter people, too, are too far to the East of the tribes with whom we have to do (and do not come farther West in their claims than the country around Mosiga[2]) to be any source of any uneasiness to us in the prosecution of our labour.

7th July. I beg leave thankfully to acknowledge the receipt of your kind favour of the 18th February last, which has just come to hand. I look anxiously for your next, as I hope it will contain something definite respecting the Interior.

I beg leave to remain,
affectionately yours,
David Livingston

[1] '. . . a fresh water lake called Mokhoro, or the lake of the boat, on account of the canoes [Tswana *mokôrô*] which are found upon it' (30.vi.43 Bennett). This apparently refers to L. Ngami (called 'Macori' in Smith, *Diary 1834–1836*, ii, p. 271), which, however, is far to the N.W., not N.E., of where the BaNgwato were then living. 'The Botletli' are the BaTeti (see below, p. 161), who live along the Botletle River, on the route that D. L. subsequently took to the Lake (1849).

[2] Mosega (now called Sendelingspos, 25° 40′ S., 26° 02′ E., about 10 miles S. of Zeerust). It was here that the Boers had defeated the MaTebele in January 1837.

6. To J. J. FREEMAN
18 July 1842

[LMS 22. Received 26 November 1842. Previous publication: *Chronicle*, vol. vii, (April) 1843, pp. 57–8 (edited); Chamberlin, pp. 37–9 (incomplete)]

Kuruman
18th July 1842

Dear Sir,

A period of twelve months has now nearly elapsed since my arrival in the country of the Bechuanas. And though during that time ample opportunities have been afforded me for ascertaining the real state of this Mission, I have not untill now felt it to be my duty to make any definite statement to the Directors respecting the amount of amelioration of which, by the devoted labours of the missionaries and Divine favour, the Bechuanas here have been the subjects. And I am not at all sorry that I have refrained so long, for, in gradually becoming conversant with their condition, some things exceeding and others falling within my expectations would probably have swayed my judgement & prevented me coming to a calm conclusion had I written sooner on this point.

Untill lately, too, I was not fully aware of the proper point from which to view the improvement which has been effected. We must not only be conversant with the present condition of the Bechuana converts, we must be intimately acquainted with others, sunk low in the same depths of degradation from which these have been raised, before we can appreciate the magnitude of the change. To me lately arrived from England, the condition of the converts presented many features of pleasing interest. But not untill after I had visited the tribes in the Interior, which may be called the facsimiles of what the converts were, was I able to see in all their greatness the wonderful works of the Lord. The contrast between what they were and have now become is most striking, and it forces on my mind with greater power than ever the conviction that the gospel has lost none of its pristine efficacy. It is still, thanks be to the Lord, the power of God unto salvation, and the evidences of its power which I here witness will, I believe, make me cherish higher ideas than ever of the efficacy of the instrument with which I am entrusted for turning the nations to God.

The number of those who give good evidence of a decided change of heart, when compared with the amount of population on the station, is very large, and we are delighted to behold from time to time large additions made to it. Many of these, too, are such as we should scarcely have expected to see made trophies of grace. These accessions are constituted of not only the young and vigorous; but the old and grey-headed, whose hearts had been subjected to a long course of induration, come forward as well, and profess their determination to devote even their eleventh hour to the service of Him who died for them. The Lord is indeed doing great things amongst us, and our hearts rejoice in the works of His hands. I can the more freely bear testimony to the mighty effects which have and do still follow the faithful and devoted labours of my elder bretheren in this place, as my instrumentality has in no way contributed to the result. And from my knowledge of the character of Mrss Hamilton and Edwards, I believe in their communications to the Directors they must have always kept considerably within what they might have told of the progress of the cause of Christ through their instrumentality.

One of the most pleasant features of the Mission is the progress made by the children in the infant school under Mrs Edwards. Founded and (with only occasional assistance from one of the natives) carried on from its commencement entirely by herself, it shews what an amount of influence may be exerted over a country by the devotedness of a single individual. The parents form a mighty contrast with their fellow-countrymen still in darkness, and it is nearly as great between them and their children. Indeed, the intelligent expression of countenance visible even to strangers, and their amount of knowledge, would almost lead one to fancy they belonged to another species, and I have no hesitation in asserting that if the efficient tuition of their instructress is in the arrangements of Providence continued to them, there will be as much difference between the intellectual developement of children and parents as we see between the physical developement of our agricultural and town population in England. I look to the infant school with peculiar satisfaction, for it furnishes me with the hope that many with their hearts embued with piety, and minds capable of being stored with knowledge, will spring up from it and go forth to make known in distant regions the unsearchable riches of Christ.

It is with much pleasure I can thus bear my humble testimony to the efficiency of the bretheren who have preceded me in this part of the missionary field, and while I magnify the grace manifested both in and by them I pray to be enabled to walk with humility and zeal in their footsteps. May the same power which supported them ever uphold and cause me to be faithful.

The church is in a most flourishing condition, and though there are still some points in the character of the converts which require the exercise of charity and forbearance in us, a visible improvement is going on. It is not a standstill church. It is making headway against the world, and in several instances the truth is beginning to prevail over their selfish national character. The person who conducted my waggon into the Interior in one of my journies is an instance, for when I paid him eighteen dollars[1] as wages he immediately laid down twelve as his subscription to the Auxiliary Missionary Society.[2] May the Holy Spirit be poured out on us more abundantly, so that the spirit of benevolence may be increased, and all the dark places of the Interior soon feel its blessed effects.

I am, Dear Sir,
affectionately yours,
David Livingston

P.S. I wrote the Directors on the 3d inst., and told them some particulars of my journey in the Interior. No instructions having in the meantime arrived, I intend in a short time to proceed thither again, and with the Divine permission remain there several months, visit the tribes north of the Bamangwato, and while making it a preaching tour will endeavour to make as much progress in the acquisition of their dialects as the time will allow.

7. To DAVID LIVINGSTON

29 January 1843

[LMS: Outgoing Letters, Africa, Box 5, pp. 521–3. Previous publication: Chamberlin, pp. 39–40 (two disconnected paragraphs)]

London
Jany. 29, 1843

Dear Brother,

We gladly embrace the opportunity offered by the return of our brother, Mr Moffat,[3] to acknowledge the receipt of your useful communication of July 18, 1842, by the perusal of which, we need scarcely say, we have been exceedingly gratified and encouraged. We desire to

---

[1] The rix-dollar, then worth about 1s. 6d.; an old form of currency surviving from the period of Dutch rule in Cape Colony (1652–1806).

[2] The members of each church were expected to contribute to its support and for the aid of mission work in the vicinity. The amount raised at Kuruman in 1842–3 was £17.15.8 (*Report*, 1843, p. cvi).

[3] Moffat embarked at London for S. Africa on 30 January (*Chronicle*, vii, 1843, p. 44).

unite in devout thanksgiving for the merciful preservation which you experienced during your several long and arduous journeys in the interior of the Bechuana country, and we heartily rejoice in the measure of success by which your efforts were attended, as well as the favorable prospects of future advancement in the Mission work among the various barbarous tribes north of Lattakoo which they appear to have opened.

It affords us unfeigned pleasure to express our entire approval of the measures you have pursued, and our grateful satisfaction at the vigor, perseverance, and fidelity with which they were prosecuted. Nor do we hesitate to state our cordial concurrence in your sentiments as to the desirableness of undertaking the permanent operations of the Society among the tribes to whom your attention has been directed. It is on this principle we have appointed the brethren by whom Mr Moffat is accompanied on his return to Africa,[1] and we trust arrangements will be made at an early period towards carrying this view into effect. . . . in a real measure . . . advancing into and labourers . . . your instrumentality,[2] but for many years to come it appears equally obvious that Native laborers will need the constant instruction and superintendance of European missionaries, and we are therefore now endeavoring to the extent of our means to provide it. The combination of the Lattakoo and Griqua Town Missions providing and organizing an efficient body of native agents for the service of both stations also appears to us very desirable, and we trust that there will be no insuperable difficulty in forming such a union.

It is with this view, and for other important purposes which will readily suggest themselves to your own mind, that we have appointed a District Committee, consisting of the brethren connected with the Griqua and Bechuana stations, of which you will be a member. In connection with the brethren thus associated, you will be able to concert the best plans for the formation of new stations and the adoption of new measures for the spiritual benefit of those multitudes who have for ages sat in darkness and in the region of the shadow of death, and we trust that through the power of God you may be honored to accomplish in those hitherto unevangelised regions changes as great and as blessed as those which have been wrought in the sphere more Southward of your honored predecessors.

We refrain from entering on the present occasion into any enlarged

---

[1] They included two recruits for the Bechuana Mission, viz. William Ashton and Walter Inglis. Both were accompanied by their wives. (*Chronicle*, vii, p. 44.)

[2] Four lines (about 30–40 words) so faintly impressed that only a few words are legible.

detail on the important subject of Native agency in reply to your communications, as you will have ample opportunity, in your official capacity as a member of the District Committee, of explaining and advocating your views or proposing any specific measures which you may deem desirable, and you may rest satisfied that the recommendations of the Committee, in support of such views and propositions, will always meet our ready and cordial consideration, inasmuch as we highly appreciate your exertions and cherish an earnest desire to respond to your solicitude and encourage your efforts on behalf of the Native tribes.

Affectionately commending you to God and to the word of His grace, and in the hope of receiving fresh communications from you at an early period,

I remain, dear Brother, on behalf of the Directors,
faithfully and affectionately yours,
for J. J. Freeman and self, Foreign Secretaries,
[Arthur Tidman]

8. To ARTHUR TIDMAN
24 June 1843

[LMS 23. Received 18 December 1843. Previous publication: *Chronicle*, vol. viii, (February) 1844, p. 20 (edited extracts); Blaikie, pp. 56–8 passim (précis and isolated paragraphs); Chamberlin, pp. 42–9 (incomplete)]

Kuruman
24th June 1843

Dear Sir,

Your kind and encouraging letter I found a few days ago on returning from another tour in the Interior, and I now beg leave gratefully to acknowledge the encouragement it imparted to my mind. It afforded me unfeigned pleasure to be informed that the measures I felt it my duty to adopt had met the approbation of the Directors. Their satisfaction in my labours I hope at all times to feel anxious to secure, and I earnestly pray the Great Head of the church may condescend so to guide my operations as that all may be for His glory. If that prayer is answered, I have no doubt but that I shall obtain not only the testimony of my own conscience but also the approbation of all His eminent servants.

In reference to two topics adverted to in yours, viz. Native agency and the appointment of a District Committee, it will be gratifying for you to be informed that, having written some of my Christian friends in Scotland in behalf of the former, I have recieved some very encourageing promises of support. One[1] has already remitted the sum of £12 to the Society, and others promise to make an effort to raise other two such sums as soon as the then depressed state of the country had been got over.

But with respect to the latter measure I confess I entertain no very sanguine hopes of its being successful. I only know of two of the bretheren, viz. Mrss Moffat & Ross,[2] at all desirous of its establishment. This, and the fact that the others will join simply because such is the expressed will[3] of the Directors, seem to augur ill for its prosperity. For my own part, although a warm admirer of the principles on which the Congregational Unions of England and Scotland are formed, my short experience among missionaries makes me not quite so sure of the propriety of missionary unions. The salutary influence of enlightened public opinion which these possess is here entirely awanting, and without it I believe we may in our corporate capacity do what as individuals no one of us should ever dare. I however endeavour to repress my private feelings on the subject, and I do so with the hope that the measure may be productive of all the advantage to the cause which a well-conducted combination is calculated to effect. But the Directors will not, I trust, consider me guilty of any impropriety if, when yielding a prompt compliance with their wish, I feel constrained to add I must reserve to myself the power of withdrawing from that Committee if at any future time I feel that to be my duty. If compelled to dissolve my connection with it, I earnestly hope it may not be in consequence of having indulged a spirit inimical to brotherly union, but that it may be the result of a humble prayerful deliberation, and with grief that the measure has failed to answer my expectations.

I shall now endeavour to give you some account of the manner in which I have been employed since the date of my last, viz. 18 July '42, and of the prospects still before us, notwithstanding the commotions which soon after that period arose. No instructions had arrived from home, and the esteemed bretheren Hamilton and Edwards having fully approved of my efforts to benifit the Bakwains, I resolved immediately to follow up these endeavours in another journey.

But when all my arrangements had been completed, the sad news were brought that Sebegwe, the chief of the Bangwaketze, had con-

---

[1] Mrs J. McRobert, wife of the Congregational minister in Cambuslang, Lanarkshire (cf. *Fam. Letters*, i, p. 73).

[2] William Ross (1802–63). He and his wife had come from England together with D. L., and were now living at Kuruman. They are often mentioned in *Fam. Letters*.

[3] 'rule' (Chamberlin, p. 42).

trary to the advice I tendered him last year from the Bakwain country left the desert of the Bakalihari, that he had been attacked by the combined forces of Mahura[1] and Sehutsane, and that very many of his people had been murdered. To add to our grief on the reception of these news, we learned that several of the believers of this station had been with Sebegwe at the very time of attack. They being ignorant of the treachourous designs of their chief had just before assured Sebegwe that Mahura was his friend & ally. The consequence was, an impression was produced on the minds of both Bangwaketze & other Interior tribes that the believers had been the means made use of by Mahura for the betrayal of Sebegwe. Some incidents which happened during their visit tended very much to deepen that impression. The accidental firing of a musket, on the night preceding the attack, by one of the visiting party, was construed as having been the signal by which they apprised Mahura of the exact situation of Sebegwe, the singing at family worship as their incantations for success, and the collecting the people together for worship (it being Sabbath morning when the attack was made) as only a pretext by which the believers tried to aid the massacre.

On being informed of these untoward events, I felt still more anxious to undertake the journey, that by my presence and explanations I might endeavour to disabuse the minds of the Heathen of their prejudices. I feared if no effort for that purpose were made the prejudices against our people might become transferred to the gospel, and thus another barrier be raised against us when we should be permitted to carry it to them. But after making every effort I found it impossible to procure people for the waggon. All the natives felt certain that Sebegwe would revenge himself on the first party from this quarter that fell into his hands. I was therefore compelled to remain in this neighbourhood for several months afterwards. This I very much regretted, as the population here is very small indeed. The majority are professors of religion, and the remainder being very few there is no scope for more than two missionaries at most.

The greater portion of my time I employed in itineracy to the ajacent tribes. But when here I took part in the routine business of the station, preaching, working occasionally at the printing press,[2] assisting at the erection of a small chapel got up by Mr Edwards & myself at one of the outstations, administering to the wants of the sick, many of whom come great distances for aid, and other duties which, though different entirely

---

[1] Chief, 1825–69, of the BaTlhaping at Taung.
[2] Established at Kuruman in 1831 for the printing of religious works, chiefly in the vernacular (Moffat, *Miss. Labours*, p. 563).

from those of the minister at home, all require to be cheerfully performed. To think of standing upon what some people at home call
'clerical dignity', in the sense they have of it, would be as much out of
the place in a missionary in Africa as his becoming entomologist would
be.

The work of God has been going on steadily here ever since we
arrived, but I am not aware of its having recieved any visible impulse
through our instrumentality. It must therefore be attributed under God
entirely to the machinery previously set in motion by our honoured
predecessors. If you could realize this fact as fully as those on the spot
can, you would be able to enter into the feelings of inexpressible[1] delight
with which I hail the decision of the Directors that we go forward to
the dark Interior. May the Lord enable me to consecrate my whole
being to the glorious work.

Most of my period of suspense here was one of great commotion in
the Interior. One tribe after another was attacked, either by the
Southern tribes or by the more to be dreaded Matibele. These wars &
rumours of wars seemed to occupy the minds of those under the preaching of the gospel, to the exclusion of everything else. This proved a
great hindrance to the work of conversion. But by the month of February last the ferment had so far subsided I was at length able to find
people to conduct the waggon.

I left this on 21st of February, and after 12 days' travelling arrived
at the village where Sebegwe with the remains of his tribe has taken up
his residence.[2] One of my men had been of the party which it was supposed had betrayed him. He entered the village along with me, and
when we arrived at the place where Sebegwe & his warriors were
seated, a most uproarious recognition of my servant followed, after
which, I having taken my seat close by Sebegwe, he turned to me and
demanded why I had attacked and destroyed all his people. I replied by
asking why he had refused to listen to my advice and thus destroy himself. Did the messengers he had sent to me last year fail to deliver my
message, or did he discredit my words? Some of the messengers being
still alive then recognized me, and Sebegwe & I soon became very good
friends. He urged in excuse for acting contrary to my advice that he was
already on his march out of the Bakalihari country when his messengers
returned, that he was most desirous again to eat corn, that great numbers of his people had been cut off by a fever which prevails near the

---

[1] 'irrepressible' (Blaikie, p. 56).
[2] At Tlhasokwane, close to the modern town of Zeerust, W. Transvaal (Schapera,
'History of the BaNgwaketse', p. 10).

Lake Mokhoro,[1] and that being entirely ignorant of the power of guns he despised the Batlapi as antagonists.

The meaning of the comet which was then visible to us in all its splendour[2] was his next enquiry. He, like all the tribes which I visited, thought that it was indicative of the approach of some dreadful calamity. Perhaps it was significant of the death of Mahura, which he had been trying to bring about by means of witchcraft, or it might be an intimation of another inroad of the Matibele, as they had seen a comet just before their first invasion.[3] I tried to convince him that there was no calamity permitted to befall man except by the will of God, and that for some object of good to those who experienced it. But the mind of poor Sebegwe is on these subjects as dark as midnight.

He however during the whole of our visit behaved in a most friendly way. It being Saturday when I arrived, I explained the nature of the Sabbath and requested an opportunity to address his people. Next morning before daybreak I was much pleased to hear a herald proclaiming that, by the orders of the chief, 'nothing should be done on that day but praying to God and listening to the words of the foreigner'. He himself listened with great attention when I told them of 'Jesus and the resurrection', and I was not unfrequently interrupted by him putting sensible questions on the subject. He told me that he once saw Mr Moffat,[4] but as Mr M. was then young and did not know the language it is not remarkable that Sebegwe had forgotten all that had been said. May the Holy Spirit be poured down upon him, for without His gracious influence nothing that we can do will penetrate the thick crust of ignorance which envelopes their benighted souls.

After remaining a few days with Sebegwe and partaking of such hospitality as his reduced circumstances now enable him to bestow, I passed on to the Bakhatla, who live a few hours to the Northwest. Their situation is peculiarly well adapted for missionary operations, more so indeed than any I have seen in this country. There is as great a

[1] In the course of his retreat from the MaTebele, Sebego had taken his people as far as the district of Ghanzi, south-west of L. Ngami (Schapera, *op. cit.*, p. 8).

[2] The 'great comet' of 1843, first seen in the southern hemisphere towards the end of February, and with most brilliancy early in March; 'one of the finest that has appeared during the present century' (G. F. Chambers, *Handbook of . . . Astronomy*, 4th ed., i, 1889, p. 447).

[3] In *Travels*, p. 10, D. L. says this was in 1816. Moselekatse's MaTebele first attacked the BaNgwaketse in 1830 (Schapera, *loc. cit.*), but the name 'MaTebele' was often also applied to the 'Mantatees' (cf. Moffat, *Apprenticeship*, pp. 84, 85), who attacked them in both 1823 and 1824. Chambers (*op. cit.*, i, pp. 524–9) records a 'very brilliant' comet in 1819, and others, 'visible to the naked eye', in 1821, 1822, and 1830.

[4] See above, p. 24.

population collected in one spot as in any other point in the Interior, and that population seems attached to the soil. There are abundant facilities for a more improved mode of agriculture, even should that be adopted by a much more numerous population than at present exists.

The manufactory of iron seems to have been carried on here uninterruptedly from a very remote period. The ore is found at the junction of the trappian & sandstone rocks in the immediate vicinity of the villages, and is scarcely anywhere covered by any depth of soil. It was very near to this spot where Mr Campbell faced about to go home, and very probably the iron founderies which he heard of but was not permitted to see are the very same as belong to them.[1] They always refuse admittance to those who have had intercourse with the other sex since the period of the year when they annually commence smelting, lest they should bewitch the iron, which is probably the very same reason which prevented Mr Campbell a sight of them.[2] Iron bewitched is when it is burned to a cinder from a too brisk use of the bellows. When the chief & principal families of this tribe fled along with Sebegwe on account of the inroads of the Matibele,[3] the majority of the tribe remained and carried on their works in iron as usual. The nature of the soil, too, is different from that at Kuruman, and it is probable we should not be mortified as here by the frequent removals of the people on account of the deaths of their cattle; and as they are situated near several other tribes, the difficulties of itineracy and superintendence of native agents among them would not be very formidable.

I lately asked the chief of that tribe if he should like me to come and be his missionary. He held up his hands & said, 'O, I shall dance for joy if you do; I shall collect all my people to hoe for you a garden, and you will get more sweet reed & corn than myself.' No instructions on the

[1] John Campbell (1766–1840), a Congregational minister in London, visited S. Africa twice on behalf of the LMS. On his second journey (1819–21) he travelled to the BaHurutshe at Kaditshwene (about 28 miles N.E. of Zeerust). He records that they worked both copper and iron, but does not mention being excluded from their 'iron founderies'. He writes, instead: 'They asserted also that copper furnaces were behind the houses of some of their captains, but we never could obtain a sight of them. They did not flatly refuse, but put it off from time to time. Perhaps they acted thus on the principle of the Birmingham and Sheffield manufacturers, being jealous lest others should obtain a knowledge of the art' (*Travels . . . Second Journey*, 1822, i, pp. 275–6).

[2] D. L. and Edwards, in 1841, were more fortunate. 'They stated that the reason why we were admitted to see the whole was that we were white men & had not been with our wives for some time, so they hoped no harm would befall the iron' (2.xii.41 Prentice).

[3] Mosielele, the Kgatla chief, was Sebego's sororal nephew and had been brought up among the BaNgwaketse. He and his dependants rejoined their own tribe after Sebego's defeat (Schapera, 'History of the BaNgwaketse', pp. 4, 7).

subject of an Interior Mission having then come to hand, I could only say in answer to his enquiries that I should inform my Christian friends in England of his desires for a missionary. I need scarcely add that his wish, although sincere, does not indicate any love to the doctrines we teach. It is merely a desire for the protection & temporal benefit which missionaries are everywhere supposed to bring. It is, however, as much as we can expect from the Heathen. If we have security for life & property, we trust the Lord will give us in His own time all the rest our hearts long for.

The village of Sechele, chief of the Bakwain, is five days beyond the Bakhatla. Last year he was exasperated with me for remaining a month with Bube, another Bakwain chief, whom Sechele considers as in rebellion against him.[1] He made known to some of the believers of this station his determination to do me mischief should I ever attempt to pass his country again. But the Lord was my shield, and Sechele was kinder than I ever saw him before. His only child was sick when I arrived, and the child of one of his principal men was reduced to a skeleton by dysentery. The means I employed were with the Divine blessing useful to both, and Sechele did not seem able to speak a single angry word.

We had much private conversation together, in the course of which he told me all his objections to the gospel we preach. Several of his questions were striking. One was, 'Since it is true that all who die unforgiven are lost forever, why did your nation not come to tell us of it before now? My ancestors are all gone, & none of them knew anything of what you tell me. How is this?' (I thought immediately of the guilt of the church, but did not confess.) I told him multitudes in our own country were, like himself, so much in love with their sins my ancestors had spent a great deal of time in trying to persuade them, and yet after all many of them by refusing were lost. We now wish to tell all the world about a Saviour, and if men did not believe the guilt would be entirely theirs.

Sechele has been driven to another part of his country from that in which he was located last year, and so has Bube,[2] so the prospects I had last year of benifitting them by native teachers are for the present

---

[1] Sechele, chief of the BaKwena 1831(?)–92, was the eldest son and lawful heir of Motswasele II, whose assassination (c. 1822) had resulted in the division of the tribe (see above, p. 15). Edwards, after his journey into the interior with D. L., wrote to Tidman (8.xii.41): 'The Bokuene chiefs are at enmity with each other. The younger [Sechele], believing he is the most legal chief of the tribe, has made several attempts in vain to attack the other [Bubi] to induce him to submit to his authority.'

[2] Sechele had been raided by the MaTebele, and Bubi by some BaRolong from Motito (*Fam. Letters*, i, pp. 64, 68, 69).

darkened. It is painful to see it. But we must not be discouraged. If we only do our duty in an energetic hearty way, the Most High will surely lift upon us the light of His countenance & bless us.

The Matibele of Mosilikatze during their last inroad upon the tribes in the Interior[1] took many of the women prisoners. These are constantly making their escape & returning to their respective tribes. When still at the town of Sechele I saw a party of these fugitives which had just arrived. They had travelled nearly two months from the period of making their escape, collecting the roots of the desert for subsistence by day, and climbing any high rock they saw in their way for protection by night. The hardships they had undergone had reduced them almost to skeletons, and it was most affecting to listen to their tale of woe. But on the part of their fellow-countrymen the recital of their sufferings seemed to excite not the smallest sympathy; they were 'women only', and the men sat & listened with the greatest indifference. Truly Heathenism has no bowels of compassion.

The tale of these females, although it had no effect on the Bakwains, had a powerful effect upon the people of my waggon. I could not prevail upon them to go an inch farther, for to go any nearer the Matibele than they were seemed like rushing into the jaws of death. Their very hearts seemed ready to die within them. I was thus reduced to the necessity of either giving up my tour & returning, or going forward on ox-back. I chose the latter, and although it has some inconveniences it possesses some advantages over the waggon.

I visited no fewer than four villages of the Bakalihari, to which with the waggon I could not have come; and as they are much more attentive to our instructions than any other Bechuana tribe, the pleasure of proclaiming the message of mercy to those who had never before seen a white face far outweighed any fatigue incurred in reaching them. By far the happiest portion of my late journey was when, sitting by their fires & listening to their traditionary tales, I could intermingle the story of the Cross with their conversation. They are a poor degraded enslaved people. The other tribes consider them as their inferiors, keep them constantly hunting for them, and although they procure all the skins which the other tribes sew into karosses they can scarcely keep as many as cover their own nakedness. Their gardens are always situated far from their villages, in order to secure the produce from the exactions of their masters; and they are always found far from water, in order to get as few visits from the servants of the chiefs as possible.

[1] About the middle of 1842, when a raiding party from the North attacked the BaKwena and several other Tswana tribes (*Fam. Letters*, i, p. 69).

To us Europeans it is wonderful how they live. But though they be in want of much that we consider almost necessary to existence, a kind Providence has supplied them with many substitutes. They have shewn me more than 40 different kinds of roots and above 30 kinds of fruits which the desert spontaneously yields them, and many of these are by no means unsavoury esculents. 'Locusts and wild honey' abound to them. Perhaps I may be excused if I mention the physiological effects of the Baptist's food. The former is excessively constipating, and the latter has quite the opposite tendency. The locusts pounded & mixed with honey are as good if not better than shrimps at home. It is not probable that he confined himself to that diet. If however 'locusts and wild honey' were as plentiful in the wilderness of Judea as they are now in the desert of the Bakalihari, he would have had very little difficulty in finding a constant supply. During a period of twelve months I saw no fewer than nineteen swarms of locusts, and yet no particular damage was done to the crops of the natives in consequence; and had I myself attended all the calls of the 'honey bird' I should never have been without a sufficiency of honey.

When at the Bamangwato I saw a son of Conrad Buys, a name both known and dreaded by the early missionaries.[1] He is apparently about 30 years of age; is dressed & speaks the language exactly as a native. He is one of their lowest menials, & is kept to tend a garden in a sort of slavery. His father, Buys, after committing many acts of injustice & murder among the more Southern tribes proceeded to the North-East of the Bamangwato, and there fell a victim to fever. The natives took possession of everything belonging to him. Even his children, of whom by different native wives he had seven, the different chiefs took and distributed among their servants. This man had been given by a former chief of the Bamangwato to his present master. Two brothers, he informed me, are still alive, but in servitude to another tribe. He has forgot all about God & Jesus, & only remembers that his father sometimes collected his children, read a book,[2] and then knelt down to pray. He does not remember a single word of Dutch, although I tried to recall it to his memory by frequently addressing him in that language. His owner

[1] Coenraad de Buys, 1761-1825(?), was a notorious Boer renegade, who after leading a turbulent life among the Xhosa tribes on the E. border of Cape Colony had moved north of the Orange River in 1814, and for the next few years figured prominently in the affairs of the southern Tswana tribes, usually as a leader of cattle-lifting parties. In 1820 Campbell heard that he was living among the BaNgwaketse (*op. cit.*, ii, pp. 141-3), but he soon afterwards went farther north, where (as D. L. mentions) he then died. Cf. Anna Schoeman, *Coenraad de Buys*, Pretoria, 1928, pp. 86 ff.

[2] 'sometimes collected his children—and a book' (Chamberlin, p. 48).

would not consent to part with him, so I was obliged to leave him in his sad position; and I could not help thinking that the passage, 'The seed of evil doers shall never be renowned', has found in him something like a fulfillment.

Both Bamangwato, Bakaa, & Makalaka have been visited during the last year by the commandoes of Mosilikatze, and they are all in a much more impoverished condition than when I saw them last. The caverns of the Bakaa & Makalaka saved their lives; their property has all been carried off. The Bamangwato in addition to the loss of property have been considerably reduced in numbers, in consequence of having been without retreats in which to hide themselves. Internal dissensions too, during which the chief killed his own brother,[1] have tended to the same result.

During my last visit to the Bakaa a native who accompanied me was seized with fever just before we entered their village. A report was afterwards circulated that he had been poisoned by the people. This year they seem determined to avoid all cause for such an imputation, for during my three days' sojourn with them they gave me nothing but a little sweet reed and a few watermelons. These were very good, but my Bakwains (of whom I had three, my own people being left with the waggon) said it was only a little water, & complained bitterly of hunger. I felt it too, but I had reason to be thankful for their stinginess. For when returning down their lofty rocks to our sleeping place below, I was so interested in the questions they were putting concerning the subject on which I had just addressed them I forgot for a moment the dangers of the path I was descending. Presently however feeling as if falling down the precipice, I made a violent effort to save myself, but in doing so struck my hand against a sharp fragment of the rock, and the Testament being in that hand it served as a point of resistance, between which & the rock a finger suffered compound fracture. I got a good splint made of a piece of sweet reed. My involuntary low diet saved me from irritative fever, and though I did not rest a day in consequence of the accident it proceeded to heal kindly.

One night however a lion, of which there are very many in that country, came very near to the bush where we were all sound asleep, & then suddenly commenced his hideous roaring. My ox leaped in among us. The poor Bakwains shrieked for fear, and I, half asleep and stupid, seized a pistol with the disabled hand [and] fired, but the rebound hurt

---

[1] Sekgoma's half-brothers Phethu and Bathoeng having seceded from him, he pursued and killed them, and brought their followers back under his rule (Schapera, *Ditirafalô tsa BaTswana*, 1940, p. 78).

me more than the shot did the lion. It rebroke my bone. The Bakwains, who were most attentive to my wants during the whole journey of more than 400 miles, tried to comfort me when they saw the blood again running, by saying, 'You have hurt yourself, but you have redeemed us, henceforth we will swear only by you'. Poor creatures, I wished they had felt gratitude for the blood which was shed for their precious souls. The second edition of the fracture was worse than the first, but as I can bear a little pain it was not nearly so great a hindrance as you may imagine, and it is now nearly well. The Lord has been exceedingly kind to me, He has shielded me in many such dangers. May my heart be stirred up to love Him more ardently, and may His name be blessed for ever and ever.

I might have proceeded farther into the Interior, but as I was more than 200 miles North from the waggon, and the people of it not very trustworthy, I deemed it more prudent to return. The only new people I saw besides the Bakalihari were a portion of the race of Makalaka. They live much farther North than the other tribe mentioned above, and are within 2 days of Mosilikatze. They assured me that that tyrant was still alive and still pursues his carreer of blood. In returning I walked over what was once the site of his town near Mosiga, and where he suffered his last dreadful defeat by a handful of Boors. The grass had recently been burned off the country, so I got a good view of the whole, and a few human bones were all that remained of what once belonged to the marauder. And these will soon be removed, for the hyaenas are so plentiful, in a few years they remove everything by which one could discover a recent field of slaughter. Mosilikatze is living at the distance of 12 days, or about 200 miles, North-East of the Bamangwato.

To one other topic I feel compelled after a long & painful deliberation explicitly to advert, and while I do so I feel tremblingly alive to the responsibility which a statement in any way calculated to influence the decisions of the Directors necessarily involves. Every time I have thought of the duty of making known my convictions my heart has palpitated with fear. But now when I hear of the glorious prospects opened up for missionary enterprise in China,[1] the dread of unfaithfulness overcomes the fear of misleading you. I feel consolation, however, in making known what I consider to be the peculiarities of this part of the world, in the belief that you do not act in consequence of the con-

---

[1] D. L. had probably seen, in *Chronicle*, Sept. 1842 (pp. 136–7), a letter from an American missionary, headed 'Opening Prospects in China', which referred to the favourable effects likely to follow from the British victory in the Opium War (1839–1841).

victions of a single mind, but from the knowledge derived from the sentiments of all your other agents in the country. The conviction to which I refer is that a much larger share of the benevolence of the Church and of missionary exertion is directed into this country than the amount of population, as compared with other countries, and the success attending those efforts, seem to call for. This conviction has been forced upon me, both by a personal inspection more extensive than that which has fallen to the lot of any other, either missionary or trader, and by the sentiments of other missionaries who have investigated the subject according to their opportunities.

In reference to the population, I may mention that I was led in England to believe that the population of the Interior was dense;[1] & now, since I have come to this country, I have conversed with many both of our Society & of the French, & none of them could reckon up the number of thirty thousand Bechuanas. But lest I should mislead I shall give the number of huts in each of the towns not yet under the immediate influence of missionaries. I do so, not with the hope that you will take my estimate as *the truth*, but with the wish that it may lead to a call for statistical information before any other missionaries are sent here. If it is thought proper to accede to this wish, & correct returns [are] made, I am confident the estimate I give below will be over, not under, the mark.

My confidence arises from the following reasons. In every instance I give a larger number of huts than actually exist, in order to obviate the possibility of mistake in counting. A large proportion of the huts are store-houses, & not inhabited by any one. There are usually one of these to the hut of every wife, and there are others appropriated as dormitories for the growing-up daughters of families. And the usual mode of reckoning five to a family ought not to be adopted where, as in heathen towns, poligamy so extensively prevails. Very many have two wives, others have four, some six, & others, such as chiefs, seven. Now each of these wives has her own hut & store hut for preserving corn &c, and this state of things operates most injuriously against the increase of children. The advantage which Christianity has over heathenism in this respect is already quite apparent in villages where the former has been adopted. On these grounds I apprehend we ought not to apply the European mode of computation here. Two or at most three to a hut is all that can be given.

---

[1] Blaikie, p. 34, quotes Moffat's recollection of telling D. L. in London (1840) that he had 'sometimes seen, in the morning sun', on the vast plain to the north of Kuruman, 'the smoke of a thousand villages, where no missionary had ever been.'

I begin with Taons, the chief residence of the Batlapi, because although very near to Mr Helmore,[1] & frequently visited by him, it is, compared to other parts, destitute of the gospel, and it is one of the largest collections of population in the country. Huts 480, last year; but it has recieved by the arrival of Sehutsane there this year about 150 more.[2] Near to Taons there is another section of the Batlapi, under a chief called Motlabani;[3] huts 770, to which for those engaged in tending the cattle of the tribe we may add 200 more. The whole of this population being situated in a valley can be seen at one view; and to us who are more accustomed to see the dreary wilderness than the pleasant haunts of men their number seems prodigiously large. Mr Owen, of the Church Missionary Society, thought there were at least 20,000 souls at Taons. But had he adopted some method of enumeration his estimate would have been less than half that number. Such as it is, however, what a mass of precious immortals is congregated there, and how sad it is to think of their state; they have fled from the gospel, and are to a man its bitter opponents.

The Bahurutse, another tribe in that direction, numbers 800 huts. But no settlement could be made with them, for though friendly to missionaries they live in a most unsuitable locality, and are constantly longing to depart from it. Their own country is in the neighbourhood of the Bakhatla, and there is every probability they will return to it as soon as they recieve certain information of the death of Mosilikatze.[4]

The villages of Litakong (Old Lattakoo), Linokaneng, and Morokueng,[5] the latter the residence of a large section of Barolongs,[6] are

---

[1] Holloway Helmore (1815–60), LMS missionary, then at Bodigelong (Gabodigelo), about 20 miles S.S.W. of Taung.

[2] After his attack on Sebego (p. 32), Segotshane was himself raided by a commando from the south; this induced him to seek the protection of his ally Mahura at Taung (Schapera, 'History of the BaNgwaketse', p. 10).

[3] Motlhabani, then living about a mile from Taung (at Sandbult). His people, the BagaMaidi, were originally BaRolong, but had long been attached to the BaTlhaping (Language, 'Geskiedenis van die Tlhaping', 1942, pp. 122, 126).

[4] The BaHurutshe, traditionally considered the most senior Tswana tribe, had moved (c. 1825) from Kaditshwene to Mosega; but when that place was occupied by the MaTebele in 1832, most of them fled south to Modimong, about 10 miles N.E. of Taung, where they now were. (Breutz, *The Tribes of Marico District*, 1953, pp. 96–7.)

[5] Dithakong (27° 04′ S., 23° 59′ E.) is about 45 miles N.E. of Kuruman; Dinokaneng (a common place-name, meaning 'at the streams') was 'about twenty miles' farther East (Moffat, *Miss. Labours*, p. 423); and Morokweng (26° 07′ S., 23° 46′ E.) is about 100 miles N.N.E. of Kuruman.

[6] BaRolong, one of the largest and most divided of all Tswana tribes; found chiefly in Vryburg and Mafeking districts (Cape Colony) and adjoining portions of S. W. Transvaal.

under the superintendance of the French bretheren of Moteeto, but I may put them into the estimate as 750 in all.

The huts of the people of Sebegwe, with those of three villages of Bamaleti,[1] 500. These villages, although some distance from each other, are not more than a single day's journey from the Bakhatla, which have 400. Of Sechele, chief of the Bakwains, 300; of Bube, 350. These are larger numbers than the Bakwain chiefs had last year. But their increase having been occasioned by the dispersion of the tribe of Sebegwe, it will probably soon be diminished.

The Bamangwato are this year so situated among rocks I could not estimate their number; but though I know they have suffered severely by the Matibele, lest I should commit an error I set them down as at my former visit, 600. The Bakaa 250, the Makalaka 200.

I do not take into account the villages of the Bakalihari, as they were all small, and cannot be given as anything like an approximation to the number of the tribe. The other section of the Makalaka I had no opportunity of estimating.

The sum total of the others is 5,750, which we may call 6,000; and applying the European average we have only 30,000 as the highest possible estimate. This is however much over the real population. Indeed, I question if there are thirty thousand Bechuanas within the sphere of our Society's operations. Certainly there are not forty thousand on this side of the 21st degree of South Latitude, unless we include those under the French & Wesleyan missionaries to the Eastward. Now for this comparatively small population we have no fewer than 12 missionaries & their wives. In this I include the two bretheren at Moteeto, also Mr Schreiner[2] and one of the bretheren at Griqua Town, as Bechuana missionaries.

In view of these facts, and the confirmation of them I have recieved from both French & English bretheren computing the population much below what I have stated, I confess I feel grieved to hear of the arrival of new missionaries. Nor am I the only one who deplores their appointment to this country. Again & again have I been pained at heart to hear the question put, Where will these new bretheren find fields of labour in this country? Because I know that in India & China there are fields

---

[1] BagaMalete, originally of 'Transvaal Ndebele' (Nguni) stock, but nowadays generally considered a Tswana tribe. They were then living about 20 miles N.E. of present-day Zeerust.

[2] Gottlob Schreiner (1814–76), then working among the BaSotho ('Basuto') N.E. of Philippolis (Orange Free State). Severed his connection with the LMS in 1846 and joined the Wesleyans. Among his children were Olive, the famous writer, and William Philip, Prime Minister of Cape Colony 1898–1900.

large enough for all their energies. I am very far from undervaluing the success which has attended the labours of missionaries in this land. No, I gratefully acknowledge the wonders God hath wrought, and I feel that the salvation of one soul is of more value than all the effort that has here been expended.

But we are to seek the field where there is a probability most souls will be converted, and it is this consideration which makes me earnestly call the attention of the Directors to the subject of statistics. If these were accurately[1] returned, and there would be very little difficulty in doing so (an individual could take a census, counting each of the population personally, in such villages as this in the course of a single day, & the largest in the country would require very little more time), it might perhaps be found that there is not a country better supplied with missionaries in the world, and that, in proportion to the number of agents compared to the amount of population, the success may be inferior to most other countries where efforts have been made.

Well supplied as this country is, it bears no comparison to the Colony. There the number of missionaries of different Societies is so large compared to the population it must strike every one with astonishment. Algoa Bay for instance or Colesberg, villages not larger than Ongar,[2] which is I believe the smallest market town in England, have each the gospel preached by three Evangelical ministers, and each of them feels convinced that he has a very large & very important field of labour. *They do believe it*. But in what way they have come to the belief I could not ascertain.

In conclusion I beg leave to say, whatever may be the views of the Directors on this portion of my communication, I feel immensely relieved by making the statement. I feel a load taken off my heart. And may the Lord in mercy guide them to the view of the subject which will tend most to His glory. I must also state that I have, since hearing of the delightful prospects opened in China, felt again the glowings of heart towards that country which were familiar to my mind when I dedicated myself to the mission work there.[3] I feel it is wrong to think more of another field than that to which in the Providence of God I have been called, & endeavour to suppress my feelings. But I tell you

[1] 'actually' (Blaikie, p. 58).

[2] A town in Essex, where D. L. had received part of his missionary training in 1838–9; about 24 miles N.E. of London. Its population (census of 1841) was 870 (*P.P. England 1843*, XXII, p. 93).

[3] D. L. had originally hoped to go as a medical missionary to China, but that was rendered 'inexpedient' by the outbreak of the Opium War (*Travels*, pp. 5, 7–8; cf. below, pp. 314–15).

of them, that you may judge how much ought to be deducted from the force of these statements by taking the existence of these feelings into consideration.

I am, Dear Sir,
affectionately yours,
David Livingston

II

MABOTSA AND EDWARDS

9. To ARTHUR TIDMAN
30 October 1843

[LMS 26. Received 1 March 1844. Previous publication: *Chronicle*, vol. viii, (April) 1844, p. 50 (edited extracts); Chamberlin, pp. 64–8 (incomplete)]

Lattakoo
30th Octr. 1843

Dear Sir,

In my last, dated 24th June, I informed you that there were again, by the establishment of peace, favourable prospects for the missionary cause in the Interior. And I likewise gave you some particulars respecting a tribe called the Bakhatla, which is situated at the nearest inhabited & at present most eligible spot northwards. At that time I had no other intention than that of remaining here, untill by the arrival of the bretheren the Committee of which you advised me should be constituted and final arrangements made for our future operations. But after waiting more than a month in suspense & daily expectation of witnessing their arrival, a letter arrived from Mr Moffat, stating that both he and his companions were detained near the coast and that probably two or three months more might elapse ere they could reach Kuruman.[1]

No one out of this country can imagine how grievously slow everything in it moves except time. But it cannot be otherwise so long as the heavy Dutch waggon and tedious pack ox are the only permanent conveyances. This disadvantage has a great effect on most missionary movements, and not unfrequently presses heavily on our spirits. For with scenes such as those of Exeter Hall[2] living and burning on our recollections, and the remembrance of the shortness of our lives, together with the sad prospects of the heathen immortals before us, it is felt hard to be called to wait or indeed do anything unconnected with the movement onward.

While here I could generally find a sufficiency of work by attending

---

[1] Moffat ultimately reached Kuruman on 13 December (*Chronicle*, viii, 1844, p. 152).
[2] A hall in the Strand (London), where the annual meetings of the LMS and other religious societies were held.

to the wants of the sick, who come in crowds from great distances as soon as they hear of my arrival. But as I believe the expenditure of much time and medicine is not the way in which in this country I can do most for the Redeemer's glory, I usually decline treating any except the more urgent cases. These, with a share of the duties of the Station, might have filled up my time untill the formation of the Committee.

But having always felt an intense desire to carry the gospel to the regions beyond, and Mr Moffat having intimated that 'The Directors would have no objection to Mr Edwards removing to the Interior',[1] and it being a fact too that a little delay would throw the commencement of a new Mission, by whomsoever formed, into the most unfavourable season for health, or else produce a much longer delay, viz. untill the hot season had passed, I concluded that it would be proper to proceed immediately and erect a hut on the spot selected near the Bakhatla. And in this decision I was cordially joined by the bretheren Hamilton & Edwards. The latter indeed resolved to accompany me, and I feel happy in being able to state that on account of his superior knowledge of the use of tools he was a much more efficient agent in the labour that ensued than I was.[2] He also afforded me much assistance by allowing me the use of a waggon, my own having previously been sent off to the Colony with Mr Ross in order to assist in bringing the luggage of the bretheren who are coming to join us.

This proceeding, in as far as I am concerned, does not preclude my being subject to the arrangements of the Committee, either with respect to my location or associate in labour. For though I believe the spot selected is the very best at present inhabited in the Interior — this, too, being the opinion of three Indian gentlemen, one an Aide [de] Camp to the Governor of Madras, who visited it with us[3] — and though I

[1] Edwards had suggested to Tidman (8.xii.41) that a Mission be established 'among the Bakatla, or at Mosiga'. On 12.vii.43 he wrote again to Tidman: 'Mr Moffat wrote me from Cape Town lately, that the Directors had sanctioned my removal from Kuruman to commence that Mission, together with Mr Livingston, with whom I am very happy to be united in that most important undertaking. He has one of the first requisites for a Missionary, good sense, & a liberal mind. We shall, I believe, act together with perfect good feeling, & be united in promoting the objects the Directors have in view by that purposed Mission. We cannot, however desirable, move forward at present. Among other considerations, Mr Moffat & the other Brethren have not yet arrived, from whom we expect further information of the Directors' views.'

[2] Edwards had been sent out to S. Africa by the LMS as an artisan; Moffat refers to his 'knowledge and experience in carpentering and building' (*Miss. Labours*, p. 563).

[3] Only two, J. R. Pringle and T. M. Steele (the aide-de-camp) were in fact visitors from India; the third, A. H. Bain, came from the West Indies. Cf. *Fam. Letters*, i, pp. 79–80.

should be delighted to call it the centre of the sphere of my labours, I shall try to hold myself in readiness to go anywhere, provided it be forward. And with respect to my future companion, as Mr Ross feels it to [be] his duty to remain near Kuruman, I should prefer from a variety of considerations one of the younger, especially Inglis,[1] to any of the older bretheren. But these with all my cares I desire to cast on the Lord, and I earnestly desire He may lead me in that path which shall be most for His glory. My short experience of missionary life fully convinces me of the excellence of the hints contained in pages 18 & 19 of the printed Letter of Instructions.[2] Indeed, close attention to them will enable one to get on pretty comfortably with even the strangest tempers, and it might have prevented much unpleasantness in Africa. May the Lord clothe me with humility and make me more like Himself.

We left this in the beginning of August, and after a fortnight spent in the journey arrived in safety among the Bakhatla. The chief eagerly enquired whether I had, as promised, told my friends of his desire that I should live with him; and on my replying in the affirmative, and that the object Mr Edwards and I had in this visit was to talk on that subject, he expressed himself much satisfied. We afterwards, in a grand 'Peecho'[3] or assembly of his people, stated fully our objects in proposing a residence with them, and desired his counsellors to mention their objections, if they had any, to our coming to teach them. One man said he had heard, 'If any one put himself under the Word of God he should be obliged to put away his superfluous wives'. To this, the only objection offered, another of themselves replied, before we could, 'that he had been to Moteeto, and saw that the missionaries there acted entirely on the voluntary principle, and neither claimed nor exercised authority over any one'. We then explained that our province was not to compell, but to teach the commands of God, to entreat and warn; but should men refuse to obey God, guilt would be incurred before Him, and He will require it. The rest were unanimous in expressing their wish that

---

[1] Walter Inglis (1815–84) had studied together with D. L. at Ongar, where they became very friendly. 'I wish it could be arranged that he should be my companion', D. L. wrote from Port Elizabeth on 13.v.41 to Rev. R. Cecil; so, too, 'O, how much I would like to have Inglis for my fellow-labourer' (8.xii.41 MacLehose).

[2] An undated booklet of 55 pages, entitled simply Letter of Instructions, &c, issued on behalf of the Directors to every LMS missionary when he first went into the field. Section XXII (pp. 18–19) deals with 'conduct to fellow-labourers'.

[3] Tswana pitsó, a mass meeting of tribesmen for the discussion of public affairs. Chronicle, April 1844, has a cover picture of the meeting mentioned; it shows D. L. and Edwards both wearing top hats and frock coats! It is reproduced here as Plate 2.

we should come & live with them. But, alas, their motives in giving us a cordial welcome are very different from ours in desiring to accept of it. They wish the residence of white men, not from any desire to know the gospel, but merely, as some of them in conversation afterwards expressed it, 'that by our presence and prayers they may get plenty of rain, beads, guns, &c &c, and be secure from death by the warriors of Mosilikatse'. May the Lord enlighten their benighted minds.

On enquiring whether they intended to remain on the spot they then occupied, we were delighted to find that they had had it [in] contemplation for some time previously to remove to the very locality selected. They, however, put it in our option whether they should remove or remain where they were. We preferred the former, as the removal was to an adjoining valley much better adapted for agricultural purposes than that they then occupied. A portion of land might have been appropriated to our use, but we preferred purchasing, with the use of the streams on each side of it. I drew up a short statement of the transaction, read it over in Sitchuana, the chief repeating it word by word after me, and when both chief & counsellors perfectly understood its nature they expressed entire satisfaction by affixing their marks. A copy of the document I beg leave to inclose.

We then proceeded to the erection of a substantial hut, 50 ft. by 18. But in this work we got scarcely any assistance from the Bakhatla. Hard work in many of the Bechuana tribes devolves entirely on females, so the males become as unfit as they are unwilling to bear it. One of the four men we took with us feigned sickness during most of the time. But Mabalwe,[1] a deacon of the church here, rendered us invaluable aid. He is willing and anxious to go with us as native teacher, and the bretheren here think him well qualified for that purpose, so I have concluded he is a proper person to recieve the assistance tendered by a friend of mine in Scotland. I have not, however, made any definite arrangement with him, as I feel anxious to hear the plans of the Directors in the Committee before doing so. I have given him a portion of the sum I have drawn in his name, viz. £12, not as remuneration for his services, as I think it undesirable to convey even in a remote way the idea of wages in the Lord's service, but as part of the assistance a believer in another country is desirous of rendering to one who spends most of his time in endeavouring to do good. The remainder will remain in my hands till definite plans are promulgated by the Committee. In the

---

[1] Mebalwe Molehane (see below, p. 102). He became D. L.'s chief assistant, and after the latter's departure from Bechuanaland continued to give faithful service to the LMS, in Matabeleland and elsewhere. He is often mentioned in *Fam. Letters*.

meantime I am endeavouring to give instruction, in order to qualify him for greater usefulness.

The Indian gentlemen above mentioned came to this country in order to have their health restored by the exercises of hunting and travelling. They were totally unlike some others of the same class who have visited this country, for they behaved with great propriety before the natives, and towards us with the greatest kindness, on various occasions supplying us liberally with game and skins to assist us in building, which with the economy we endeavoured to maintain will render the whole expense of journey & building a very small item only in the expenses of the Interior Mission.

We have been here nearly a month again,[1] and the bretheren do not yet appear, but we recieved information yesterday which leads us to conclude that they must now have reached Colesberg. Patience has her perfect work here if anywhere.

Believe me, Dear Sir,
Yours affectionately,
David Livingston

Copy of the Agreement between the Chief &
missionaries respecting the portion of land allotted
to the latter

I, Moseealele,[2] chief of the Bakhatla, with the full consent and approbation of my counsellors and people, do sell and make over for the use of the missionaries of the London Missionary Society that parcel of land which is bounded on the South-East and North-East by the stream Tlomesho, on the North & North-West by the stream Manuane, on the South & South-West by the watercourse winding along the bottom of the hill Mabotsa,[3] extending thence Eastward to the point where the above-named streams meet. And I renounce all claims of sovereignty over the said land. And I make over the said streams for the use of the missionaries, with as much wood & pasturage from the lands in my district as they or successors may require.

In testimony of my full approbation of the disposal of this land, wood, & pasturage, I Moseealele do here annex my mark   +

[1] Since 27 September (*Fam. Letters*, i, p. 86).

[2] Mosielele, chief of the BaKgatla-baMmanaana 1842–73.

[3] The new station, which in accordance with D. L.'s suggestion (see p. 51) became known by the name of the hill, was located at 25° 19′ S., 25° 46′ E. (about 30 miles N.W. of Zeerust, and immediately adjacent to the modern Hurutshe village of Gopane). In tribal traditions the site is usually called Maanwane, after the stream (D. L.'s 'Manuane').

I request my under-chiefs and counsellors in testimony of their approbation to do the same:

Seema	+
Kalaote	+
Monotse	+
Thokoe	+
Mogotse	+
Mabalwe	
Motating	+

We, the undersigned, do hereby certify that we purchased the above-mentioned land, use of said streams, wood and pasturage, on behalf of the London Missionary Society for a gun, some powder, lead, and beads; that both chiefs & people fully understood the nature of the transaction; and that it was with their full consent they were made over to be the property of the London Missionary Society for ever.

David Livingston
Rogers Edwards

Done at Mabotsa on the
28th August 1843

The land is about a mile & a half in breadth, and about two in length. The whole of it can easily be irrigated, and will form excellent gardens for the people. The above document may seem foolish, but it is not without power even in this country. The present location of Lattakoo was bought in a similar way,[1] and to that circumstance its present possession by the missionaries seems mainly to be owing. Those who go to the Interior will be in exactly the same position as the missionaries here were. This consideration induced us to bargain as we did. A gun and ammunition for the purpose of killing game is of much more value than beads. On this ground we gave the musket, & by that means the price is very much less [than it] would have been by any other article of [trade]. As it is, however, the whole will not amount [to] £4.[2] A hill immediately in the rear of the [spot][3] selected is called Mabotsa, a marriage fe[ast]. Perhaps this would be an appropriate name for a [station] in that dark land whence, benighted though it is, we [earne]stly hope many will be admitted into the 'marriage supp[er of] the Lamb.'

D. Livingston

[1] In 1823, for a price variously described by Moffat as 'a comparatively small sum (about £5)', and '40 lbs of beads' (*Apprenticeship*, pp. 113, 189).

[2] Lovett (*History of the LMS*, i, p. 610) says that the land was purchased 'for a gun, value £4'.

[3] Paper torn. From here on, the words in brackets are taken from the extract published in *Chronicle*; those preceding are guesses.

10. To ARTHUR TIDMAN
9 June 1844

[LMS 27. London postmark: 13 January 1845. Previous publication: *Chronicle*, vol. ix, (March) 1845, p. 43 (edited extracts); Blaikie, p. 69 (short paragraph); Chamberlin, pp. 68–72 (almost complete)]

Mabotsa
9 June 1844

Dear Sir,

The Lord having in tender mercy restored me to my wonted health, I have much cause for gratitude in being able again to communicate with you. The affliction from which I have been raised was both painful and protracted, as the wounds discharging profusely prevented the union of the fragments into which the bone was broken,[1] and these having seldom been properly secured, every motion of the body produced a grating irritation which reacted on the wounds. But through the mercy of our Heavenly Father the whole has healed well beyond my most sanguine expectation, and the bone is perfectly straight and firm. It was a severe trial of patience to be laid aside so long, and at a period, too, when every assistance that can be rendered is required. But though I fear I have not learned all that was intended by the chastisement, I trust I have realized much which, though I knew, I did not fully feel before. And I hope I am now more anxious than ever that my spared life may be entirely consecrated to the glory of my great Deliverer.

The Bakhatla are at present busily engaged in removing from their former location to the spot on which we reside, and it is cheering to observe the subordinate chiefs have, with one exception, chosen sites for their villages conveniently near to that on which we purpose to erect the permanent premises. We purpose to build a house to serve as school and meeting-house as soon as possible, and then we hope our efforts to impart a knowledge of saving truth will assume a more regular form than at present.

Among a people so degraded as Bechuanas, no very decided result can be expected unless there is a continuous application of the truth to their minds. And for this missionaries in Africa have superior advan-

---

[1] Early in February, soon after returning to Mabotsa with Edwards, D. L. had been attacked by a wounded lion, which mauled his left arm (*Fam. Letters*, i, pp. 90–1, 93; *Travels*, pp. 11–13). 'The lion left me eleven ugly gashes and a shattered humerus, and these discharging excessively made me as weak as possible' (28.v.45 Hayward).

tages to those in countries more densely populated. There the mass of the population cannot be addressed very frequently, or the address followed by continued and pointed appeals to the same individuals, while here we generally have opportunities of directing the light on to the same minds continuously, and it appears by the Divine blessing to ensure greater results than desultory efforts between which considerable periods intervene. Conversion among Bechuanas is in general by no means a quick process. Their depravity being subnatural, some time elapses ere they are raised to the level of sinners in other countries, and then they seem to require time again before they can accomodate their minds to the change of thought and motive. There may be a leaning to the side of holiness for a long period, but generally a thorough revolution is wrought out before their convictions become embodied in action.

I visited the Bakhatla frequently before the establishment of the Mission. But it was not untill my fifth visit that sufficient confidence was inspired to draw forth a cordial invitation for me to settle among them. And this is the only good I can ascertain effected by my itineracies to them. The reason seems to have been, too long periods intervened between each journey to produce any lasting impression. And this is not to be wondered at, for nothing can exceed the grovelling earthliness of their minds. They seem to have fallen as low in the scale of humanity as human nature can. At some remote period their ancestors appear to have been addicted to animal worship, for each tribe is called by some animal. By it they swear, and in general neither kill nor eat it, alledging as a cause that these animals are the friends of their tribe.[1] Thus the word Batlapi, literally translated, is 'They (of the) Fish', Bakuain 'They (of the) Crocodile', Bakhatla 'They (of the) Monkey', &c.[2] But if the conjecture is not wrong, they have degenerated from even that impure form of worship, and the wisest among them have now no knowledge of it, but suppose some of their ancestors must have been called by these names.

They have reached the extreme of degradation. When we compare the Bakhatla with the inhabitants around Lattakoo, the latter appear quite civilized, and their present state of partial enlightenment shews that the introduction of the gospel into a country has a mighty influence even over those by whom it is either not known or rejected. I am not

---

[1] These usages and beliefs are part of the totemic cult of the BaTswana, now obsolescent (cf. Schapera, *The Tswana*, 1953, p. 35, where the relevant literature is also cited).

[2] Chamberlin, p. 70, has '*Men*' for '*They*'; e.g., '*Men* (of the) *Fish*', etc.

now to be understood as speaking of the converts, nor of the new phases of character the transforming power of the gospel has developed among them, but I allude to the unconverted, and to those other than saving influences of Christianity which so materially modify the social system at home. On many these influences have operated for years, and they have not operated in vain. Hence the mass of the population in the Kuruman district are not now in that state the gospel found them, and in which the poor Bakhatla now are. There, the existence of Deity is tacitly admitted by nearly all, the exceptions denying it rather on account of attachment to their lusts than in sober seriousness. And I believe the number is but small who have not the idea floating on their minds that this life is but the beginning of our existence, and death but one event in a life which is everlasting. But the Bakhatla have had no thoughts on the subject, their mind is darkness itself, and no influences have ever operated on it but those which have left it entirely selfish. It is only now that Christians have begun to endeavour to stop[1] the stream which has swept generation after generation of them into darkness. And O, may [the] Holy Spirit aid our efforts, for without His mighty power all human efforts will be but labour in vain. That power exerted over Bechuanas, raising them from the extreme of degradation and transforming them into worshippers of the Living God, constitutes *the* wonder and *the* cause for gratitude in the Bechuana Mission.

Our native assistant Mebaloe has been of considerable value to the Mission. In endeavouring to save my life he nearly lost his own, for he was caught and wounded severely.[2] But both before our being laid aside, and since recovery, he has shewn great willingness to be useful. The cheerful manner in which he engages with us in manual labour on the station, and his affectionate addresses to his countrymen, are truly gratifying. Mr Edwards took him to several villages near the Kurrechane[3] lately in order to introduce him to his work, and I intend to depart tomorrow for the same purpose in several villages of the Makone,[4] situated N.E. of this. In all there may be a dozen considerable villages situated at convenient distances around us, and we each purpose to visit them statedly.

It would be of immense advantage to the cause had we many such agents. But after being assured by bretheren on the spot, whom I pre-

[1] 'have begun to stop' (Chamberlin, p. 71).

[2] Cf. *Travels*, pp. 12–13.

[3] Kaditshwene (on the farm Bloemfontein 223, Marico District, Transvaal), close to Enselsberg, *c.* 25° 22′ S., 26° 15′ E., and about 30 miles E.S.E. of Mabotsa.

[4] BaKoni, a generic name used by the southern BaTswana for the Sotho-speaking tribes east and north of the Marico River (*Travels*, p. 202).

"In a grand *Peccho*, or assembly of the people, we stated fully our object in proposing a residence with the tribe, and desired the Counsellors to mention their objections, if they had any, to our coming to teach them. They were unanimous in expressing their wish that we should do as we proposed."

2. 'THE DAWN OF MERCY ON A DARK LAND'

sumed to be intimately acquainted with the state of the Mission, that many such could be got, and after most earnest pleading for and recieving assurances of support from my friends at home, I am sorry to say I cannot succeed according to my desire. Suitable individuals are generally so wedged and dove-tailed among their relatives, I fear some time must yet elapse ere that means of spreading the gospel can be extensively brought into operation. Still, believing that it is extremely well adapted to the state of this country, and having seen that it has been extensively blessed for the conversion of souls, I shall never lose sight of it, and constantly pray that God may incline the hearts of his converts to feel more compassion for their countrymen.

Believe me,
Dear Sir,
Yours affectionately,
David Livingston

11. To DAVID LIVINGSTON
11 September 1844

[LMS: Outgoing Letters, Africa, Box 6, pp. 203–8. Previous publication: Chamberlin, pp. 72–4 (incomplete)]

London
Sept. 11, 1844

Dear Brother,

You will be assured it was with strong and affectionate solicitude we received the intelligence of the alarming disaster which occurred to you at Mabotsa in the month of February last. The information reached us in a letter from Mr Moffat, which was dated on the 24th of that month,[1] and since it arrived we have received no further communication on the subject. You will therefore judge of the anxiety we have felt, & continue to feel, as to the results of the serious injury inflicted on your person, under circumstances & in a situation which would render it all but impossible to obtain proper surgical treatment. Our only consolation has been to know that you were in the hands of a gracious God, whose mercy and resources are alike unbounded, and who watches over the lives of his servants with unceasing care. From your own knowledge of

---

[1] D. L. had written to Moffat on 15 February, describing his encounter with the lion and asking Moffat, because of 'inability on my part', to communicate the news to the Directors (*Fam. Letters*, i, pp. 90–2).

surgery, we trust you were able to direct your fellow-labourer Mr Edwards, & others at the Station, to do what was needful on the occurrence of the accident, as well as in its subsequent treatment. We feel that we cannot be too thankful to the God of mercy for your deliverance in the moment of imminent danger, and we earnestly hope the next communications we receive may bring us the cheering intelligence of your entire recovery from the injury you then received.

We also hope that an event which so nearly proved fatal will impress you with the necessity of being very careful for the future how you expose yourself to similar risks. In the country you now inhabit the temptations to personal exposure must be continually recurring, & it will therefore be the more needful for you to observe the greatest caution, remembering the peculiar value of a life devoted, as yours is, to the spread of the Gospel among the thickest shades of heathenism in a region as barbarous as it is remote. We believe that God has graciously endowed you with qualifications especially suited to the exigencies of your present arduous position; and we are therefore the more anxious that no circumstances should arise to withdraw you from it. There we trust your labours will be greatly blest in extending the reign of Christ and diffusing the blessings of his salvation. Your past exertions appear to have been attended by many tokens of his favor. He has honored you to penetrate the untrodden wilds of heathen guilt & misery, and to carry the glad tidings of the Cross where no sound of mercy had ever before been heard, and now he has led you to a spot on which it seems to be his wish that you should concentrate your energies and reap a harvest to the glory of his grace.

We thank God that he has given you the desire, not only to preach Christ among tribes already partially evangelised, but to make known his name in those more distant parts of the wilderness on which not a ray of heavenly truth has ever beamed. Your reception at Mabotsa, & the circumstances under which your labors were there commenced, encourage us to indulge the assurance that the God of Missions is with you, that his grace will be afforded to give saving power to the word which you preach, and that probably ere long you & Mr Edwards will be enabled, with the assistance of Native teachers, to extend your sphere of labor & advance yet further towards the interior of the country.

Having adverted to the subject of Native Agency, of which we rejoice to know you have from the first been a zealous and decided advocate, we would say that we should be glad if you would take the young man, Mokitera Serian, under your immediate superintendence, with a view to his being employed in that capacity.[1] We fear he will not do much good at the Kuruman Station, since *that* is but a comparatively limited field of labour, affording, we apprehend, little opportunity or stimulus to his exertion, especially as through some reason or other it appears he has fallen under censure, the effect of which would naturally be to depress his mind & tend to disqualify him for active service at that Station. When he left this country we felt great interest in him, & indulged the hope that he would prove a valuable labourer; and if, in any way, he has erred from the path of Christian consistency, we hope from a consideration of his youth and inexperience he will be treated with tenderness, & an effort made to restore him to his right position and bring him into some station of respectability and usefulness in connection with the Missionary work. We have written to the Secretary of your Committee on the subject, and thinking that a change of scene and associations might, by God's blessing, have a happy influence on his mind, we have requested that measures might be taken for his removal to Mabotsa, where we are assured you will make every endeavour to promote his welfare and bring him forward into the ranks of Missionary service.

Your letters of Oct. 30 and June 24[2] have reached us in due course, and to the former of these we have already, in preceding parts of this communication, substantially replied. Your letter of June contains[3] two or three points to which we would now briefly advert. With reference to the District Committee, we are grateful that you so readily accepted your appointment from the Directors to act as a member of that body, and we trust experience will have removed any apprehensions you might have felt in the first instance as to the satisfactory working of a plan which has been long tried & found highly beneficial in other parts of the world. The affairs of our Missions in India, the South Seas, & the West Indies, are all conducted by Missionary Committees similarly constituted, and no objection has hitherto been raised against such a mode of operation by those who have to carry it into effect.

The power of a Committee is precisely of the same nature as the

---

[1] Mokotedi was a protégé of Moffat's, who had taken him as a servant to England. There he became spoiled by the fulsome attentions of some LMS supporters, and greatly offended Moffat by his vanity and impudence, which persisted after his return to S. Africa (Moffat to Tidman, 3.xi.45). The Directors hoped he would be used as a 'teacher', but the District Committee decided (Jan. 1844) that 'his character and conduct having been from the period of his departure so utterly inconsistent with the Christian profession', it could not 'recommend his being employed in any way in Missionary operations'. Hence the present appeal to D. L.

[2] 'Your letters of October 21 and January 24th' (Chamberlin, p. 72).

[3] 'Your letter of January explains' (Chamberlin, p. 72).

power of the Board of Directors. In both cases, it is a delegated power, & no more, and the objections which would be fatal to a Committee would also be fatal to a Board, as they are both based simply on the principle of representation and possess no absolute or final authority. The Committee is accountable to the Board, and the Board is accountable to the Members of the Society, to whom, in every case, there is an appeal from the decisions of the former two bodies. In such cases no individual Missionary can suffer wrong from a Committee. If wrong be attempted, he has the remedy in his own hands, by refering the case to the Board, or (if he fails to receive redress there) to its constituents, to whose decision he must clearly either submit, or retire from the service of the Society. We have thus endeavoured to give a correct idea of the nature of a District Committee, because we feel persuaded that, when viewed in its true light, no reasonable objection can be urged against the appointment, & Agency, of such a body for conducting the local affairs of an extensive Mission.

Your statistical notices of the population of the Bechuana Country will be useful for our future guidance in the adoption of measures for extending the Gospel in that part of Africa. On comparison of its population with that of India or China, we fully agree with you as to the superior claims of either of the latter countries on the resources of the Christian Church, and we shall certainly feel it our duty to act upon the principles which you have so properly and earnestly urged upon our attention. At the same time, there will be no diminution of our interest on behalf of the Bechuana Mission, nor shall we ever feel that your own energies could be better employed than in labouring to widen its boundaries and multiply its triumphs.

In the hope of hearing from you directly, at an early period, and commending you meanwhile, with your fellow-labourers and your work, to the Lord's constant favour and protection,

We remain,
Dear Brother,
yours faithfully and affectionately,
Arthur Tidman ⎱
J. J. Freeman ⎰ Foreign Secs.

12. To ARTHUR TIDMAN
2 December 1844

[LMS 31. Received 1 July 1845. Previous publication: Chamberlin, pp. 76–8 (in full)]

Mabotsa
2d December 1844

Dear Sir,

Having in my communication of June last adverted to the causes which prevent native agency being called more extensively into operation, you will readily percieve the reason why in the enclosed I have recommended that £15, of which Mrs Philip[1] recently advised me as 'collected by a Sunday school in Southampton for the support of a native teacher', should for the present year be appropriated to the general objects of the Society.[2] And the reason why I venture to address the contributors is, if the plan of correspondence with this school is calculated to increase or keep alive the interest they already feel in the cause of Christ, I may be honoured to do in one school what you at home now so successfully attempt in all. For though situated, as Roman soldiers once said of Britain, 'out of the world', we look with intense interest on the grand efforts made for enlisting the rising generation, and we have no doubt but by the Divine blessing a phalanx will be raised destined to effect more noble achievements than those of Caesar's soldiers. If you think my letter calculated to draw on the contributors in the path of liberality untill I find a laborer whom I can conscientiously recommend, be so kind as address it to the proper quarter.

Various considerations connected with this new sphere of labour, and which to you need not be specified in detail, having led me to the conclusion that it was my duty to enter into the marriage relation, I have made the necessary arrangements for union with Mary, the eldest daughter of Mr Moffat, in the beginning of January 1845.[3] It was not without much serious consideration & earnest prayer I came to the above decision, and if I have not decieved myself I was in some measure guided by a desire that the Divine glory might be promoted in my increased usefulness. I hope this will be considered a sufficient notification of the change contemplated, and that it will meet with the approbation of the Directors.

[1] Wife of Rev. John Philip, LMS Superintendent at Cape Town. She died in 1847, and an obituary notice in *Chronicle* (xii, 1848, p. 29) records that she assisted her husband with 'zeal and dignity . . . in the discharge of his important and varied duties through a long succession of years'.

[2] 'The enclosed' (a letter, LMS 29, to the donors of the money, dated 17.ix.44) describes the difficulty of finding native teachers, exhorts the readers to seek salvation in Christ, and concludes with a few brief remarks about mission work among the BaKgatla. It subsequently transpired that the money was not in fact intended for D. L.'s use (see below, pp. 85, 102).

[3] D. L. had become engaged to Mary Moffat (1821–62) in July, while on a recuperative visit to Kuruman. They were married there on 2 January 1845.

I may mention that I do not regret having come out single. I rather think it would be advantageous if many of our young missionaries would spend at least as much time previous to marriage as would enable them to acquire the language and become acclimatized. In cases where young men would be kindly cared for by older bretheren, a much longer delay would be advantageous for the mission, but when there is an almost total deprivation of European society & civilization long delay would be improper.

The arrangements connected with the above caused an absence from this station of nearly two months lately,[1] and probably an equal period will be lost by my next visit to Kuruman. But the necessary supplies being obtained at the same time will enable me to devote myself unremittingly to the great work for the future. On my return lately I found that Mr Edwards had nearly finished the walls of a small but substantial school. On its completion the native assistant Mebaloe and I commenced the instruction of the children, and though we found them exceedingly shy at first we by degrees overcame their fears. The attendance, however, is extremely irregular. Sometimes we have fifty, at other times not five. But we hope to overcome all difficulties connected with it by perseverance. The attendance on our other services is also very fluctuating, & when we have a good meeting it is entirely by the influence of the chief. All are at present much deluded by a rainmaker, concerning whom I shall furnish some information which may be appropriate for the Juvenile Magazine.[2] May we be enabled to be faithful to their souls, for if we are there is no doubt but that the Divine blessing will attend God's own word.

After the school was finished, I commenced the erection of a dwelling house, and it is now nearly finished. The dimensions are 52 feet by 20 ft., and it is built of the same material as the school. Mud is heaped on about a foot in thickness at a time, then cut straight, and the heat of the sun is so great in a day or two it becomes both hard & strong. It is therefore both a cheap & easy mode of building. This you will understand when I mention that though my house is large enough to be a church for the station, the whole expense is about £25. The greater heat of the climate required greater dimensions than at stations farther South.

[1] D. L. had left for Kuruman towards the end of June, and was back at Mabotsa on 13 August (*Fam. Letters*, i, pp. 102, 104).

[2] *The Juvenile Missionary Magazine* (a monthly, price ½d., designed for 'the youthful friends of Christian missions throughout the Empire, especially . . . those connected with the London Missionary Society'). The first number appeared in June 1844.

Having engaged to furnish information to a Welsh missionary magazine through the late Revd. E. Williams,[1] I am unable to furnish it directly to the Editor, Mr Roberts of Llanbrynmair,[2] in consequence of being ignorant of his address. If you kindly forward a letter which I send by this post to your care, you will very much oblige,

Yours affectionately,

David Livingston

13. To ARTHUR TIDMAN
23 March 1845

[LMS 32. Received 15 July 1845. Previous publication: *Chronicle*, vol. ix, (September) 1845, pp. 137–8 (edited extracts); Chamberlin, pp. 78–82 (incomplete)]

Banks of the Molopo[3]

23d March 1845

Dear Sir,

As an attempt at response to your circular respecting the Juvenile Magazine,[4] I beg leave to enclose a sketch of the station Mabotsa, kindly furnished by A. H. Bain, Esqre, a gentleman who recently visited that quarter.[5] *A* is placed behind the temporary residence erected previous to our actual removal to the locality and in a native garden, the waving line around being the hedge row, *B* the school, and *C* in the

---

[1] Edward Williams (1814–44), LMS missionary at Hankey (Cape Colony) 1837–1843 (*Register*, pp. 38–9). After his return to England owing to ill health (he died in June 1844), he wrote to D. L., who had met him in 1841. 'He has been the means of establishing a Welsh missionary magazine, and his letter contained earnest entreaties for correspondence for it' (28.i.45 Pyne).

[2] Samuel Roberts (1800–85), 'social and political reformer; ... pastor of Llanbrynmair, 1834–57; became a leader of public opinion among Welsh nonconformists' (*D.N.B.*).

[3] Having gone to Kuruman at the end of 1844 for his wedding, D. L. was now on his way back to Mabotsa with his wife. The Molopo River, where he struck it (near present-day Mafeking), is about 40 miles S.S.W. of Mabotsa.

[4] A printed leaflet, dated 3 May 1844, had announced the forthcoming appearance of the Magazine, and 'earnestly' solicited 'original contributions on subjects affecting the Religious Interests of the Young'. D. L.'s contribution was in fact published not there, but in *Chronicle* (see above).

[5] Andrew Hudson Bain (1819–94), one of the 'three Indian gentlemen' previously mentioned (p. 47), visited Mabotsa again in August–September 1844 (Methuen, *Life in the Wilderness*, 1848, pp. 47, 154 ff.). He subsequently settled in the Orange Free State, where he became a leading citizen and considerable landowner (Williams, *Some Dreams Come True*, [1948]. pp. 153–9). The original of his sketch has not been found. A block made from it appeared as the cover picture of *Chronicle*, May 1846, and is reproduced here as Plate 3.

distance is that point of Kurrechane at which Mr Campbell turned round to go homewards, *D* my own dwelling, *E* the intended site of Mr Edwards's house, *G* the Mission gardens. The line from *H* in the direction of *G* is the watercourse, *F* the principal village with the round cattle-pen of the chief near the centre, *I* a portion of another village, and *J* the beginning of the ascent of the hill Mabotsa. Near to *H* may be observed the long stumps of trees, the remains of the wood in which we commenced.

The spot from which the sketch was taken does not afford the most picturesque view of the station, but it takes in the range of Kurrechane in the extreme distance, & I preferred it on that account to any other. We can look to Mr Campbell as a missionary pioneer with something more than satisfaction, for though there is now comparatively no danger in traversing these regions, scientific expeditions have as yet penetrated but a very small way beyond him.[1]

The following information concerning a 'rainmaker' is presented with the same object. And it may be well to remember that the Bakhatla among whom we dwell in some respects resemble the Batlapi of old. All the maxims of their conduct are based on the absolute ignorance of the present life. The body, with its appetites and desires, is regarded as the whole of man. Unlike the Batlapi of old, however, they treat missionaries with respect. Yet notwithstanding the deference paid us, they cling with astonishing pertinacity to their antient superstitions. Unlike what young people might suppose, they have no curiosity about God and eternity, and this although all that can be said of their own vaguely floating ideas on these subjects is, those who are better informed think they can distinguish in them something like broken planks floated down on the stream of ages from a primitive faith. I have sometimes asked them why, since we had come so far to tell them of these things, they never question me about them. They reply by another question, 'Do we know to ask?' The subject has to be pressed upon them, and they appear as persons dosing towards one who would wake them up. They prefer to get rid of the disturbance that they may again quietly compose themselves to sleep. Alas, they know not that the sleep of sin is the sleep of death.

A belief in witchcraft is characteristic of all the tribes. Many if not all have a fear lest by means of the mysterious powers of plants & roots some of their neighbours may influence the prosperous or adverse

[1] Presumably a reference to the 'Expedition for Exploring Central Africa', 1834–1836, led by Dr Andrew Smith, which went as far north as the Tropic of Capricorn, in long. 27° E. (Smith, *Diary*, i, p. 49; ii, p. 13; and map.)

events of their lives, and like those in our own country who are subject to superstitious fear they never investigate the cause of it. It is exceedingly difficult to induce them to examine for themselves. In the case of the rainmaker who came to Mabotsa I found it impossible. He came with large pretentions, was called 'Morimo' or God, and asserted that he had power to cure diseases, make rain, and charm game for the hunters. He is most insignificant in appearance: of low stature, his hair twisted or plaited like that of a female; the numerous wrinkles around his eyelids nearly obscure the white of his small cunning eyes; wide nostrils, and irregular teeth. His body was without ornament, and his 'karros' filthy, yet some of the most intelligent among the Bakhatla were literally afraid of him. One man, who has scars on his body shewing that twenty-three have fallen by his hand in battle,[1] confessed that he was afraid of him, and took off some of his ornaments as an offering to the rainmaker.

On the day of his arrival the clouds seemed propitious. But though on that and several other occasions he experienced pointed disappointment, the people could not or would not percieve that the excuses he advanced were mere pretences. Having spoken to him in private on the folly and wickedness of his course, I was very soon afterwards blamed as the cause of the departure of the clouds. The chief sent for me and enquired in the presence of a number of his counsellors why I had driven away their rain. I repeated all I had said to the rainmaker, and added I was sorry to see my friends decieved by an impostor. One asked if I did not know that he could not only give rain, but kill people by lightning? Having besought them to put his powers to the test by experiment, an old man gravely remarked that God had made white men wise in many respects, but those who had come forth of Lōey (a cavern in the Bakwain country, with marks in the rocks around somewhat like footprints, from which Bechuanas imagine they were produced in the beginning),[2] these were skilled in other things of which white men were ignorant. White men know how to make guns, and black men know how to make rain, and the latter ought not to be interfered with.

Having admitted our ignorance of rainmaking, and induced them to

---

[1] In some Tswana tribes, warriors were scarified on the back or chest for every foe slain in battle. Methuen, *op. cit.*, pp. 266–8, mentions both this particular man, and also the rainmaker described by D. L.

[2] Lôwê (also called Matsieng), about 12 miles N. of Mochudi (24° 26′ S., 26° 09′ E.), is said by the BaTswana to be the place from which the first human beings and animals emerged on earth. D. L. visited and described it in 1848 (*Fam. Letters*, i, pp. 283–4).

confess our mutual obligations to instruct each other, I offered myself as pupil to the rainmaker. Nothing daunted, he made allusion to the fee of an ox. I offered three if he would only exhibit his power by collecting the clouds during the time we were sitting. He excused himself by saying that he must first go and dig medicines, but promised to bring the clouds in our presence in a few days. But though I placed the whole of my waggon oxen at his disposal, he declined to have me for a pupil when I stipulated that he should make some little difference between his rain and the 'rain from Heaven', such as causing it to rain on my garden one day & on none of the others, or on all the other gardens & not on mine. I wished to test his godship before them by killing a kid by prussic acid and then offer a little of it to him. But the people were afraid of exasperating him, for several called out, 'We have done with him', evidently anxious that I should not proceed to provoke him.

By inducing him subsequently to name the periods in which he would give rain, his failures were pointed out again and again. And on one occasion, when making a great smoke by burning old bones, bulbs, roots, &c, for the purpose of, as he said, healing the clouds,[1] when it was pointed out to them that his smoke was all going to the leeward while the clouds were all situated in the opposite direction, many laughed outright. But though they did so, they still continued to fear, honour, and sing his praises, and instead of believing that we wished to undecieve them, the endeavours seemed to produce the impression that the missionaries did not wish them to obtain rain. They think it is enough to be as their fathers were, content in the power of superstition, and the very indefiniteness of their superstition seems to hold together the system. Power Divine, and that alone, can burst the chain which holds them in bondage.

It may not be known to the Directors that though the Bakhatla have the reputation of being workers in iron, only a very few families in the tribe possess the knowledge of the art. The rest believe that it can be smelted only by means of certain medicines, and that though others who have not the knowledge of these medicines should attempt to smelt the ore, their attempts would prove quite abortive. There are not half a dozen families in the tribe who work in iron.

Being now with my partner in life on our way to resume our labours in connection with that Mission, I purpose on our arrival to commence, in addition to our other services, an evening lecture on the works of God in creation & Providence, and endeavour so far as is in my power

[1] The Tswana verb *alafa*, here translated 'heal', means the use of 'medicines' for either magical purposes or the treatment of disease.

to illustrate the subject on the following day. I intend to commence with the goodness of God in giving iron ore by giving, if I can, a general knowledge of the simplicity of the substance, &c, [and] endeavour to disabuse their minds of the idea which prevents them in general from reaping the benefit of that which abounds in their country. If this fails, I shall try other means to break the power of this superstition. I intend also to pay more particular attention to the children of the few believers we have with us, as a class for whom, as baptized ones, we are bound especially to care. May the Lord enable me to fulfill my resolutions. I have now the happy prospect before me of real missionary work. All that preceded has been preparatory.

> Believe me,
> Dear Sir,
> Yours affectionately,
> David Livingston

14. To ARTHUR TIDMAN
17 October 1845

[LMS 36. Received 13 April 1846]

Mabotsa
17th October 1845

Dear Sir,

As an answer to your most welcome letter of 11th Septr. '44 is now more than due, I begin a narration of the painful events which have transpired since the date of my last, viz. 23d March '45. We were then in our progress hither, and certainly did not anticipate that on the very day of our return a state of mind should be developed by Mr and Mrs Edwards, involving the annihilation of all hope of cooperation in either native or European labour.

Our parting had been one of apparent cordiality, and marked by the expression of abundance of good wishes, and as they had given me no intimation of the commencement of opposite feelings I was totally unprepared for our first interview, which was begun by Mr Edwards in the following words: 'Your conduct has been dishonest, dishonourable, and mischievous; at least this is my opinion, and I don't believe there is another instance on record as bad', &c. Having in his presence taken notes of these and other denuntiations, I interrupted him and asked to what part of my conduct he referred. He replied with still greater vehemence, 'You went to natives, Sir, you went to natives, and there is not a better way for destroying their confidence in my integrity than this'. But being still utterly ignorant of the cause of all his excitement, I had to repeat the request several times, and untill words containing a reference to a case of discipline which occurred six months before had crossed his lips I could not concieve wherein my offence consisted. I then endeavoured to pacify him by giving all the explanations which at the time I recollected, but appealed to him in vain when I besought him to allow for some of the same feelings in my mind which he so repeatedly declared had actuated his own. He refused by declaring with great emphasis, 'I shall always maintain you went to natives'.

Mr Edwards then proceeded formally to demand '*a second apology*' for an offence alledged to have geen given about fourteen months before. 'For', said he, 'I have no right to be satisfied with your first apology'. He likewise informed me that he had, during my absence, written 'what he thought of me to the other bretheren', 'that Mrs Edwards had desired him to say, that she had formerly written favourably of my character to Mrs Moffat, &c, but that she too had' (in my absence) 'thought it her duty to write what she thought to Mrs Moffat, &c.'

Mr E. next produced a long letter for the Directors, in which, by taking a view of himself and all he has done since his connection with the Society in 1823, he comes to the conclusion 'that he is not the mere appendix Mr Livingston wishes him to be'. Notice is also taken of all he has done for the Mission in the Interior: the Directors are told of a journey undertaken by Mr E. and myself into the Bakwain country about three years ago, 'as mentioned in Mr Moffat's work',[1] 'that Mr Livingston has boarded in his house' during his abode at Kuruman, 'that he furnished Mr Livingston with a cart in which to put his bed and baggage on the occasion of proceeding to erect a hut at this station', 'that he furnished provisions and paid the wages of the men who accompanied us', 'that he spoke first at the Peecho which was then held', 'that he did not hear certain statements Mr L. says he heard'. Our first journey to the Bakwain country is said to have been for the purpose of forming a station 'somewhere in the vicinity of Kurrechane, his original destination'. By these, and a number of similar statements, a connection between a journey to a part of the country eight days distant from Kurrechane, and the formation of Mabotsa, is endeavoured to be ex-

---

[1] Cf. *Miss. Labours*, 1842, p. 608 n.: 'Mr Edwards accompanied by one of the younger missionaries [viz., D. L.] has lately gone into the Interior, with the prospect of commencing a mission among the Bakone tribes'. This refers to the journey of 1841.

hibited. And as my account of the formation of this Mission does not include all the events of the three or four years preceding that event, Mr E. attempts to impugn my veracity.

The letter to the Directors contains several other statements, but for each it is difficult to assign an object. There seems to be something like compassion, as when he speaks of 'Mr Livingston's prevailing weakness'; desire for peace, as when he tells the Directors 'how desirable it is that harmony should exist among us', and reveals the fact that there has been a want of concord on this station, for 'alas, peace has been broken on the score of honour.' There is also the desire to communicate information, for the Directors are informed that 'on Mr Livingston's return from the Interior, he (Mr L.) thought a commencement ought to be made at Mabotsa without waiting for the instructions of the Directors, but I (Mr E.) thought it better to wait for the sanction of the Board'. And 'Mr L.'s well-known sentiments are that native teachers are superior to European laborers', that Mr L. 'thinks that no one ought to have anything to do with native teachers except the one who pays their salary', 'that Mr L. engaged the native Christian Mebaloe privately and for private ends', 'that though Mr E. respected that individual, as a Christian whose conversion he had witnessed, yet he had looked upon him as a private individual on the station', and that he has reason to believe 'that Mr L. has accused him to other bretheren'.

The above extracts are given as near the original document as the state of bewilderment Mr E.'s unexpected conduct produced would allow me to take them down at the moment. Mr E. has since recieved the advice for his own sake to alter several of the phrases, but as I have not seen the amended copy I cannot give him the benifit of the milder form in which they may reach the Directors.[1]

A day or two after the interview, Mr E. informed me by note that 'In consequence of the unsatisfactory nature of our meeting, he had resolved to appeal to a Committee of the bretheren and would proceed immediately to the quarter where the bretheren principally reside'. He accordingly did leave the station, and took up his residence at Motito in April last. He made one visit of a few days to Mabotsa about two months ago for the purpose of preparation for a journey to the Colony, in which he is now engaged and which will probably detain him till some time next year. During his recent visit he in a note requested to be informed whether I still entertained the desire, mentioned in last meeting of

[1] The letter from which D. L. quotes was in fact not sent (see below, p. 93), but in another, dated 20.ix.46, Edwards did refer to some of the points mentioned. For comparison, the relevant passages are given below (pp. 83–5).

Committee, to extend missionary labour to another tribe,[1] adding, 'I cannot but regret that I was not previously aware of that your wish. Had I been, I might have waived all matters of difference between us'.

In appearing before the Directors, although for the first time, on an unpleasant topic, I am conscious that in the absence of other evidence I shall just be considered as engaged in a quarrel. But though that view of the matter may produce a diminution of confidence, the following facts seem to shew that I have no other alternative than to appear in a single capacity. Mr Edwards has revealed 'that there has been a want of harmony and peace between us, that' (at the very commencement of the station) 'he thought that I wished to drive things all my own way', and that the native teacher has been regarded with feelings certainly not such as favoured unity of effort in his employment and direction of his energies.

Now of the prevalence of the above feelings, except in one instance which I endeavoured immediately to rectify, I solemnly assure the Directors I lived in ignorance. I did not even suspect unkind feelings in reference to myself. Certain circumstances, however, made me suspicious of their existence in relation to the native teacher, and as a feeling of isolation was produced, the efficiency of that department of labour suffered in consequence. But had I concieved that there existed a state of feeling equal to what Mr E. now reveals, I certainly could not have united with Mr E. in all the duties of family, social, and public devotion for more than a twelvemonth without the least notice of it. Had I only been aware of its existence, the mind of my young partner in life would have been prepared for the shock.

But the letters of Mr and Mrs E. not having reached their destinations in time to throw a gloom over our marriage, did arrive only two days after our departure in happy ignorance of the reception which awaited our return to Mabotsa. If these letters have in no instance swayed the mind towards prejudging the case, the facts that Mr E. since his residence at Motito has visited the bretheren who must form the Committee, and not only to them but to travellers — mere men of the world — accused me of faults and failings tenfold more numerous than the above, and of the mere existence of which I had not an idea

---

[1] The minutes of that meeting (at Kuruman in Feb. 1845), which Edwards did not attend, contain no reference to D. L.'s 'desire'. But that he had already contemplated moving away is evident from his writing, on 28.i.45 (from Kuruman), to B. Pyne of Ongar: 'At Mabotsa matters go on pretty well. But I don't expect to remain there long. The sphere is too small for two missionaries. As I am the younger I purpose to go on to the Bakwains of either Bubi or Sechele.' Cf. also below, pp. 78–9.

untill recently informed through the medium of public notoriety —
these have the effect of destroying the confidence I should otherwise
feel in the decision of the Committee.

I have felt most reluctant to trouble either Directors or Committee
with a subject which, besides its prolixity, is sufficiently unpleasant. But
it seems a duty to notice aspersions which, if not public, I could afford
to pity.

The first offence, or that which recieved the epithets 'dishonest, dishonourable, and mischievous', happened six months previous to our
interview, and to the best of my recollection was as follows. Some unpleasant words having occurred between Mrs Edwards and the wife of
our native assistant, in reference to the exchange of the meat of certain
kinds of game, a remark or two fell from Mr Edwards, such as, 'I shall
take care she eats less of the meat procured by my powder & lead', [and]
made me aware that something unpleasant had taken place.[1] But being un-
desirous of further information, I made not a single observation in reply.

In this state of comparative ignorance I remained untill, when offici-
ating at next ordinance, I saw the woman rise up & go out previous to
the celebration of the Supper. The remarks above referred to, and a
rush of other feelings, came into my mind as I saw the appearance of
discord in our little community. As Mr E. had maintained entire silence
on the subject of exclusion, it seemed to me to be duty to ascertain
whether improper feelings were not indulged by the woman. And I
accordingly enquired of Mebaloe, who has always acted as deacon, the
reason of his wife's absence. But he, having recieved a hint from another
member on the subject of quarrel, had refrained from conversation with
his wife. I therefore directed him to make enquiry, saying perhaps it
was sickness, perhaps something else. The answer I recieved through
Mebaloe was, 'Mr Edwards had sent a message to her to the effect that
she was expelled from the communion'.

Having thought and prayed over the subject for a week, and Mr E.
still maintaining silence, I mentioned the subject privately to Mr E.,
and told him the question I had put and the answer recieved, and
added, 'as a missionary on the station, I had after a week of consideration & prayer thought it my duty to ask why a member had been excluded & not a word said on the subject'. I at the same time stated my
desire not to offend him, the time which had been occupied in hesitancy
lest I should give offence, &c. He denied the fact of expulsion, by repeating a message which did not amount to pointed excommunication,

[1] The incident occurred during D. L.'s absence from Mabotsa in the middle of
1844 (*Fam. Letters,* i, p. 106).

it having been in the form of a question, as, 'If you are so & so, can or will you come to the ordinance?' To this I replied that I believed his testimony fully, but the woman having recieved a wrong impression something ought to be done to remove it, in order that discipline might have its proper effect. This Mr E. declined, on the ground that 'as the affair had happened in his own house, he did not feel at liberty to enter on or proceed in the matter', adding two or three times, 'But if you choose to enter into the subject you may; the woman has already confessed to Mrs E. that she had spoken improperly in the presence of a heathen man', and again added, 'But if you feel inclined to settle the matter you may, I don't feel at liberty to proceed in it'. Having stated that I should endeavour to remove the false impression from the woman's mind, I observed that such a step was proper. 'We must always bear the ends of discipline in recollection, and as these are the good of the offender and the purity of the church, we must always be careful to prevent the impression of discipline being the effect of revenge'. To which Mr E. rejoined, 'I shall do right, and don't care what impression is produced'; and on my remarking that we were required to have a good report even of them which are without, he concluded by, 'But she is within'.

Having called the woman, I proceeded entirely on Mr Edward's testimony of her guilt, and never asked one question on the comparative innocency of the parties. Before next ordinance, she had not only asked the forgiveness of Mrs E. a second time, but had explained to the heathen who was present at the altercation that improper speech such as he then heard was not in accordance with the religion of Christ. As Mr E. had so repeatedly expressed dislike to enter on the subject, I without again calling on him to do so signified to the woman that no objection to her admission to the Supper could now exist, and at the same time warned her to be more circumspect in future.

During the space of three months after this I was in constant contact with Mr E., yet not one single hint was ever given to disturb the full persuasion I entertained that in quashing this affair without the least enquiry into the merits of the quarrel I had done a kindness to Mrs Edwards and all concerned. After, however, it had lain dormant for six months, it was revived among the natives by Mr Edwards, and as his examinations were made when I was within a few miles of Mabotsa, although nothing was elicited but what I had told six months before his mind was prepared for recieving me as he did.

In reading the above account, and bearing in mind that such is put forth as the cause of the denuntiations 'dishonest, dishonourable, and

3. MABOTSA

mischievous', &c, it is probable the Directors will suspect that some important feature is kept out of view: the exasperation and cause assigned will not appear proportionable. Yet I can solemnly declare I am not aware of a worse light in which my conduct can fairly be put. A slight alteration, the addition of a letter, alone renders the charge odious. Instead of saying, 'You went to a native, and you frankly informed me of your motives for doing so', the charge is made general: 'You went to natives'; and the plural without any explanation, though quite unfair, leaves room for many injurious inferences. Another accusation is founded on the above, viz. that I charged Mr E. with having 'excluded a member in revenge'. Mr E. is more excusable in thinking that I did than in the other charge, but he is mistaken. The allusion to revenge was exactly as above. The reference to exclusion was put in the form of a question, and with the enquiry was joined the expression of desire not to offend. But though my reason for asking was simply a belief of duty *as a missionary &c*, the last phrase is interpreted by Mr E. as 'standing up for my honour'.

The offence for which a second apology was demanded occurred while I was superintending the digging of our watercourse, about fourteen months previous to our interview. An under-chief was among the number employed, and one day, presuming on his greatness, he refused to do his portion of the work. As he expected the same wages as the others, I endeavoured to convince him of the impropriety of sitting idle, and after coaxing him in vain for several hours I took his spade and worked with it myself. The man went home immediately and appealed to Mr Edwards, then returned in a sort of triumph, demanding his spade. Having put the question, 'Do you intend to work now?', he without answering went off again, and in still greater triumph brought Mr Edwards, who asked me 'if nothing could be done to allow the man to work', adding, 'if *he* is not allowed to work he will go off and take all the others with him'. I told Mr Edwards that the man had refused to work during the whole morning, and all I had asked him on his return from appealing to Mr E. was, 'Do you intend to work now?' Mr E. replied, 'O, you demand apologies from natives; leave the work alone, and I shall carry it on myself, and never have a word with them'. In declining to obey this order, which was given with the outstretched hand, I told Mr E. that it was quite improper to allow a native to appeal to him, as such conduct could make a nonentity of me, a fellow-laborer; this man had refused to work to me, and I must settle it. When Mr E. departed, the same question not only elicited a promise to work, but he actually did work well ever afterwards.

G

About five months afterwards, a note was put in my way by Mrs Edwards, containing the information that ever since the above circumstance her husband had entertained feelings towards me which would prevent the Divine blessing on our labours, and that as these bitter feelings were increasing she felt very uneasy, &c. I waited on Mr E. immediately, and apologized for having in some way or other offended him. I stated that, having no recollection of having ever intentionally given offence, I supposed he had observed something in my manner which had displeased him. As he seemed unwilling to mention my fault, I pressed him to it by saying, 'As you are so much older than I am, I have always expected that if I ever offended either in word or deed you would immediately tell me of it'. Mr E. then stated that 'he had in the matter above mentioned been offended, because he thought I wished to drive things all my own way', but that after I had been bitten by the lion he had thought no more about it (Mrs E.'s note being unknown to him).

After again telling him that I had had no intention of offending in what I said, I requested him two or three times, 'If ever I should again offend him, either in word or deed, immediately to call me aside and tell me of it'. And Mr E. having assented by saying, 'Yes, let us do so, and I shall take better care of my temper', I firmly believed I had secured a preventative to public disgraceful discord such [as] this into which I am now drawn.

This belief threw me off my gaurd, and when fourteen months afterwards a second apology was amongst denuntiations demanded, my replies were less meek than a more expected attack might have elicited. I declared, what I had never before hinted, that at the very period of time when he had taken offence for my refusing to allow him to be made a source of appeal, numerous appeals were attempted to be made to me against Mr E.[1] And my refusals were usually answered by reproaches, such as, 'Why did you bring that man with you? We know you, but we don't know him, *and all the people to the Southward tell us that he is Satan*', &c. To which reproaches I invariably answered by defending the character of Mr E., denying the truth of the reports they had heard and ascribing all to the malice of the enemies of the gospel. As Mr E. had stated, at the time of my making the first apology, that his reason for taking offence was 'he thought I wished to drive things all my own way', I referred to this by reminding him that no sooner

---

[1] The workmen on the mission station had complained to D. L. that Edwards was cheating them in regard to wages (*Fam. Letters*, i, p. 130).

had I been laid aside (by another cause than obedience to the order he gave me to leave the work to him) than the work had gone so far wrong as to require to be done again three times over.

Having asked my opinion of his letter to the Directors, I replied that there was a twist running through it, and asked how he could tell the Directors, in order to impugn my veracity, that he had been for years following a plan in reference to Mabotsa, which he knew to have been at one time a desire to go to the Bakwains, at another to Mosega, and at other times to have been a great desire to get away from Kuruman in order that, as he himself habitually expressed it, '*Moffat should not keep him to be his lackey*'.

The above expressions are the worst I uttered. A plural cannot be inserted with truth where I have put down a singular. Nor can the epithets with the lines under them[1] be ascribed to me in any other sense than as quotations. No epithets whatever were made use of by me reproachfully. The last question was put in his own phrase, in order that he might not be able to deny the facts. But I confess the replies to the demand for a 'second apology' savoured more of indignation than I now approve. The statements though literally true may not have been expedient. I feel sorry that they were uttered too, because Mr E. in his communications with the bretheren leaves out of sight my 'dishonest, dishonourable conduct', and by a few slight changes forms a list of 'charges & reproaches' out of these explanations, and in contrast to these refers to his own conduct as having been characterized by meekness and wisdom.

During the period when, as now appears by the revelations of Mrs E., a certain state of feeling existed both in reference to the native teacher & myself, I can distinctly recollect having been conscientiously desirous to promote a return of honour and influence of Mr Edwards among the natives. Certain statements made by Mr E. without my knowledge or consent seem to have led to the decision that we should occupy Mabotsa. A concurrence of circumstances at the time of appointment alone made me willing to be silent concerning these statements as to my desire for Mr Edwards's cooperation. But no sooner was it determined on that we should be fellow-laborers than I resolved to do everything in my power to promote Mr Edwards's usefulness, and in this I had the fullest persuasion that I should thereby promote the professed object of all our labours.

One hour, however, had not elapsed after our appointment in Com-

---

[1] Italicized in the text above.

mittee[1] before jealousy was manifested lest Mebaloe should pay more respect to me than to Mr Edwards. This I supposed quashed by my immediately appealing to Mr Moffat whether I had not requested him publicly to charge that individual to make no distinction between Mr E. and myself. Mr E. heard the response, it was by his own explicit recommendation I was induced a little before that period to select Mebaloe. I requested Mr Moffat to give the charge because I believed it would from the man's spiritual father come with more force. But though Mr E. got the subject of Mebaloe's probable conduct to himself introduced into Committee, he now assures the Directors that Mebaloe was 'engaged privately'. This manifestation of feeling in Committee induced me to propose to Mr E. at Mabotsa that he should draw & pay Mebaloe's salary. But having one half year's portion already drawn, I could do no more then than hand him the receipt. He took it, and afterwards put it into my room without a single remark.

In order to increase his influence too among the natives, I freely allowed him to expend all the funds of the station. These priveleges, however, in connection with the unfortunate idea that he now occupied a different position from that at Kuruman,[2] seem to have operated injuriously on his mind. A new missionary maxim was repeated so frequently ('Let every man do as he likes'), and journies &c being undertaken without even mentioning whither, I had to refrain proposals & remarks on our work from a feeling of complete isolation & noncooperation. On no occasion did Mr Edwards ever deign to take the least notice of the school. As soon as I was sufficiently recovered, Mebaloe and I commenced teaching, and we have carried it on alone ever since. But though left to build the whole of this house at the same time, I never once complained that Mr E. preferred going about the country to assisting a fellow-laborer.[3] (He gave 4½ days' assistance in the roof.) My nearest friends can testify that I refrained from naming what I could not praise. But Mr E. believes that I have told, and tells the Directors that he 'has reason to believe I have accused him to the bretheren'. I fear it is only suspicion. But I never complained. Yet now, when Mr E. knows that during the whole of my absence at Kuruman

---

[1] The Committee did not in fact 'appoint' D. L. and Edwards. It merely noted that the Directors had approved of their proceeding 'to commence a Mission among the Bakhatla tribe', and it accordingly recommended that £50 be granted to them 'towards the object' (Minutes, 1st Meeting, 6.i.44).

[2] Where he had ranked as an artisan, not a full missionary.

[3] D. L. does not mention (what he wrote to Mary Moffat on 12.ix.44) that Edwards had been unable to help him owing to a crushed finger (*Fam. Letters*, i, p. 105).

Mebaloe carried on the school without one single visit from him (Mr E.), and could only give the paltry answer for non-attendance, 'I did not know that I had leave to attend', I do feel inclined to complain of the charge of 'privacy' as really unfair.

And had Mrs E. pursued the course she with such honourable assiduity followed at Kuruman,[1] she might not have found time for the unique specimen of female missionary correspondence which she composed for my newly-constituted mother-in-law. Perhaps her sympathies might have been drawn in another direction than that of 'thinking it her duty' to descend to the phraseology which her letter contains.

In adverting to Mr Edwards's letter to the Directors, I am not conscious of a desire to abate from the honour he deserves; nor shall I attempt to represent the journey to the Bakwain country, in which he was at least seven weeks absent from his family, as of less importance than he describes it. But I am compelled to refer to it, because the fact that I did not, in my letter published in the Chronicle of April '44, exhibit a connection between that our first journey and the establishment of the Mission at Mabotsa, constitutes the root of bitterness from which most of the other evils have sprung. The letter of Mrs E. informs us that even she was ignorant of the offences to which, with a devout expression of trust in the Lord, she applies the terms 'shabby', 'ungentlemanly', 'unchristian', &c, untill her husband came to the knowledge of the above fact. And as Mr E. fancied that my silence respecting his journey robbed him of all the honour he deserved,[2] a laboured but indirect attack on my veracity followed.

I have examined all my notes again in order to discover whether I ought to have mixed up my recollections of Mr E.'s journey with my account of the establishment of the Mabotsa Mission. And I now do most solemnly declare I cannot percieve that the facts of the case would have justified me in doing so. Even had I been aware of Mr E.'s desire to exhibit a journey undertaken three years before as the cause of the formation of this Mission, I could not have acceded without a direct violation of the truth. Having, in consequence of performing the same journey in his company, been well acquainted with both the object & effects of our visit, it could not possibly occur to my mind to introduce '*Kurrechane, Mr E.'s original destination*' into a plain narrative of events which had no connection therewith.

[1] Where she had conducted an 'infant school' (see above, p. 27).

[2] An editorial foreword to the published extract from D. L.'s letter of 30.x.43 states, *inter alia*, 'Our intrepid Missionary, Mr. Livingston, . . . has made preparatory arrangements for the opening of a station among the tribe of the Bakhatla' (*Chronicle*, viii, p. 50). Edwards is not mentioned.

But Mr E. now assigns the object of our first journey as the formation of a Mission 'somewhere in the vicinity of Kurrechane', and from this the inference may be drawn that he had even then Mabotsa in view.[1] But the route of our journey having been to a portion of the country eight days distant from Kurrechane, and in a totally different direction,[2] how could I exhibit a connection which in Mr E.'s own mind is at best only inferential? I appeal to Mr E.'s own letter to the Directors, and to the unpublished portion of mine, as evidence that in my narrative of the formation of the Mabotsa Mission there is not even carelessness, but that, as ought to be in writing to such a distance, the only statements are given which the circumstances would allow.

Mr E.'s own letter informs the Directors that in our first journey we ascertained from the two detached portions of Bakhatla visited *'that they had no authority to invite missionaries in consequence of being without their chief'*. This continued to be the case with them for nearly three years afterwards. And when by certain commotions the whole tribe was collected under one chief,[3] and that chief gave me an invitation to settle in his country, Mr E. refers to my return from this event, which happened at the conclusion of a five months' sojourn in the Interior, by stating that *'Mr L. thought we might make a commencement immediately with the Bakhatla'*, but he (Mr E.) *'thought it better to wait for the sanction of the Board'*. This, from whatever motive adduced, is a fact. On returning to Kuruman after having recieved the invitation of the chief, although with the expectation that my companion Mr Inglis must have arrived, I left next day in order to meet Mr Edwards, then at an outstation; and my first words after salutation were, as in the unpublished portion of my letter, that a commencement should be made for whoever might be the occupants. To this proposition, made to him in consequence of Mr Hamilton having charge of the school, Mr E. gave a pointed refusal. I then sent off my waggon & oxen to the assistance of the coming bretheren; and when, about two months afterwards, Mr E. did accede to my proposition to make certain preparations at Mabotsa, as my vehicle was doing missionary work elsewhere I did not concieve that the loan of which Mr E. gravely informs the Directors involved any degradation.

[1] Edwards, on returning from that journey, had written to Tidman (8.xii.41) urging the establishment of a mission station 'among the Bakatla and Baharutse at Mosiga' (about 30 miles S.E. of Mabotsa); his letter does not mention 'Kurrechane', i.e. Kaditshwene.

[2] D. L. fails to mention that before proceeding to the BaKwena he and Edwards had first visited the BaKgatla in the neighbourhood of Mabotsa, i.e. about 30 miles W.N.W. of Kaditshwene.   [3] See above, p. 35, and below, p. 89.

The reasons why Mr E. refused to accede to the proposition for preparation were desire to know the will of the Directors relative to leaving Kuruman, and prediliction for Mosega, for which deserted station[1] he even made windows which are now lying unused at Kuruman. And he persisted in his desire to follow the advice of Revd. F. Owen, even though told that the place was quite destitute of inhabitants and moreover insalubrious, untill informed by a chief of the Bahurutse that in the event of the tribe removing they would proceed, not to Mosega, but to Pōe.[2] Mr E. on hearing this came & asked me where Pōe was situated, and on my informing [him] that that locality was about 8 miles from Mabotsa, he then and then only consented to assist in making preparations for this station. As he was then quite unaware of the importance of the tribe, he assented with the distinct avowal that all he would do had a reference to the future approach of the Bahurutse to Pōe. My object in soliciting his assistance was that the then favourable aspect of this portion of the Interior should be taken advantage of as soon as possible. I was not aware of what necessity has since taught me, that building could be carried on without the aid of another; and, as the unpublished portion of my letter mentions, 'though I should be delighted to think the spot selected the sphere of my future labours, yet I should endeavour to hold myself in readiness to go anywhere else, &c.'

I feel ashamed to refer to these and several other points concerning which Mr E. has gravely adverted in his letter to the Directors. But not knowing what effect they may have at such a distance, I feel anxious to allude to the whole, in order that by an extended notice my own mind may be allowed to turn to the objects with which it ought to be engrossed. I did, as Mr E. remarks, board with him during my delays at Kuruman, but neither that, nor the provisions he furnished for the journey, were gratuitous.[3] It is, however, by mistake he informs the Directors that he 'procured men for the journey'. I procured each of mine, and as the feigned sickness of Mr E.'s principal workman was the means of exciting the deacon of the church to really gratifying exertions, I mentioned these efforts with gratitude. The idea of detraction in

[1] Mosega had been occupied successively by agents of the Paris Evangelical Missionary Society (1832), American Board of Commissioners for Foreign Missions (1836-7), and Church Missionary Society (Owen, 1839-40).

[2] Pôwê, a hill immediately north of Dinokana village (25° 27' S., 25° 52' E., about 20 miles N.W. of Mosega). The locality was long, and still is, an important site of Hurutshe settlement, though when D. L. wrote most of its inhabitants were living in the south, near Taung, as refugees from the MaTebele.

[3] Cf. *Fam. Letters*, i, p. 176, where D. L. mentions having been charged '6d. a day for my board'. The same letter (1.vii.46 Moffat) contains other details of the financial affairs referred to above.

reference to Mr E. never entered my mind. But on returning, Mr E. without my knowledge paid one of my men, and on enquiry I found that he had put down all the expenses of the journey to the account of the Society. This was the only instance in which the whole expense of a journey did not come from my own salary; and as I afterwards insisted that the beads, &c, which I furnished for the purchase of gardens should be erased from the account he had drawn out, why should the Directors be informed of the provisions, men, &c, *he furnished*, when he knows that all the expenses were paid by the money of the Society?

The statement that 'he spoke first at the Peecho' calls up recollections which had nearly passed into oblivion. He did speak first, and the use he makes of this fact is 'he did not hear certain things I heard'. I am sure Mr E. would not relish a paltry insinuation conveyed in the other half of the fact of his 'speaking first'. I was called upon by the chief to speak first, but turned round & beckoned to Mr Edwards, believing it comely to give my senior the preference.

The degradation involved in answering these childish charges is more painful than any sacrifice I have yet been called to. That I must stoop to notice them, because made against me in a public capacity, seems indispensable, yet the details leading to the notice of mere trifles suffuse my cheeks with burning blushes. I hope neither my thoughts nor time may ever be so employed again.

Mr E. founds another accusation on the fact that the preparations we made were not mentioned by me in Committee. They were matters of as public notoriety previous to the meeting as the employment of Mebaloe was. They were the subject of conversation untill every man of us knew what had been done, and nothing else but positive knowledge of what we were doing induced us to vote money for the expenses of which Mr E. had already begun a list. And if my silence involved criminality, what must his have involved? He was equally silent on the subject of preparations, and probably for the very same reason — there was no necessity for a formal enumeration.

Whether Mr E.'s fears had any foundation when he supposed that I wished to make him a 'mere appendix' may be ascertained by the fact that, previous to my being aware of anything but determined non-cooperation, I consulted with the bretheren in Committee on the propriety of having two instead of one station in the Interior. Having recieved their approbation, the only consideration which prevented this resolution from being put into effect was, Mr E. might have been put to inconvenience in reference to a projected Colonial journey. I am not conscious of having at any time spoken of Mr E.'s conduct as influenc-

ing my decision. It was my intention to leave Mebaloe with Mr E. as a
valuable and tried assistant, reserving the burden of taking an untried
and perhaps inferior assistant for myself; and in resolving on this mode
of procedure I conscientiously believed that with one native teacher &
one European in each, the gospel might be introduced into two tribes
simultaneously.

I should probably have remained at Mabotsa untill the return of Mr
E. from the Colony. But when I found that my presence not only induced him to avoid communion when here, but caused him to take up
his residence on a station of another Society nearly 200 miles off,[1] I felt
at liberty to alter my plans. When Mr E. visited this for the purpose of
preparation for his Colonial journey, and informed me that had he only
known of my previous intentions he might have waived all matters of
difference between us, as these were *not between us* (had it only come in
a manly way between us, how much better it had been than talking
untill his words were carried by his children to the natives), but in his
own mind, I immediately resolved to yield up Mabotsa to his care. As,
however, his absence may be prolonged till March or April of '46, we
intend to keep up the usual services untill his return. Even after I was
informed by Mr E. of his feelings respecting Mebaloe, I informed the
latter that my intentions were that he should assist Mr E. at Mabotsa.
Having earnestly enquired whether I were dissatisfied with him, and
entreated to be allowed to go forward, his entreaties, joined with the
knowledge that Mr E. only considered him a private individual on the
station, induced me to consent to his removal.

The Directors may concieve that in reference to my leaving Mabotsa
I have acted with too much precipitancy. But every hope of cooperation
being annihilated, remaining in expectation of usefulness would be a
waste of life.

As a specimen of the charges he made before the bretheren at Kuruman, I may mention a statement imputing most odious conduct to me
in reference to a native garden.[2] The bretheren agreed to put a pointed
question on that charge, and though his statement was made only the
day previous he literally eat in his words. It is not wonderful if, after
the bretheren had by one single enquiry elicited the nature of his
charges, I should recieve the advice to follow out my previous intentions
immediately. Although the bretheren demanded that Mr E.'s charges
&c should be written out for my use, Mr E. has persisted in with-

[1] Motito was then a station of the P.E.M.S.

[2] Edwards alleged that D. L. had appropriated gardens started by Mebalwe and
another native (cf. *Fam. Letters*, i, pp. 126–8).

holding them, preferring to appear on the defensive as if I had made an attack on him. Justice seems to require that the charges which Mr E. has to the neglect of his own duties been circulating through the country should be reduced to writing.

With respect to my 'well known sentiments' respecting native teachers, I never did maintain the idea of irresponsibility, but I did maintain that no one ought to have authority over them who had no authority over his own temper. This sentiment, though uttered at first without any reference to Mr E., seems to have been to him especially galling. I have thought, too, that the native teachers should remain in connection with their spiritual fathers, because the latter are likely to have more influence over them for good than others not so related to them. If wrong, Mr E. might have tried to put me right. Another sentiment is attributed to me in Mr E.'s letter to the Directors, viz. 'that I consider native teachers superior to European laborers'. This is founded on the belief I entertain that the indirect benifits of missionaries are more numerous than the direct. The conviction was founded on the increase of the outstations of Griqua Town and Kuruman as compared with the head stations. My object in pointing this out was to induce more attention to the indirect means of spreading the gospel. But though this sentiment may be interpreted into condemnation of the modes of operation adopted by other bretheren, I deny that any such condemnation existed in my mind. Both direct and indirect success in this country I have ever ascribed as, under God, the result of the labours of our predecessors.

The tribe to which we have transferred our labours is the Bakwain under Sechele, a chief concerning whom I made some remarks in a former letter.[1] He is situated about forty miles N.N.East of Mabotsa, and though the locality is much less inviting than this station the prospect of usefulness is much greater. When still undecided whether to accede to the warm invitations the chief gave, a question put by one of his people greatly assisted in fixing our resolution. 'When we reach the presence of God', said he, 'will you be able to say you have taught us? I shall tell Him you have not'. This from an entire heathen startled me, and when I asked if he had not heard what I had just been telling them all he added, 'But can we know by being told once?' I began school and the foundation of our house on the same morning. The chief acquired a perfect knowledge of the large & small alphabets in two days, and has since made considerable progress in learning to read. Fear of divorce in the event of his becoming a Christian makes his wives unwilling to

[1] See above, p. 36.

follow his example, but he compells them to learn and is himself their teacher. He says he wishes we had come to his country before he married so many.[1] May the Lord enlighten his darkness.

I am now engaged on the roof of our new dwelling, and hope after again going through all the preparation of a house and garden I shall be allowed to devote my time to the proper duties of a missionary. Mrs L. has with the native teacher assisted in carrying on the school at Mabotsa during my frequent visits to the town of Sechele. Paul, a deacon of the Church at Kuruman,[2] has recently come to the Interior for the purpose of spreading the knowledge of the gospel among his countrymen. He intended on leaving Kuruman to fix his residence with another portion of the Bakwains, a few days distant from Chonuane,[3] the town of Sechele. But a considerable dispersion of that section of people having lately occurred in consequence of the death of Bube their chief,[4] we considered that a temporary residence at Chonuane [was] more advisable than an attempt with the scattered and disturbed remains of the tribe of Bube. We intend as soon as possible to begin a regular itineracy to the tribes Eastward of the new station, which being situated about three days nearer to them than Mabotsa will facilitate our operations.

The Directors will percieve that the unfortunate circumstances which occurred immediately after I had with much labour prepared the only house and garden deserving the name on the station have prevented my attending to duties of much more importance. As I now go through the same round of preparation, I cannot recommend anything in reference to the young man Mokoteri. Had I been allowed to leave Mabotsa in the manner I contemplated, I could have pointed to it as exactly the situation your letter specifies. But the state of mind Mr E. manifested towards the only native teacher employed excludes all hope of an arrangement in the case of Mokoteri. It is to be regretted that the Directors have not been furnished with more ample details concerning that young man. Our unanimous opinion, founded on the united testimony of the bretheren who witnessed his conduct, was that he was

---

[1] Sechele at that time had five wives.

[2] As mentioned below (p. 102), he was 'of the same family' as Mebalwe. One of Moffat's earliest converts, and the 'oldest deacon' of the church at Kuruman, he was already being employed as a catechist in 1834 (*Miss. Labours*, p. 589).

[3] Chonwane, 24° 52′ S., 25° 58′ E., on the farm 'Secheli's Oude Stad No. 224', about 47 miles N. of Zeerust (Trigonometrical Survey Office, Pretoria, 1.x.1958). The BaKwena under Sechele had settled there in 1844.

[4] He was accidentally killed, by an explosion of gunpowder, in August 1845 (*Fam. Letters*, i, pp. 137–8, and below, p. 89).

then quite unfit to be employed in missionary labour.[1] He was not then, nor has he at any subsequent period been, an inhabitant of Kuruman. He has always resided with a man who had for many years kept the mother of Mokoteri as his concubine, and whom he usually designates his father. Their residence being about 150 miles from Kuruman, we have had but little opportunity of ascertaining whether our first decision ought now to be altered. Our only means of information were the bretheren at Griqua Town, and a short visit made by Mokoteri to Kuruman in the capacity of waggon driver to a trader. These did not allow us to entertain any more favourable opinion. As, however, the subject will in obedience to your instructions be fully discussed in next meeting of Committee, I shall leave it entirely in the hands of the bretheren.[2]

In conclusion, I regret having been compelled to write this tedious and most unpleasant letter. I never contemplated that such a production should leave my pen, and hope it may not again be my lot to notice other facts of the same nature. In thinking of Mr Edwards's condi[tion][3] I wish to forgive as I hope to be forgiven, and though pa . . . in order to give full proof that I have no desire to make any one an 'appendix', I hope to be allowed to live in peace, devoted to the service of our Redeemer.

[Signature cut out]

The name of the new station is C h o n u a n e; the uane is pronounced as waney.

[As already mentioned, the letter from Edwards quoted above by D. L. was apparently never sent. On 20 September 1846, however, Edwards wrote another letter to Tidman (from Mabotsa), in the course of which he refers to his association with D. L. in the foundation of the Mission to the BaKgatla. After remarking that 'The sphere I now occupy is not the result of a sudden resolution from the example or influence of others', he states that from the time he joined the L.M.S. in 1823 'my destination was to this quarter'; that Dr Philip had diverted him successively to various stations in Cape Colony, but was ultimately

___

[1] See above, p. 57 n.

[2] The Committee, at its third meeting (March 1847), decided, 'upon the testimony of the Griqua Missionaries, in whose district he has been living for the last two years', that Mokotedi 'is totally unfit for any department of Missionary labor, & therefore we cannot conscientiously comply with the request of the Directors to recommend him either to Mr Livingstone or to any other Missionary in the country.'

[3] Small triangular cut in paper.

persuaded by Moffat, 'finding I was still desirous of going north', to let him join the Mission at Kuruman; and that he had lived and worked there 'nearly 14 years'. The letter (received in London on 25 February 1847) continues:[1]

'When the brethren Ross & Livingston reached the Cape, with assurance of other missionaries to follow, I resolved to visit the northeast, with a view to a mission in this vicinity, but waited their arrival at Kuruman in order that Mr Hamilton might not be left alone in my absence. When making preparations I mentioned to the brethren, at one of our prayer meetings, what I purposed, & invited one of them to join me. Mr Ross was anxious to go, but Mrs R.'s situation was such that [he] could not leave her.[2] Mr Livingston replied, "I shall be happy to accompany you". We set out direct to the Bakhatla living near here. To enquiry if they wished to have missionaries, they referred us to the Chief living on the Molopo River & with the Baharutse. We visited also the Bakuene under Bobe & Sechele, & on our return a Uanketse town on our way to the Bakhatla on the Molopo, where they also referred us to the other chief at the Baharutse.[3] (See Moffat's book, page 608.)

Shortly after our journey home I forwarded a brief account of our visit, & took the liberty of intimating to the Directors that I believed it practicable & desirable to begin a Mission at the northeast, & expressed a wish to be allowed to enter on it. While waiting their reply, I began some preparations for the future, by visiting the Colony to arrange for some of our children, & to purchase supplies for ourselves & a few things which might be useful to carry on public work at the Station we had in view. Having been referred to the Chief of whom I have spoken, I purposed to see him on [my] way down. Mr L., wishing to see that part of the country & the Baharutse tribe, agreed to go also. The Chief whom we visited, after consulting with the others, replied that he had no objections that missionaries live among the Bakhatla. Sanction being thus obtained, I pursued my journey to the southward, concluding that

---

[1] I have normalized the punctuation and corrected the many spelling mistakes, except of proper names.

[2] She was expecting the birth of a child.

[3] In his original description of this journey (letter to Tidman 8.xii.41), Edwards does not mention asking the BaKgatla if they wished to have a missionary. The first group visited lived 'north-west of Mosega' (i.e., near Mabotsa) and consisted of people who had been captives of Moselekatse; the second, fugitives from the MaTebele, lived on the Molopo River 'two days westward' of the BaNgwaketse ('Uanketse') under Segotshane (see above, p. 24). Other refugees, including the tribal chief Pheko (elder brother of Mosielele), were with the BaHurutshe near Taung.

if the Directors approved of the mission we should commence as soon as possible after my return.

The only reply I received to my application to the Board was in a joint letter to Mr Hamilton & myself from Mr Moffat, then in England, in which he remarked, "The Directors have no objection that the brethren Edwards & Livingston begin a mission in the interior if a suitable spot is found". Before that intimation was received, Mr L. was of opinion that we might commence without the sanction of the Board. I, however, did not feel at liberty to leave Kuruman on my own responsibility, more especially as I was supplying for Mr Moffat as far as I was able, for which the Directors kindly expressed their satisfaction in a letter he brought from them to me.

What Mr M. had communicated was encouraging as far as it went, but really I did not consider it as official, & still looking for his return I wrote him at Cape [Town] & remarked that it would have been as well had the Directors given me the black on white themselves. He was astonished that I was doubtful, & wrote immediately that if I would have black & white, here it is: "The Directors have appointed you & Mr Livingstone to the interior mission." This I was obliged to receive as the minds of the Directors, & began immediately to make preparation for the future house. When Mr L. returned from the northeast he found that authority had arrived for us to begin the Mission, & that I had got rushes & frames ready & was at work on the doors for the hut.

Being informed that Mr M. had landed at the Cape, we determined on another visit to the Bakhatla to make arrangements for a residence with them. I collected tools & implements & put them into working order, procured men for the journey & for the work at the Station, made provision for them & ourselves, & loaded my waggon with doors, frames, tools, & the provisions, & lent Mr L. a vehicle & oxen for his bed & other baggage. (We had each sent a waggon to meet Mr Moffat. Mr L. lived in my family from his arrival at Kuruman till his marriage.) Having arrived, I urged for a public meeting [with] Chief & people in order that we might understand each other. When they met (about 80 to 100 men), Mr L. wished me to bring the object of our visit to their view, followed by himself on the same subject. See Missionary Magazine for Apr. '44.

As soon as matters were settled for a residence, we went to work, put up poles & roof on them, & one layer of reed merely as a shade from the sun, fixed 3 window frames & 2 door frames (these I made on the spot), having in view to complete the hut on our return from Kuruman, to where we hastened to meet the brethren from England, & where soon after, when met in Committee, they placed on the minutes, "That the brethren Edwards & Livingston proceed to the Interior Mission agreeable to appointment of the Directors".[1]

I have in few words given you some idea of the way in which I have been led to this distant sphere of labour in the neighbourhood of my original destination, but not before 20 years had elapsed from leaving England. I am, however, grateful for being now permitted to spend part of my life in this heathen land. . . .'

The letter contains no further reference to D. L., and does not mention any of the 'charges' which he complains Edwards had made against him.]

15. To DAVID LIVINGSTON
30 December 1845

[LMS: Outgoing Letters, Africa, Box 6, pp. 408–10]

London
Dec. 30, 1845

Dear Brother,

We have the pleasure to acknowledge the receipt of your letters dated June 9 and December 2, and are happy to take the present opportunity of writing in reply. It concerned us to find that you were not able to appropriate the contribution from Southampton, although you subsequently found that it was not committed to your own disposal, but was intended for the support of a particular teacher labouring in connection with the Kat River Mission.[2] From the increasing importance of Native Agency it was discouraging to learn that not a single appointment could be made in the Bechuana Country, even when the funds were offered for the purpose. This fact plainly demonstrates the necessity for immediate & earnest attention to the subject; and we trust you will make a point of bringing it, at an early period, under the special notice of the brethren. In former communications you expressed yourself so strongly in favour of the employment of Native Agents that we felt it would be superfluous to press the matter upon your personal consideration, but we hope you will see it your duty to endeavour to awaken a more powerful interest in this branch of Christian instrumen-

---

[1] For what was actually 'placed on the minutes', see above, p. 74 n.
[2] An LMS Mission attached to the Hottentot colony established by the Government in 1829 in the Kat River valley, north of Fort Beaufort, in what was then the eastern borderland of Cape Colony.

tality than yet appears to exist among the members of the Bechuana Mission, and to urge the brethren to serious deliberation on the most suitable & efficient means for extending its application to the work of God in the extensive regions lying North and East of Kuruman. The subscription from Southampton has been transferred to Kat River, and Dr Philip & Mr Read[1] have been informed accordingly. Your letter addressed to the friends there was duly forwarded, and led in fact to the discovery of the error which had been made in the first appropriation of the money.

You will be assured of our deep and grateful interest in the accounts of your proceedings & prospects at Mabotsa. It is evident that the hand of God has directed you to a field of labour requiring a more than ordinary exercise of zeal and wisdom & fortitude. The extreme degradation of the tribe, both morally & socially, and the lamentable indifference, if not antipathy, evinced by the majority to the grace of the Gospel & the blessings of salvation, render a peculiar combination of qualifications requisite in the Missionary who would attempt to raise them in the scale of existence and unite them with the redeemed family of God. We trust, dear brother, the spirit of the Lord will direct you in your arduous work and replenish your mind with an abundance of those gifts & graces which it demands. Nor shall we cease to pray that his presence & blessing may eminently attend your labours, rendering them the means of lifting the savage from his sinful and brutish condition to the advantages of civilised life & blessed fellowship with the living Redeemer. It is an occasion of thankfulness that in the beloved partner of your days you have the comfort & advantage of being associated with one like minded with yourself, who is no stranger to missionary work, who is acquainted with the language of the people, and inured to the burning climate of the wild scenes of an African desert. We sincerely congratulate you on the union, and desire for yourself & Mrs Livingston every blessing & comfort which God loves to bestow upon his people, with an abundant measure of prosperity in your united labours.

Your information respecting the Native Assistant Mebalue afforded us much pleasure, and if you would furnish a more enlarged account of his history, conversion, & labours, it would be acceptable. You do not state how he is supported, whether by a subscription from England or elsewhere, or by his own exertions. Should it be by a contribution from this country, we should be glad if you would mention by whom it is given, and whether there is an English name attached to it.

[1] James Read (1777–1852), LMS missionary at Kat River 1829–35, 1838–51 (*Register*, p. 4).

We were thankful to hear of his entire recovery, as well as your own, from the effects of the serious injury received in the early part of last year. His prompt & courageous conduct on the occasion, in your own defence, was indeed valuable, and claims the grateful acknowledgments of all your friends. We trust, dear brother, you will be careful never voluntarily to expose yourself to a similar danger in future.

With very kind regards to Mrs L. and Mr & Mrs Edwards, and affectionately commending you all to the unfailing protection & increasing favor of our divine Lord,

I remain, Dear Brother,

Ever faithfully and affectionately yours,

[A. Tidman]

Forn. Secy., L. M. Society

We are much obliged for your communication of March 23, enclosing sketch of Mabotsa Station, sent in reply to our circular respecting the Juvenile Missionary Magazine. We shall be happy to receive further articles of the same kind.

Your letter addressed to Mr Roberts was also forwarded in due course. I hope shortly to write to your fellow-labourer, Mr Edwards.

III

BAKWENA AND BOERS

16. To ARTHUR TIDMAN
10 April 1846

[LMS 38. Received 23 December 1846. Previous publication: *Chronicle*, vol. xi, (February) 1847, p. 26 (edited extracts); Chamberlin, pp. 87–90 (incomplete)]

Mabotsa[1]
10*th April* 1846

Dear Sir,

As the commotions which occur among the tribes in this region usually possess features of interest in relation to our Mission, I shall relate a few particulars concerning the more recent changes which have occurred; and though these are calculated to awaken emotions more of pain than pleasure, the information may tend to excite prayer that He who is head over all things to his Church may overrule the course of events for the establishment of His glorious kingdom.

Wars, or rather expeditions for plunder, seem to have been of frequent occurrence in this country from time immemorial, & the narration of the deeds performed in their forays forms a prominent feature in native conversation. But though generally the occasions of the most wanton cruelty, they are regarded in much the same light as our own wars were thirty years ago. As with the antient Highlanders, 'lifting cattle' is not considered by the Bechuanas synonymous with stealing. Some do not like the term robbery to be applied to these deeds of plunder, while they could talk with composure when the term 'lifting' is applied.

In former years more severe scourges swept over the tribes, by the irruptions of Mantatees[2] and Matibele. Compared to these, Bechuana

---

[1] Although D. L. had moved to Chonwane towards the end of 1845, he continued to visit Mabotsa occasionally while Edwards was still away in the south (cf. *Fam. Letters*, i, pp. 161, 171). It was presumably on such a visit that the present letter was written.

[2] BooMmantatisi, a name referring specifically to a tribe of BaTlokwa ruled by the chieftainess Mma-Ntatisi (as regent for her young son Sekonyela), but used collectively for both them and several other groups of BaSotho who, fleeing before invaders from the East, from about 1820 onwards harried and plundered the peoples of southern Bechuanaland.

marauding inflicted but little lasting injury. All the tribes in the Interior
were dreadfully thinned by these sweeping scourges, so there are but
few old men now alive to tell the history of bygone years. Old Makabba,
mentioned by Mr Campbell, fell by the hands of the Mantatees,[1] and
his son Sebegoe was driven away into the desert. More recently Sebegoe
was driven by fever from the banks of the Lake Mampoore[2] back to
the country of his father, and there his power was completely broken by
an attack of Mahura, chief of the Batlapi. This latter event seemed
very unfavourable at the time, as the natives here could not be expected
to understand that though Mahura had for many years heard the gospel
he had no connection with believers. But the ruin of Sebegoe's influence
allowed the chief of the Bakhatla to escape from a state of vassalage to
him and collect the scattered remnants of his tribe into one body at
Mabotsa. They now enjoy priveleges they might not have had under
Sebegoe. The severe trials through which all have passed were probably
designed to produce humility and make the native mind more susceptible
to the influences of the gospel.

The Bakuains or Baquanes were formerly divided into two portions
under Bubé and Sechelé, the division having been effected by the murder
of Sechele's father.[3] The two parties were always at variance. In August
last Bubé, having recieved some gunpowder in a present from Sechele,
and concieving that coming from such a quarter it must be bewitched,
he endeavoured to dissolve the charm by holding some medicines in a
state of combustion over it. But his incantations were interrupted by an
explosion, which inflicted so much injury as subsequently to cause his
death. Poor Bubé, being dreadfully scorched, sent messengers off to
Mabotsa immediately to entreat assistance, as he believed no one but a
white man knew the remedy for a burn inflicted by gunpowder. But
being at Chonuané at the time of their arrival, and without that which
might assist their chief, his sorrowing servants were obliged to go round

[1] Makaba II, chief of the BaNgwaketse since c. 1790, was killed in 1824 while
resisting an attack by Sebetwane's people (part of the 'Mantatee' horde). Campbell
often refers to him, in both *Travels* (1815) and *Travels ... Second Journey* (1822,
esp. i, pp. 314–17).

[2] A name sometimes applied to Lake Ngami (cf. *Oswell*, i, p. 242). It really applies
to the BaTawana living there, who were also known as MaMpuru (cf. Smith, *Diary*,
i, p. 407), 'Mpuru' being the praise-name of Tawana, their first chief (Schapera,
field notes, 1940).

[3] See above, p. 36. The conspiracy to assassinate Motswasele (Sechele's father)
had been headed by his cousin Moruakgomo. The latter was himself killed by
Sebetwane's people in an attack on the BaKwena c. 1828, and was then succeeded
as chief of his division of the tribe by Bubi, his half-brother (Schapera, *Ditirafaló*,
pp. 43–7).

again by Mabotsa, and ere they reached their master must have travelled nearly 200 miles.[1]

About a month previous to the accident which caused his death, this amiable heathen chief visited us at Mabotsa and when spoken to said, in his usual way of endeavouring to please, 'I love the word of God'. On hearing of his death, it was a good opportunity for pressing on the messengers and Bakhatla the truth of the eternal destiny of man. But though listened to with attention when telling them how different the feelings of Bubé in relation to the Divine word *now* were from what they had been, we have still to long and pray for the conviction to take place that they need a Saviour from the wrath to come.

After the chief was departed who by his influence kept most of that section of Bakuains together, many of the principal people preferred escaping to Sechele to remaining with Khake,[2] the successor of Bubé. It then became necessary for Sechele to demand the goods and dependants of those who had returned to their allegiance. The tribe being weakened, it would in general have been considered a good opportunity for revenging antient wrongs. But Sechele, having promised not to shed blood, on approaching the town of Khake left the great body of his people at a distance and, nearly unattended, advanced to entreat the people to return to their allegiance. Entreaty having failed, Sechele told them that he refrained from the usual course on such occasions simply because of 'his promise to his missionary', and only demanded the goods of those who came over to his party. With these, others took the opportunity of changing sides. But every article brought which formerly belonged to Bubé was instantly returned. Sechele then returned to Chonuane.

Subsequently to this transaction, an old man who had been an accomplice in the murder of Sechele's father was concerned in instigating some of Khake's men to an assault on some of Sechele's people; and to the abuse inflicted an insulting message was added, upbraiding the latter chief for cowardice, '*pretending* he did not fight because of his missionary, &c.' We endeavoured to allay the irritation produced, & hoped that as the men who were wounded & abused were of an inferior rank the affair would pass over.

An expedition was planned under the appearance of an elephant hunt, and the first intimations of our disappointment we recieved were the sight of the wounded carried past to the town, which was soon followed

[1] Bubi's death (August 1845) is described more fully in *Fam. Letters*, i, p. 138; cf. also Cumming, *A Hunter's Life*, 1850, i, pp. 234–5.

[2] Kgakgê, younger brother of Moruakgomo (and therefore Bubi's half-brother).

by the sounds of heathenish joy mingled with the loud wailing of those who had lost their friends. These events caused us much sorrow. The chief justified his conduct on the ground that these people were his own subjects, and the deciet he employed lest we should again have prevented him avenging the indignities done to their hereditary chief. His conduct has in no way been altered for the worse, although we were not sparing in manifesting our detestation of the crime of murder. In desire for general information, & assiduity in reading, he surpasses all the chiefs except Waterboer[1] with whom I have come in contact. May the Lord incline his heart to righteousness and make him a blessing to his people.

Khake with the remaining portion of his people came about a week ago to this station.[2] These commotions have thus ended by the whole of these two tribes being brought into closer proximity to the gospel. We pray that we may yet see that the plans of Divine mercy have been carried right through the midst of all this human wickedness, and that those who now feel no compassion for each other may have mercy shewn to themselves.

12 April. While engaged in writing the above, I was informed of the approach of Mr Edwards on his return after about twelve months absence. On leaving he produced the impression on my mind, by a note still in my possession, that he went 'for the purpose of appealing to the Committee' against myself. On finding that so far from wishing to lord it over him I had been asking counsel of the bretheren in Committee as to the propriety of giving him and the native teacher the entire charge of the station, he came back and informed me in another note that had he known of these my intentions before he went to Kuruman he 'would have waived all notice' of what he called 'differences between us'.

As his accusations were by himself made *public* over the whole country even before I knew that he was offended, and he had produced his 'letter to the Directors' and read it before Mrss Hamilton, Moffat, Ashton, myself, and others, and had also to them declared his intention of bringing the subject before the Committee, fully expecting that I should thus have an opportunity of defending myself I sent the two

---

[1] Andries Waterboer, chief of the Griquatown community 1820–52. A convert and former school-teacher, he was 'by far the ablest Captain the Griquas ever had' (Marais, *The Cape Coloured People*, 1939, p. 37); cf. *Travels*, pp. 105–6.

[2] i.e., to Mabotsa. He remained there until after the Boer attack of 1852, when he submitted to and went to live with Sechele. He was killed in 1880, while raiding the BaKgatla-bagaKgafêla, then at war with the BaKwena (Schapera, *Ditirafalô*, pp. 52, 54).

requests put upon the minutes of the meeting[1] — the first in order that the men with whom I have associated might honestly state whether I had in any instance acted as he (Mr E.) in his letter to the Directors stated, the second in order that, as it was impossible for me to leave the Interior in the then state of the tribes and while building my house, I should have a fair opportunity of meeting the charges at next meeting of Committee. But when these requests were attempted to be read by the secretary, Mr Edwards & Inglis uproariously opposed their production.[2] Mr Edwards vociferously declared that he had never written to the Directors the letter to which I have referred, that he never had accused me, and though reminded by those who had recieved his letters and heard his statements he boldly denied all, and demanded the production of the letters &c.

As it is now to me apparent that the course of conduct pointed out in the regulations never contemplated a case such as this, I take my leave of the subject, believing, although most unwillingly so of one whom we hope that he is a channel of Divine truth, that there is either a large amount of forgetfulness peculiar to Mr Edwards, or something else which in a missionary would be utterly confounding. Sitting here nearly separated from the stirring influences which press around the path of duty at home, I feel much sorrow of heart that I have allowed my mind to be so deeply engrossed & perplexed in brooding anxiety over slanders which their author thought at last better to leave in a state of bastardy. To how much better account both our time[s] might have been spent we shall both know, I hope, in that region where strifes are ceased for ever.

> Believe me, Dear Sir,
> Yours affectionately,
> David Livingston

[1] D. L. did not attend the meeting (held at Taung on 9 March 1846), but sent in two written requests: (a) that the 'brethren' should be asked if any of them had ever heard him making accusations against Edwards; (b) that the 'brethren' should furnish him with a copy of Edward's charges 'for my use at the next Committee meeting'. (The full text is quoted in *Fam. Letters*, i, p. 181, n. 11).

[2] They were nevertheless read, and are appended to the Minutes.

17. To DAVID LIVINGSTON
29 October 1846

[LMS: Outgoing Letters, Africa, Box 6, pp. 503–5]

London
Octr. 29, 1846

Dear Brother,

We perused with deep and painful concern the principal portion of your letter dated in October last, explanatory of the circumstances which led to your separating from Mr Edwards and your removal to another Station. From our previous knowledge of your character & disposition, we are inclined to take the most favourable views of your conduct in this transaction, though we should feel it unjust to pass any positive opinion on the proceedings of Mr Edwards, from whom *no communication on the subject* has been received. You will readily believe that of all the trials connected with the affairs of the Society, none have ever occasioned us so much anxiety, embarrassment & sorrow, as the disagreements of our Missionary brethren; and we earnestly hope it may not again be your lot to be associated with circumstances so distressing as those which your letter discloses. The whole affair shews the extreme importance of mutual forbearance, generosity & meekness, on the part of brethren labouring together at the same Station; and we trust the lesson it has supplied will not be forgotten either by yourself or Mr E. The Directors are satisfied that the circumstances of the case required a separation, and though the present state of our funds is unfavourable to the adoption of new Stations[1] they much prefer your entrance on an entirely new sphere of labour to your continued residence at Mabotsa subject to the unhappy and detrimental influences which prevailed there. They have therefore sanctioned your removal to Chonuane, in the strong hope that you will there be able to bestow your undivided attention on the work, enjoy the peace of God in your heart, and largely experience His blessing on your labours.

We were gratified to learn that you have enlarged prospects of usefulness at the new Station, and we devoutly hope the Lord will give you favor in the eyes of the people, clothing his word with power and making your labours effectual to the salvation of many. Among a tribe so barbarous and unenlightened as the Bakwain, your work will be peculiarly arduous, making constant demand on all your intellectual resources as

---

[1] Expenditure during the preceding year had exceeded 'ordinary income' by some £4,500 (*Report*, 1846, p. 19).

well as on all your spiritual energies. We pray that in wisdom & knowledge and grace you may ever find yourself equal to your position, and from year to year be privileged to reap the fruits of your zeal in increasing abundance. Let your ardour be sustained by incessant communion with Christ and your consolation drawn from the conviction of his power and sympathy, and then you will neither be faint or wearied in your mind, whatever obstacles may exist or trials arise.

In the assurance of our continued confidence and affection, and with very cordial regards to Mrs L.,

I remain, Dear Brother,
On behalf of the Directors of the London
Missionary Society,
Yours very truly,
[Arthur Tidman]
Foreign Secretary

18. To ARTHUR TIDMAN
17 March 1847

[LMS 41. Received 18 August 1847. Previous publication: *Chronicle*, vol. xi, (October) 1847, p. 155 (edited extracts); Chamberlin, pp. 96–110 (incomplete)]

Kuruman[1]
17th March 1847

Dear Sir,

As a considerable period has elapsed since I had an opportunity of transmitting letters to the Directors, and those which I have now brought with me seem out of date, I shall endeavour to embody their contents in a general sketch of our proceedings during the last eight months. This will include a short account of two journies in an Easterly direction, undertaken in order to attempt the removal of certain obstacles to the establishment of a native mission in one of the tribes located there. And in order that you may understand the nature of these obstacles, and the circumstances which rendered it desirable to make an effort for the settlement of at least one of our native teachers in that direction, I may mention that the country situated Eastward of our station & North of the 25° degree of South Latitude has been taken

---

[1] D. L. had recently come south with his family, partly in order to attend the fourth meeting of the District Committee, held on 8–9 March at Dikgatlhong, about 100 miles S.E. of Kuruman.

possession of by certain Dutch emigrants, who consider themselves sole masters of the soil by virtue of having assisted in the expulsion of Mosilikatze.

While still engaged in the erection of our dwelling at Chonuane, we recieved notes from the Commandant & Council of these emigrants, requesting an explanation of our intentions &c, as also an intimation that they had resolved to come and deprive Sechele of his firearms.[1] We recieved too, about the same time, several very friendly messages and presents from an influential chief called Mokhatla,[2] who lives about four days Eastward of the station; and at last, during my absence at Mabotsa, he paid a visit to Chonuane, and expressed satisfaction with the idea of obtaining Paul as his teacher.

As soon as our house was habitable, Paul and I proceeded to the Eastward. After crossing the River Marikoe,[3] our attention was attracted by villages which were scattered over the country in numbers to which we had been unaccustomed. One cannot travel far in the Bakwain country without seeing large trees broken, bent, and twisted, and other indications of the presence of elephants and rhinoceros, or he may come upon herds of the giraffe, eilands, buffaloes, and other varieties of game. But here we found wild animals comparatively scarce, and we beheld instead the more pleasant haunts of man, & though travelling we had the pleasure of addressing immortals on their eternal destiny at least once every day.

On reaching the town of Mokhatla, we found him busily engaged in drawing copper wire and manufacturing ornaments. (He works also in wood and iron with considerable dexterity, which is remarkable, as manufactures are not hereditary in his family.) He was still of the same mind in reference to Paul, but told us that the settlement must be effected with the Commandant of the emigrants, as the only mode whereby peace could be secured to himself, he being no longer considered master of his paternal territory. Mokhatla is chief of a large section of the Bakhatla.[4] He mentioned about fifteen villages who own his authority, and he has a good name among all the other tribes. In the distance we saw the residence of another Bakhatla chief called

[1] This message was received early in February 1846 (*Fam. Letters*, i, p. 165).

[2] Mokgatlê, chief 1835(?)–89 of the BaFokeng, a Tswana tribe living about 90 miles E.S.E. of Chonwane (and immediately N. of the modern town of Rustenburg.

[3] About 30 miles E. of Chonwane. The Marico (Tswana 'Madikwe') is a major tributary of the Crocodile River. The journey mentioned was made in July 1846 (*Fam. Letters*, i, p. 177).

[4] D. L. was mistaken. As he himself subsequently mentions, (see below, p. 283), Mokgatlê's people were 'Bahukeng' (BaFokeng).

Pilanie,[1] whose people are still more numerous than those we visited. Compared with these, the Bakhatla to whom most of our efforts have hitherto been directed appear a mere fragment of a tribe. The people of Mokhatla had never heard the gospel before, except from Paul and Mebaloe.

Proceeding Eastward through his villages untill we crossed the River Ourie[2] or Limpopo, we then came to a large tribe of Bakwains, and spent the Sabbath with them. The chief, a most friendly man, shewed me the scars on his back of stripes which had been inflicted by those who consider themselves masters of his country. While standing in his town, we counted eleven villages in the plain below, all of which acknowledge him as their chief. Everywhere we were recieved with kindness and confidence as soon as we were known as missionaries, and some of the chiefs informed us that they had formed part of the train of Mosilikatze in his frequent visits to the waggon of Mr Moffat.[3] They seem then to have acquired an idea of what teachers are.

The Commandant lived near to this tribe, and being a well-informed man we found no difficulty in persuading him that an attempt to disarm the Bakwains would break up our Mission, and that he ought to delay the execution of the orders of Council untill I should lay the whole matter before it. This I did by letter, and likewise stated my intention of introducing the gospel amongst the Eastern tribes by means of native agents.

As soon as we arrived at Chonuane, we commenced the erection of a school, 50 feet by 20. Having finished this in less than two months and set systematic instruction fairly into operation under Paul & his son Isaac, Mrs L., Mebaloe & self proceeded again to the Eastward.[4] Our course was straighter than formerly, and we thereby visited many villages we had not seen in our previous journey. We had resolved to call on the Commandant and Mokhatla on our way home. After spending another Sabbath with Mamogale,[5] the chief of Bakwains on the Eastern bank of the Ourie, we continued our Eastern course. On our right lay a considerable tribe under Samogoe.[6] We did not visit it, but

---

[1] Pilane, chief 1825(?)–48 of the BaKgatla-bagaKgafêla, then living in the vicinity of Saulspoort, about 40 miles N. of Rustenburg. The BaKgatla-baMmanaana (of Mabotsa) claim to be an early offshoot of theirs.

[2] Odi, the Tswana name for the Crocodile (Limpopo) River.

[3] In 1835, when Moffat had accompanied Smith's expedition into the Transvaal, spending about two months with Moselekatse (*Miss. Labours*, pp. 578–84; *Matabele Journals*, i, pp. 36–130).

[4] This journey was made in the last two months of 1846 (*Fam. Letters*, i, p. 187).

[5] Mmamogale, chief 1835(?)–84 of the BaKwena-baMogôpa, a Tswana tribe living about 25 miles E.N.E. of Rustenburg.

[6] Seamoge, chief 1834(?)–88 of the BaKgatla-baMmakau, living about 45 miles E. of Rustenburg.

proceeded to the Bamosetla,[1] a large tribe consisting of about a dozen villages grouped together on a plain. They knew nothing of missionaries, but we found no difficulty in collecting them in large numbers.

Six days beyond the Bamosetla we came to a cluster of tribes. We could at one view behold the localities of seven, and these in amount of population seemed to exceed the whole of the Batlapi and Batlaros.[2] The natives say the population is still denser the nearer we approach the coast. They are called Bagalaka.[3] Their dialect is somewhat different from that we use. But we were readily understood, and they easily accommodated their language to ours. In appearance they resemble Matibele, and the men cultivate the fields. We procured specimens of the spindle and distaff with which they spin cotton. The plant seems to be indiginous. They smelt iron, copper, and tin, and in the manufacture of ornaments know how to mix the tin & copper so as to form an amalgam. Their country abounds in ores. And the Ourie or Limpopo, after recieving many considerable streams, becomes, as the natives call it, the 'mother of all rivers', being at least 400 yards in breadth. It is said to enter the sea a little to the North of De Lagoa Bay.[4]

The people are rich in cattle, and were never subject to Mosilikatze. They recieved us in general with fear. Indeed, on approaching the town of Mañkopane,[5] the chief to whose people we had promised a visit, we saw the men all armed and running up the rocks at the foot of which their town is built. This arose from the impression that we were enemies and might make use of our firearms. When their fears subsided. we found the chief & people kind, but their confidence was far from full. We preached several times, but there was far more palaverish ceremoniousness than we could relish. Their chief, though not more than 20 years of age, had 48 wives and 20 children. The latter in feature all very much resemble himself.

While here, we recieved a pressing invitation from another chief to visit him, and heard of another tribe which exceeds all others in manufacturing skill. *'They have never been known to kill any one.'* Hearing such a character from their bretheren, our desire to visit them was great.

---

[1] BaKgatla-baMosêtlha, living at Makapaanstad, about 65 miles E.N.E. of Rustenburg; traditionally considered the most senior tribe of BaKgatla.

[2] BaTlharo, a Tswana tribe living westward of Kuruman. The LMS had several outstations among them.

[3] Originally of 'Transvaal Ndebele' (Nguni) stock, these people are (as D. L. indicates below) divided into several different tribes. They live chiefly in Potgietersrus district, N.W. Transvaal.

[4] The mouth of the Limpopo is in Lat. 25° 13' S., and Lourenço Marques (Delagoa Bay) in Lat. 25° 58' .

[5] Mankopane, chief 1845(?)–77 of the BaMapela, one of the Laka tribes.

But being between 2[00] & 300 miles from home, we were obliged to defer seeing this 'lily among thorns' till some other opportunity.

The state of the three tribes of Bagalaka we visited may be stated in the words 'hateful & hating one another'. Crowds followed our waggon from one tribe untill we approached the next. They returned then, lest, as they said, 'they should be killed'. But though surrounded by such crowds, our conversational opportunities were but few. If either Mrs L. or myself made any movement towards them, a general rush backwards and treading over each other occurred. Mebaloe was better able to quiet their fears, and held many conversations on revealed truth. Very little can be effected in one visit.

In speaking of the relations between Dutch & natives, I shall confine myself chiefly to the statements of the former. They have taken possession of nearly all the fountains, and the natives live in the country only by sufferance. Each chief when called upon is obliged to furnish the emigrants with as many men as any piece of work may require, and except in the case of shepherds no wages are paid for labour. Labour is exacted as an equivalent for being allowed to live in the land of their forefathers. In this system of unrequited labour all the emigrants, from the Commandant downwards, unanimously agree. In other ways of maltreatment they are not so unanimous. The better disposed emigrants lament the evils they witness. But the absence or laxity of law leaves the natives open to the infliction of inexpressible wrongs.

A short time previous to our visit to Mañkopane, a few emigrants galloped up to the herds of that chief, singled out 30 of the finest cattle & 50 of the largest sheep, and then, driving them off, proceeded to act in a similar manner in an adjoining tribe. On complaining of this to the Commandant, he professed entire ignorance of the transaction, and promised to investigate the matter and apply the law in the case. The deed was the more galling to the natives because a son of Conrad Buys was among the marauders; and this man,[1] when his father died & left him an orphan among this people, was kindly treated and enabled by them to discover his relatives.

A misunderstanding occurred [between] Melechoe,[2] chief of a large

---

[1] Probably 'Doors' or 'Doris' (Theodorus ?) Buys, 'a brigand born', who in those days was often used by the Boers of northern Transvaal as interpreter and go-between in their dealings with the local native tribes (cf. Agar-Hamilton, *Native Policy of the Voortrekkers*, 1928, pp. 66–9, where he is named 'David').

[2] Moletsi, chief of the BaKwena-baMoletsi, living about 15 miles N.W. of Pietersburg. Official Boer records confirm that he was attacked in 1846 by a 'commando' with which Buys was closely associated (*Voortrekker-Argiefstukke 1829–1849*, pp. 251–3).

& powerful tribe, and some of these emigrants. The latter ordered three tribes to assist them in an attack upon Melechoe. These formed a living bulwark in front of one hundred mounted whites. The illfated tribe was driven back by the battle axes of their own countrymen, and the whites found it an easy way of fighting to fire over the heads of their sable assistants. Melechoe held out long, but by employing their allies to capture the cattle immense booty was secured. 10,000 sheep and 400 captives were included in the spoils. On asking the natives why they had been so foolish as to assist in the murder of their countrymen, their reply was that they feared that, had they refused to go, they themselves would have been attacked. An *English trader*, too, joined in the attack made on Melechoe.[1]

Now the emigrants invariably admit that in reference to them the Bechuanas are an honest and peaceable people. I have frequently put the question whether the Dutch ever knew Bechuanas guilty of stealing cattle from white men, as the Caffres near the Colony have done, and the uniform answer has been, 'No, they are honest and peaceable towards us'. The above-mentioned massacre, for such it was, the natives having no firearms, may however teach them to be neither. On the side of the oppressor there is power. The black man may yet obtain a knowledge of that power, and then it may appear that the emigrants have industriously sowed the seeds of some future 'Caffre war'. The lawless alone may now be guilty, but vengeance may be wreaked on both good and bad, as is now the case in the Colony.[2]

(On returning to the Commandant's, we found that the representation I had made to the Council had met with a favourable reception. Mokhatla still of the same mind, but another obstacle presented itself in an emigrant who lives near him, a most inveterate enemy to missionaries, and one who shewed displeasure twice with Mokhatla by demanding why he had not killed *'that missionary'* according to previous instructions. Mokhatla answered, 'I avoid that which you avoid. I took him to your chief, and he did not kill him.' Having been more than two months from home, I could not go to endeavour to remove this man's enmity, and feel disinclined to send Paul untill I have made some

---

[1] Elsewhere D. L. gives his name as Hartley (20.v.47 Dyke). Henry Hartley (1815–76) was a professional hunter living in W. Transvaal, who subsequently figured prominently in the European opening-up of S. Rhodesia (cf. Le Roux, *Pioneers and Sportsmen of South Africa*, 1939, pp. 88–92).

[2] The 'Seventh Kafir War', between the Cape Colony and the Xhosa ('Caffre') tribes on its eastern border, had begun in March 1846; it lasted until the end of December 1847. (Theal, *History*, vii, pp. 1–63).

attempt for the purpose. He & Mebaloe are well employed at Chonuane. This paragraph may be regarded as *private*.)

I now gratefully acknowledge the receipt of your letter some months ago, in which you appear to consider that I needed to be stirred up on the subject of native agency.[1] In the absence of information respecting my efforts to induce the bretheren to commence the systematic training of a native agency, it was quite reasonable to suppose that I had cooled down on the subject. I could not, however, inform you of those efforts without appearing to criminate those who opposed them. I preferred silence, though with the conviction that to you that silence must appear a diminution of zeal. An expression in a letter from the Directors, which I recieved some time previous to our first meeting of Committee, led me to believe that some definite plan would be promulgated in that meeting.[2] When the business was nearly over, and nothing likely to be said on the subject, I put the question, 'What is to be done in reference to training native teachers?', and found that my impression derived from the Directors' letter had been erroneous.

At our next meeting of Committee (1845), I presented a paper on the subject to the bretheren. In it I expressed my convictions on the subject of systematic training of agents, & ventured to suggest that an Institution for the purpose be organized at   and be requested to act as Tutor of the same. The clause runs verbatim thus: 'While then I have no idea of superseding by any new arrangement the duty of each missionary making every effort in his own sphere for raising up suitable individuals, I earnestly entreat your serious deliberation on the suggestion that an Institution for the education of native teachers be organized at   and that   be requested to act as Tutor of the same.' The reason why I left blanks was simply because I concieved the filling up of these would come better from the elder bretheren. Some approved of it heartily. Others assailed [it] with such logic as, 'Suppose we made you professor in this college, there are no individuals in the churches fit for a course of training'; and it was more than insinuated that in bringing forward that paper I 'wished to appear well with the Directors'. This last induced me to withdraw it.[3]

The conviction seized my mind, when I witnessed the opposition of

[1] See above, p. 85.

[2] See above, p. 29 f.

[3] The minutes of the 1845 meeting contain no reference to D. L.'s proposal. It was opposed by all the senior missionaries, including Moffat, 'so I withdrew the paper altogether, and will not again bring it forward. If the old gents don't of themselves commence an institution, it won't succeed. It did not appear in the minutes for that reason' (23.v.45 Watt).

some honoured bretheren, that by bringing the subject forward myself, instead of waiting till it emanated from those of higher standing, I had retarded instead of furthering this most important mode of spreading the gospel. This conviction caused me months of bitter grief. Every time the subject arose in my mind I felt a pang.

I could not possibly leave the Interior Mission to attend the meeting of Committee for 1846. The fact that nothing was said at that meeting, nor yet at this ('47) untill the evening of the second day, has freed my mind from the conviction that in 1845 I acted prematurely. I waited untill we were proceeding to elect the office bearers for the ensuing year before making the motion which you will see in the minutes.[1] Had I put it in any other form I might have been foiled by the assertion, which I could not have disproved, that there is a lack of men suitable for training. As it was stated that I made the motion for 'returns' with a view to founding a motion for systematic training and employment of native agents thereupon, I fear the returns will be sought for by each according to his wishes for the success of such a motion. At present I have not very sanguine hopes of success in inducing the bretheren to cooperate in the undertaking, and unless the cooperation is hearty no good will result.

I feel inclined to say, though I do it with diffidence, that the probabilities of success would be greater if Mr Ashton[2] were appointed by the Directors Tutor of all suitable individuals who can be found willing to dedicate themselves to the Divine glory among the distant heathen. I know he would most willingly enter into such a work, for he has always supported the suggestion which was made, and from his zeal & energy we might hope for good results. He would, however, require the cordial cooperation of the bretheren who have charge of churches. I hope to be able to demonstrate before another year that native teachers may be placed even among very distant tribes. The objects of my present visit to this quarter have been to attend the meeting of Committee and procure a supply of food.

It will afford me much pleasure to furnish you with some account of the conversions of Mebaloe and Paul. I have requested the former to

---

[1] The motion, seconded by Moffat and carried unanimously, was as follows: 'That returns be made by the different Brethren having the oversight of Churches how many members there are whom they can recommend for Missionary labour among the distant Heathen, & that the Brethren in the interior endeavour to ascertain the suitability of that field for such agency: the subject being of more immediate importance on account of the dangerous position of the Interior Tribes arising from the neighbourhood of Foreign Immigrants.'

[2] William Ashton (1817–97), stationed at Kuruman; one of the recruits who had accompanied Moffat from England.

write it out himself. The whole will be included in my next communication. His name is David Molehane. He always signs himself so. Molehane is the family name, David was given at baptism, but not being partial to changing their expressive names I have always called him by his common one Mebaloe. Paul is of the same family, but as he disliked his former name, viz. 'Father of Darkness', he has always been called by his Christian one.

David has been supported by the contributions of certain friends in Glasgow collected by a Mrs McRobert, now in Islesteps near Dumfries.[1] I intended to place Paul to the account of a certain school in Southampton, but Mrs Philip informed me that £15 collected there was not intended for me but for some one under Mr Solomon,[2] & your subsequent notice that that sum was intended for the Kat River Mission convinced me I had nothing to do with it. I have been advised of a contribution of £10.10.0 by Ralph Lindsay, Esqre, but do not know anything of that gentleman.[3] I have drawn £12 for Paul, and should prefer his name being connected with some school or church, as it may be the means of exciting to greater interest in the Mission. But I leave the matter to your discretion. He is an excellent man, the best preacher among the Bechuanas, and one of the oldest converts. David, however, possesses far more energy and decision of character. I thought at one time that the two together would constitute an efficient mission to Mokhatla, but my friends here dissuade me from parting with Mebaloe, and strong mutual attachment, and the fact that had I no assistant I could not itinerate, render it easy to decide on keeping him at Chonuane.

We have now been a little more than a year with the Bakwains. No conversions have occurred, yet real progress has been made. The indications of advancement may be more interesting to myself than to any one else, yet I believe it may be apparent to all who may witness it. The Sabbath is observed so far that no work is done in the gardens on that day & hunting is suspended. There is a general impression among the people that we are their real friends. This is manifested in a variety of ways.

When we came, the belief in rainmaking was universal. They believed that as God had given the white man guns & other things whereby he excelled the black, so he had conferred the knowledge of

---

[1] The McRobert family had left Cambuslang about the middle of 1846.

[2] Edward Solomon (1820–86), LMS missionary at Griquatown 1842–51 (*Register*, p. 52). For the Southampton contribution, see above, p. 59.

[3] He was a life member of the LMS, living 'in London and its vicinity'. In *Report*, 1845, p. viii, he is listed as having donated £10.10.0 'for a native teacher under the inspection of Rev. D. Livingston'.

rainmaking on them as one thing in which they might excel the white. It availed nothing when told that their rain medicines produced no visible effect. 'Your medicines', said they, 'produce no visible effect either when you administer them, but they enter into the inward parts, do their work, and then the cure follows many days afterwards. In like manner our rain medicines enter into the clouds, heal them, and we have rain some time afterwards.'

Sechele was chief rainmaker himself, and had unbounded confidence in his own powers. Last year, however, proved one of unusual drought. The clouds went round & round us untill the people were saying, 'These clouds make sport of us'. Our house was supposed the cause why no rain came down, and we were requested to allow them to sprinkle it with medicine. To this we had no objections, provided the stuff did not smell badly, yet no rain came. The crops were lost. When I asked Sechele whether he intended to make rain this year, he replied, 'You will never see me at that work again'. A rainmaker came from a great distance. He asked a sheep, and promised rain at a certain period. But the time having arrived, and no rain, when he asked another sheep he was answered by banter & laughter. Many still fear the rainmaker, but formerly no one dared to laugh at him.

Formerly all believed that preaching, praying, observance of the Sabbath, were just the customs we had derived from our ancestors, and many felt jealous lest compulsion should be used to make them part with their superfluous wives and other practices and become Makoas[1] (or white people in customs, &c). But after some time they began to enquire why some white men only observed the customs of their ancestors, and others observed neither the Sabbath nor any custom whatever. 'To be plain with you', said one, 'we should like you much better if you traded with us & then went away, without forever boring us with preaching that "word of God" of yours'.

They were exceedingly anxious to obtain medicine which should enable them to shoot well. A Griqua came & sold a little bit of sulphur at a high price, and some of it was inserted under the skin of the hand of the chief. This was shewn to me as a great acquisition. I told them they had been decieved, [and] handed the chief a cupful of sulphur as a proof that it was not niggardliness that prevented me from giving the 'gun medicine'. He looked at it some time & then said, 'I wish you would decieve me too; it would be pleasanter, though you cheated me out of my goods'. He returned the sulphur, apparently feeling that falsehood was sweeter than truth.

[1] Tswana *makgowa*, Europeans.

The people in general have more curiosity than any other I have come in contact with. Most of the principal men attempt to acquire a knowledge of reading. The famine caused by the loss of the crops has, however, prevented many from making much progress. After attending a few days they are obliged to go to the fields in search of the roots on which they have subsisted. The chief, having always had food, has never been absent. He & his wives have therefore been our best scholars. He can read the Testament pretty well, & always seems to relish explanations of what he does read. He has adopted European clothing, and is most desirous of making progress in civilization.[1] We are encouraged by these things to hope that his example will have a good effect on the people. We trust that our supporters do not cease to pray for the influence of the Holy Spirit to change their hearts. Unless they are converted, advance in civilization will be a poor reward for our toils.

You are already aware that by the advice of my bretheren here, and in accordance with my own previously expressed wish to carry the gospel to another tribe, I left Mabotsa and proceeded Northwards to Chonuane. Mrss Ross, Inglis, and Edwards uproariously opposed the introduction of my reasons for leaving that station, and it was voted 'informal' to accede to the requests I had made in the belief that the subject would be introduced by Mr Edwards.[2] That being the case, I have waited for the sanction of the Directors to my new station, and that not having arrived[3] I could not bring forward the expenses I have incurred in building a house and school. I am not aware by what process of reasoning the same individuals, viz. Ross and Inglis, could vote the introduction of my reasons 'informal' last year, and move for their production this year.[4] I am left to conclude, from the expression oft repeated in the ears of all present while I was discharging a sacred duty in reference to the funds of the Society, 'Wait till Livingston brings

[1] 'That he is desirous of civilization I think we may conclude, since he sent out goods with us to purchase a matrass, 4 lanterns, 6 candleboxes, a baking pot, a smoothing iron, a table, &c, and soap is an article which both he & others eagerly buy' (10.vi.47 Murray, from Kuruman).

[2] In 1846 the District Committee (over which Moffat presided) had unanimously passed the following Resolution (moved by Inglis, seconded by Helmore): 'That a paper from Mr Livingstone having been read, it be rejected as informal and contrary to the Regulations'. See above, p. 92.

[3] D. L. had evidently not yet received the Directors' letter of 29.x.46, which sanctioned his removal to Chonwane (see above, p. 93).

[4] At the 1847 meeting, Ross moved: 'That Mr Livingston be called upon to give his reasons why he left the Bakhatla Station, to which he was appointed by the Directors, without the concurrence of the District Committee'. He was seconded by Inglis, but all the others present (except D. L., who abstained) voted against him.

forward his expenses', that there was some feeling akin to revenge prompting the motion.

Mr Inglis, having taken up his residence in my house at Mabotsa, where certainly there is no work for two missionaries, continued to talk of a station among the Bahurutse untill actually expelled by the Bakhatla. He then offered himself to the Wanketze & was rejected, proceeded to Colesberg for supplies, and now imagines that the Bahurutse will go with him to form a station at Mainaloe.[1] As there is not the smallest probability of any movement of the sort, I felt it a solemn duty to endeavour to prevent the loss of another year's salary in mere talk by recommending Mr Inglis to act according to the pointed instructions of the Directors.[2]

I might have remained at Mabotsa untill the Bakwains removed to a better locality, and had I done so I should not have incurred the expenses which now press heavily on my spirits. But having gone, although to a place where water is scanty and bad, been obliged to sow corn at a fountain forty miles distant,[3] [and] lost it all by buffaloes and rhinoceros, yet our pleasing prospects of success prevent us from regretting the exchange; and we believe the people will soon remove to a better locality from a conviction of the advantages to be derived from European improvements.

In wishing to fix Inglis to do something for his salary, I am conscious of having acted from a solemn conviction of duty to Him who knows my heart. In Mr Ross's case, although not recorded in the minutes, I feel I acted under the same conviction. I am opposed to Mr R. taking a trip to England, whether for the sake of taking his children thither, taking unto himself another wife,[4] or anything else unconnected with public missionary business. Even in cases of failure of health I believe

[1] Mainelwe, the Tswana name for the Klein Marico River, near Zeerust.

[2] The District Committee in 1846 had recommended Inglis to start a Mission among the BaHurutshe, 'who have recently gone to their own country'. As he did not do so, the Committee in 1847 resolved that he 'be requested to state his views & prospects respecting the Baharutse Mission to which he was recommended last year'. Immediately afterwards, D. L. (seconded by Moffat) moved: 'That in obedience to the instructions of the Directors now received, & the fact that no Station has been commenced during the present year amongst the Baharutse by Mr Inglis, we now recommend him to devote his labours to the Bamaires [BagaMaidi] or to some Station connected with the Kuruman or Griqua Town.' Inglis, and two others of the eight members present, voted against, and so defeated, the motion. He did in fact soon afterwards settle among the BaHurutshe at Mathebe (Pôwê), 'on the eastern side of the Mainaloe River' (*Report*, 1848, p. 117).

[3] At Kolobeng (*Fam. Letters*, i, p. 187).

[4] Mrs Ross had died at Motito in December 1846 (*Chronicle*, xi, 1847, p. 132). 'Mrs Ross is dead, and Mr R. talks of going home' (*Fam. Letters*, i, p. 198: 4.v.47 Mrs N. Livingston).

we ought to make our wills, for the climate of England is not to be compared to this. But for a little heat too much this is the finest climate in the world. Cases of consumption have been known to recover by coming up hither from the Colony. Mr Ross could not have premeditated his motion, for he agreed to the amendment of Mr Ashton, although that annihilated his own.[1]

I have intimated above that it is probable we shall remove with the Bakwains to a locality suitable for a permanent station. We wish the removal to take place during the ensuing cool season. All the bretheren here agree as to the desirableness of the step. I have spent every farthing I have in the world, worked hard & fared hard, and am not ashamed to say that I am in debt £29 for building expenses. £3.8.0 of this sum were expended at Mabotsa. £15 or £20 more will be expended in commencing the new station, and as our corn was eaten by buffaloes while I was looking out for a proper sphere for Paul, nothing can come from my salary for the purpose of building. But for the assistance of the native teachers I could not have succeeded with so little expense to the Society.

The above is what I wish the Directors to take into consideration. The movement I have made has not been sanctioned by them, yet I should not act otherwise were I in the same circumstances again. The debt, I confess, presses heavily on my spirits. Although Mr Edwards entreated Mr Moffat to 'use all his influence with me to induce me to yield up Mabotsa to him', I am morally certain the same man would vote against any grant of money being made for the new station. So would Inglis and perhaps Ross, so unanimity being awanting I should recieve only a rebuff. I am resolved therefore not to bring either expenses or station before the District Committee.

A circular from Dr Philip has lately come to hand concerning the depressed state of the funds of the Society, and that the Directors had resolved to diminish the sum annually expended on our South African Missions.[2] In this resolution I most cordially concur, and my concurrence is founded on the impressions I recieved in passing through the Colony. I did not then communicate my convictions to the Directors that the Colony was no longer a missionary field, because I believed

[1] See above, p. 104 n. Ashton's amendment, seconded by Moffat, reads: 'That as we are now unable to enter into all the circumstances which led Mr Livingston to leave his Station, we avoid at present entering into the subject'. Ross voted for it, D. L. again abstained, and Inglis was the only dissentient.

[2] I have not located a copy of the circular; but the Directors reported, at the general meeting of the LMS in May 1847, that owing to 'the limited resources of the Society' they had decided, *inter alia*, to reduce expenditure on their S. African Missions by £1,500 per annum (*Chronicle*, xi, pp. 77, 79).

that from a mere novice such a broad assertion would be considered mere censorious conceit. I shall now give my reasons for believing that too much has & is being expended on South Africa, and need scarcely premise that I state my impressions always with the conviction that the Directors, having superior sources of information and, of course, better means for forming a correct judgement, will take my statements only for so much as they are worth. It is easy to recommend changes, but there is great responsibility connected with every change in missionary operations.

At Algoa Bay there are two missionaries connected with our Society, a Wesleyan, a Government schoolmaster qualified & willing to teach all, both white or black. The clergyman is, I believe, non-evangelical. The village is as like Ongar in Essex as regards population & appearance as two places can be. The only exception is a small clump of native huts a little apart from the *one* street of which the village is composed. Suppose a Wesleyan missionary, an English clergyman (non-evangelical), a salaried Government schoolmaster, and Mr Passmore, with a small clump of Fingoes, alongside Mr Cecil at Ongar,[1] and you have a correct picture of one missionary field. Uitenhage[2] appears a mere village, not twice the size of Ongar, yet it has an evangelical clergyman of the Dutch Church, a Wesleyan missionary, one of our Society, and a Govt. schoolmaster. Graaf Reinet[3] has a population equal to a very small country town in England, yet here we have an evangelical clergyman of the Dutch church, one of the Church of England, a Wesleyan missionary, Mr Gill, and Mr van Lingen.[4] Colesberg, when I saw it, was not equal in size to Ongar, yet it too had an evangelical schoolmaster, a Wesleyan, and London Missionary Society's agent. Graaf Reinet has a Govt. schoolmaster too.

These are the only Colonial fields I saw, and can say, without the smallest personal feeling towards any of the respected brethren who occupy these fields, I wonder what our Society's agents do there. The

---

[1] William Passmore (1802–52) was the LMS schoolmaster at Port Elizabeth ('Algoa Bay'), where he worked chiefly among 'Fingoes', refugees dislodged from Natal by the Zulu conquests of *c*. 1815–25 (*Register*, p. 45). Richard Cecil (1799–1863) was the Congregational pastor at Ongar 1838–47; there he also conducted an 'academy' for training missionary students, which D. L. had attended (H. C. Tibbutt, in *Bedfordshire Magazine*, v, no. 40, Spring 1957, pp. 321–3).

[2] 20 miles N.W. of Port Elizabeth, in 33° 46′ S., 25° 25′ E. D. L. had passed through it (and the other places named) on his original journey to Kuruman in 1841.

[3] Graaff Reinet, 32° 15′ S., 24° 32′ E., 160 miles N.N.W. of Port Elizabeth.

[4] Albert van Lingen worked for the LMS at Graaff Reinet 1830–46; Joseph Gill (b. 1814), who had come out with Moffat from England, was there temporarily in 1846–7, owing to the 'Kafir' war (*Register*, pp. 31, 56).

Colonial market is literally glutted with missionaries. I do not believe that equal advantages are enjoyed by any town or village in the United Kingdom as those which are pressed on the people of Algoa Bay, Uitenhage, Graaf Reinet, & Colesberg. With such an overflowing supply from Europe, will the Hottentots ever bestir themselves so as to become preachers? I fear, never.

I am more and more convinced that in order to [effect] the permanent settlement of the gospel in any part, the natives must be taught to relinquish their reliance on Europe. An onward movement ought to be made, whether men will hear or whether they will forbear. I tell my Bakwains that if spared ten years I shall move on to the regions beyond them. Now is their opportunity, and if they do not learn the guilt will rest on their own heads. If our missionaries would move onwards now to those regions I have lately visited, they would in all probability prevent the natives settling into that state of determined hatred which I fear now characterizes most of the Caffres near the Colony to all Europeans.

If natives are not elevated by contact with Europeans, they are sure to be deteriorated. It is with pain I have observed that all the tribes I have lately seen are undergoing the latter process. The country is fine. It abounds in streams and has many considerable rivers. The Boors hate missionaries. But by a kind & prudent course of conduct one can easily manage them. Medicines are eagerly recieved, and I intend to procure a supply of Dutch tracts for distribution amongst them.[1] The natives who have been in subjection to Mosilikatze place unbounded confidence in missionaries. The Boors spoke disrespectfully of me to the natives as soon as my back was turned, but they always came and related it with shouts of laughter. If the Boors knew this and many other things I have mentioned, they would become more exasperated against them, and probably shew their hatred towards myself.

If in consistency with your financial plans, may I be favoured with £5 or £10 of medicines? My friend Dr J. Risdon Bennet[2] would procure them cheaper and better than any one I know. He knows, too, which will be most useful for me. I have spent more than £30 of salary

---

[1] On 10.vi.47 D. L. wrote to Rev. Andrew Murray, minister of the Dutch Reformed Church, Graaff Reinet: 'My heart's desire is to do good to all, as I have opportunity, & have as little to do with politics as possible. Have you any Dutch tracts at your disposal? I should much like to have it in my power to give a tract when I can do nothing else. Will you help me in this respect?'

[2] (Sir) James Risdon Bennett (1809–91), 'physician; ... F.R.S. 1875; knighted and made president Royal College Physicians, 1876; published medical treatises' (D. N. B.). D. L. had studied medicine under him in London, and wrote him several times from S. Africa (Blaikie, pp. 31–2 and passim; Chamberlin, pp. 4, 28, 49, 83).

in this way, which may be an inducement to you to accede to my request. It is necessity alone makes me trouble you. But if it is not in accordance with your usual plan of operations, you have only to say No.

With Christian salutations,

I am, Dear Sir,

Yours affectionately,

David Livingston

An opportunity having occurred of transmitting this direct to Colesberg, I prefer embracing it to rewriting & correcting this. I hope the erasures &c will not be ascribed to carelessness.   D. L.

19. To DAVID LIVINGSTON

6 September 1847

[LMS: Outgoing Letters, Africa, Box 6, pp. 558–60]

London

September 6, 1847

Dear Brother,

We had the pleasure to receive in due course your letter of March 17, containing the details of your recent journies in the Eastern part of the Bechuana Country and of your proceedings in the new sphere of labour at Chonuane, to which your attention was directed when circumstances indicated the desirableness of your removal from Mabotsa. Of the propriety of that measure we have no doubt, especially as it appears that the labours of one Missionary will be sufficient to meet the claims of the latter Station. We hope your arrangements for a permanent course of labour at Chonuane are tolerably complete by the present time, and we fervently pray that the divine blessing may abundantly succeed your Missionary exertions in that locality. The Directors have kindly considered your statement of the expenses incurred in building, and have passed a resolution by which you are entitled to draw for £30 to liquidate the debt upon your dwelling house. We have issued a corresponding advice to the District Secretary, Mr Helmore, and the amount will be paid in the usual way.

We are happy to find that your views in relation to Native Agency remain unaltered, and as the attention of the Committee has been specially directed to the subject we trust it will not be long before an united effort is made with a view to the adoption of some definite plan to promote this important object. The experience of each successive year only serves to deepen our conviction of its close alliance with the future interests of the Missionary work, and the wisdom of putting forth, without delay, every practicable effort for its furtherance. We have therefore sanctioned the call for returns, proposed and adopted at the last meeting of the Committee; and, in addition to this, have appointed Mr Ashton to undertake the instruction of any suitable young men who may be found willing to place themselves under a course of training for Missionary service. We commend these incipient measures to the divine guidance and approbation, and trust they may finally issue in the production of a large and efficient body of Native labourers for the extension of Christianity and its blessings in the extensive regions towards the centre of Africa.

We notice with considerable regret your statements as to the movements and designs of the Dutch Emigrants, and fear there is reason to apprehend that their presence in the Bechuana Country will occasion serious obstruction to the evangelisation and improvement of the Native tribes. It is obvious that great wisdom and prudence will be requisite on the part of our brethren in dealing with these men. To keep the Natives in subjection and strip them gradually of their hereditary possessions, their lands and their cattle, they will naturally endeavour to hold them in ignorance and shut out that light which elevates the oppressed & condemns the oppressor. It will therefore be of importance, without compromise of principle, to disarm their prejudices and gain their goodwill; and in this we trust our brethren will be eminently successful, so that even before the face of its fiercest enemies the Gospel may have free course and be glorified.

Desiring our kindest regards to Mrs Livingston, and commending you afresh, in all your concerns and labours, to the unfailing protection and abundant grace of our Divine Lord and Saviour,

I remain,
Dear Brother,
Ever faithfully and affectionately yours,
[Arthur Tidman]
Forn. Secy., London Missionary Society

P.S. Your letter of April 10, 1846, was also duly received. We have the pleasure to add that the Directors have granted your request for a supply of medicines, leaving the purchase and selection to Dr Bennett, as you suggest, and it will be forwarded to your address at the earliest opportunity.

We shall feel obliged by your transmitting to us, on receipt of this letter, information respecting any Native teachers who may be under your superintendence, supported by special contributions from England, with accounts of their labours, mentioning particularly any instances of the divine blessing which may have attended them, and stating both their Native and English names.

The subscriptions advised and committed to your appropriation, according to our list, are as follows: £24 from Mrs McRobert for a teacher or teachers, whom for the sake of distinction we will call the Cambuslang Teachers, and £10.10.0 from Ralph Lindsay, Esq., for a teacher who may be called Lindsay's teacher. It will be best to apply the latter amount to the support of the Agent mentioned in your letter under the name of Paul, and report accordingly to us, and we will take care to forward the communication to Mr Lindsay. It is possible we may have advised other subscriptions, they may have escaped insertion on our list; if so, we depend on you to send us information respecting them.

20. To ARTHUR TIDMAN
30 December 1847

[LMS 41.A. Received 9 May 1848]

Kolobeng, Bakwain Country,
30 Dec. 1847

Dear Sir,

Having proceeded to the Kuruman in March last for the purpose of attending a meeting of Committee, we were compelled by circumstances connected with the birth of our second child[1] to an absence of nearly three months more than we had anticipated. I shall not therefore attend the next annual meeting, but endeavour to communicate with the Committee and Directors by the pen.

At the date of my last, my mind was oppressed by many topics of a depressing and irritating nature, but the arrival of your kind letter of 29th October 1846 tended to soothe the bitterness of spirit under which I laboured. The admonition to 'let my ardour be sustained by incessant communion with Christ' was most appropriate. I have to lament that my zeal is not all drawn from that source. Incidents, which when viewed in connection with the glorious work in which it is my privelege to be engaged ought to dwindle clean out of sight, too often exercise an

---

[1] Agnes, born at Kuruman in May (*Fam. Letters,* i, p. 199); married (1875) Alexander Low Bruce; died 1912 (Alice Z. Fraser, *Livingstone and Newstead,* 1913, pp. vii, 240–3).

undue influence on my thoughts, and I hope that in your prayers for your agents I may always be remembered as requiring a larger infusion of the spirit of the gracious Redeemer. I felt considerable anxiety in reference to pecuniary affairs, but am thankful to say much of my anxiety was unnecessary.

When we returned to Chonuane,[1] we found that though the season for sowing had arrived the chief had forbidden his people beginning with their gardens untill he should ascertain whether we could make another trial of the locality. He stated to us that some of his people were opposed to removal to another situation, because Chonuane afforded abundance of native produce, and the only direction in which we could move would be nearer the dreaded Mosilikatse. 'But', added he, 'I see you are unable to live in comfort here, and though all my people should leave me I am determined to cleave to you wherever it may be needful to go'.

We had two wishes. We felt extremely anxious to settle Paul with the tribe of Mokhatla, and equally so to obtain a permanent abode for our own tribe. After prayerful consideration we decided on the latter, and feel truly grateful to the source of all influence we had obtained so much favour in the eyes of the Heathen as induced a simultaneous movement of the whole tribe, the very next morning after our decision was known, to perform a journey of about 40 miles to the North-West and build a new town entirely on our account. The stream on which our new settlement is formed is called the Kolobeng,[2] and in as far as temporal matters are concerned we have the prospect of abundance of both native and European produce. And, better still, I believe we can now reasonably indulge the hope that through the Divine blessing the gospel will not only be permanent here, but sound out to dark regions beyond.

When still engaged in cutting wood for a temporary dwelling, the chief, without a single suggestion from us, intimated his intention to erect the school. 'I desire', said he, 'to build a house for God, the defender of my town, and that you be at no expense with it whatever.' Had we been able to bestow the requisite superintendance, a substantial building might have been secured, for more than 200 workmen were employed on it. But being engaged in erecting our own huts, and such numbers of uninstructed workmen, all anxious to do something, being

[1] In July (*Fam. Letters*, i, pp. 200, 201).
[2] The 'new settlement', named after the stream, was located at *c.* 24° 40′ S., 25° 40′ E., about 270 miles N.N.E. of Kuruman. D. L. and the BaKwena went there in August (*Fam. Letters*, i, p. 203).

difficult to manage, I was obliged to plan a small building and of the materials which, though frail, they knew best how to use. It was with no small pleasure we found ourselves so soon after our removal able to resume regular services. The people also undertook our watercourse, in exchange for our assistance in erecting a square house for their chief. We should have been glad to render assistance in their efforts to improve, without any equivalent, but an interchange of friendly services brings us into closer contact with the people, and developes feelings of confidence which we hope at no distant day may by Divine grace ripen into glorious fruit. Forty of the older men made the watercourse, and a younger band of sixty-five built the dam.

When Sechele's house was finished, he requested us to establish a prayer meeting in it. He said: 'Although I have not yet given up my sin (polygamy), I greatly desire to have prayer in my house every evening'. He invites his people to attend both it and our other services, and we are sensible of an increase of knowledge in many. Some of the most influential men in the tribe have made persevering efforts to acquire a knowledge of reading. Their progress has not, however, been so great as a witness of their patience might expect. They seem to experience considerable difficulty in the mental effort required to join letters into words, probably from not having been accustomed to anything of the sort in their youth. They remark, if I should give them medicine which would enable them to conquer the difficulty, they would gladly drink it. Sechele and his brothers are our best scholars. The former has read the Testament and Selection[1] through twice, and never allows me, in my frequent visits to the town, to retire without requesting me to read & explain a chapter or two with him. Our present position is one of hope, and all our dependance for success is on the Arm of Him who is almighty to save. We expect your prayers that Jesus may be glorified here, and that we may have grace to ascribe to Him alone all the glory.

Mrs Livingston has recently commenced an infant and sewing school, but as it still possesses the attraction of novelty we cannot form an opinion as to the ultimate success of the measure. Paul and David continue to render valuable assistance in all our operations. But for them, the work of instruction would have been at a stand during itineracy and our visit to the South. We have school early in the morning, and having attended that we are all engaged in manual labour till near the time for our evening services. The labour has been incessant ever

---

[1] *Likaélo tse ri tlaocoeñ mo likualoñ tsa Morimo* ['Lessons selected from the Books of God'], 2nd ed., London 1841; Moffat's translation of 'Scripture Lessons used in the Borough-road and other schools' (*Miss. Labours*, p. 561 n.).

since our removal, and completely prevented us from extending our efforts to the ajacent tribes. Paul & I had made preparations for an itineracy a fortnight ago, but an Englishman, having gone down the Limpopo elephant shooting, lost all his cattle by the bite of a small fly[1] (a very little larger than a common house fly), & sent to us for assistance. As all our oxen were sent to extricate him out of his difficulties, our journey will not commence till the second week in January.

I ought now to furnish some account of the conversion of our native teachers.[2] But a younger brother, Charles Livingston, having nearly finished the course of study pursued in the Oberlin College, Ohio, U.S., and resolved to dedicate his life to the service of Christ in China, has written to me requesting an introduction to the Directors of our Society. The relationship I sustain to him makes me anxious, in submitting the case for their judgement, to impart as much of his history as will enable them to form an opinion whether his desire is of the romantic & evanescent cast, or whether it possesses a character of stability sufficient to warrant the trouble & expense of examination as to suitability in other respects. This is all I can do in the case.

His resolution to become a missionary has not been formed on my recommendation. My letters to him have nearly all miscarried. But when I found by his to me that he had resolved to dedicate his life to the service of Christ among the heathen, I felt desirous that he should think of China and that he submit himself to the judgement of the Directors, as men of experience in such matters, in order that it might be ascertained whether he were a suitable individual or not. I wished to introduce him to the Directors of our Society simply because I have confidence in their wisdom & desire to act for the best, such as will produce satisfaction whether their deliberate opinion is favourable or otherwise. I am not aware that my influence has extended farther.

During my residence in England in 1839 in connection with the Society, my brother was hopefully converted, and became a member of the Congregational Church in Hamilton.[3] He had then a strong desire to obtain a liberal education, but neither he nor our parents possessed the necessary means. He began, however, to make some efforts towards

---

[1] The tsetse fly (*Glossina morsitans*). The 'Englishman', whom D. L. elsewhere calls 'a mad sort of Scotchman' (13.ii.48 Watt), was the famous hunter Roualeyn Gordon Cumming (1820-66), who made several expeditions into Bechuanaland 1845-9. In his book (*A Hunter's Life*, 1850, ii, pp. 228, 231) he gratefully acknowledges the help given him on this occasion by D. L.

[2] As requested by the Directors (see p. 86), and promised by D. L. (see p. 102).

[3] A town 11 miles S.E. of Glasgow. D. L.'s parents moved there *c.* 1840 from Blantyre, 3 miles away.

mental improvement after the labours of the day were over. But having myself experienced the immense difficulty of pursuing a course of study with no resources but those of indoor manual labour, I advised him to endeavour to obtain admittance into one of the colleges in America in which students support themselves by labour in the open air. By this means I hoped his frame might be invigorated for future service. I never once advised him to become a missionary, but approved of his desire for mental improvement, on the ground that if qualified the Lord Jesus would certainly employ him in some way in promoting his glory.

While my advice was on its way to Scotland, I recieved a letter asking counsel as to the propriety of proceeding to Oberlin. I had just recieved the quarterly allowance of £5 from Mr Arundel, and answered my brother's letter by transmiting that sum to pay his passage, and very shortly afterwards he, being sixteen years of age,[1] embarked at Liverpool. We had not seen each other for a period anterior to his conversion, and we could not then, because I had given my all. It was nearly his all too, for after paying his passage, landing at New York, and selling his box and bed, he had only £2.13.6 in the world.

Having purchased a loaf and piece of cheese as provisions for the way, he set out for Oberlin, a distance of either 3[00] or 700 miles.[2] His money, and provisions too, were all spent long before he reached his destination. But kind Providence helped him. He never begged. He obtained work, as soon as he arrived, in the bookbinding establishment of the College, and supported himself through the preparatory department. In the third year he entered on the Collegiate course, and in that department each student is required to deliver certain theses in the College Chapel. The junior students are allowed during a portion of the course to read their productions, but Charles, with the approbation of his Tutor, resolved to recite his from memory during the whole period; and while preparing for his first appearance, on the banks of a river, subjected himself by the exposure to an attack of pleurisy.

I am thus minute because the remedial measures employed so reduced his strength as made him subsequently relinquish the hope of becoming a missionary. His bodily weakness prevented him from working with his hands, and rather than run into debt he left his lodgings in the town, although his landlady remonstrated against it, and lived entirely in his

---

[1] Charles L. (who died in 1873) was born in 1821 (*D.N.B.*) 'Sixteen' should therefore presumably read 'eighteen'.

[2] It is actually about 550 miles (Secretary, Oberlin College, 18.v.60).

own room in the College. His diet, cooked by himself & consisting of potatoes and salt butter, was not calculated to strengthen his debilitated but growing frame, and want of means to purchase books compelled him to borrow from his fellow collegians and work hardest over them after they had retired to sleep. When the first session was over, he went to Canada in quest of a home in another brother's house,[1] in which to recruit his strength, but had to perform most of the journey on foot. In subsequent vacations he adopted the plan of setting out in some direction and walking on till he found a school, and the salary assisted him in the next session.

And now, at the date of Decr. 1846, [he] writes me that he has attained the degree of A.B., and may in two years from that time have the degree of A.M.,[2] but does not care much about the latter, for he can hardly spare money to pay for the parchment. And after stating his reasons for believing that it is his duty to dedicate his life to the cause of Christ as a missionary rather than as a minister, he adds, 'I should prefer to go out under the London Missionary Society to all others. As for the American Missionary Society, I can never submit to go out under their patronage. A Society composed of slaveholders & of those who apologize for slavery is not the thing for me. All its members are not pro-slavery. Still, so long as they tolerate slaveholders among them as Christians, recieve their money — think of it, the blood & sweat and groans of the downtrodden slave supporting a missionary — who would want to recieve such money? Not only do they this, but they also tolerate polygamy in some of the mission churches among the Indians.' But I think it may be better to enclose his letter to the Secretary.[3] It was designed for no eye but mine, and he will kindly use his discretion whether it ought to come before the Board. I do so lest in mine there may be the least colouring which can mislead.

If the Directors should think it right to examine the case, I concieve Dr Wardlaw[4] might obtain information as to his character before he

---

[1] D. L.'s elder brother, John (b. 1811), was then living in Lanark, Ontario, where he had settled in 1838. Cf. *Fam. Letters*, i, p. 73, and below, p. 164.

[2] Charles L. 'entered the Preparatory Department of Oberlin College in 1840, ... was graduated with a Bachelor of Arts degree in 1845, and was enrolled in the Oberlin College Theological Seminary for the next three years, but transferred to Union Seminary [New York] for his final year and for graduation in 1849' (Secretary, Oberlin College, 18.v.60).

[3] The letter, dated 'Lafayette, Dec. 17th 1848', is now in the LMS archives. D. L.'s quotation from it is almost verbatim.

[4] Ralph Wardlaw (1779–1853), 'congregational minister in Glasgow 1803–1853, and from 1811 divinity professor in the congregational seminary there' (*D.N.B.*); a Scottish Director of the LMS.

left Scotland from a Mr Henry Drummond,[1] who was my brother's employer, a deacon of the church in Hamilton but now of Dr Wardlaw's or of one of the Independant churches in Glasgow. Revd. Mr Laing,[2] an Independant minister settled somewhere in Scotland, was instrumental in the conversion of my brother. Revd. J. Kirk[3] was pastor of the church in Hamilton subsequently to his joining it. He & two deacons accompanied my brother to the ship. In America, Professor Finney is one of the teachers in Oberlin, Rev. A. Mahan is president of the College.[4] Any other in whom the Directors have confidence might be induced to ascertain the qualifications of the young man without incurring expense.

Another point, but which I cannot comprehend, is, he has found time in the midst of his difficulties to think of a helpmate, and has actually become engaged to a young lady, although a stranger in a strange land.[5] I should have advised him to have attempted the acquisition of some medical knowledge previous to the former step, but the fact of a matrimonial connection being in prospect renders the case somewhat more complex. His address is: Charles Livingston, student, Oberlin Collegiate Institute, Loraine County, Ohio. U.S.

Hoping you will be guided to that which will conduce most to the Divine Glory in all your measures,

[Signature cut out]

P.S. I have advised my brother, in a letter of same date as this, to make a personal application to the Directors, but it is uncertain whether my letter will reach him.[6] It will be desirable, after the foregoing introduction, that the case be ascertained from those who are not related to him.

---

[1] A lace manufacturer in Hamilton until about 1844, then moved to Glasgow (cf. *Fam. Letters*, i, p. 32). Three of D. L.'s letters to him from S. Africa are included in Chamberlin's book (at pp. 24, 59, 118).

[2] Possibly James Byre Laing, one of the theological students who preached at Hamilton between October 1838 and September 1839 as candidates for the vacant post of minister (W. Naismith, *Centenary of St. James' Congregational Church*, Hamilton 1907, p. 10); pastor of Woodside Church, Aberdeen, 1840–58 (J. Ross, *History of Congregational Independency in Scotland*, 1900, pp. 245, 258).

[3] John Kirk, the successful candidate (see preceding note); ordained 1839; minister of St. James' Church, Sept. 1839–August 1845, then moved to Edinburgh (Naismith, *op. cit.*, pp. 10, 64; Ross, *op. cit.*, pp. 231, 248, 251, 258).

[4] Charles Grandison Finney (1792–1875), Professor of Pastoral Theology at Oberlin 1835–75 and President of the college 1851–65; Asa Mahan (1799–1889), President of Oberlin College 1835–50 (Secretary, Oberlin College, 18.v.60).

[5] Charles L.'s description of his future wife, Harriet C. Ingraham, is quoted in *Fam. Letters*, i, p. 224, n. 46 (where I have misdated his letter as 'October 1846'). She was an Oberlin graduate of the Class of 1847, and died in December 1900 (Secretary, Oberlin College, 18.v.60).

[6] I have not located it.

21. To ARTHUR TIDMAN
1 November 1848

[LMS 44. Received 28 April 1849. Previous publication: *Chronicle*, vol. xiii, (August) 1849, pp. 115–16 (edited extracts); Chamberlin, pp. 123–8 (incomplete)]

Kolobeng
1st November 1848

Dear Sir,

No portion of our lives ever seemed to glide more swiftly past than the year which has elapsed since our location on the Kolobeng. Our operations have been characterized by a pleasant variety, but of necessity chiefly confined to our own people. The results, though considerable compared with nothing, are trifling indeed when contrasted with what remains to be done. Many discussions & incidents have occurred to cheer us in our solitude, and an interest has been imparted which often lightened the manual labour in which, during the intervals of service, it was necessary constantly to engage. Circumstances have also developed considerable opposition, but it has been of a kind which afforded much encouragement, for our most bitter opponents seemed to entertain no personal animosity, and never alluded to their enmity to the gospel in our presence unless specially invited to state their objections.

An event which excited more open enmity than any other was the profession of faith and subsequent reception of the chief into the church. As the circumstances which led us to recieve his confession as genuine are somewhat peculiar, I may be allowed to mention a few particulars in order that the Directors may form an opinion as to the propriety of the step we have taken.

The state of the Bakwains about three years ago was very unlike that of the tribes ajacent to the Kuruman, among whom the gospel had been in silent operation for nearly a quarter of a century previous to their obtaining the present ample supply. I have never been able to contemplate the condition, especially of the old, without a painful foreboding that our entreaties & warnings would only render their doom the more terrible. They generally resist an invitation, or if they listen to our message it is with the firm persuasion that they have been preserved to old age by some medicine or other, and it would be folly to think of another saviour now.

Sechele, though generally intelligent, had imbibed largely of the prevailing superstition, and in addition to being the chief rain-doctor of the tribe we have had evidence that he was reckless of human life. Indeed, although he had the reputation among other tribes of being addicted to witchcraft, he thought it highly meritorious to put all suspected witches to death. From the first day of residence with the Bakwains to this, he attended school & all our services with unvarying regularity. The first indication of deep feeling observed in him was when, sitting together under our waggon during the heat of the day, I endeavoured to describe 'the great white throne', 'the Judgement se[a]t', &c. He said, 'These words shake all my bones, my strength is gone'; and the existence of our Lord previous to his appearance among men, & Divine nature, surprised him greatly.

We have often during the three years in which we have been with the tribe witnessed that the word of God was with power, and as his knowledge increased he professed among his own people firm belief in the divine truth, and great thankfulness because the gospel had been sent to him while so many were left in darkness. A poor scoffer from one of the Southern tribes having visited him, we felt anxious lest his taunts should have an injurious effect, but felt relieved when we ascertained that while Sechele treated his visitor with the deference due to his station in his own tribe,[1] instead of argument generally sat down by his side & read four or five chapters of the Testament to him. 'His taunts are very bitter', said he, 'but I fear only for my people, lest they too should believe as he does'.

The greatest sacrifice he had to make was the renuntiation of polygamy. Of all other sins, they had possessed the idea that they were wrong, but this practice had never been imagined as possessed of moral turpitude. His superfluous wives were decidedly the most amiable females in the town, our best scholars too; and hoping that their souls also might be given to us, we did not feel called upon otherwise to press the point in question than by publicly endeavouring to declare the whole counsel of God. Two of them were the daughters of under-chiefs through whose influence, after his father's murder, he had been enabled to succeed to the chieftainship. This circumstance made his parting with them assume the appearance of ingratitude, and led him to propose to remove to some other country for four years, in order that they might in the interval forget him & become married to others.[2] As we had

---

[1] He was a petty chief of the Ba Tlharo, who had visited Sechele late in 1847 (*Fam. Letters*, i, pp. 220–1, 227).

[2] 'He is bound by his wives. Has a curious idea: would like to go to another country for three or four years in order to study, with the hope that probably his wives may have married others in the mean time. He would then return and be admitted to the Lord's Supper, and teach his people the knowledge he had acquired. He seems incapable of putting them away, he feels so attached to them' (13.ii.48 Watt).

observed a gradual change in his disposition, & an improvement in his character, and add to these facts were the sending them to their parents, with the message that 'the word of God had come between him & their daughters', and a proffessed desire to observe the laws of Jesus, we did not hesitate to recieve him. A third wife was taken to her own tribe because she had no relatives among the Bakwains, & left us with many tears. A fourth, although in the same situation, we thought ought to remain because she has a little daughter. Each took all the goods which belonged to her, and he furnished new clothing besides, previous to sending them home to their friends.[1]

On the morning after it was known that Sechele had renounced his wives on account of the gospel, a general consternation seemed to have seized both young & old.[2] The town was as quiet as if it had been Sunday. Not a single woman was seen going to her garden. Pichos[3] were held during the night in order to intimidate him and make him renounce his purpose. But after having been tried in various ways for two months, we proceeded to administer the ordinance of baptism. Many of the spectators were in tears, but these were in general tears of sorrow for the loss of their rainmaker, or of grief at seeing some of the ties of relationship to him completely broken. We commend him to your prayerful sympathies, that he may be preserved to the day which will declare each man's work, what sort it is. To the Great God Our Saviour Jesus Christ, through the influence of whose Spirit alone we hope for success, be the undivided honour and glory for ever.

Rainmaking to Christians in England may seem a simple absurdity too ridiculous for sober argument, but the people here having no graven images, that is the mode in which they most openly give that glory to the creature which belongs to the Creator & Lord of all. The rain doctor, having abundance of expedients, generally contrives to keep up the attention of the people by his trifles till the rain comes. Their minds are thus relieved from the irksomeness which withering winds and a cloudless sky would otherwise produce. In vain we tell them he does nothing more. 'He charms the clouds by his medicines, & without his charms no rain would ever fall.' 'But we see no effect from his charms. He burns his medicines & we often obtain no rain till a month afterwards.' 'That is the way of all medicine', is the reply; 'you give medicine, and the patient may become well in a day or two, but sometimes

---

[1] For other details, including the names and parentage of the wives sent away, see *Private J.*, pp. 298–9.

[2] 'seemed to surge both young & old' (Chamberlin, p. 125).

[3] *Pitsó*, a tribal assembly.

not for a month afterwards, & sometimes he dies, but we cannot say
your medicine has no effect'. It is of little use to point out the difference
which exists between the application of medicines, having known
effects, to living beings and inanimate objects, for they apply medicine
to their houses, hoes, gardens, shoes, indeed to everything. They never
relinquish their follies untill they feel the love of Christ constraining
them, and preaching His unsearchable riches has always more effect
than argument, and I believe it will be found so all over the world.

We have erected a substantial house, 50 ft by 20, and a workshop of
smaller dimensions. This work prevented us from proceeding with the
settlement of Paul with Mokhatla's people so soon as we intended. We
went[1] in order to erect a small hut as a commencement, but the opposition of the Boers or emigrants was such we felt assured they would burn
it in our absence. We contented ourselves by providing the materials,
and will return in two months with his family. I hope then to be able to
remain two months more on the spot & build a small school, & think
that our presence will prevent any actual outburst of hostility. The
French missionaries in the Basuto country lately sent 5 native teachers
to one of the tribes in that direction. The Commandant of the Boors
tore their letter of introduction & threw it into the fire, & sent them
back with contumal scorn.[2] Apprehension of a similar treatment for
Paul is the reason why I prefer going with him and acting in what may
appear to you an over-cautious manner. We shall now have more time
to devote to the Eastern tribes, and they form a most interesting field
for missionary labour. If we cannot furnish native teachers soon, the
field will in all probability be lost in as far as our Mission is concerned.

The infant school under the care of Mrs L. afforded us much encouragement. The attendance during the past year may be stated as
from 60 to 80. The failure of the native crops has lately had considerable effect on the regularity of their attendance, for the children have
been obliged to go great distances in search of locusts and roots on which
to subsist. Mrs L. must also soon discontinue it for a season, but it will
be resumed after her confinement.[3]

A lady in Cambuslang collected from her friends in Glasgow for the
assistance of Mebaloe. She has since removed from that place, and I
believe a Mr Whish in Glasgow[4] will now occupy her place. I shall en-

---

[1] Early in February (13.ii.48 Watt).

[2] For further details, see *Fam. Letters*, ii, p. 11.

[3] Her third child, named Thomas Steele, was born on 7 March 1849 (*Fam. Letters*,
ii, p. 33); he died at Alexandria (Egypt) on 15 March 1876 (Blaikie, p. 451 n.).

[4] Charles Whish, owner of a millinery warehouse, and one of D. L.'s many
correspondents (cf. Chamberlin, p. 90). He is often mentioned in *Fam. Letters*.

close in my next a communication for Mr Lindsay respecting Paul and his labours. I have considerable hope that the attempts of Mr Ashton will be crowned with success, and that others will be induced soon to enter on the same errand of mercy and field of labour as Paul. But success will almost entirely depend on those of the bretheren who are pastors of churches. If the members refuse to give themselves to this work, it may become a question whether a different distribution of the European force of the Mission will not be advisable. The instances in which the majority of the population is Christian might be left with only occasional superintendance. A teacher from the Kuruman has, I am happy to state, lately made preparations for commencing among the Wanketse to the westward of Kolobeñ.[1]

A vote of disapprobation with the mode in which the Directors favoured me with £30 for building expenses at Chonuane[2] makes it necessary that I allude to the circumstances in which I applied for it, in a manner more minute than I should otherwise have done. I have in spending my salary always acted on the conviction that it was wrong to go to the Colony merely because there we could obtain supplies much cheaper than from the traders who occasionally visit us. By a journey to Grahm's Town[3] or Algoa Bay I could have saved more than £30 of each year's salary, but it would have been at a loss of from six to nine months each time to the Mission. I have bought from traders often at a price double, sometimes three times more, than I should have done at Algoa Bay. The salary was sufficient for all I wished,[4] but when it became necessary to remove to Chonuane the expenses of removal [and] building house & school having been superadded to ordinary outlay reduced our resources to nothing. We endured for a while, using a wretched infusion of native corn for coffee, but when our corn was done we were fairly obliged to go to Kuruman for supplies. I can bear

---

[1] Cf. *Fam. Letters*, i, pp. 259, 263–4. After Sebego's death (November 1844) his followers, headed by his son Senthufe, had returned to their ancestral home at Kgwakgwê, about 30 miles S.W. of Kolobeng.

[2] Cf. above, p. 109. At the fifth meeting of the District Committee (May 1848), which D. L. did not attend, the following resolution (moved by Hughes, and seconded by Helmore) was carried unanimously (Moffat being among those present): 'That this meeting transmit to Mr Livingstone an extract from the Directors' letter of 3rd Septr. 1847 containing a resolution relative to his station and a vote of £30 to defray the expenses of erecting a dwelling house at Chonuane — at the same time expressing its dissatisfaction at the *irregular* way in which that money had been voted by the Directors, inasmuch as no application was made *to the Committee* by Mr Livingstone for any sum of money to defray his expenses.'

[3] Grahamstown, 33° 19′ S., 26° 32′ E., capital of the Eastern Province of Cape Colony.

[4] Married missionaries received £100 per annum.

what other Europeans would consider hunger and thirst without any inconvenience, but when we arrived, to hear the old women who had seen my wife depart about two years before exclaiming before the door, 'Bless me! How lean she is! Has he starved her? Is there no food in the country to which she has been?', &c, this was more than I could well bear.

I went to the meeting of Committee[1] with the full persuasion that the building expenses would be given, so that I should be able to procure supplies for my return. But before I had stated the case Mr Helmore brought forward a motion expressive of disapprobation at my leaving Mabotsa, and withdrew it. Another & another followed, exhibiting a spirit which prevented me from making known my necessities. I then returned to the Kuruman to muse over my position. I had come for supplies, & had not a penny in the world to buy them with. The bretheren of the Committee would not probably be more willing to sanction the new Mission on another occasion more than this. Mr Moffat willingly advanced the money, but then no one likes to be in debt; so, thinking that now was the time in which I really ought to make known the case & ask the aid of the Directors, I did so,[2] and believe I acted properly, though all the world should disapprove.

Mr Hughs mentioned in Committee that he had recieved £30 through Dr Philip for his project on the Vaal River.[3] It is surprising he did not see that that was equally an irregularity with mine, & being then on the point of starting for the Colony he might have had a little consideration in his motion for those who do not go thither. Colonial journies are in general serious drawbacks to the Mission. Mabotsa will again be left desolate for six or eight months. I have often thought of bringing the subject under the consideration of the Committee, but my motives will now be suspected, and I am not sure but they would be justly so. Man is a complex being, & we greatly need our motives to be purified from all that is evil.

We have purchased a bell, & it was with joy we mounted it. It relieves us from the task of going through the town with a small hand bell. I made an application to the Committee on the subject, as also on the subject of expenses for building on the new station,[4] but they seem to

---

[1] At Dikgatlhong, in March 1847. See above, p. 94 n.

[2] MS. reads: 'and I did so'.

[3] Hughes had left Griquatown in 1845 to start an irrigation settlement 40 miles away on the Vaal River, at Backhouse (Freeman, *Tour*, 1851, pp. 232–5). The only reference to this in the minutes of the 1847 meeting is that the District Committee voted him £7.10.0 'for finishing his house'.

[4] The minutes contain no reference to this application.

have thought only on the £30 which they had no power to refuse. I shall apply again by letter, for I do not feel it my duty to go out this year merely to attend its sittings.

I shall feel obliged if the Directors will forward the sum of £20 to Mr Henry Drummond, 62 Queen St., Glasgow, to defray the expense of clothing which I have ordered from him.[1] I shall advise Mr Rutherfoord of Cape Town[2] of the amount, to be deducted from the salary. Mr Drummond will apply for information as to the conveyance to Algoa Bay. We have sustained considerable loss from the boxes having been broken open there, & do not know who is now the Society's agent there. Friends unknown to us send boxes without invoices, & we do not know who to thank or blame. The ladies connected with Carr's Lane Chapel, Birmingham, sent two chairs to Sechele. They came safely, and arrived just two days before that on which we had resolved to baptize him.[3] They were to him highly interesting, as tokens of love from those he had never seen.

[Signature cut out]

22. To DAVID LIVINGSTON
23 December 1848

[LMS: Outgoing Letters, Africa, Box 7, pp. 171–3]

London
December 23, 1848

Dear Brother,

We have to acknowledge your letter of December last informing us of your removal from Chonuane to a new station on the Kolobeng River. We have been encouraged by the account which you have given of the suitableness of the locality as a Missionary post; and we hope we may now regard you as permanently settled, knowing well the disadvantages attending frequent changes of this nature. We bless God for your continued health and strength, and for the prospects of enlarged

---

[1] D. L. and his family had much of their clothing sent to them from Scotland by Drummond (cf. Chamberlin, pp. 59–60, 119–20; *Fam. Letters*, i, pp. 72, 121–2, ii, p. 124; and below, p. 143).

[2] Howson Edward Rutherfoord, a prosperous merchant actively interested in religious and educational movements, and a S.A. Director of the LMS.

[3] Sechele was baptized on 1 October 1848. The annual Reports of the LMS for this period show that the members of Carr's Lane Chapel were zealous supporters of the Society, contributing on the average more than £500 p.a. to its funds.

usefulness and more systematic effort with which you are now favoured. We also rejoice in the favour shewn to you by the Chief and people, and the willingness which they manifest to sustain your labours and establish the Mission on a firm basis. The industry of the Natives, and their desire for the advantages of civilisation, are also very encouraging; and the Station you occupy will, we doubt not, furnish another instance of the concurrent progress of civilisation and Christianity, and exhibit the beneficial influence of each upon the other.

It gratified us to be informed of the desire of your brother to enter upon Missionary service; and, in accordance with your suggestion, we have opened a correspondence with Dr Wardlaw on the subject, and thro' him with Mr Drummond; and the information which has been received from the latter is very gratifying.[1] Apart, however, from this, there are difficulties in the way, which we fear it will not be easy to remove: 1st, the present inability of the Society, on account of its pecuniary position and prospects, to send out more Missionaries; 2nd, a personal interview with your brother would be essential, and the expense of this the Society could not incur, and we apprehend he has not himself the means of defraying it; and 3rd, his engagement to marry.

The obstacles arising out of these circumstances are formidable, and would, even on the supposition that the way was clear in other respects, greatly militate against the accomplishment of those earnest Missionary desires which your brother entertains. As we have lately sent out several Missionaries to China,[2] some time must elapse before we can attempt to add to their number; and if your brother wished to go out married, as we presume he would, the Directors could not consent to such arrangement without violating a general rule which it has been deemed expedient to establish, namely, that every Missionary proceeding to the East go out in the first instance unmarried, and that a fair trial of health and Missionary capability be given before he involves himself in domestic responsibilities. Our experience has taught us, by many severe lessons, the importance of a steady adherence to this regulation; and we should not, unless for the most weighty and urgent reasons, feel at liberty to depart from it. We will, however, further communicate with your brother, and give him these particulars for his guidance.

We are now in daily expectation of receiving your reports of the Native teachers labouring under your superintendence, namely, Lind-

[1] This correspondence (including the letter to Charles L. mentioned below) cannot be traced in the LMS archives; it may have been among the records destroyed during the bombing of London in World War II.

[2] Four recruits for the China Mission had left England in March and April 1847, and another seven followed in February 1848 (*Chronicle*, xi, pp. 51–7; xii, pp. 36–41).

say's teacher (Paul) and the Cambuslang Teachers. We addressed you on the subject under date Sept. 6, 1847,[1] and we have relied upon your making the necessary effort for supplying us with the information then requested. We had anticipated its arrival at a much earlier period, and can only hope that it is now very near at hand.

In a few months hence we trust you will see our brother Mr Freeman in the Bechuana Country.[2] He may not be able to visit your own station, on account of its comparative remoteness; but we doubt not you will feel a pleasure in attending the general Meeting of the brethren which we expect will be convened for the purpose of receiving him, and of which due notice will be given by the District Secretary.

With kindest regards to Mrs Livingston, whose efforts in the instruction of her own sex we duly appreciate, and commending you both in all your interests, personal, domestic & public, to the constant care and abundant blessing of our divine Lord and Saviour,

I remain,
Dear Brother,
Ever faithfully and affectionately yours,
[Arthur Tidman]
Foreign Secretary, London Missionary Society

23. To ARTHUR TIDMAN
26 May 1849

[LMS 46. Received 9 October 1849]

Kolobeng
26th May 1849

Dear Sir,

The state of this Mission, which at the date of the last letter I had the pleasure of addressing you wore rather a pleasing aspect, has for the last few months assumed quite another phase. We have had an intensely hot and dry season. Only five inches of rain have fallen during the year, and the thermometer has ranged higher than we have ever seen it. The Kolobeng is nearly dry, and the native crops, which during the last three years have been scanty, have this season entirely failed. The men

---

[1] See above, p. 110.

[2] Freeman had recently been deputed to visit and report upon the Society's Missions in S. Africa and Mauritius. He left England in December, and reached Cape Town in February (1849). After returning home, he published (1851) *A Tour in South Africa*, a general account of his travels and observations.

are therefore compelled to frequent hunting of the larger game, and the women & children must make almost daily excursions in search of roots or locusts. Our meetings are in consequence very thinly attended, and the school has dwindled away to a mere skeleton. Instead of quiet and comparatively well observed Sabbaths, it is quite common to see pack-oxen laden with meat, or crowds of women burdened with locusts, returning home on that sacred day. And all, in their eagerness to procure that which will satisfy the wants of the body, seem but little disposed to attend to the unfelt wants of the soul. The natural indisposition to conversation on divine subjects has now a plausible excuse, and though we deeply deplore the present accession of apathy, yet, knowing the severity with which the scarcity presses on them, we cannot feel surprised at it.

Another tribe, called the Bakaa, having suffered considerably by the repeated attacks of the Bamangwato, lately came a distance of about 150 miles in order to join the Bakwains.[1] They had no sense of security in their own country, and were attracted hither by the report that Sechele had embraced the 'word of peace'. They came, as they said, in order 'to enjoy sleep; they had none at home'. They seem to be about a thousand in number.[2] While we feel thankful for their arrival, as an increase to our immediate sphere of usefulness, for the present they act as a fresh infusion of heathenism into the present unchristian mass.

In December last I made another attempt to place Paul in the centre of a population of many thousands, the tribe selected being that of Mokhatla, because this chief had of his own accord urgently requested Paul to become his teacher. But the Boers have taken possession of the whole country, & though their Commandants have always expressed themselves in a most friendly way towards our objects, they made me aware of a strong undercurrent of opposition. Being unwilling to believe that this would be developed in any other way than it had always been in our itineracies, yet feeling anxious lest it should prove a hindrance to Paul in his work, I delayed going untill our arrangements at home were such as would admit of my spending a few months with him at the commencement.

When the Commandant, who was in Mokhatla's vicinity, learned that it was no longer mere itineracies we contemplated, he suddenly altered his tone, and threatened in a most furious manner to send a commando against the tribe with which we meant to settle; that my

---

[1] They had arrived on 3 May (*Private J.*, p. 304). Their troubles with the BaNgwato are described more fully in *Fam. Letters*, i, pp. 213–14; ii, p. 25.

[2] According to a census D. L. made soon afterwards, they numbered 1,236, and the BaKwena 2,384 (Freeman, *Tour*, pp. 279–80).

object was to take possession of the country for the English Government, that I wished to introduce fire arms among all the tribes as I had done among the Bakwains, &c &c. I replied by denying connection with Government, having, as he knew when on a former occasion I entreated him to refrain from a projected expedition against Sechele,[1] distinctly refused to be in any way connected with even his own, from principle, and that I should certainly proceed in my work by the authority of Christ, and if he obstructed it, by driving the people away, the blood of their souls would be required at his hand. He offered to present no impediment if I should 'promise to teach the natives that the Boers are a superior race to them'!

We immediately made preparations to build a school, but before we had made any progress we were informed that a deputation from the Dutch Synod had come to within forty miles of us. Believing that the Boers might be won over to forbearance by their ministers, and that the Commandant's mind might be disabused of his fancies, we went towards the deputation.[2] Both Potgeiter[3] and his sub-commandants had preceded us, and were now all flattery towards my person and objects; and all they would request of me, previous to a thorough and permanent removal of all obstacles out of the way, was about one month's delay. During this period they solemnly and repeatedly promised that they would exert themselves to the utmost of their power to win over such of their subjects as were opposed to missionary operations. As they even entreated me not to force, or appear to force, the matter by building now, and the preachers thought I ought to concede the point, I agreed to return for a short period to Kolobeng, and, having visited some other tribes, I came home in January.

On taking leave, I publicly saluted the deputation, the Commandant, & sub-commandants, and was not a little surprised shortly after my return by hearing that a Boerish bull had been sent to our Committee demanding my recall.[4] I have lately seen the document. It is untrue from end to end. The postscript tickles me rather, for I do not like even

---

[1] See above, p. 96.

[2] Cf. *Fam. Letters*, ii, pp. 9–10; and, for D. L.'s encounter with the Commandant (Potgieter), *ibid.*, ii, pp. 8–9, and *Private J.*, p. 302. The members of the deputation, sent by the Synod of the Dutch Reformed Church in Cape Colony, were Revs. W. Robertson and P. E. Faure.

[3] Andries Hendrik Potgieter (1792–1852), Chief Commandant of the Boers in the Transvaal.

[4] On 23.i.49, shortly after the meeting described, Potgieter had written to Ross (as Secretary of the District Committee), demanding D. L.'s immediate and permanent recall from Kolobeng, failing which the Boers themselves would take steps to expel him. (LMS archives, Philip papers, A.2.3.)

to think of running away like a coward.[1] It is, however, quite evident that their blandness before their ministers was a mere feint to get me out of the way till they had secured an entire riddance by writing to the Committee. The expression of their intended policy towards the natives, combined with the threats in case of non-compliance on the part of the Committee, clearly shew that they have bloody designs. At present I have as little intention of deserting my post in the hour of danger as I had when it is said I ran away. The Boers believe that I have sold Sechele 500 guns and a cannon.[2] This belief has tended to keep them from slaughtering the Bakwains as they have done to several other tribes. Knowing this, although applied to for information I have declined speaking on the subject.

The period of my visit was immediately after they had suffered a defeat by the English.[3] But living North of them I was unaware of the circumstance. I had no wish to come into contact with them, but unintentionally became acquainted with Pretorious, on whose head the Governor had placed £2[000] or £3,000.[4] Several others have had large sums offered for their capture, so my appearance may have seemed to their uninformed minds as that of a Government spy. I was pursuing my vocation in entire ignorance of their peculiar position, and only became fully aware of it on reading the Colonial newspapers some time afterwards. No other missionary having ever visited the numerous tribes in that direction, the Commandants repeatedly asked why I did not remain with the Bakwains till they were all converted. I suppose they concluded if they could procure the recal of this one they would be permitted to follow their future policy towards the natives undisturbed.

But I hope other missionaries will be induced to pity the condition of these perishing thousands, and if not of our Society, of some other.

---

[1] Cf. *Fam. Letters*, ii, pp. 22–4, where D. L. comments more fully on Potgieter's letter. Its postscript asserts that when asked to answer various charges made against him, 'he hastily fled without daring to greet anybody'.

[2] The Boers certainly believed that D. L. furnished the BaKwena with firearms, but Potgieter did not actually say so in his letter, nor did he mention the figure '500'. Cf. *Fam. Letters*, ii, p. 35, n. 5.

[3] In Feb. 1848 the British Government had annexed the territory that became known as the Orange River Sovereignty (subsequently termed Orange Free State). In July some of its Boer inhabitants revolted, with the aid of reinforcements from the Transvaal. They were defeated at the battle of Boomplaats (29 August), which ended the rebellion. (Theal, *History*, vii, pp. 277–91.)

[4] Andries Willem Jacobus Pretorius (1798–1853), Commandant-General of the Boers in W. Transvaal, had headed the unsuccessful invasion of the O.R.C. After his defeat at Boomplaats, the Governor of Cape Colony had offered a reward of £2,000 for his apprehension (Theal, *op. cit.*, p. 292). D. L. had met him while visiting the D.R.C. deputation (*Fam. Letters*, ii, p. 10).

There are no elements in the Bechuana character calculated to encourage the belief that conversions will occur precipitously. They are truly *slow* of heart to believe. It is therefore imperatively necessary to endeavour to extend the *gospel to all* the surrounding tribes. This, although it involves a great many weary journies, is the only way which permits the rational hope that when the people do turn to the Lord it will be by groups. When native teachers can be furnished, that is of course still better than occasional visits, and now that the way to the East seems in a measure closed for the latter mode of working, we have turned our thoughts northward.

When I had made every preparation for a journey thither, a party of seven men, who had never before seen a white man, came from the Lake in order to invite us to come.[1] I am on the point of starting, and have just heard of the proposed visit of the Revd. J. J. Freeman to the African stations. I am not aware of how far he intends to come. If no further than Kuruman, I shall go thither as soon as I return, although, having sent Mrs Livingston out for the sake of refreshment,[2] I had no intention of visiting that quarter this year. A deputation such as he is well calculated to stimulate our flagging zeal and quicken us to renewed efforts for the glory of our common Lord.

In the full persuasion that you participate in our joys & sorrows, I may mention that Sechele, in his peculiarly difficult position, fell before the power of temptation once since he was baptized.[3] Both for his own sake and that of others, we concluded it to be our duty to exercise discipline. He has all along manifested a most becoming spirit, and never changed in the least his conduct towards us, or his appearance as decidedly on the Lord's side towards his people. We have frequently heard prayer among the bushes by those whom we knew to be *not* in any way connected with us.

Mrs L. was safely delivered of a son in March last, and will probably resume her infant school as soon as she returns from Kuruman. The medicines kindly sent by the Directors have come safely, are excellent in quality, and called forth very thankful emotions.

[Signature cut out]

[1] They were messengers from the chief of the BaTawana, and reached Kolobeng about the beginning of May (*Fam. Letters*, ii, p. 50).

[2] She and her children had left for Kuruman 'a few days' before 20 April (*Fam. Letters*, ii, p. 32).

[3] Less than four months after being baptized, Sechele had impregnated one of his discarded wives. For this offence he was suspended from communion. Cf. *Fam. Letters*, ii, pp. 29–30, 41–3; *Private J.*, p. 304; and below, p. 225.

IV

LAKE NGAMI

24. To ARTHUR TIDMAN
3 September 1849

[Received 31 January 1850. Now in Livingstone Memorial, Blantyre (Lanarkshire). Previous publication: *Chronicle*, vol. xiv, (March) 1850, pp. 35–7 (edited version, omitting postscript); *JRGS*, vol. xx (1850), pp. 138–42 (edited extracts, combined with others from a letter to Steele)]

Banks of the River Zouga[1]
3d September 1849

Dear Sir,

We left Kolobeng on the first of June last, in order to carry into effect the intention of which I had previously informed you, viz. to open a new field in the North by penetrating the great obstacle to progress called the Desert,[2] which, stretching away on our West, Nor-West, & North, has hitherto presented an insurmountable barrier to Europeans. A large party of Griquas in about thirty waggons made many & persevering efforts at two different points last year, but though inured to the climate, & stimulated by the prospect of much gain from the ivory they expected to procure, want of water compelled them to retreat. Two gentlemen to whom I had communicated my intention of proceeding to the oft-reported Lake beyond the Desert came from England for the express purpose of being present at the discovery,[3] and to their liberal and zealous cooperation we are especially indebted for the success with which that and other objects have been accomplished.

While waiting for their arrival, seven men came from the Bataoana,[4] a tribe living on the banks of the Lake, with an earnest request from their chief for a visit. But the path by which they had come to Kolobeng

---

[1] Nowadays commonly known as the Botletle. The name used by D. L. is said to have been that of a Yeei chief living on its banks (Wellington, *Southern Africa*, 1955, i, p. 420, n. 1).

[2] The Kalahari Desert.

[3] D. L. is referring to Oswell and Murray (see below). On 26.ix.48 Oswell, replying to a 'long letter' just received in London from D. L., had said he would be at Kolobeng 'towards the close of May, 1849 ... Steele will not accompany me; Murray perhaps may' (*Oswell*, i, p. 171).

[4] BaTawana, an offshoot of the BaNgwato; they had migrated from Shoshong and settled at L. Ngami *c.* 1800.

was impracticable for waggons, so, declining their guidance, I selected the more circuitous route by which the Bamangwato usually pass, and having Bakwains for guides[1] their self-interest in our success was secured by my promising to carry any ivory they might procure for their chief in my waggon. And right faithfully they performed their task. When Sekhomi, the Bamangwato chief, became aware of our intentions to pass into the regions beyond him, with true native humanity he sent men in front of us to drive away all the Bushmen and Bakalihari from our route, in order that, being deprived of their assistance in the search for water, we might, like the Griquas above mentioned, be compelled to retire. This measure deprived me of the opportunity of holding the intercourse with these poor outcasts I might otherwise have enjoyed. But, through the good Providence of God, after travelling about 300 miles from Kolobeng we struck this magnificent river on the fourth of July, and, without farther difficulty in so far as water was concerned, by winding along its banks nearly 300 more we reached the Bataoana on the Lake Ngami by the beginning of August.[2]

Previous to leaving this beautiful river and commencing our route accross the desert, I feel anxious to furnish you with the impressions produced in my mind by it and its inhabitants, the Bakoba or Bayeiye. They are a totally distinct race from the Bechuanas. They call themselves Bayeiye (or men), while the term Bakoba has somewhat of the meaning of 'slaves', and is applied to them by the Bechuana.[3] Their complexion is darker than that of the Bechuana, and of 300 words I collected of their language only 21 bear any resemblance to Sitchuana. They paddle along the rivers and Lake in canoes hollowed out of the trunks of single trees, take fish in nets made of a weed[4] which abounds on the banks, and kill hippopotami with harpoons attatched to ropes. We greatly admired the frank manly bearing of these inland sailors. Many of them spoke Sitchuana fluently, and while the waggon went along the bank I greatly enjoyed following the windings of the river in one of their primitive craft and visiting their little villages among the reed.

[1] They included a man who had already visited L. Ngami (*Oswell*, i, p. 185).

[2] The route taken, and the incidents of the journey, are described much more fully in a letter from Oswell to Vardon, 10.i.50 (*JRGS*, 1850, pp. 143–6); cf. also *Private J.*, pp. 304–6, and *Travels*, pp. 53–65.

[3] The BaYeei (Tswana 'MaKoba') were immigrants from N.W. Rhodesia, who had settled in Ngamiland early in the 18th century. They were found there by the BaTawana, who made serfs of them. Their language also belongs to the Bantu family, but, as D. L. mentions, differs appreciably from SeTswana. Cf. Schapera and van der Merwe, *Some Bantu Languages of Ngamiland*, Cape Town, 1942.

[4] Possibly a slip of the pen for 'reed'.

The banks are beautiful beyond any we had ever seen except perhaps some parts of the Clyde. They are covered, in general, with gigantic trees, some of them fruit-bearing and quite new. Two of the boabob[1] variety measured 70 & 76 feet in circumference. The higher we ascended the broader it became, untill we often saw more than 100 yards of clear deep water between the broad belt of reed which grows in the shallower parts. The water was clear as chrystal, and as we approached the point of junction with other large rivers reported to exist in the North it was quite soft and cold.

The fact that the Zouga is connected with large rivers coming from the North awakens emotions in my mind which make the discovery of the Lake dwindle out of sight. It opens out the prospect of a highway capable of being quickly traversed by boats to a large section of well-peopled territory. The hopes which that prospect inspires for the benighted inhabitants might, if uttered, call forth the charge of enthusiasm — a charge, by the way, I wish I deserved, for nothing good or great, either in law, religion or physic, has ever been accomplished in the world without it. However, I do not mean the romantic flighty variety, but that which impels with untiring energy to the accomplishment of its object. I do not wish to convey hopes of speedily effecting any great work through my poor instrumentality. I hope to be permitted to work as long as I live beyond other men's line of things and plant the seed of the gospel where others have not planted. But every excursion for that purpose will involve separation from my family for periods of four or five months. Kolobeng will be supplied by native teachers during these times of absence, and when we have given the Bakwains a fair trial it will probably be advisable for all to move onward.

One remarkable feature in this river is its periodical rise & fall. It has risen nearly three feet in perpendicular height since our arrival, and this is our dry season.[2] That the rise is not caused by rains is evident from the water being so pure. Its purity & softness increased as we ascended towards its junction with the Tamunakle,[3] from which, although connected with the Lake, it derives the present supply. The sharpness of the air causing an amazing keeness of appetite at an elevation of little more than 2,000 feet above the level of the sea (water boiled at 207½° Th.[4]), and the reports of the Bayeiye that the waters

---

[1] D. L. habitually uses this spelling for 'baobab' (*Adansonia digitata*).

[2] 'Our dry season extends from May to October' (*JRGS*, 1850, p. 140).

[3] Thamalakane, flowing towards L. Ngami from the N.E. It joins the Botletle at 20° 08′ S., 23° 23′ E.

[4] 'The point of ebullition by Newman's thermometer was 207½°' (*JRGS*, 1850, p. 140).

came from a mountainous region, imparted the idea that the increase of the water at the beginning and middle of the dry season must be derived from melting snow.

All the rivers reported to the North of this have Bayeiye upon them, and there are other tribes on their banks. To one of these, after visiting the Bataoana and taking a peep at the broad part of the Lake, we directed our course. But the Bataoana chief managed to obstruct us by keeping all Bayeiye near the ford on the opposite bank of the Zouga. African chiefs invariably dislike to see strangers passing them to tribes beyond. Sebitoane, the chief who in former years saved Sechele's life, lives about 10 days N.E. of the Bataoana.[1] The latter sent a present as a token of gratitude. This would have been a good introduction. The knowledge of the language is, however, the best one can have. I endeavoured to construct a raft at a part which was only 50 or 60 yards wide, but the wood, though sun-dried, was so heavy it sunk immediately. Another kind would not bear my weight, although a considerable portion of my person was under water. I could easily have swam accross, and fain would have done it, but landing stark naked and bullying the Bakoba for the loan of a boat would scarcely be the thing for a messenger of peace, even though no alligator met me in the passage.

These & other thoughts were revolving in my mind as I stood in the water, for most sorely do I dislike to be beat, when my kind and generous friend W. Oswel,[2] Esqre, with whom alone the visit to Sebitoane was to be made, offered to bring up a boat at his own expense from the Cape, which after visiting that chief & coming round the North end of the Lake will become missionary property. To him and our other companion, W. Murray,[3] Esqre, I feel greatly indebted, for the chief expense of the journey has been borne by them. They could never have reached this point without my assistance, but for the aid they have rendered in opening up this field I feel greatly indebted, and should any

[1] Sebetwane was chief, 1825(?)–51 of the MaKololo. After being driven by invading tribes from his home in the (present) Orange Free State, he and his people gradually migrated north and ultimately (c. 1840) established themselves as the ruling community in Barotseland and adjoining districts (N.W. Rhodesia). How he 'saved Sechele's life' is described below, p. 154.

[2] William Cotton Oswell (1818–93), 'African explorer; . . . during his ten years in Madras civil service won reputation as linguist and elephant hunter; spent two years' furlough in hunting over unexplored South Africa; took part in Livingstone's discovery of Lake Ngami, 1849, and the Zambesi, 1851 (D.N.B.). He had first met D. L. at Mabotsa in 1845, became one of his chief friends and benefactors, and is often mentioned in his letters and publications, usually with warm appreciation. Cf. W. E. Oswell, *William Cotton Oswell: Hunter and Explorer*, 2 vols., 1900.

[3] Mungo Murray, of Lintrose, Cupar Angus, Forfarshire. He had previously accompanied Oswell into the interior in 1845; cf. *Oswell*, i, pp. 104, 108.

public notice be taken of this journey I shall feel obliged to the Directors if they express my thankfulness.[1]

The Bayeiye or Bakoba listened to the statements made from the Divine word with great attention, and if I am not mistaken seemed to understand the message of mercy delivered better than any people to whom I have preached for the first time. They have invariably a great many charms in their villages. Stated the name of God in their language (without the least hesitation) to be 'Oreeja'.[2] Mentioned the name of the first man & woman, and some traditionary statements respecting the Flood. I shall not, however, take these for certain till I have more knowledge of their language. They are to be found dwelling among the reed all round the Lake and on the banks of all the rivers to the North. With the periodical flow of the rivers great shoals of fish descend. The people could give no reason for the rise of the water, farther than that a chief who lives in a part of the country to the North called Mazzekwa[3] kills a man annually and throws his body into the stream, after which the water begins to flow. When will they know him who was slain that they might obtain admittance to the leaves of the tree which is for the healing of the nations, that the pure river of water of life might flow that whosoever will might drink freely?

The sketch on the next page [see *Plate 4*] is intended to convey an idea of this river and the Lake Ngami. The name is pronounced as if written with the Spanish Ñ, the g being inserted to shew that the ringing sound is required. The meaning is 'great water'.[4] The Latitude, taken by a sextant on which I can fully depend, was 20° 20' S. at the North-East extremity or junction with the Zouga. (Longitude about

---

[1] In *Chronicle*, March 1850, p. 36, the words 'for the chief expense of the journey has been borne by them', were italicized. The editorial foreword (pp. 34–5) also contains the following paragraph: 'In the month of July last, an opportunity was presented to this enterprising Missionary of gratifying his long-cherished purpose, by the visit of two benevolent travellers, Messrs. Murray and Oswell, who requested his co-operation in attempting to cross the Desert, and exploring the unknown regions to the north. This overture Mr. Livingston gladly embraced . . .'

[2] In the modern orthography, Oreza (Schapera and v.d. Merwe, *op. cit.*, p. 97).

[3] I cannot identify this name. It may be a corruption of WaWikwo, applied by the BaYeei to the MaMbukushu of Andara (western Caprivi Strip), whose chief 'is the hereditary Great Rain Maker of the Okovango' (A. G. Stigand, 'Ngamiland', *Geog. J.*, lxii, 1923, p. 416; cf. J. Chapman, *Travels in S. Africa*, 1868, i, pp. 139, 307).

[4] The more commonly accepted version is that the name is derived from the Central Bushman word *nghabe*, 'giraffe'. Methuen, in 1844, rendered it as 'Ngabi (*Life in the Wilderness*, p. 156), and Oswell gives Ngami and Inghabé as alternatives (*JRGS*, 1850, p. 148).

No. CLXVI.]   [MARCH, 1850.

THE

Missionary Magazine

AND

CHRONICLE.

JOURNEY OF DISCOVERY OF THE REV. D. LIVINGSTON, IN THE INTERIOR OF SOUTH AFRICA.

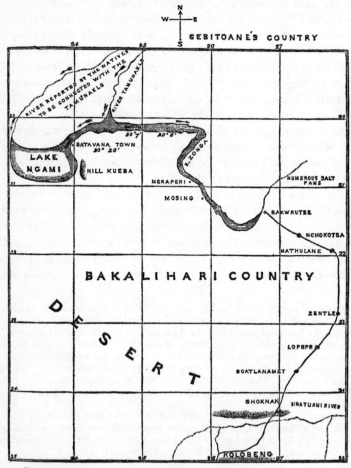

The *Single line* marks the route of the Travellers from Kolobeng.
The *Stars* mark the position of small streams or fountains on the route of the Travellers.
The *Dotted lines* distinguish the Rivers *reported* by the Natives.
The *Arrow-heads* indicate the course of the Rivers.

24° East. We do not know it with certainty.)[1] The waggon stood near
the Bataoana town. We rode on horseback about 6 miles beyond to the
broad part. It gradually widens out into a frith about 15 miles accross
as you go South from the town, and in the South-South-West presents
a large horizon of water. It is reported to be about 70 miles in length,
bends round to the North-West, & there recieves another river similar
to the Zouga. The Zouga runs to the North-East. The thorns were so
thickly planted near the upper part of this river we left all our waggons
standing at about 180 miles from the Lake & went thither in that of Mr
Oswel. But for this measure our oxen would have been unable to return.
I am now standing at a tribe of Bakurutse,[2] and will in a day or two re-
enter the desert. I fear I shall not have the pleasure of seeing Mr Freeman. This journey has taken longer than I expected.

The breadth put down [see Plate 4] is intended to shew the
difference between the size of the Zouga after its junction with the
Tamunakle & before it. The farther it runs, it becomes the narrower.
The course is shewn by the arrow heads. The rivers not seen but
reported by natives are put down in dotted lines.

The dotted lines running North of the river & Lake shew the probable course of the Tamunakle and another river which falls into the
Lake at its North-Western extremity. The arrow heads shew the
direction of its flow. It is narrower below than it is nearer its junction
with the Tamunakle. At the part marked by the name of the chief
Mosing[3] it is not more than 50 or 60 yards in breadth, while at 20° 7′ it
is more than 100 and very deep.

The disease reported to prevail at certain seasons appears from the
account of the symptoms the natives give to be pneumonia & not fever.
When the wind rises to an ordinary breeze, such immense clouds of
dust arise from the numerous dried-out lakes called salt pans, the whole
atmosphere becomes quite yellow, & one cannot distinguish objects
more than two miles off. It causes irritation of the eyes, and as wind
prevails almost constantly at certain seasons the unpalpable powder
raised may act as it does among the grinders in Sheffield. We observed
cough among them, a complaint almost unknown at Kolobeng. Musquitoes swarm in summer, and the banyan & palmyra give in some
parts an Indian cast to the scenery.

[1] On modern maps, the N.E. extremity of L. Ngami is at 20° 23′ S., 22° 57′ E.
(The words in parentheses are a marginal addition.)
[2] BaKhurutshe, an early offshoot of the BaHurutshe. They were then living on
the Botletle River in the vicinity of Lake Dow.
[3] Masenyo, a Khurutshe headman living at c. 21° 08′ S., 24° 36′ E.

Who will go in to possess this goodly land in the name of Him whose right it is to reign?

Affectionately yours,
David Livingston

Kolobeng, 14*th October*

Having reached home on the 10th currt., I am happy to find that I have still the prospect of meeting Mr Freeman. Two boxes (one from Mr Young's congregation[1]) have come to hand & been acknowledged.

The compiler of the Report for 1847[2] has been led into an error, which is scarce worth noticing except to correct an impression the Directors seem to have recieved that the conduct of the Bakwains rendered it necessary for me to return to Mabotsa.[3] The impression may have been derived from my own communications, for I have always endeavoured to state matters in as sober & cool a manner as possible. But the conduct of the Bakwains, from the very commencement, has been so uniformly kind & respectful towards us, and they have attended so perseveringly on our instructions, neither the entire want of corn & vegetables nor the badness of the water at Chonuane ever raised a wish to return to Mabotsa. And I now only feel sorry that the Directors have not had the opportunity of joining with us in our gratitude to Him who has given us so much favour in the sight of the Heathen. I advert to this topic now because, having given a true but unfavourable report of the state of the Mission in my last, you may concieve it to be worse than I have stated. I do not believe there is, in the present or past state of the people, the least cause for despondency.

D. Livingston

25. To J. J. FREEMAN
14 November 1849

[LMS 47. *Address:* Revd. J. J. Freeman, Kuruman or elsewhere]

[1] Possibly Rev. John Young, in whose church (Albion Chapel, Finsbury, London) D. L. had been ordained in November 1840 (*Chronicle,* 1841, p. 14).

[2] MS. has '1827'.

[3] The 'error' was worded thus: 'In last Report it was stated that Mr. Livingston had removed to Chonuane, intending to commence a station in that locality, but circumstances have induced him to resume his labours at Mabotsa, as his resident station, retaining the other as an outpost' (*Report,* 1847, p. 112). The misunderstanding may have arisen from the fact that D. L.'s letter of 10.iv.46 was headed 'Mabotsa'; see above, p. 88

4. THE ROUTE TO LAKE NGAMI

Kolobeng
14th Novr. 1849

Dear Sir,

We have indulged the hope for several months past that you would find it convenient to visit us, but having lately heard from Mr Moffat that you seemed inclined to make Kuruman your farthest point North, I now take the liberty of entreating you to reconsider your resolution. I hope our Kuruman friends will press on your attention the superior claims of the stations in this quarter to those of the French bretheren by which you propose to return. But before I urge any other consideration, I may mention that before undertaking my late journey I expected to return in time to meet you at the Kuruman before the departure of Mrs L. My journey was much longer than I expected, and Mrs L. waited 2 months here alone.[1] I have been eight months from home this year. Two of these were spent in trying [to] place Paul with the tribe of Mokhatla. There is always a great deal of work to be done after an absence from a station. Our house is yet unfinished. But there were no other considerations.[2] The oxen are altogether unfit to travel. One half have been worked for six months, and have done & endured more than oxen ever did before; the others have all been affected by a disease which renders them unable to travel.

For your coming in I have to urge that when you have visited the Colonial stations you have only seen one end of the chain, and as your advice at home will probably vitally affect the onward movement of the whole you ought for your own satisfaction to see the other end. This is the more necessary because the Directors seem, by an expression in the Report for '47, to have imbibed an erroneous impression as to the position a missionary occupies when beginning with a new tribe. It is stated that I had been under the necessity of returning to Mabotsa, a step I never dreamed of, for although put to shifts from the beginning till now for vegetables & corn, the uniform kindness of the people endeared us to them; and I am fully persuaded that any missionary may live in perfect security with any tribe in so far as the natives are concerned, if he have only a decent smack of common sense. So strong is my conviction on this point I do not believe there is any necessity for two Europeans to be present with any one tribe, and I should consider giving countenance

---

[1] She and her children had left Kuruman at the beginning of August (*Fam. Letters*, ii, p. 67). D. L. returned to Kolobeng on 10 October (see above, p. 138).

[2] The succeeding mention of 'unfit oxen' suggests that 'no' should perhaps have been deleted.

to a colleague to settle here as inflicting a wrong on some other tribe which might otherwise be enjoying his services.

Then again you stated, I think most truly, in a speech delivered in Cape Town, that since the failure of the Niger expedition[1] this must be considered the key to the Interior. Now we have sailed on the Southern end of a navigable highway to a large tract of country. This discovery belongs to Missionaries. Will you not come in & give your advice as to how we are to take advantage of it? If I incur any expense, I have the rod of 'a vote of disaprobation' in Committee over my head. And then the world we have beyond in the North (is that to be left to traders & Boers?) presses hard on the other side. I do most sincerely wish you may be induced to come, for many reasons, but hope you will be guided by His counsel who cannot err.

Affectionately yours,
David Livingston

26. To J. J. FREEMAN
9 January 1850

[LMS 49. *Address:* Revd. J. J. Freeman, care of H. E. Rutherfoord, Esqre, Cape Town]

Kolobeng
9th January 1850

My dear Sir,

In the hope that this may reach you before you depart from the Cape, I take the liberty to state a few things which I quite forgot to mention during your short but pleasant visit here.[2] That which I regret most is having failed to bring before your mind *all* the circumstances connected with the region to the North of this. But this may supply the deficiency.

I believe I stated that I had no wish to leave the Bakwains on account of anything unpleasant in their conduct toward us or in their disposition in regard to instruction. When the present hungry season is past, we have every reason to hope that their former desire for instruction will

---

[1] An expedition, sponsored by leading English philanthropists, which had been sent to the Niger delta (W. Africa) in 1841, in order to develop 'natural resources and legitimate trade' as a means of displacing the traffic in slaves. Owing to the many deaths causes by malaria, the enterprise was abandoned within a few months. Cf. Groves, *The Planting of Christianity in Africa*, ii, 1954, pp. 4–12.

[2] Accompanied by Moffat, Freeman had been at Kolobeng 'on the last days of 1849 and beginning of 1850' (*Private J.*, p. 306; cf. *Fam. Letters*, ii, p. 74). He gives an account of the station in *Tour*, pp. 279–81, 291–2.

return. But feeling the importance of having that field occupied before the Boers can enter their claims to the exclusion of those of missionaries, I feel strongly drawn to the North. The plan you proposed in reference to keeping that field open for our Society is very satisfactory in as far as other Societies are concerned. But pre-occupation is the only remedy in so far as the Boers are concerned.[1]

It is of importance, too, to have the way to another tribe open for us in case it should happen here as in other tribes in this country, the whole people resolving unanimously to reject the gospel but keep the missionary for the sake of the temporal benefits he brings. The Barolongs at Motito did so, and when we came to Mabotsa I ascertained that their chief had earnestly advised Mosielele to adopt the same policy. I concieve that the efforts of Mrss Lemue & Lauga for many years previous to their leaving were a mere waste of life,[2] and that that & other cases which have happened ought to have some weight in causing removals. It would perhaps conduce to the efficiency of missions if it were known that, except in special instances, a tribe would not be favoured with a European missionary beyond a certain number of years.

The statements of the Bakhoba led me to believe that the people around & North of Sebitoane are numerous & more civilized than Bechuanas. The Bakhoba themselves, if I am not greatly mistaken, possess much more traditional knowledge than the people farther South. Four tribes were specified; and the Bakhoba themselves were reported to have larger villages, canoes, &c, on the Tamunakle than those we saw on the Zouga. The former river is so large several others branch off from it and flow, some to the East, others to the West. You know enough of waggon travelling now to understand that the prospect of having a mission where itineracies to great distances could be performed in short periods of time is rather pleasing to those who have no locomotives except the ox waggon or riding ox. But against this we have musquitoes in such numbers the very natives complain of them, a kind of gadfly which is also very troublesome, sparrows by the million, making the prospect of raising English corn dwindle into nothing, an epidemic (probably pneumonia) frequently fatal but said to be less so now than in

[1] D. L. had contemplated making another attempt 'this summer' to reach Sebetwane; but, wrote Freeman to Tidman (2.ii.50, from Bloemfontein), 'We have advised him not to go again at present, & he has therefore changed his plan & will remain at home.' As the sequel shows, Freeman was mistaken. What his own 'plan' was I have not ascertained.

[2] Jean Louis Prosper Lemue (1804–70) and Jean Lauga (1811–87), of the P.E.M.S., had come to Motito in 1832 and 1838 respectively; in 1847 both were transferred to Basutoland, to start a new mission station there. Cf. Jousse, *La Mission Française au Sud de l'Afrique*, 1889, i, pp. 97, 217, 287.

former years, and last, though not least, an additional 600 miles of land carriage. We are about 270 miles beyond Kuruman, and these make an impression on the salary sufficient to make us look unutterable things at the distance beyond.

But I cannot help earnestly coveting the privelege of introducing the gospel into a new [land][1] and people. When I heard the new language and saw a few portions of the people, I felt that if I could be permitted to reduce their language to writing, & perhaps translate the Scriptures into it, I might be able to say that I had not lived in vain. I have had a strong desire ever since to be the first in this great undertaking. Perhaps it arises from ambition, but it is not of an ignoble sort. I have wished for a long time to have the uvula excised, and thank you heartily for your kind invitation to accompany you for the purpose, but besides the want of preparation for the journey I have felt so drawn to the new region, and a desire to go South having never entered my mind, I could not come to a decision.

I have no inclination to meddle in the work of revisal or translation, believing with you that it will be best for the present to leave it in Mr Moffat's hands. His attention having long been directed to that department of labour, he excels us all in critical knowledge of the language; and Kuruman having been a place of refuge for the dispersed from many tribes,[2] his style has fewer provincialisms than it would have had had he been located anywhere else. That you may have an idea as to whether Mr Lemue's assistance deserves the name,[3] I may mention that while still at Motito he took several portions of the New Testament to the French district committee which he had *re*translated, and when the bretheren referred the subject to Mr Cassilis,[4] as best able to judge whether they ought to be printed, he decided that Mr Moffat's Testament was all that they required. Several notable blunders occur in his Proverbs.[5] Wherever the word 'honour' ought to be, the word to 'strain out' a liquid is used, &c. Insofar as I am able to give an unbiassed opinion, I think we are well quit of his assistance.

Boxes containing clothing for the natives seem to be made up by the

[1] Word inadvertently omitted in starting new page.
[2] MS. has 'from many of many tribes'; 'of many' are the first words of a new page.
[3] In 1846 the District Committee had resolved to invite Lemue's cooperation in translating the Scriptures. He duly submitted a version of Isaiah, which was, however, not considered good enough to be published without revision (Minutes, 1847, 1848; cf. *Fam. Letters*, i, pp. 180–1).
[4] Jean-Eugène Casalis (1812–91), missionary in Basutoland 1833–56; author of *Études sur le Langue Séchuana*, Paris 1841.
[5] *Liperoverebia tsa Salomo*, Lemue's translation of 'Proverbs', had been published in Basutoland in 1846.

friends in England with the idea that a little money spread out into a large surface of cheap & often very useless calico becomes a very handsome sum. If our good friends knew how much their kind intentions cost the Society for freight, and us for land carriage, and the little satisfaction cheap goods afford Africans, it might tend to change their minds. I have paid as much as £4.10.0 for goods the prime cost of which could not have been half that sum in England. We cannot get the expense of carriage by sale. Some kind person sent me several large packets of plates & bits such as are used for the heels & toes of ploughmen's shoes. He might as well have sent skates or curling stones. But probably it was an expression of real sympathy towards the cause in which we are engaged. But in many cases the question might be whether sending the hard cash into the treasury of the Society would not be the best way of investing it. We purchase our own clothing in Scotland,[1] and though we bear most of the expense such boxes are always the most satisfactory — their value bears some proportion to their expense. Hardware in general is useful, but soft weak goods, although expensive to us, do not answer the intentions of the kind donors.

In your visit to Sebube,[2] you may not have been told that in former years much fighting took place between him & the Wanketse. On one occasion, as I have heard an old man relate when last over there, a man was observed among the slain, whom they believed to be Sebube. The whole tribe danced with joy, and in their songs of victory they repeated to each other, 'Now that Sebube is dead we have no one else in the world to fear'. 'And after all', said the old man laughing, 'here he is among us as our teacher'. The great change which has taken place in many is not visible to one who is unacquainted with their history.

I am sorry the lion's skin did not come till four days after your departure. It has a good mane, & would have been a good specimen for you. The people could not have overtaken you on this side Mamusa,[3] so I concluded the expense of sending was more than it is worth. I quite forgot the salt from the Lake. Had I known that you would have been pleased with curiosities, I might have had a lot laid out in one spot for you. Your visit has been very refreshing, and we thank you sincerely

---

[1] See above, p. 124.

[2] A Tlharo tribesman who had recently gone to the BaNgwaketse as 'native teacher' (see p. 122). He worked among them for many years, dying in 1891 at Ranaka (near Kanye), where some of his descendants still live. Freeman had visited him on the way back from Kolobeng (Tour, p. 292).

[3] Now known as Schweizer Reneke (27° 11' S., 25° 20' E.); about 230 miles from Kolobeng (Freeman, Tour, p. 293). Occupied since 1846 by the BaTlhaping under Mahura, with Ross as resident missionary (Report, 1847, pp. 110–11). Freeman was there on 11.i.50 (Notebooks).

for it. The only cause for regret is that it was so short, & our accommodation so poor.

The idea has got into my head since your departure that a triennial deputation might be as efficient as either Committee or Superintendant. At any rate a trip to this salubrious climate would do no harm to any of our London ministers. If Mr Tidman could be persuaded to exchange the smoke of London for the pure air of this country for about a year, it might add ten to his life. He certainly would increase in weight, for it is really a fine climate. There is neither consumption nor scrofula, and people apparently consumptive have been cured without medicine by being brought up to Kuruman.

Hoping that you will be safely protected & restored to the bosom of your family by our Heavenly Father, and presenting our Christian salutations,

We remain yours affectionately,
David Livingston

Will you at some future time favour me with the names of the stones which puzzled me?

27. To DAVID LIVINGSTON
5 August 1850

[LMS: Outgoing Letters, Africa, Box 7, pp. 280-2]

London
5 August, 1850

Dear Brother,

At the beginning of the present year reports had reached us from various quarters of the success which had crowned your efforts to penetrate to the great interior lake, but it was not until the receipt of your letter of the 3rd Sept., written from the banks of the River Zouga, that we were made acquainted with the full and authentic particulars of your most interesting discovery.

Anxious that the friends of Africa, and especially of the African Missions in this country, should participate in the welcome tidings, we gave insertion to your letter in the Missionary Chronicle for March, and I need scarcely add that your statements have awakened the most lively interest, not only in the discovery itself as a valuable contribution to geographical science, but as opening up prospects of the ultimate civilisation of tribes and nations hitherto deemed inaccessible by Europeans.

The announcement of the important discovery achieved by yourself in conjunction with the companions of your journey, Messrs Murray & Oswell, having brought us into communication with the Geographical Society, I cannot perhaps give you a more concise and connected view of the proceedings taken by that Society and by our Directors, than by transcribing the following extract from our Board Minutes of the 23rd ult. :

'The Foreign Secretary stated that, in consequence of the important discoveries made in South Africa by the Rev. Dr Livingston, the Royal Geographical Society had this year awarded to their enterprising missionary 25 guineas, being one half the Royal Premium for the encouragement of Geographical Science and discovery annually placed at their disposal, and that Mr Alderman Challis[1] and himself had at the request of the Council, and as the representatives of the Board, attended the last Annual Meeting of the Society to receive the Royal Premium, together with a letter addressed by the President, Capt. W. H. Smyth,[2] R.N., to Dr Livingston. That letter and the address of the President to Alderman Challis and himself had since been published in the Report of the Society,[3] and made honourable mention of the value of Missionary enterprise and of the London Missionary Society. Very gratifying extracts from these documents having been read to the Board, it was

Resolved: That this Board expresses its high admiration of the intrepidity and benevolent aim of the Rev. Dr Livingston in pushing his discoveries in South Africa, and cordially concurs in the estimate of the important discoveries formed by the Royal Geographical Society.'

The letter addressed to you by the R. G. Society and referred to in the foregoing extract was forwarded to Kolobeng a few weeks since, and its printed report will be transmitted to you by the same ship that conveys the present letter. I beg further to advise that the 25 guineas, the amount of the premium awarded to you, has been duly paid into our hands and passed to the credit of your account.

It might be premature to anticipate the probable results of the successful exploration of extensive regions now for the first time laid open

---

[1] Thomas Challis (1794–1874), hide merchant; Lord Mayor of London, 1852; M.P. for Finsbury, 1852–7 (J. J. Baddeley, *The Aldermen of Cripplegate Ward,* 1900, p. 104); a Trustee of the LMS, 1845–69.

[2] William Henry Smyth (1788–1865), 'admiral and scientific writer' (*D.N.B.*); president of the R.G.S., 1849–51.

[3] *JRGS*, xx, 1850, pp. xxviii–xxxii (copy of Smyth's letter, pp. xxix–xxx); reproduced substantially in *Chronicle*, xiv, (Sept.) 1850, pp. 156–9.

to European enterprise. The friends of Missions cannot but recognise in the event the hand of a gracious providence opening up a highway for the entrance of the Gospel into regions which have scarce yet been enlightened by its beams, and which appear to present local advantages for the formation of settlements upon a more permanent footing than has yet been realised in the existing Stations of the Society. In the meantime we shall not fail to watch the progress of events with the liveliest interest, and upon Mr Freeman's return to this country we shall in conference with him be able to form a more correct estimate of the probable bearings of the recent discovery upon the future interests and objects of the Society in connection with its African Missions.

We were exceedingly concerned to hear from your letter of the 26th May, 1849, of the annoyance you had suffered from the opposition and violent proceedings of the Boers. The subject has also been adverted to in the correspondence of the Kuruman brethren. A bitter and unrelenting hatred of any measures taken with a view to the introduction of the Gospel among the Native tribes is no doubt at the bottom of these hostile demonstrations, and although it may suit the purpose of the influential leaders among the Boers to render you personally obnoxious, we may reasonably conclude that any other Missionary, had he been brought into similar circumstances of juxtaposition with them, would have encountered no less opposition. Upon this subject also Mr Freeman will no doubt be able to furnish us with valuable information.[1]

Congratulating you upon your safe return to your field of labour, and wishing you and Mrs Livingston the continued and enlarged enjoyment of every spiritual blessing, I have the pleasure to subscribe myself,

Dear Brother,
Very truly yours,
Arthur Tidman
Foreign Secretary of the London Missionary Society

28. To J. J. FREEMAN

24 August 1850

[LMS 52. London postmark: 7 JA 1851. Previous publication: Lovett, *History of the LMS*, 1899, vol. i, pp. 612–14 (incomplete); Chamberlin, pp. 133–8 (incomplete)]

[1] Freeman wrote to Tidman on 2.ii.50 that D. L. had not been further troubled by the Boers, and that 'the charges brought against him of having supplied Natives with firearms and powder are altogether groundless. . . . We do not imagine that any further steps will be taken by the Dutch authorities against Livingstone or any of the brethren in connexion with *that* affair. All *that* has passed, & we imagine it has closed.'

Kolobeng
24th August 1850

My dear Friend,

I have to acknowledge the receipt of two letters from you, one a circular relating to Mr Thompson,[1] and the other dated 23 May in answer to one you had recieved from me before you left the Cape. The belief that in one or two points in the latter[2] I ought to try and effect your conversion induces me to trouble you with another letter. I hope you will kindly excuse the infliction.

You object to the 'idea of giving a people a trial with the gospel for a certain number of years, on the ground that in nearly all cases where Christian Societies are now reaping success a considerable time elapsed before there were indications of that success', and you allege that '*had there been any precipitate removal of the missions, under the impression that it was useless and hopeless to give them a longer trial, then humanly speaking all the present success had been lost.*' I agree with you entirely in reference to the time which has usually elapsed before success became visible. But the history of the Bechuana Mission forbids assent to the inference you draw. At least that is my conviction, and if you will only review that history I have strong hopes that you will view the matter in the same light.

The Bechuana Mission began at the Kuruman, and the attention of the missionaries was directed chiefly to the Batlapi. No visible success attended their labours, but the tribe got a fair *trial*, and instead of the missionaries removing at the conclusion of the trial the experiment was performed for our instruction in the opposite way: the Batlapi left the missionaries. The tribe divided into several fragments soon after leaving, and without following their wanderings we may just note their positions as: those under Motheebe at Lekatlong, Lingopeng, and Borigelong,[3]

---

[1] William Thompson (1811–89); after missionary service in India, settled in Cape Town (June 1850) as pastor of Union Chapel and Agent for the S.A. Missions of the LMS (in succession to Dr Philip, who had retired owing to old age and illness) (*Register*, p. 38). The circular referred to his LMS appointment (see below, p. 164).

[2] 'the letter' (Chamberlin, p. 133).

[3] Mothibi, elder brother of Mahura, was chief of the BaTlhaping 1812–45. In 1825 he had left Kuruman with part of the tribe, ultimately settling about 100 miles to the S.E. at 'Lekatlong' (Dikgatlhong, the junction of the Vaal and Harts Rivers). He subsequently moved with the heathen section of his following to 'Borigelong' (Gabodigelo, now called Springbokfontein, about 35 miles to the N.N.E.), where he died in November 1845, 'much enfeebled by age and sickness' (*Chronicle*, x, 1846, p. 104; Mackenzie, *Austral Africa*, 1887, i, p. 43). 'Lingopeng' (Dingopeng) was 19 miles S. of Gabodigelo (Moffat, in *Chronicle*, 1846, p. 43).

those under Mahura and Motlabani & Tlaganyane[1] at Taong, Mamusa, & Lithako.

You will remember that Mr Moffat in his work mentions that the first success they subsequently had at Kuruman was among a small tribe of Balala called Bachaine[2] (of which Paul & Mebaloe here are members) and a lot of refugees from the Interior. But the seed had been sown in the hearts of the Batlapi too. The *trial* had been made, and the results were as follows. When the party which settled down at Lekatlong had got a little time for reflection, they actually sent a deputation of their number to the nearest mission station, Griqua Town,[3] to beg instruction. And the bretheren there being unable to supply them with a missionary, the people sent individuals statedly to Griqua Town to recieve a little instruction, and while they returned to Lekatlong to impart that little others were sent to recieve a fresh supply. This system went on till many were fit for fellowship, and when the missionaries went for the first time they were surprised & delighted with the progress they had made. The visits of the bretheren ever afterwards were for the purpose of examining candidates and recieving them into fellowship. Before a European missionary came to settle among them there were upwards of one hundred in the Church, and when I visited Lekatlong a short time after Mr Helmore's settlement there religious profession was rather too fashionable.[4] He found it necessary rather to restrain than urge to a confession of Christ. As we are reviewing the subject privately, no one's feelings will be hurt by supposing we think little of his labours. But I think you will agree with me in thinking that *up to the period* of Mr Helmore's settlement the fruits were those of the *trial* made at Kuruman. Mr Wright did not, so far as I recollect, look upon the work in any other light.

The distance has always prevented the Kuruman bretheren from visiting with any regularity the next division of Motheebe's people, settled at Borigelong. But the seed was sown before they left that

---

[1] Possibly Thaganyane, son of Mothibi's half-brother Saku, and head of the BaTlhaping at 'Lithako' (Dithakong).

[2] 'Balala' is the generic Tswana term for 'serfs, servants, inferior people' (Brown, *Secwana-English Dictionary*, p. 14). The 'Bachaine' (BaTshwene, BaTshweneng, BaTshweng) 'were vassals of the Batlaping, and . . . to this day are regarded by that tribe as inferiors' (Mackenzie, *Ten Years North of the Orange River*, 1871, p. 143). Moffat, in *Miss. Labours*, pp. 8–12, briefly describes the status and treatment of 'Balala', but neither mentions their conversion nor names the 'Bachaine'.

[3] About 80 miles away.

[4] Helmore was at Dikgatlhong 1840–2, 1843–56 (*Register*, p. 45). D. L. went there in March 1847 to attend the fourth meeting of the District Committee. The local church about that time had more than 200 members (*Report*, 1846, p. 113).

station. The native teacher was sent after a wish had been expressed by the people, and when he went his position was totally different from that to Sebubi among the Wanketse. The gospel having been deposited, the influences of the Holy Spirit soon caused the fruits to appear, and the result of the trial has been especially satisfactory, for we have a Church planted in the midst of a mass of Heathenism, and every year there has been what Dr Chalmers[1] called 'an excavation' going on. This experiment clearly proves that a respectable church may result from such a trial as I advocate, and that church be anything but a feeble standstill one, though it does not recieve a European missionary as its pastor. Lingopeng is a twin experiment, and equally satisfactory. The future will determine which will furnish the healthiest children, those who have recieved little or much nursing.

The division under Mahura, including the Bamaeris and Tlaganyane, exhibits another important feature in the Bechuana Mission. Let the chief of any locality exhibit determined opposition to the gospel, few or none of his people ever profess their faith in Christ till he alters his conduct or is removed by death. Mahura altered his conduct in order to increase his town by drawing a number of believers from other parts. Had he not done so, it would have been a mere waste of life for a European to have lived with him. Tlaganyane never altered his conduct, and he had no believers under him. Mochuara, who with his Barolongs enjoyed the ministrations of Lemue & Lauga for a great many years, acted on the principle of getting all the temporal good out of the missionaries he could, while fully determined never to believe the gospel, and not a single individual under him ever attempted to profess Christ.[2] Mochuara even sent an advice to the above effect to Mosielele at Mabotsa when we removed thither. In the cases of Mahura, Tlaganyane, & the Bamaeris, we have no fruits from the trial apparent *up to the period* of Mr Ross's settlement.[3] But no one will deny the existence of a preparedness, and not even that appeared in the Barolongs of Mochuara, although Mr Lemue & Lauga spent half a lifetime upon them.

[1] Possibly Thomas Chalmers (1780–1847), 'principal and divinity professor of the Free Church College, Edinburgh, 1843–7; . . . author of theological, philosophical, expository, and devotional treatises' (*D.N.B.*).

[2] Motshwari was chief of the Mariba section of BaRolongbooRratlou, formerly settled at Morokweng (an outstation of Motito). In December 1849 Freeman found him at Setlagodi (about 80 miles E.N.E. of Motito). 'He is aged, blind, and very deaf. He is much respected, and has been a man of peace; and although not embracing Christianity himself, he has always respected and encouraged the Missionaries' (*Tour*, p. 269).

[3] Ross settled with Mahura at Taung in January 1844, and in 1846 moved with him to Mamusa (*Register*, p. 51).

As it is with the Bechuana Mission in its private developement I am most familiar, I can only point you to its history, and request you to say whether it warrants the inference that the removal of a Mission would cause an ultimate loss of success. To me those who never heard the gospel are greater objects of compassion than those who have heard it for seven years & rejected it. The plan of trial would perhaps tend to the more rapid extension of the knowledge of Christ in the world. The full persuasion that this is the great desire of your heart makes me presume to give you this long lecture, and if I fail to effect your conversion you will not take the *trial* amiss.

I have had thoughts of writing a paper[1] on the above subject for one of the periodicals. But people have got so much into the habit of laying everything to the account of the Directors I have had fears lest my heresies should implicate them. One scarcely wonders at anything that comes from Europe now, but the resolutions of our friends at Leeds, which lately came to hand, almost took away my breath. A poor out of the world African like myself would have no objection to any amount of cross-examination 'after a lapse of 50 years' repose; but in my un-utterable stupidity I imagine that their 'most valued secretary' might have recollected that 48 years are wanting to complete the 50 at which period there was quite as much friendly sifting of affairs and hostile poking at the Directors as would have satisfied most merciful men. Did the Leeds worthies never hear of the committee of investigation which sat in the Mission House?[2] We *did* in Africa, and it certainly was not 50 years ago. And then to see Mr Baines,[3] whom we have been accus-tomed to look up to as one of our big wigs, bringing forward a resolu-tion resembling one of Pharaoh's lean kine, for it eat up that which preceded it and was none the fatter. 1st: Directors, don't you lord it over these mission churches; we have had our suspicions, but we won't allow the mission churches to be anything but independant, self-sup-porting, self-governed. 2nd: Directors, why do you allow the indepen-dant self-supporting self-governing mission churches to act out their independance in reference to Govt. grants for education? Out and out

---

[1] 'writing on paper' (Chamberlin, p. 136).

[2] In April 1849 a Select Committee of the LMS had met to inquire whether, after 'more than fifty years of honour and usefulness', any modification of the Society's constitution or mode of administration was practicable, 'which may promote the stronger attachment of its Constituents, or increase its efficacy'. Its report was pub-lished in *Chronicle*, xiii, (December) 1849, pp. 179–83.

[3] Edward Baines, of Leeds, a prominent figure in Congregational circles; life member and Country Director of the LMS.

voluntary as I am, I don't like to see the Directors forced to vote for independancy & coercion with the same breath.[1]

But I could have forgiven it all had they not parted with a puff about 'the excellent spirit which pervaded this meeting'. Was it a liberal spirit? If it had been so, then the 'most valued secretary', Mr Miall,[2] might have concocted a resolution such as the following: 'Seeing our suspicions have proved groundless, and our agents both at home and abroad being allowed by the extreme conscientiousness of the Directors to exist on smaller salaries than those of any other Society,[3] we do hereby bind ourselves to double the amount of our annual contributions, and otherwise increase the revenue of the Society during the present year, so that both Directors and their agents may see that these suspicions alone prevented the full developement of the generosity of our natures.' But I shall look with some curiosity to the contributions from Leeds to see what fruits the 'excellent spirit' will produce. Mr Tidman might have astonished them had he compared the salaries of our Society's[4] officers and missionaries with those of other Societies. I see 38 Wesleyan missionaries cost about £3,000 more per annum than 36 of our missionaries do. It would not look well in any of us to make the comparison, but to think of Directors, Secretaries, & every one of us, looked upon with suspicion tends strongly to beget discontent.

The Dr's manifesto[5] has not yet come to hand. I have mentioned to Dr Tidman my reasons for proceeding again to the Lake.[6] Having only

---

[1] The resolutions criticized were passed at a meeting of 'Ministers and Delegates connected with the West Riding Auxiliary to the London Missionary Society', held at Leeds in January 1850 and reported in *Chronicle*, xiv, (Feb.) 1850, pp. 28–9. After considerable discussion had 'removed the impression that the directors wished to prevent the Mission churches from being self-sustained and self-governed', Mr Baines moved that the Directors should require their missionaries in Cape Colony 'to decline Government grants for schools'.

[2] Rev. J. G. Miall, of Bradford, secretary of the West Riding Auxiliary; responsible for the establishment of the Select Committee, of which he had been a member. The Leeds meeting passed a resolution which, after expressing 'perfect confidence' in the officers of the LMS, declared that 'in the lapse of 50 years many things may have arisen in relation both to its constitution and working, which would warrant friendly inquiry and discussion. That therefore it views the conduct of its most valued Secretary, . . . in moving for the late Select Committee, with entire satisfaction' (*Chronicle*, 1850, *loc. cit.*)

[3] 'Salary for an unmarried missionary in our Society is £75, for a married one £100. Our Society gives the least. The Wesleyans have considerably more. The French have £20 to £50 to be expended on improvements at the Stations, £80 being considered as a supply for the Missionary's personal wants. I cannot specify the salaries of other Societies' (9.x.46 Whish).   [4] MS. has 'Societies'.

[5] 'The Directors manifesto' (Chamberlin, p. 136). I cannot explain the allusion.

[6] See above, p. 141n., and below, p. 154. D. L. had left Kolobeng in April, and returned at the end of July.

one establishment to support, the expense was less, but we lost eleven oxen by pitfalls, lions, &c. The sum you thought of, if sanctioned, would be amply sufficient.[1] Mrs L. promises me a twelve months leave next time.

We met Oswel on our return.[2] Brought supplies for us from the Colony, and returned a bill of £40 which was to be spent in purchasing them. Seemed very anxious to get me to promise to allow him to accompany me next trip. I don't well know how to get rid of him, and he feels he cannot go any distance alone. I sometimes think I might employ him to find a way down to the sea coast.

I shall not involve the Society in any expense till I have the sanction of the Directors. If I go down to the Colony to get my uvula excised, I should procure supplies by drawing a year in advance rather than subject you to the suspicions of the Leeds worthies.

I begin to fear we have established a branch of what Sidney Smith[3] called 'the great Irish manufactory'. Mrs L. got a daughter seven days after we reached Kolobeng.[4] Sechele sends you many salutations. The Boers are more than ever troublesome, waylaying travellers between Sentuhe's & the Molopo[5] in order to rob them. The rebel Pretorious sent an order lately to him to stop all English travellers & traders, and many other indications of a coming storm present themselves. I have but small hope for the stability of the station. In the present posture of affairs it would be impossible for Sechele to leave. I never have had a wish even to return to England, but what you suggest would answer extremely well.[6] Sechele does not make any progress in English. This is rather surprising, for he is a first rate speaker in his own tongue and comprehends most subjects readily.

---

[1] 'Mr Freeman thinks I ought to have my extra expenses paid, which I suppose is as good as done' (18.viii.50 Watt). Cf. below, p. 193.

[2] Oswell was to have accompanied the recent expedition, but on reaching Kolobeng in May found that D. L. had already left the month before. He therefore went on to hunt along the Botletle, and after meeting D. L. also revisited Lake Ngami (*Oswell*, i, pp. 214–21).

[3] The famous English divine and wit (1771–1845). D L. evidently liked reading (and quoting) him; cf. *Fam. Letters*, i, p. 98.

[4] The child, named Elizabeth Pyne, died in September, when 'just six weeks old' (*Fam. Letters*, ii, p. 103). See below, p. 188.

[5] 'Sentubes and the Moloso' (Chamberlin, p. 136). Senthufe, son and successor of Sebego (see p. 122n.), had with his people returned, *c*. 1845, to the old tribal home at Kgwakgwê (*c*. 24° 59′ S., 25° 19′ E.), where Freeman had visited him (and his 'teacher', Sebubi) early in January, immediately after leaving Kolobeng (*Tour*, p. 292).

[6] I have not ascertained what Freeman suggested.

Wilson and Mr Edwards's son[1] went in company this year and got nothing but a terrible squeeze from the king of terrors. We found him in high fever. Gave him some medicine which relieved him. He again exposed himself, had a relapse, and sent after us to the Botaoana for more medicine. Before that reached him he had been lying two days insensible, large bed sores formed, &c &c &c, and is not yet perfectly recovered. The Botaoana chief would not give him guides, although he offered anything he chose to ask as wages. The same chief took a great liking to a beautiful gun I recieved as a present from Lieut. Arkwright after setting his collar bone and also the broken thigh bone of his servant.[2] It must have cost him £25. When I asked guides to Sebitoane, he promised meat for my family during my absence, guides, &c &c &c, adding if I only knew him I would have no hesitation in trusting him anent both family & *gun*. I handed it to him at once. An act of entire confidence goes a long way with these people, for instead of refusal, as in the case of Wilson, he was ready to do everything for me, and but for the fever I should have been more than paid for my gun.

Of the anti-rhinocerists you saw at Bloemfontein,[3] Rider the young artist & a Hottentot died of fever. Rider took some views of the Lake. Harris, who now has them in his possession, never went down to see it.[4]

With kind salutations from Mrs L. & self,

Believe me, yours affectionately,

David Livingston

Your beautiful telescope[5] shews the satellites of Jupiter well, and were it not that my plaguey watch[6] is dead again I could observe an

---

[1] J. H. Wilson was a trader who had settled at Kolobeng early in 1849 and accompanied the first expedition to Lake Ngami; Samuel Howard Edwards (1827–1922) was the son of D. L.'s former colleague at Mabotsa. Both subsequently travelled extensively in the Interior, and Edwards also figured prominently in the opening-up of S. Rhodesia. There are short biographical sketches of both in Le Roux, *Pioneers and Sportsmen*, pp. 95–105.

[2] 'the broken thigh of one of his servants' (Chamberlin, p. 137). Robert Arkwright, 1st Dragoon Guards, had visited Bechuanaland on a shooting trip in 1846, when he spent several days with D. L. at Chonwane (*Fam. Letters*, i, pp. 178–80).

[3] Capital of the Orange River Sovereignty; 29° 07' S., 26° 14' E. Freeman and Moffat were there at the beginning of February 1850 (*Fam. Letters*, ii, p. 86).

[4] 'Mr Alfred Rider, an enterprising young artist who had come to make sketches of this country and of the lake immediately after its discovery, had died of fever before our arrival' (*Travels*, p. 75). The illustration of L. Ngami facing p. 66 of that book was based on an 'unfinished drawing' made by him and 'kindly lent for this work by his bereaved mother' (*loc. cit.*). On the illustration his name is given as 'Ryder'. Harris, a 'cousin' of the famous traveller William Cornwallis Harris, is described in *Fam. Letters*, ii, pp. 86–7, as a man of disreputable character.

[5] See below, p. 170: 'a small telescope kindly presented to me by Mr Freeman'.

[6] 'my plague watch' (Chamberlin, p. 137).

occultation by the moon's dark light sufficiently well for the Longitude.

May I ask you to pay Mr Snow £10 out of the salary of 1851 for books I now order?[1]

D. L.

29. To ARTHUR TIDMAN
24 August 1850

[LMS 51. Received 9 January 1851. Previous publication: *JRGS*, vol. xxi (1851), pp. 18–24 (edited version, omitting last six paragraphs); Chamberlin, pp. 138–9 (most of third paragraph)]

Kolobeng
24th August 1850

My dear Sir,

The attendance on our services having greatly declined soon after the refreshing visit of the Revd. J. J. Freeman, in consequence of the attention of the people being engrossed by their gardens, and knowing that such would continue to be the case till the harvest was past, I considered it again advisable to proceed to the North. Mrs Livingston and Mebaloe, the native teacher, had joined in my desire to visit Sebitoane; and Sechele, having purchased a waggon, the first service he wished it to perform was to place him in the presence of the man who, in former years, when assaulting the Bakwain town, ordered his warriors[2] to be sure and spare the lives of the sons of Mocoasele (Sechele's father).[3] The attack having been made in the dark, Sechele was badly wounded & lay insensible till the morning. When recognized, Sebitoane gave orders to his doctors to attend to the wounds, and subsequently restored him to liberty.[4] Had we succeeded in reaching Sebitoane, the interview between the two chiefs might have been interesting. Our chief sent a present to his former benefactor last year, but his messengers were prevented going in the same way that we were. They have been more successfull this year. So though we have not been able to go as far as we intended, we are thankful to hear that the way has been opened by them.

[1] John Snow was a publisher and bookseller in Paternoster Row, London. Among the works he issued were Moffat's *Missionary Labours*, Freeman's *Tour*, and the LMS *Chronicle*.

[2] 'survivors' (*JRGS*, p. 18).

[3] Motswasele II was chief of the BaKwena *c.* 1807–22; he ruled so despotically that he was ultimately assassinated at a tribal assembly (see above, p. 89); cf. Schapera, *Ditirafalô*, pp. 43–4.

[4] Fuller and somewhat different versions of this story are given in *Fam. Letters*, ii, pp. 43–4 (May 1849) and *Travels* (1857), pp. 14–15.

Having no apprehension that Sekhomi would throw obstacles in our way, we visited his tribe both in going and returning. As he is an old friend, I apologized for passing to the Westward of him in our last trip, on the ground that, as I knew he was very much opposed to our finding a passage to the Lake (he having twice refused our request for liberty to pass), I had determined to go in spite of him, and yet without contention. He replied, 'U 'ntsitile, mi kia boka', 'You beat me, and I thank you or acknowledge it'.[1] His entire conduct was the opposite of what it was last year.

We had more intercourse with the Bakalahari, especially with the inhabitants of a large village about 40 miles North of the Bamangwato; and as we passed through their country in April, before the pools which are usually filled by the rains are dried up, we suffered no inconvenience from want of water. After visiting the Bakurutse who live at the lower end of the Zouga, we crossed that river and ascended on its Northern bank. Stumbled on a native grave for the first time since I came into the country. It was that of a Bushman. An old tortoise shell which they use as a dish, a stick used in digging roots, some grass and bushes, were placed above it, and a fire had been made on the edge of an old pitfall which the relatives had used to save themselves the trouble of digging a grave. On enquiry, the Bakhoba informed us that the Bushmen in burying their dead address them in reference to these articles thus: 'You have all that belongs to you; go away to your God, and let us eat what we can get here'. A little farther on we came upon an old man, quite naked and hopelessly diseased. He informed us that he had been deserted some days before by his two daughters; that he suffered much from thirst, for though lying under the large trees which line the banks of the river he could not crawl down for water. Having supplied him with a covering & some food, we offered to carry him to the next village. 'O', said he, 'if they saw me they would flee from me'. Socialism has but sorry fruits among these unsophisticated specimens of humanity.

Our intention in passing alone the Northern bank of the Zouga was to follow the course of the Tamunakle untill we reached Sebitoane. But when near the junction of the two rivers we were informed by a Bakhoba chief, called Palane,[2] that the fly called Tsetse abounded on the Tamunakle. As its bite is fatal to oxen, horses, & dogs, though harmless to men and goats, and we had no more oxen than were sufficient to

---

[1] The verb *bóka*, here translated 'thank' or 'acknowledge', normally means 'praise, applaud'.

[2] Phalane, whom D. L. had previously met when going to L. Ngami in 1849; he lived near Makalamabedi, 20° 19′ S., 23° 51′ E. (*Private J.*, p. 305).

draw our waggons, I proposed proceeding alone. But Mrs L. preferring to wait during my absence among the Bataoana, we recrossed the Zouga and went down towards the Lake. Lechulathebe,[1] the chief, furnished guides, and informed us that the distance would be performed partly by land & partly by water, as the Tamunakle had a very zigzag course; that the riding ox would certainly die soon after I returned, in consequence of being bitten by the fly; and promised to furnish my family with meat during my absence, but objected to Sechele going along with me, because his messengers had not yet returned to tell how Sebitoane's mind stood affected towards him.

Everything seemed favourable, and before starting I took Mrs L. down to take a peep at the Lake. We had rather more curiosity than an Englishman who came to buy ivory from the Bataoana had, for though within 6 miles of it he informed us he had never visited it, and he actually never did.[2] Our children took to playing in the water with as little fear and as much glee as if they had lived from birth in another than this thirsty land. On the day following, our driver and leader were laid up by fever, and subsequently to that two of our children and several of the people besides. A young English artist called Rider, who had taken some views of the Lake scenery, and a Hottentot belonging to another party, died of it. As the malaria seemed to exist in a more concentrated form near the Ngami than in any other part, we were compelled to leave after spending two Sundays with the Bataoana; and as the time at my command would have been spent before I could safely leave my people, the fever & fly forced me to return to Kolobeng.

I was mistaken last year in supposing that the epidemic of which we heard was pneumonia.[3] There is undoubtedly a greater amount of cough on the river than at Kolobeng, but that which came under my observation this year was real marsh fever. The paludal poison is evolved every year as the water begins to flow and moisten the banks of vegetable matter. When the river and Lake are full the fever ceases, but it begins again when evaporation has proceeded so far as to expose the banks to the action of the sun. Our visit last year was made when the river was nearly at its height. The Lake had retired about 20 feet from the spot on which we stood last year; this might be about three feet in perpendicular height.

In the natives the effects of the poison imbibed into the system appear most frequently as bilious fever, and they generally recover after a

[1] Letsholathêbê, chief of the BaTawana 1848(?)–74.
[2] This refers to Harris (see above, p. 153).
[3] See above, p. 137.

copious evacuation of bile. In some it appears as continued fever, in a child there was the remittent form, while in two cases there was simple intermittent fever. In one the vascular system of the abdomen became greatly affected, he became jaundiced & died. In another there were only muscular pains and rapid decline of strength, while in several others there was only pain in the head, which a dose of quinine removed. Mr Wilson (an enterprising trader stationed at Kolobeng; I omitted to mention his name as having accompanied the expedition last year, in consequence of referring to it in its missionary aspects only),[1] who had it in its most severe form, had several violent fits of intermittent fever when recovering from the other, and at a distance of 400 miles from the Lake. This disease seems destined to preserve intertropical Africa for the black races of mankind. If the Boers, who have lately fallen upon the plan of waylaying travellers between Kuruman and this, should attempt to settle on either Lake or river, they would soon find graves.

As the Ngami is undoubtedly a hollow compared to Kolobeng, and the Teoge,[2] a river which falls into the Lake at its North-West extremity, is reported to flow with great rapidity, the region beyond must be elevated. A salubrious spot must be found before we can venture to form a settlement. Then that alone will not suffice, for Kolobeng is 270 miles by the trocheameter from Kolobeng, and the Lake by the same instrument is 600 miles beyond this station. We must have a passage to the sea, on either the Eastern or Western coasts. I have hitherto been afraid to broach the project on which my, perhaps dreamy, imagination dwells. But, as you are aware, the Bechuana Mission was virtually shut up in a cul de sac, on the North by the Desert and on the East by the Boers. The Revd. Mr Fridoux of Motito lately endeavoured to visit the Bamapela, and was forcibly turned back by an armed party of them.[3] You at home are accustomed to look upon a project as half finished when you have secured the cooperation of the ladies. My better half has promised me twelve months' leave of absence for mine. Without promising anything, I mean to follow a useful motto in many circumstances, and try again.

---

[1] The words in parentheses were added in the margin. (The names of the various other patients mentioned are given in *Fam. Letters*, ii, p. 83.)

[2] Taoge, the main channel on the western side of the Okovango delta.

[3] This incident, which occurred in March, is described more fully by Jousse, *Mission Française*, i, pp. 313–16; cf. also J. S. Moffat, *Lives*, p. 278. Jean Frédoux (1823–66), of the P.E.M.S., had come to Motito in 1845 (and in September 1850 married Moffat's daughter Ann). The BaMapela were Mankopane's tribe (see above, p. 97).

The following information, gleaned from intelligent natives, may be interesting, and probably is not far from the truth, as they could have no object in decieving me. The Ngami is merely a reservoir for the surplus waters of a much larger lake or marsh, containing numerous islands, about 150 or 200 miles beyond.[1] Sebitoane, who was defeated by the Griquas near Motito or Litakon in 1824 (he was one of the Mantatees on that occasion),[2] lives on one of these islands. The river which falls into the Ngami at its North-West extremity is called Teoge. It runs with so much rapidity, canoes ascend with great difficulty, & when descending no paddling is required; the force of the current suffices to bring them down rapidly. Large trees are frequently brought down, and even springbucks and other antelopes have been seen whirling round & round in the middle of the stream as it hurried on their carcases to the Lake. But this flow only occurs at one period of the year, and whence the increase of water in the upper lake is derived no one can tell. Other rivers are reported as existing beyond Sebitoane's district, and a large population is said to live on their banks. The names of these tribes are: Bagomae, Barovoia, Barosia, Batongka, Banambia, Banami, Bazatoa, Bachorongka, and Babiko.[3] The last named tribe are famed for their skill in manufactures, are lighter in colour than Bakhoba, and have longer hair and beards. All the iron used among the people near the Lake comes from the North. But though the Bakhoba are much more inquisitive than Bechuanas, I never met with one who had even heard of the existence of the sea. They had heard of a people whom we conjectured to be Portuguese, and we saw an old coat which we believed to be Portuguese manufacture.

Although we have seen the Zouga flowing and even rising considerably, the natives assert that soon after the small reservoir near the Bakurutse villages, called Kumatao,[4] is filled by the Zouga, the latter

[1] 'The Ñami is only a reservoir for the surplus waters of the real Lake, which Lake has never yet been seen. But this, though you don't like secrets, I tell to no one but yourself. The honour of discovery would naturally fall to you' (8.vii.50 Moffat: *Fam. Letters*, ii, p. 85). The 'real lake' was presumably the Okovango Swamps, whose waters drain into L. Ngami.

[2] In June 1823 (not 1824) the 'Mantatees', advancing on Kuruman from the north, were defeated at Dithakong by a combined force of Griquas (armed with guns) and BaTlhaping (cf. Moffat, *Miss. Labours*, pp. 354–63, and *Apprenticeship*, pp. 88–103). Motito is about 7 miles to the west.

[3] Of these names, which D. L. apparently got from Yeei informants, I cannot identify Barovoia, Banami, Bazatoa, Bachorongka. The others, in the order given, are nowadays usually written Makoma, BaRotse (MaLozi), BaTonga (BaToka), BaNambywa (BaNanzwa), and BaWiko (MaMbukushu), the forms in parentheses being recognized variants.

[4] Kumadau, on modern maps termed Lake Dow; *c.* 21° 15' S., 24° 40' E.

ceases to flow. The rains do not affect it in the least, and in many parts its bed becomes quite dry. This is also the case, according to report, with the Tamunakle & Teoge. During a certain portion of the year the beds exhibit only a succession of pools with dry patches between.

The fishes, which we saw so abundant in July & August last year, had not yet descended from the North in June. The Bakhoba seemed quite sure they would appear in the month following. They enumerated nine varieties of fish in the Lake & rivers, two of which are said to attain occasionally the length of a man. Of the 5 varieties which came under our observation, four were very good eating. The fifth, called by naturalists Glanis Siluris, had attained a length of about three feet. There are crockodiles or alligators and hippopotami, but the latter are scarce now, in consequence of the Bakhoba frequently hunting them. They kill them by means of a large harpoon, to which a strong rope is attached, in somewhat the same manner as whalers do. They use nets made of the hibiscus, baskets, & assegais, for killing fish. Their canoes are flat bottomed & scooped out of single trees.

The banks of the river are in many parts lined with trees of gigantic growth. I observed twelve quite new to us at Kolobeng. The banyan and palmyra were recognized as Indian trees by our friend Mr Oswel. The boabob, the body of which gives one the idea of a mass of granite from its enormous size, yields a fruit about the size of a quart bottle. The pulp between the seeds tastes like cream of tartar, and is used by the natives to give a flavour to their porridge. Other three bear edible fruits. One, called 'Moporotla',[1] yields a fruit an unripe specimen of which measures $20\frac{1}{2}$ inches in length and $7\frac{1}{2}$ in circumference. The seeds are roasted & eaten, the body of the tree is used for making canoes. Another, called 'Motsouri',[2] is a beautiful tree & very much resembles the orange; we did not see the fruit. The natives pound the root of a kind of flag and obtain flour not greatly inferior to that from wheat in taste & appearance. This flag is called 'Tsitla',[3] & it grows abundantly in both Lake & river. The root of a water lily is used as a vegetable, but it is not so good as the tsitla. The people sow when the river has risen high enough to moisten the soil of the flats in which their gardens are situated. They do not require to wait for rains as the other tribes must do, for they have good crops though but little rain falls. Rainmakers are

---

[1] *Kigelia pinnata*, 'sausage tree' (Miller, *Woody Plants of Bechuanaland*, 1952, p. 79).

[2] Tswana *motsaodi*, used for both *Garcinina livingstonei*, 'African mangosteen', and *Guibourtia coleosperma*, 'Rhodesian copalwood' (Miller, *op. cit.*, pp. 32, 58).

[3] Probably *Prionium serratum*.

consequently at a discount among the Bakhoba. Besides the usual native produce they cultivate an excellent ground nut.

The banks of the Zouga are studded with pitfalls, which the Bakhoba dig for the purpose of killing game. Some of these are very neatly smeared over with mud, and if a sharp look out is not kept one finds himself at the bottom, with the sand running down on him, as the first intimation of the presence of the trap. They are from eight to ten feet in depth, and the wild animals are so much afraid of them they drink during the night and immediately depart to the Desert. Elephants abound in large numbers, but previous to our first visit the ivory was of no value. The tusks were left in the field with the other bones. I saw thirteen which had been thus left and were completely spoiled by the weather. In our first visit [the] Bataoana would have preferred to sell a tusk for a few beads to parting with a goat for twice the amount. They soon, however, acquire a knowledge of the value of ivory. In one village the headman informed me that two of his wives had been killed by elephants entering the village during the night and turning over the huts, apparently by way of amusement. Besides elephants, rhinoceros, buffaloes, &c &c &c, we observed a new species of antelope called 'Lechoee'.[1] It is rather larger than the pallah.[2] The horns in shape are like those of the waterbuck, the colour of the skin is a beautiful brownish yellow. Its habits are those of the waterbuck. Mr Oswel has this year secured a new variety of the khoodoo.[3]

The country beyond the Bamangwato, so far as we have penetrated, is quite flat, only intersected here & there by the dry beds of antient rivers. The Desert does not deserve the name, except from its great want of water, for it is usually covered with abundance of grass, bushes, and trees. Nor is it destitute of inhabitants. Both men and animals exist in considerable numbers. Man, however, has a hard struggle to keep soul & body together. The Bakalahari children are usually distinguished by the large protruding abdomen and thin ill-formed legs & arms. The listless eye shews that youth has few joys for them. Although much oppressed by the Bechuanas who visit them annually in order to collect skins, they are often at variance among themselves.

They obtain water in certain hollow parts, called 'sucking places', where there is a stratum of wet sand about three feet below the surface, by means of a reed. A bunch of grass is tied round one end of it, to act as

[1] *Kobus leche*, Lechwe waterbuck.

[2] *Aepyceros melampus*, impala (Tswana *phala*).

[3] Kudu, *Tragelaphus strepsiceros*. The 'new variety' secured by Oswell was actually *Tragelaphus spekei*, the marshbuck or sitatunga (Afrikaans *waterkoedoe*, 'water-kudu', Tswana *nakong*); cf. *Oswell*, i, pp. 219–20.

a sort of filter. This is inserted in the wet sand, and that which was taken out in making the hole is firmly rammed down around it. The mouth applied to the free extremity draws up enough of water to fill a load of ostrich egg shells.[1] By making wells in these spots we several times obtained water sufficient for our oxen. The natives were always anxious that we should not in digging break through a hard layer at the bottom of the wells, asserting that if we did the water would be lost.

The Bushmen of the Desert are perhaps the most degraded specimens of the human family. Those near the river Zouga look much better. The river supplies them with fish and 'tsitla', and they seem expert in the use of the bow & arrow, for they have killed nearly all the lions. The Botletli are real Bushmen in appearance and language, yet about twelve years ago were in possession of large herds of cattle.[2] (We saw specimens of their cattle, the horns of which measured from six to eight feet from point to point.) The Bushmen are very numerous on all sides of both Lake and River. Their language has as much klick[3] as it has farther South.

Of the animals which live in the Desert the eiland[4] is perhaps the most interesting. He is the largest of the antelope kind, attains the size of a very large ox, and seems wonderfully well adapted for living in that country, for though they do drink a little if they pass near the water, they can live for months without a drop. They become very fat. The meat is excellent, and as they are easily run down by a good horse it is surprising they have not been introduced into England.

The soil is generally sandy. Vegetation is not much more luxuriant, except in the immediate vicinity of the river, than in this portion of Africa generally. All the rocks we saw consisted of calcareous tufa, travertin, and sandstone. On the banks of the Lake there is a rock of igneous origin. The tufa contains no shells, but the salt pans near the lower end of the Zouga are covered with four varieties of recent shells.

---

[1] Used by both Bushmen and BaKgalagadi as water-containers. The method here described of obtaining water is still practised nowadays by inhabitants of the Kalahari.

[2] These people, whose common name is usually pronounced 'BaTeti', call themselves BaUra, and claim to have migrated into their present habitat from N.W. Rhodesia towards the end of the 18th century. As D. L. indicates, they are culturally more advanced than the Bushmen, but their language (which, however, has not yet been fully studied) is apparently of the same family. Cf. Schapera, *Ethnic Composition of Tswana Tribes*, 1953, p. 83.

[3] The famous 'clicks' (injected consonants) that are so characteristic a feature of the Bushman and Hottentot languages. They also occur in several Bantu languages, including Zulu, Xhosa, and Yeei.

[4] Eland, *Taurotragus oryx*.

It is probable these flats, called salt pans because sometimes covered with an efflorescence of salt, were reservoirs, such as the Kumatao is now, at a period when the flow of the Zouga was greater than it is at present. The country generally is unquestionably drying up. Streams and fountains which in the memory of persons now living supplied towns with water are now only dry watercourses. And as antient river beds are now traversed by more modern streams, giving sections which shew banks of shells, gravel, & rolled boulders, it is perhaps not unreasonable to conjecture an alteration in the elevation of the entire country. At present, wherever the bed of the Zouga may lead (perhaps towards the Limpopo), water seldom flows far past the Bakurutse villages.

In returning we met out friend Mr Oswel at the ford by which we recrossed the river. We hastened back to Kolobeng, and in recrossing the Desert suffered more from want of water than we did in going in. The rain water was all dried up. If Mr Oswel makes any discovery I shall inform you of it. Our messengers to Sebitoane are the only guides one can have.

You will gather my views from the former part of the letter, and if Mr Freeman will shew you a private communication you may collect some of my reasons for those views.

The present state of the Bakwain Mission is unsatisfactory. The Kolobeng has not answered our expectations. Three remarkably dry seasons have dried it up. This would be of little consequence in so far as we are concerned, because we can purchase corn at Kuruman, but the soil at Kolobeng does not seem to retain the moisture sufficiently for rearing native produce, and the people have consequently been compelled to suffer much hunger. They removed hither entirely on our account, they have given the locality a fair trial, and it appears but fair and reasonable that we should remove with them to some spot more suitable for them. Before coming to a final decision, Sechele has resolved to try gardens a few miles higher up the stream, but I have but small hopes of success — the soil is the same. Successive years of hunger have had a most depressing effect on our Mission, for our enemies have not been slow in making comparisons between the years of plenty of heathenism and those of scarcity under the gospel. House building at Mabotsa, Chonuane, & Kolobeng partook of the nature of amusement, but I now feel my ardour in that line cooling.

The Boers lately sent an order to Sechele to stop all English travellers and traders proceeding to the North. The order was accompanied with a request that he should inform them whether he intended to comply or not, so that they might understand whether he was their friend or enemy. The note was signed by one named Standers,[1] sub-commandant to the General-Commandant Pretorious, for whose head the Government had offered £2,000 reward. I advised no notice to be taken of it. as a refusal to obey the order would only excite them the more. Indeed, many of them would be as much disgusted & astonished by the disobedience of a black man as Balaam was with the altercation of his ass. They have waylaid the path to Kuruman, in order to plunder English travellers, for some time back, and but for our knowledge of the country assisting strangers many would have fallen into their hands. Potgeiter lately put a chief to death, and put one of his own creatures into the chieftainship instead. The people in revenge killed the latter. He put another chief to death last year.[2] A deputation from the Dutch Reformed Church baptized last year hundreds of the children of such murderers, and some of Potgeiter's among the number. Africa seems a long way off from the Millenium.

(Private) That which inspires more fear than anything else in the Lake country is mosquitoes. They are dreadful. Their bite is more venemous than anywhere else, at least so said those who have been in India, New South Wales, & Brazil. They are really painful, and the pain continues for several days. Sleep is out of the question when you come to a den of them. I could not touch a square half inch on the bodies of the children unbitten after a single night's exposure.

I have not had the pleasure of being able to acknowledge any letter from you for a long time. Yet. . . .

[Ending and signature cut out]

A few errors occur in the printed sketch of the country,[3] and are doubtless the result of my bad penmanship. In my simplicity I imagined I had written very plainly: Z o u g a, not Z o n g a; B a t a o a n a, not Batavana; S e r o t l e, not Zentle; S h o k u a n, not Shoknan. Except Zouga & Bataoana, the other names here referred to are unimportant. Teoge is the name of the other river referred to. Many others are referred to as existing, but beyond the Lake. I could not help feeling sad as I looked down on the steady flowing waters of the Zouga (exactly like the Clyde just above Bothwell Bridge[4]), and thought of the thousands who have paddled over them in total ignorance of Him who bare

---

[1] Adriaan Hendrick Stander (1817–96), commandant since April 1850 of Marico District, Transvaal (*Fam. Letters*, ii, 88–9).

[2] I have not discovered who those chiefs were.

[3] The map on the cover of *Chronicle*, March 1850, which was made from D. L.'s sketch in his letter of 3.ix.49 (see above, p. 136).

[4] Near Blantyre, Lanarkshire (Scotland).

our sins on his own body on the tree. How many more must have passed their lives on these other rivers which have never yet been seen by a European.

D. L.

30. To WILLIAM THOMPSON
27 August 1850

[LMS 53. Received 13 November 1850. Previous publication: Chamberlin, pp. 139–41 (incomplete)]

Kolobeng
27th August 1850

My dear Sir,

I recieved a few days ago the circular announcing your appointment to the Agency at Cape Town,[1] and to which your kind note of 3d July was appended. I now beg leave to accept of your offer of service in reference to the transmission of letters to & from America. My brother Charles is settled as pastor of a church in Lakeville, Livingstone county, New York.[2] He was educated at Oberlin and Andover. Indeed, he is a naturalized citizen of the United States. I have another brother settled in Lanark, Canada West.[3] My parents are also in that country,[4] and having so many relatives there I begin to feel anxious to have a more direct means of communication than that which I have hitherto availed myself of, viz. by way of England. Both brothers would like to send me books, periodicals, &c, but the expense by way of the Mission House we found to be so enormous we were obliged to forbid them sending.

That which I shall be much obliged to you if you can conveniently do for me is to enquire of the United States consul, — Chase,[5] Esqre, if he acts as agent in such matters. If not, is there any American house which does? And what is the firm in New York to which, in the event of Mr Chase or another American gentleman acting as agent, my brother ought to address letters & parcels? Also, what is likely to be the

---

[1] See above, p. 147.

[2] Possibly because the LMS could not accept him, Charles L. had abandoned his missionary aspirations (*Fam. Letters*, ii, p. 74). But he did not remain long at Lakeville: '3 sermons on Sunday & poor health was too much for him' (*Fam. Letters*, ii, p. 129: 26.iv.51 Moffat).

[3] His elder brother John (see above, p. 116).

[4] They had contemplated going there, but finally decided to remain in Scotland (*Fam. Letters*, ii, pp. 92, 114).

[5] Isaac Chase, U.S. consul in Cape Town, and local agent for many American insurance companies (*ibid.*, ii, p. 100).

cost of agency in reference to letters, parcels of books, &c? I am quite willing to pay any reasonable amount that may be thought proper. If you can obtain a satisfactory answer from Mr Chase, will you state in a note the name of the firm in New York to which my brother ought to send, and address it to Revd. Charles Livingston, Lakeville, Livingston County, State of New York? Perhaps a mere slip inserted into a letter which I now send him addressed to your care would be sufficient, as I explain to him in the body of it that I intend applying for the assistance of Mr Chase.

So it seems we not only met at Mrs Sewell's,[1] but we shall yet meet up in the Interior of Africa, perhaps on the banks of the Lake. You will never think of turning round in your visitations without seeing us all, & you will be sure of a welcome if you come our length. We lately returned from another visit to the Lake country. Were compelled by fever and fly to return without going any farther than last year. Met Mr Oswel on our return, and do not know where he is now.[2]

I must conclude this hasty note by noticing the bills which I have drawn for 1850:

No. 3　£50　in favour of Revd. R. Moffat; salary
No. 4　£40　August 1st, in favour of Charles Alexander Green,[3] Esq.; salary
No. 5　£15　Do., Do., C. A. Green, Esqre; salary
No. 6　£20　4th August; Do.; Robert Moffat, Esqre; salary
　　　£125

In the last statement of accounts from Mr Rutherfoord, a balance of £10.15.6 was stated to be overdrawn. This sum ought to have been put down as £5.15.6. I explained the reason to Mr Freeman when here. As we have four children, the salary may be put down as £120;

deduct　£　6　in order to have even money
　　　114　amount of salary
　　　125　amount drawn for 1850
　　£ 11　overdrawn and due by me to the Society.

I mention it before you can have found it out by the appearance of

---

[1] Keeper of a boarding-house (with LMS connections) at 57 Aldersgate Street, London, where D. L. had stayed in 1838 and 1840. Thompson was in England, on furlough from India, in June–October 1840 (*Register*, p. 38).

[2] On 27.x.50 D. L. wrote to Moffat: 'Oswel is about 80 miles beyond this', i.e. on his way back to Kolobeng from the Botletle (*Fam. Letters*, ii, p. 112).

[3] A hunter and trader, born in Canada, from whom D. L. had just bought a wagon for some ivory and '£40 in money' (*Fam. Letters*, ii, p. 89).

the bills, for I have no apprehension that you will catch your fellow servant by the throat, saying, Pay me that thou owest. I have still to draw £12 for a native teacher, and may perhaps be obliged to run a little more into the Society's debt, for in my late trip I lost a great many oxen. I do not, however, advise you that I certainly will do so.

Shall write you more at length soon. This is by an opportunity I did not expect, but which I embrace to write the Directors, &c. By excusing this, & attending to my request, you will very much oblige,

Yours affectionately,
D. Livingston

You might have told me how our old friend Mrs Sewell looked.

V

SEBETWANE'S COUNTRY

31. To DAVID LIVINGSTON
1 March 1851

[LMS: Outgoing Letters, Africa, Box 7, pp. 329–30]

London

1st March, 1851

Dear Brother,

Since writing to you under date the 5th of August ult., we have received yours of the 24th of the same month, containing a detailed account of your second journey with Mrs L. to the scene of your recent discoveries.

From the narrative we learn with regret that although your progress through the territories leading to the Lake was retarded by few of the obstacles you had encountered in the former journey, a concurrence of untoward events compelled you to hasten your return without accomplishing the important objects you had in view. The prevalence of the venomous insects on the Tamunakle, and of the still more fatal fever around the region of the Lake, proved a barrier to the onward march of discovery which your previous experience had in no way taught you to expect. In regarding these formidable obstacles as an intimation that it was your duty to retrace your steps, we consider that you not only exercised a very proper discretion, but that to have acted otherwise would have been an unjustifiable exposure of the health and lives of yourself and companions.

While we in common with the friends of African civilisation most decidedly sympathise with you in the disappointment attendant upon this second journey, it may gratify you to know that we are not disposed to regard the results of this journey as wholly valueless, nor to relinquish the hope of ultimately obtaining a footing in those regions, until it can be shewn that this periodical malaria is so extensively prevalent as to form an insurmountable barrier to the success of the undertaking.

You have already gleaned important information in regard to the geography of the countries traversed, the character and disposition of the inhabitants, the climate, the natural history, etc. You have also ascertained the position of the Lake and the bearings of the circumjacent rivers. All this information will be available at a future time.

When we further consider the perilous situation of those of the Native tribes connected with our Stations beyond the Colony, continually exposed to the encroachments of the Emigrant Boers, and when we lastly reflect upon the parlous condition of the heathen tribes located at and about the Lake region, yet unvisited by the light of the Gospel, we find strong inducements to encourage you to prosecute your investigations whenever a favourable opportunity may occur, and at a period of the year when it can be done without risk to your health. We feel the less reluctant in giving our countenance to the undertaking, since we perceive that Mrs Livingston has already evinced her self-denial and magnanimity by giving it her sanction.

As you might readily suppose, our hope of an ultimate solution of this interesting problem is mainly grounded upon your statement that the River Teoge, which falls into the Lake at its North-West extremity, is reported to flow southward with great rapidity, leading to the inference that the region beyond must have a considerable elevation, and that consequently hopes may be entertained of finding localities in that direction unexceptionable on the score of health. In giving our general sanction and encouragement to the further prosecution of your investigations, with a view to the earlier introduction of the Gospel into these newly-explored regions, we are aware that much must necessarily be left to your own discretion in regard to the ascertained or probable facts upon which the hopes of ultimate success are grounded, the most suitable way and time for carrying the object into effect, the period of absence, etc. We trust, however, you will be directed by the Spirit of Grace and Wisdom, and commending you and all your interests to the Divine Care and effectual benediction,

I remain, dear Brother,

Very truly yours,

[Arthur Tidman]

Foreign Secy. of the London Missionary Society

Your recent references to the affairs of the Kolobeng Station have been so meagre as to afford no topic for remark.

The Board has recently adopted the following resolution, viz.,

That Mr Livingston be encouraged as opportunity may offer to direct his attention to the preparation of a Dictionary in the Sichuana, if he can do it without abstracting his time from more necessary labors.

Captain Steele[1] of the Royal Geographical Society has sent us a gold watch, of which he requests your acceptance as a mark of his esteem. We shall avail ourselves of the first safe opportunity for transmitting it to you.

32. To ARTHUR TIDMAN
30 April 1851

[LMS 55. Previous publication: Chamberlin, pp. 144–8 (in full)]

Boatlanama
30th April 1851

My dear Sir,

After a silence prolonged since 1849 I had the pleasure of again hearing from you on the 19th currt. But being then engaged in putting our provisions &c into the waggons, I defferred answering your favour till some leizure hour should occur on the journey. That opportunity has occurred while the people are drawing water for the cattle out of the deep wells of Boatlanama,[2] and one of the Bakalahari will take this back to Sechele.

Your letter is dated 5th August 1850, nearly ten months ago, and I am sorry to learn that my letter from the Zouga, 3d September '49, was quite as long on its way to you. One reason I had for writing there was that you might have the information before any of my friends should, and it was dispatched to the Colony a few days after I reached Kolobeng.[3] Letters sent direct to Colesberg seldom remain longer in the way than five months. I have recieved them at Kolobeng in a little more than four from the date of their leaving England. But if sent to the care of any one at the Cape, much longer time is required, and nothing is gained in either expense or safety. Be so kind therefore as to address letters (& newspapers when sent) to the care of Mr David Arnot,[4]

---

[1] (Sir) Thomas Montague Steele (1820–90), Coldstream Guards, the 'aide-de-camp' who had visited Bechuanaland and met D. L. in 1843 (see above, p. 47, and *Fam. Letters*, i, p. 80). D. L.'s second son was named after him; he communicated to the R.G.S. on 11.ii.50 D. L.'s account of the discovery of L. Ngami (Oswell's came two months later); and the gift mentioned was but one more instance of his 'great kindness' to D. L. (cf. *Fam. Letters*, ii, p. 33). He was not an officer, but an ordinary Fellow, of the R.G.S.

[2] A well-known watering-place, in 23° 37′ S., 25° 48′ E. D. L., again accompanied by his wife and children, had left Kolobeng on 24 April (*Private J.*, p. 3).

[3] On 10 October 1849 (see above, p. 138).

[4] An attorney at Colesberg, who 'acts as our agent' (10.i.51 Watt). For some details about him, see *Fam. Letters*, ii, p. 123, and Williams, *Some Dreams Come True*, pp. 97–103.

Colesberg, South Africa. But parcels, periodicals, &c, may come in the usual manner. I beg to call your attention particularly to this, as all the letters &c except your own to which you refer as leaving in the same ship reached me in November last,[1] nearly seven months ago.

In consequence of not knowing that you had recieved the sum awarded by the Royal Geographical Society till many months after the letter of the President arrived, I requested my friend Captain Steel to purchase a watch with it, suitable for observing occultations of stars by the moon in order thereby to find the Longitude. Mr Maclear, the astronomer at the Cape,[2] having publicly invited any one to make observations on certain stars, engaged to observe them simultaneously and make the calculations. As it would not require much time, and a small telescope kindly presented me by Mr Freeman with my own sextant are all that are required besides the watch, I felt anxious to comply with Mr Maclear's invitation. And as the watch might have an inscription, it would serve as a memorial of the occasion on which the money was given. As I am not sure whether Captain Steel is in England, or whether it may be convenient for him to attend to my request in consequence of having met with an accident, I am unable to say anything more about the money, except that if he applies for it you have my authority for furnishing it to him.[3]

In my last I gave you an account of our unsuccessful attempt to reach Sebitoané. We were driven back by fever. We are now on our way to try again, and should we find a suitable people and locality will commence a station. You are aware that the Bakwains have for successive years suffered either partial or entire failure of crops. The want of corn has been contemporaneous with the possession of the gospel, and as some of the ajacent tribes who have shewn considerable opposition to the 'Word of God' have been favoured with years of plenty, many of the people associate teaching and hunger as inseparable. The dearth caused by repeated droughts has operated most injuriously on our success, for those who were willing to be taught, and these were not a few, have always been compelled to leave the school for the purpose of obtaining food by hunting, &c. The Boers, too, by perpetual meddling have distracted the mind of the tribe. And to crown all the Kolobeng, which for the first year after our settlement was a fine large stream

---

[1] D. L. was then at Kuruman (*Fam. Letters*, ii, p. 114).

[2] (Sir) Thomas Maclear (1794–1879), astronomer-royal at the Cape of Good Hope 1834–70. 'I shall never cease to remember his instructions and help with real gratitude' (*Travels*, Preface, p. v).

[3] In *JRGS*, 1851, p. xxiv, it is stated that the Royal Premium of 25 guineas awarded to D. L. had been 'since, by request, converted into a Chronometer Watch'.

capable of irrigating land enough for the subsistance of the whole tribe, has gradually dried up, and renders a removal to a new locality absolutely necessary. All the streams & fountains in the tract of country inhabited by the Bakwains & Bangwaketse have been subjected to the same cause of desiccation. The chief of the Bangwaketse lately shewed me nine streams which were perennial when Mr Moffat visited Makabba,[1] but now during the greater portion of the year they present the spectacle of dry watercourses.

The only course left for the Bakwains is removal to some other part of their country, equally destitute of flowing water with the Kolobeng, but where native corn may be raised. They propose to go about 10 miles higher up its course to a part called Limaoe.[2] We quite approve of the step. But with the prospects God has opened up for us in the North we cannot see it to be our duty to incur the expense and undergo the toil of building in that locality. There is no probability that they will remain there permanently, and it is quite certain we cannot raise the necessaries of life in the spot. And under existing circumstances we have little real missionary work among them, not more than a native teacher could effect. On the other hand, the Bakwains have increased in knowledge since our residence among them, they have uniformly treated us with respect and kindness, and though the numbers willing to be taught, both of adults & children, are small compared with what might be, the Bakhatla & Bahurutse combined do not furnish so many. We know them too, and we love them. The attachment is reciprocal, and I have a strong impression they will yet in numbers turn to the Lord and be blessed. The seed sown will not be lost.

But we have an immense region before us. Thousands live and die without God & without hope, though the command went forth of old, Go ye into all the world and preach the gospel to every creature. It is a venture to take wife & children into a country where fever, African fever, prevails. But who that believes in Jesus would refuse to make a venture for such a Captain? A parent's heart alone can feel as I do when I look at my little ones & ask, Shall I return with this or that one alive? However, we are His, and wish to have no interests apart from those of His kingdom and glory. May He bless us and make us blessings even unto death.

The country around Sebitoané is described as quite a network of

---

[1] At Kgwakgwê, in August 1824 (*Miss. Labours*, pp. 396–414; *Apprenticeship*, pp. 133–44).

[2] Dimawê. The BaKwena did in fact move there in August (*Private J.*, p. 78).

large rivers, 'Linokanoka',[1] river upon river. We may require to go beyond him for an elevated locality. We shall seek such, though the people may not be very numerous. The Bakoba carry intelligence far, and may be instrumental in assisting us in various ways. We feel the necessity of making a venture at once, as so much time is consumed in the weary 600 miles beyond Kolobeng before we reach the Lake country. Mr Oswel is on his way in too. We are separated at present by want of water.[2] He is unwearied in his kindness, for all which may God bless him.

On the subject of expenses, I may mention to the Directors that these have been considerable. Two spans or teams of oxen alone cost £40. Tear & wear of waggons, extra wages, &c, are considerable. But the Leeds luminaries might advert to the twenty-five guineas I have got, so I beg to refer you to the opinion of Mr Freeman on this point. I have overdrawn the salary for this year considerably. I shall feel obliged if you pay on demand to Mr Pyne £10 for female clothing which we order by the same post,[3] & £10 to my father, part payment for clothing already sent by Mr Drummond.[4] These £20 to be put to the account of salary for 1852. I shall advise Mr Thompson of the sum. If as successful as we hope, we shall not return before the beginning of '52.

As I cannot possibly write the Secretary of the Geographical Society at present, I shall feel much obliged if you communicate the following corrections which I have made on a map sent by Mr Arrowsmith for the purpose,[5] and in which Mr Oswel fully concurs. He paid considerable attention to the course of the River during last year's trip,[6] and

---

[1] *Dinokanoka,* from *noka,* river. The reduplication of the stem indicates 'intensification of the idea conveyed by the simple form, large numbers', etc. (D. T. Cole, *An Introduction to Tswana Grammar,* 1955, p. 118).

[2] Oswell was travelling together with D. L., but had gone ahead at this stage of the journey 'to clean out the watering-places for us' (*Private J.,* pp. 3, 4).

[3] Mr Benjamin Pyne and his family, of Ongar, had become very friendly with D. L. when he was studying there under Rev. R. Cecil in 1838–9. He often wrote to them from South Africa, and said in the letter referred to (also dated 30 April): 'We send a notice to Dr Tidman that he is to pay Mr Pyne £10 on demand; this is to be laid out in clothing for my better half & children'; then follows a short list of the garments required.

[4] In October, D. L. wrote to his parents: 'We wrote you from Boatlanama, and I fear I neglected to tell you to apply to the Directors for £10 [to] defray my balance with Mr Drummond. I advised them to pay it to you, and if you write them a note it will be forthcoming' (*Fam. Letters,* ii, p. 140).

[5] John Arrowsmith (1790–1873) was a well-known cartographer who did much work for the R.G.S. The map mentioned was enclosed by D. L. in a letter to Moffat, 26.iv.51, with the request to 'address & forward it' (*Fam. Letters,* ii, p. 129).

[6] After he had met D. L. returning from L. Ngami, Oswell remained for some time on the Botletle (see above, p. 152).

naturally feels anxious that three or four mistakes which we made in our first visit should be corrected by ourselves rather than by anyone else.

The river is highest in the end of August and lowest in January, March & April. At the end of April the flow has fairly begun all along its course. This is the reverse of what we stated, and led to the second error, for supposing the river to be at its lowest when we saw it in August '49, Mr O. calculated that when full it must in some parts be 500 yards broad. But as the result of longer & more accurate observation he is convinced it does not exceed 300 yards anywhere. It does not actually flow farther to the Eastward than the Bakurutse villages, and only so far when the small lake called Kumadow is filled by the river & overflows. There was water in the bed of the river at the farthest or most easterly Bakurutse villages when we first struck it on the 4th July 1849, but none in 1850. The Kumadow is about 5 miles broad and 15 long. It is opposite the hill Kiria.[1] The Lake Ngami itself we believe, on the report of intelligent natives, to be seventy or seventy-five miles in circumference. Mr Oswel has no doubt from observations made during his second visit but that the Lake recieves the Teogé or Teophé and the Kunyeri.[2] He was shewn the mouth of the latter.

We have both concurred in these corrections and indicated on Mr Arrowsmith's map what we concieve ought to be published as correct. But we did not apply the measurement according to the scale furnished, on account of being in the act of departing. There is a correction, too, on the bend of the river. We feel anxious that these corrections should not be published by Mr Arrowsmith while the Secretary of the Royal Geographical Society is unaware whence the corrections have proceeded. He will feel an interest in them besides.

[Rest of letter missing]

33. To ARTHUR TIDMAN
1 October 1851

[LMS 57. Received 31 January 1852. Previous publication: *Chronicle*, vol. xvi, (March) 1852, pp. 52–3 (edited extracts); Blaikie, pp. 119–20 (three paragraphs); Chamberlin, pp. 148–53 (virtually complete)]

[1] Kedia Hill, 21° 26′ S., 24° 37′ E., a few miles S.W. of Lake Dow. (In *Private J.*, p. 248, n. 1, the longitude is misprinted as 23° 47′ E.).
[2] Kunyere, a channel from the N.E. that joins the Nghabe River (a continuation of the Thamalakane) at Toteng (20° 23′ S., 22° 57′ E.).

Banks of Zouga
1st October 1851

Dear Sir,

Availing myself of the kindness of a party of Griquas who leave this river tomorrow and proceed direct to Philipolis,[1] I hope you will recieve this letter at least as soon as any of my friends can obtain information respecting the movement of which I informed you from Boatlanama.

We left our old route at 'Nchokotsa,[2] and proceeding nearly due North crossed the bed of the Zouga and certain salt pans remarkable for their extent. One, called Ntwétwé, was about 15 miles broad[3] and probably 100 long. Beyond these we passed through a hard flat country covered with mopané trees[4] and containing a great number of springs in limestone rock. A considerable number of Bushmen live in the vicinity, and they seem to have abundance of food. Leaving this district of springs, and guided by a Bushman, we crossed an excessively dry and difficult tract of country and struck a small river called Mababi.[5] Visiting a party of Bushmen and another of Banajoa,[6] we after some days reached the Chobe[7] in 18° 20′ S., the river on which Sebitoane lived. The tsetse abounded on the southern bank, and as the depth is from 12 to 15 feet we could not cross with the waggons. The cattle were taken over to an island, and Mr Oswel and I proceeded about 30 miles down the river in a canoe. It was propelled by five rare good rowers, and to us who are accustomed to bullock waggons the speed seemed like that of boat races at home.

Sebitoané recieved us kindly, and offered to replace our cattle, which were all believed to have been bitten by tsétsé. He returned to the waggons with us, and subsequently fell sick and, to our great sorrow, died.[8] He formed one of the party of Mantatees repulsed by the Griquas at

---

[1] Philippolis (named after Dr John Philip); a Griqua settlement and LMS station at 30° 16′ S., 25° 16′ E., about 18 miles north of the Orange River. The Griquas mentioned above were a hunting party whom D. L. met on his way back from Sebetwane's country (*Fam. Letters*, ii, pp. 136, 154).

[2] Chukutsa Pan, 21° 17′ S., 25° E.

[3] MS. has 'long', an obvious slip of the pen. Ntwêtwê Pan is the name commonly applied to the western half of the Makarikari Depression.

[4] *Colophospermum mopane.*

[5] A watercourse in the general vicinity of 19° S., 24° E.; connects the Ngoga River (a branch of the Okovango) with the Mababe Depression to the north-east.

[6] BaNambywa, BaNajwa, or BaNanzva, a people of Kalaka stock who had fled from the MaTebele and settled on the Mababe Flats. In *Private J.*, p. 14, there is a brief description of the village visited by D. L.

[7] Also called the Linyanti; a major tributary of the Zambesi, which it joins at Kazungula (17° 45′ S., 25° 20′ E.).　　[8] On 7 July, of pneumonia (see below, p. 181).

Old Lattakoo, and since then he has almost constantly been fighting. An elderly man, his almost constant companion, was the individual who killed Makabba of the Wanketze.[1] He several times lost all his cattle, but being a man of great ability managed to keep his people together, and ended his days richer in cattle, and with many more people under his sway, than any other chief we know in Africa. He had long wished to open up intercourse with Europeans and obtain the weapons[2] he saw used with such fatal effect at Lattakoo, but when he had reached the summit of his wishes, in seeing a path made into his country, he was compelled to lie down and die. A doctor who attended him interrupted with rudeness when I attempted to speak about death, and his people took him away from the island when not far from his end. Mr O. and I went over to condole with his people soon after the news of his death came, and they seemed to take our remarks thankfully.

We remained two months with them. They are by far the most savage race of people we have seen. But they treated us with uniform kindness, and would have been delighted had we been able to remain with them permanently. Such was my intention when I left Kolobeng, and, having understood that there were high lands in that region, to avoid the loss of time which would occur in returning for my family I resolved that they should accompany me. The deep rivers among which they now live are a defence to them against the Matibele. To have removed them to the high lands would have been rendering them defenceless. And the country itself was so totally different from anything I knew or could have fancied, I feel[3] convinced that two years alone in it are required for the successful commencement of a station.

To say it is one vast swamp for hundreds of miles, with patches of hard ground covered with date, palmyra, and other trees, conveys but a poor idea of it. It is for hundreds of miles intersected with numerous rivers and branches of rivers coming out of these & returning into them again. These are flanked with large reedy boggy tracts of country. Where trees abound, if not on an island, the tsetse exists. Indeed, we seem to have reached the limits of waggon travelling. The intentions of our kind friend Mr Oswel were to proceed down one of the rivers, perhaps to the sea, while we remained at our settlement. But the tsetse and country presented insuperable barriers.

[1] See above, p. 89.

[2] Fire-arms. 'He had the idea that our teaching was chiefly the art of shooting and other European arts, and that by our giving him guns he would thereby procure peace' (*Private J.*, pp. 16–17; cf. below, p. 181).

[3] Altered in MS. from 'felt' (which is the word given in both *Chronicle* and Chamberlin).

We proceeded on horseback about 100 miles farther than the place where the waggons stood, to see the Sesheke or river of the Borotse.[1] It is from 300 to 500 yards broad, and at the end of a remarkably dry season had a very large volume of water in it. The waves lifted the canoes and made them roll beautifully, and brought back old scenes to my remembrance. The town of Sesheke is on the opposite shore; the river itself, as near as we could ascertain by both instruments, 17° 28′ South. It overflows the country periodically for 15 miles out. Contains a waterfall called (smoke sounding) Mosiatunya,[2] the spray of which can be seen 10 or 15 miles off. There are rapids in it between Sesheke and the chief town, situated 8 days up the river, of Sebitoane's daughter, who is now in power.[3] It is a large river so far as they know it, and its general direction from Sesheke up may be gathered from the native expression, 'When you look up the river the sun rises on one cheek[4] & sets on the other'. The river of the Bashukulompo[5] is about 80 yards wide, and when it falls into the Sesheke it is called Zambesi. There are numerous rivers reported to connect the two, and all along the rivers there exists a dense population of a strong black race. Their country abounds in corn and honey, and they shew much more ingenuity in iron work, basket work, and pottery, than any of the people south of them. We have indicated in the map[6] the positions of the principal towns of these dark races, but these do not comprise all from whom Sebitoane recieved tribute.

That which claims particular attention is the fact that the slave trade

[1] The upper Zambesi, 'called by the whole of the Barotse the Liambai, or Leeambye. This we could not ascertain on our first visit, and, consequently, called the river after the town, "Sesheke". This term Sesheke means "white sand-banks", many of which exist at this part' (*Travels*, p. 208). The town was subsequently moved several times, but retained its old name; in 1853 it was located, according to D. L., at 17° 31′ 38″ S., 25° 13′ E. (*op. cit.*, p. 203).

[2] The Victoria Falls, situated 'about 4 days or 80 miles below the town of Sesheke' (see below, p. 182); first seen, and given its present name, by D. L. in November 1855.

[3] 'Hear that Mamochisane [Mma-Motsisane], Sebitoane's daughter, is successor to him in the chieftainship' (13.vii.51: *Private J.*, p. 29). The only surviving child of his senior wife, she was then living at Naliele (*op. cit.*, p. 28, n. 2).

[4] MS. has 'chief', evidently a slip of the pen, since elsewhere D. L., in quoting the 'expression', always writes 'cheek' (*Private J.*, p. 40; *Fam. Letters*, i, pp. 138, 148; and below, p. 185).

[5] The Kafue. The 'Bashukulompo' (MaShukulumbwe), who call themselves BaIla, live on both sides of the river, mostly in what is now known as Namwala district.

[6] Not located. Another, made by Oswell, is given in facsimile in *Oswell*, i, facing p. 262 (reproduced in Debenham, *The Way to Ilala*, facing p. 64). A redrawn version was published in *Bulletin de la Société de Géographie* (Paris), IV, Oct. 1852.

only began in this region during 1850.[1] A party of people called Mambari,[2] from the West, came to Sebitoane, bearing a large quantity of English printed and striped cotton clothing, [and] red, green, and blue baize of English manufacture, and with these bought from the different towns about 200 boys. They had chains & rivets in abundance, and invited the people of Sebitoane to go on a marauding expedition against the Bashukulompo by saying, 'You may take all the cattle, we will only take the prisoners'. On that expedition they met with some Portuguese, and these gave them three English guns, recieving in return at least 30 slaves. These Portuguese promised to return during this winter. The people confessed that they felt a repugnance to the traffic, but they (the Mambari & Portuguese) refused cattle for their clothing and guns. It seems to me that English manufactures might come up the Zambesi during the months of June, July, & August or September, by the hands of Englishmen & for legitimate purposes, as well as by these slave dealers for their unlawful ends. There is no danger from fever if people come after May & leave before September. The Govt. might supply information to traders on the coast. I shall write you fully on this subject, as also on another of equal importance, but at which I can only now hint.

You will see by the accompanying sketch what an immense region God has in his Providence opened up. If we can enter in and form a settlement, we shall be able in the course of a very few years to put a stop to the slave trade in that quarter. It is probable that the mere supply of English manufactures in Sebitoane's part[3] will effect this, for they did not like it and promised to abstain.

I think it will be impossible to make a fair commencement unless I can secure two years devoid of family cares. I shall be obliged to go southwards, perhaps to the Cape, in order to have my uvula excised and my arm mended[4] (the latter if it can be done only). It has occurred to

---

[1] Chamberlin, p. 151, has '1856', obviously a misprint. Oswell, reporting what D. L. had learned from Sebetwane's messengers who came to Kolobeng in Sept. 1850, writes: 'Sebitoané has only seen one of them [the Portuguese], but with the under slave-dealers he has had traffic for the last three or four years' (*Oswell*, i, p. 230, letter dated 4.iv.51).

[2] In *Travels*, p. 218, D. L. says these people 'are of the Ambonda family' (i.e. OviMbundu of Central Angola), but Dr J. T. Tucker (quoted in *Fam. Letters*, ii, p. 146) asserts that they were really 'slaves or descendants of slaves, who acted as agents for white traders'.

[3] 'on Sebituane's part' (Blaikie, p. 120).

[4] D. L.'s left arm had recovered fully from the wounds inflicted by the lion (cf. above, p. 52: 'the bone is perfectly straight and firm'); but he subsequently injured it twice, in 1844 and 1849, during building operations (*Fam. Letters*, i, pp. 104–5; ii, p. 60).

me that, as we must send our children to England soon, it would be no great additional expense to send them now along with their mother. This arrangement would enable me to proceed alone and devote about two, perhaps three, years to this new region. But I must beg your sanction, and, if you please, let it be given, or withheld, as soon as you conveniently can, so that it might meet me at the Cape.

To orphanize my children will be like tearing out my bowels, but when I can find time to write you fully you will percieve it is the only way, except giving up the region altogether. Kuruman will not answer as a residence,[1] nor yet the Colony. If I were to follow my own inclinations, they would lead me to settle down quietly with the Bakwains or some other small tribe, and devote some of my time to my children. But Providence seems to call me to the regions beyond, and if I leave them anywhere in this country it will be to let them become heathens. If you think it right to support them, I believe my parents in Scotland would attend to them otherwise.

I send you the map, but you must please to understand that it was constructed entirely for my own use, and many points are put down merely for future enquiry. I have not put down all the rich towns from which Sebitoane gets tribute, but what I have put down will give you an idea of the population. The rivers only which we have seen are likely to be correct. The others were drawn by natives on the ground or on paper,[2] and as they were drawn by many and different individuals, and all gave the same general outline, we hope the sketch may assist future observers. Please to hand a copy to Captain Steele, & another to the Royal Geographical Society. I shall write the latter soon.

The Griqua who takes this is waiting here. His waggon [is] about 12 miles down the river. I cannot detain him longer, and therefore beg leave to remain,

Affectionately yours,
David Livingston

34. To ARTHUR TIDMAN
17 October 1851

[LMS 58. Received 15 March 1852. Previous publication: Blaikie, pp. 122–3 (some disconnected extracts); Chamberlin, pp. 153–64 (many omissions)]

[1] The reason is given below, p. 190.
[2] Cf. *Private J.*, pp. 31, 33, 40.

Banks of the Zouga
17th October 1851

Dear Sir,

I wrote you a note on the 2d currt.,[1] and inclosing a rough sketch of what we believe to be the main branch of the river Zambesi sent them forward by a party of Griquas from Philipolis; and I shall now endeavour to give you a fuller and more connected account of our visit to the country of Sebitoane than it was then possible for me to furnish.

The objects I had in view in proceeding thither were not simply those of discovery. Conversation with the people Sebitoane sent out to Kolobeng last year[2] led me to the conclusion that I ought immediately to form a settlement in a hilly part of their country; & to the important ends which I still hope to see accomplished I shall in a subsequent part of this letter more particularly refer. Having been rather sanguine in my hopes of effecting a settlement, I resolved to obviate the necessity of a wearisome journey back for my family by taking my whole establishment with me, & though now obliged to return to a certain extent unsuccessful, I think I erred on the right side in attempting much. Those who may view it as a mere journey of exploration ought perhaps to remember that we bring to view a large section of the human family, and others who have tried to discover only rivers &c &c have not accomplished so much, though quite unencumbered with 'impedimenta'. The people, too, whom we visited were wonderfully well pleased with the children, and the presence of the little ones playing merrily among them was of itself sufficient to dissolve all suspicion.

We followed our old route, only diverging a little in order to visit Sekhomi in his sickness.[3] It is good policy, as well as duty, to do good as we have opportunity. Sekhomi seemed much gratified by our attention, medicines, &c, and we found his good graces of essential service to us at a subsequent part of the journey.[4] You may remember the obstructions he endeavoured to throw in our way to the discovery of the Lake, but had we not enjoyed his countenance in this trip we should either have found great difficulty in reaching Sebitoane, or failed altogether.

---

[1] That letter is, however, clearly dated '1st October' (see above, p. 174, and below, p. 181).

[2] Cf. below, p. 198, and *Travels*, pp. 76–7. They reached Kolobeng in September 1850 (*Fam. Letters*, ii, p. 103).

[3] D. L. had heard of Sekgoma's illness before leaving Kolobeng (*Fam. Letters*, ii, pp. 125, 129). 'He had a large ulcer on the pit of the stomach, the result of an abscess having burst there' (*Private J.*, p. 4).

[4] D. L. was allowed to engage one of Sekgoma's men, who subsequently helped to secure a Bushman guide from an obstructive Ngwato headman (*Private J.*, pp. 5, 9).

We left our old route at 'Nchokotsa with Bamangwato guides, and proceeding nearly due North passed over several very large salt pans, each of which is furnished with a spring of brackish water on one of its banks. Beyond these the country is covered with mopane & boabob trees, and there exists a great number of springs in soft limestone. In the vicinity of these live many Bushmen, who own the sway of Sekhomi. One of them, called Shobo, acted as our guide alone the Westerly course indicated in the sketch, and after considerable difficulty, caused by the meandering course he pursued through a sandy bushy country destitute of water, we at last reached the small river Mababi. Chombo, the headman of a Banajoa village situated on the banks of a reedy swamp (10) ten miles broad into which the Mababi flows, became our guide accross this marsh, through the river Sonta,[1] and to the banks of the Chobe. We were informed that the tsetse existed on the Sonta, but, being likewise assured that we could pass through the district inhabited by the insect by night in safety, we went through that river on the night of the 18th June, and early on the morning of the 19th unyoked on the banks of the Chobe, but found ourselves still in the midst of the venomous fly. Having swam the cattle over to an island in which the tsetse is said not to exist, we proceeded down the river in a canoe about 25 or 30 miles. Sebitoane kindly assured us that though our cattle were bitten by the tsetse, and should certainly die, he would replace them. He next proposed to take the waggons accross the river in canoes, there being no ford in the Chobe, and as the people of Mosilikatse frequently come along it seeking a passage in order to steal cattle, he was afraid they might pounce on us in one of their forays. We were quite willing to cross with the waggons, but untill he had seen them he had no idea what ponderous lumber these were. We remained two months on the banks of the Chobe without molestation from the Matibele.

Sebitoane was one of the Mantatee horde which was butchered by the Griquas in 1824 near Old Lattakoo. An old man, by whose hand old Makabba fell, very soon after our salutations were over asked why we Makoa (white men) had attacked & killed so many of them then. I replied by asking him if he had not seen a white man inviting them to come to a parley.[2] He answered, 'We saw three men on horseback capering about in front of the others'; & on my explaining their object he added, 'Then we killed ourselves not knowing what they wanted'.

---

[1] Now known as the Savuti channel, it links the Chobe River with the Mababe. For Chombo, see *Private J.*, p. 14.

[2] Before the battle started, Moffat had vainly tried to reason with the invaders and prevent any fighting (*Miss. Labours*, p. 357; *Apprenticeship*, pp. 91-2).

Long before it was day, Sebitoane was by our fire relating many of the adventures & difficulties of his most eventful life.[1] He has been fighting almost constantly for about 30 years, has several times lost all he possessed, only last year narrowly escaped drowning by his canoe being upset by an ambuscade of Matibele, but ended his days richer in cattle, & having more people subject to his sway, than any chief we know in Africa. We had two services on the following day, and to these I look back with mingled feelings of sorrow and satisfaction, for these were the only meetings he was ever well enough to attend. For many years he has been anxious to open up an intercourse with Europeans, chiefly I believe with a view to the purchase of firearms. With these he hoped to rid himself of the troublesome visits of the people of Mosilikatse. Large presents were sent to different chiefs with the request that they would guide white men to his country, and guides were actually sent down to the Zouga last year after we had left it. These were seen by Mr Oswel.[2] And others came as far as Kolobeng, but during our visit to Kuruman[3] they were in accordance with African tactics sent home again, and we experienced as much difficulty in penetrating into his country as if he had done nothing.

After, however, seeing in the opening up of a path into his country his long cherished wishes respecting European intercourse accomplished, he was seized with pneumonia, and after lingering about a fortnight in our vicinity his people removed him towards the Linyanti.[4] But while still in the way he expired in his canoe. The people recieved our condolence and advice thankfully, saying, 'Do not leave us; though Sebitoane is dead his children remain, and you must treat them as you would have done himself.' It was no part of my plan to leave soon. Messengers were dispatched to inform his son[5] & daughter of the decease of their father, and as they live near the town of the Borotse, or at least 200 miles up the river from the town of Sesheke, some time elapsed before we heard from them.

---

[1] Details are given in *Private J.*, pp. 18–22, 25–7.

[2] While hunting along the Botletle (after D. L. had left him), Oswell received a message from the BaTawana that some of Sebetwane's people 'had arrived there with orders from their captain not to return without seeing a *makooa* or white man'. He therefore went to L. Ngami and interviewed the 'guides', but could not persuade them to take him to Sebetwane: 'they asserted . . . that their chief wished to hear their report of the white man before seeing him' (*Oswell*, i, p. 215).

[3] D. L. and his family, needing recuperation, went to Kuruman in November (1850) and returned to Kolobeng in March.

[4] The village of Dinyanti (18° 17′ S., 23° 50′ E., according to *Travels*, p. 203), where Sebetwane was living at the time of his death.

[5] Sekeletu, 'a son or stepson by an inferior house' (*Private J.*, p. 29).

During the two months of our stay on the Chobe, we saw great numbers of people and obtained much valuable information. Some of that, however, jotted down on the sketch was only intended for my own guidance in future investigations. I did not intend to send that map to you, but finding I could not write you fully I presumed it would partially supply what was lacking in my note.

Sebitoane having promised to take us to see his country, and particularly a large river of which we had heard as the Sesheké, we proposed to his people after his death to take us thither. But to this they would not consent till orders came from Mamochisané (Sebitoane's daughter and his successor in the chieftainship) to treat us exactly as if the old man were still alive. We then proceeded on horseback about one hundred miles from the waggons, and were gratified exceedingly by a sight of the largest river either of us had ever seen. At the end of a remarkably dry season the water was from 300 to 500 yards broad. And though the banks are from 16 to 20 feet in height, we saw evidence of its annual flow extending fifteen miles beyond. When the wind blows waves of considerable size rise on its surface, and accidents frequently occur in crossing, in consequence of the broad side of the canoe being kept to the wind. It was quite calm when I went over to hold a service in the town in the morning, but as the time for taking an altitude of the sun approached, the waves were running so high it was only by great persuasion I could induce the people to paddle me back again. We found the Latitude to be about 17° 28′ South.

And as this river is said by the natives to flow a little beyond Sesheke southwards, then turn due East, and at a great distance is joined by the Bashukulompo or Maninché river,[1] which is only from 80 to 100 yards broad, we presume the Sesheke is the main branch of the Zambesi. Several of them informed us that beyond the junction it assumed the name Zambese. Slave dealers, either true Portuguese or bastards, have been seen on the Maninche or Bashukulompo river, but never, so far as we can ascertain, ascended the Sesheke. They may have been prevented by a waterfall situated about 4 days or 80 miles below the town of Sesheke. It is called 'Mosioatunya', or 'resounding smoke'. The noise it makes can be heard at a considerable distance, and the spray seen ten or fifteen miles off. The bed of the river immediately beyond it is narrowed by rocks, but this narrowness does not extend very far down; the river is said soon to widen, and the waters become placid again.

The Borotse had intercourse with some people in the Nor-West,

[1] The Kafue (see above, p. 176); 'Maninche' may be a local name.

who possessed abundance of European goods, before Sebitoane came into these parts.[1] *The slave trade, however, only began on the Sesheke in 1850.* A party of a tribe called the Mambari came to Sebitoané last year, carrying great quantities of English manufactured goods, viz. blue, printed, and striped cottons, blue, green, and red baize, and a few very old Portuguese muskets. They declined everything in exchange for these except boys of about fourteen years of age. The barter in these being repugnant to the Basuto or Makololo, as Sebitoane's people are called,[2] they offered both cattle and ivory, but the Mambari preferred slaves to either. They subsequently incited the Makololo to go on a foray against the Bashukulompo or Babolebotle,[3] stipulating that in consideration for the use of their guns they should recieve all the captives, while the people of Sebitoane would take all the cattle. While on this expedition the Makololo met a party of slave dealers on the Maninche, and gave them about 30 captives for three English muskets. The Mambari carried off, bound in chains, about 200 slaves, chiefly boys & girls; for though the Makololo would not part with their own children, they had no objection to sell those of the tribes living in subjection to them. Both Mambari and Portuguese were so well satisfied with their new customers they promised them a visit during the present year. We were in hopes of meeting them, but they did not come during the period we remained in the country. The price of a boy was one old Portuguese musket or about 9 yards of cotton or baize.

When we reached Sebitoane's people we were much pleased to see so many wearing European articles of clothing. And since our country's manufactures are so highly valued in the very middle of Africa, it is a pity the market cannot be supplied by legitimate commerce. There seems to be a large demand. Many tribes were mentioned to us as possessing an abundant supply. The Makololo purchased eagerly, and though they promised to refrain from traffic in slaves, the only effectual means of stopping the trade would be by supplying the market with English goods in exchange for the produce of the country.

That Christian merchants who may have enterprise enough to commence a trade in these parts would be no losers in the end may be in-

---

[1] The BaRotse (nowadays termed MaLozi) were the dominant tribe in the valley of the upper Zambesi until their conquest by Sebetwane, *c.* 1838. Cf. Gluckman, 'The Lozi of Barotseland', 1951, pp. 1, 5.

[2] Sebetwane himself belonged by origin to the BaFokeng-baPatsa, a Southern Sotho ('Basuto') tribe; but, as D. L. mentions below (p. 186), the people who accompanied him into Barotseland included members of various Tswana tribes. The name MaKololo reputedly became applied to them because Sebetwane's favourite wife was a woman 'of the Makollo tribe' (Ellenberger, *History of the Basuto*, 1912, p. 307).

[3] Apparently a nickname applied by the MaKololo to the BaIla ('Bashukulompo').

ferred from what has taken place on this river (the Zouga) since its discovery. There being formerly no market, we saw many instances of ivory rotting in the sun. The people called the tusks 'marapo hela', 'bones only', and they shared the fate of other bones. Indeed, they were much more anxious to sell a tusk worth in Grahm's Town 4/6 per lb. than to part with a goat for a larger price, the whole value of which was not more than 2/6. We know of 900 elephants having been killed on its banks since that period, and, independantly of quantities of ivory which have found their way to the Colony by other channels, a merchant at Kuruman[1] took 23,000 lbs of that article thither during the present year, and the greater portion of it came from this river alone. If one river tends to swell the amount of the commerce of the Colony, what may not be expected from numerous rivers all much more densely populated than the Zouga? The supply of this one article cannot be expected to continue always so large, but the natives readily acquire the habit of keeping articles (in expectation of the return of the trader) which at present are allowed to run to waste. The only use the ivory found on the rivers indicated in the map is turned to is the formation of armlets, and half an inch is lost in the formation of each, the saw employed being $\frac{1}{4}$ of an inch in diameter. They would all prefer brass wire to ivory for armlets. Honey abounds, but the wax is always thrown away; and the only use hitherto made of ostrich feathers is to adorn the head in dancing. The return of the slave dealer is never longed for by the poorer classes, but all classes are glad to recieve the visits of the English trader.

Since it is found profitable for those engaged in the coast trade to pass along picking up ivory, beeswax, &c &c, would it not be much more advantageous to come up the Zambesi and recieve those articles from the producers themselves? I venture to put this forth, though entirely ignorant of the commerce on the coast. But I feel assured, if our merchants could establish a legitimate commerce on the Zambesi they would soon drive the slave dealer from the market, and be besides great gainers in the end. Europeans may come up the Zambesi in the months *June, July, & August*. We had frost on the Chobe in June & July. But no one ought to venture sooner. September is safer as respects liability to being seized by fever than May. Would the Government supply this information to those engaged in the coast trade? Or would it be better to wait untill I can point out, by my own residence in & knowledge of the country & climate, a spot of known healthiness & easy of access by the Sesheké, to which commercial men might be invited to carry their

---

[1] David Hume (see above, p. 9).

enterprise? The Portuguese have a sanatorium far in the Interior, and Tete[1] is reported comparatively healthy. The history of our stations renders it doubtful whether the rearing of such is the best way of propagating Christianity, comfortable establishments presenting such strong temptations to remain, though the tribes for which they were reared have departed. And though I have undergone much fatigue & manual labour in rearing three such, I would cheerfully undergo much more if it would prove a sanatorium for more unhealthy districts. Let it once be found that Christian missionaries and Christian merchants can remain throughout the year in the Interior of the continent, & in ten years the slave dealer will be driven out of the market.

In referring to the countries drained by the Zambesi, I concieve we speak of a large section of the slave-producing region of Africa. Of this, however, you will be better able to judge when I state that the towns of the Borotse and Mamochisané are situated 8 days above that of Sesheke, and the people know the river as very large at least 8 days or other 200 miles beyond. Its direction may be guessed at by the drawings of the natives always indicating a great deal of Northing, and their expression is, 'When we look up the river as far as we know it, the sun rises on one cheek and sets on the other'. And its size may be inferred from an independant fact. Seunturu, the chief of the Borotse whom Sebitoané expelled,[2] made a canoe, of planks sown together, which was so large it required 20 men to paddle it. It was roofed in with cloth, & Sebitoane's people distroyed it. The only obstruction to navigation above Sesheke consists in a series of four rapids, but the natives manage to drag their canoes along the bank when opposite them, & others might do the same.

Several of the rivers which connect the Bashukulompo & Sesheke are said to be as large as the Chobe, and that being from 12 to 15 feet deep, & from 40 to 50 yards wide, were its course not so very winding a small steamer might sail on it. The roots of the reeds preventing it from encroaching on the land, it is as deep two feet from the bank as in the middle. Several of our people, in stepping out of canoes into what appeared a few inches of water, were surprised to find themselves plomp in up to the neck. The Lonta has light-coloured water, and when it flows into the Liambae the clear water of the latter flows on some dis-

---

1 'The farthest inland station of the Portuguese' in East Africa (see below, p. 302); situated on the Zambesi R. at 16° 10′ S., 33° 35′ E.

2 Better known as Mulambwa, 'Santuru' (as D. L. calls him in *Travels*) was chief of the MaLozi *c.* 1780–1830 (Gluckman, op. cit., p. 2). The traditional version is that he died before the Kololo conquest, which was in fact facilitated by a dispute among his sons for the succession (Jalla, *Litaba za Ma-Lozi*, 1934, pp. 39, 41).

tance in the same channel unmixed.[1] The Lobale, whether river or lake,[2] is always spoken of as the source of all the water, and both it, the Moeng or Moenye, Macoma,[3] &c &c, have numerous tribes on their banks. And all are well supplied with guns & clothing from the West or North-West. Seunturu formerly sent people up to the Lobale to barter for crockery, cloth, &c.

All the rivers indicated in the sketch are navigable by canoes. They are inhabited by a black race. They are deep chested, and their muscular system is largely developed. The Bechuana who live among them appear a puny sickly set. And, indeed, those who came in with Sebitoane are fast dying out. In our ride to Sesheke we saw more people moving about in one day than we should have seen in ten in any part of the Bechuana country as yet supplied with missionaries. I have noted only a portion of the towns, and these only the large and rich ones. More might have been added, for some we saw contained a larger population than any of our chief missionary stations.

This black race speak a language quite distinct from that of the Bechuana. There are many dialects of it, and if I may judge by a comparison of 300 words collected from the Bayeiye or Bakoba, and about an equal number from each of the following tribes, Bashubea, Barotse, Batōka, Banyeñiko, Bamaponda, and Balojazé, it sustains the same relation to Sitchuana as the Latin does to the English.[4] The different dialects differ from each other as much as Provincial English does from broad Scotch. Sebitoane has done good service by introducing the Sitchuana. His people being a mixed multitude of Basuto, Bakwains, Bamangwato, & the Black races, we found people who could readily understand us everywhere. It is probable a good expressive language will spring out of the materials he has brought together.[5]

The Black race designate the Supreme Being by the name Nyampi or Reza. The latter is identical with the Oreeja of the Bayeiye. If a

[1] 'Lonta', as used here, is the Zambesi above its junction with the Kabompo (D. L.'s 'Liambae'); cf. *Private J.*, pp. 41, 219.

[2] Cf. *Private J.*, p. 29: 'What is Lobale? Is it a Lake or river?' It is, in fact, the region immediately N.W. of Barotseland, inhabited by the tribes collectively termed BaLuvale.

[3] 'Moenye' (Mwenyi) and 'Macoma' (Makoma) are the names, not of rivers, but of tribes living on the banks of the Luanginga, a tributary of the upper Zambesi (cf. *Private J.*, pp. 41, 212).

[4] The tribes listed (BaSubiya, BaRotse, BaToka, BaNyengo, MaMbunda, and BaLuchazi) all speak Bantu languages of the 'Central' or 'West-Central' zones, whereas Tswana belongs to the 'South-Eastern' zone (Doke, *Bantu*, 1945, pp. 31, 74, 105). D. L.'s vocabularies are described more fully in *Private J.*, pp. 30–1.

[5] A sound prophecy. Lozi, a modified form of Kololo, is now the *lingua franca* in Barotseland.

person dies, they say he is 'lifted' by Nyampi or by the Lord (Morena).[1] It is remarkable that, of those who were found about 30 years ago destitute of the knowledge of God & futurity, no specimen now occurs. But they are degraded low enough in the scale of humanity, and no one more than the African needs the humanizing influence of the gospel of Christ. Having this message to deliver to these lost souls, we can go anywhere in safety. A merchant can do the same. We each have an end in view which appears feasible to all. But slave dealers produce discord and a feeling of insecurity wherever they go. The Mambari felt it necessary to hoist a white flag when they came to the Makololo. We must however give the slave dealer his due. The Mambari came all decently clothed in European clothing. We have never seen a party of Bechuana of which as much could be said. Civilization, the lower end of our missions, ought perhaps to sink lower still. If the love of Christ enters the heart, civilization follows in due course.

You will by this time be able to understand the course matters took. We could not cross the Chobe at first, and before any plan could be proposed Sebitoane fell sick and died. We waited for Mamochisané the queen, but she having been in childbed could not come. All the people were pleased with the prospect of our remaining with them. They even promised to plant for us, and they will do it too. The chief next in power was sent down to us to act in her behalf. But we ascertained that the hilly part to which they were willing to go was without defence from the Matibele, and Mosilikatse constantly sends expeditions against them. Their deep reedy rivers are a protection. It would have been wrong in me to remove them thither merely for my safety.

Then the rainy season was at hand, and should the Chobe fill so would the Sonta behind us. The Chobe rises 8 or 10 feet in perpendicular height, and should the Sonta rise three we should be brought to a standstill on its banks, and every ox would be bitten by the tsetse. The Chobe ought to have filled during our stay, and that it did not was ascribed by the people to the death of Sebitoane. The drought which has prevailed over the whole country probably extended to the sources of the river. Then would it be right to expose my family on swamps of an extent such as we never dreamed? The whole country is one vast level intersected by numerous rivers, and when these fill, as they do periodically, all the country we saw must present the appearance of an immense marsh with numerous islands scattered over its surface. The

[1] *Nyambe* ('Nyampi') and *Leza* ('Reza', 'Oreeja') are names widely used for the Supreme Being in various parts of Central Africa; *morena* is the Tswana word for 'lord, master', but may also be used for God (more correctly, *Modimo*).

highest land is raised above the surrounding low annually flooded country by only a few feet. We saw earthen dykes for catching fish about a mile beyond where our waggons stood.

And though both Mrs L. and myself did and do still regret leaving so soon, had we remained till another moon should enable us to travel through the tsetse by night, this would have been no protection, for we were informed that as soon as the nights become warm the insect bites by night as well as by day. We seem to have reached the limits of waggon travelling, at least of such heavy vehicles as this country furnishes. Mr Oswel would have proceeded along one of the numerous rivers had it been possible, but bogs and tsetse presented insuperable barriers. I regret this the more, as I had hopes that he would find a passage for us down to the coast while I was prosecuting my mission among the Makololo. We returned, as we had hitherto travelled, together, he assisting us in every possible way. May God reward him. The route through Shobo's country being now impracticable, we came down the Tamunakle, and crossing it wended our way along its Southern bank.

I need not say anything about the importance of immediate action in reference to this highway into the Interior. Considering the immense distance we have to traverse before we reach the country of the Zambesi, the existence of the African fever (one child has been attacked by it three times on this river in our progress down), the nature of the country (all swampy except where Mosilikatse extends his forays, and beyond the Borotse), it seems as if it only remained for us to make an effort for a settlement in the latter direction. Less than two years' absence, and entire freedom from domestic care, will not suffice for even a feasible effort. The tokens of Divine care which have been already bestowed, and a full conviction that I am in the path of duty, induce me to offer myself for the service.

There are considerations for, and others against, my doing so. I shall mention some of the latter first. Some of the bretheren do not hesitate to tell the natives that my object is to obtain the applause of men. This bothers me, for I sometimes suspect my own motives. Then, after our return last year, Mrs L. was delivered of a daughter. An epidemic was raging in the town at the time. The child was seized by it and cut off at the age of six weeks. The mother had an attack of paralysis of the right side of the face. One eyelid was motionless, and the mouth was drawn to the opposite side. As the uvula was unaffected, I was of opinion that it was the result of inflammation spreading along the bone from some carious teeth producing pressure on the nerves as they issue from their foramina, & that rest, counter-irritation, & tonics, were the proper treatment. We went to Kuruman, and the complaint was partially removed. I postponed my own wants, & did not proceed to the Cape in order to have my uvula excised, in order to allow her rest. The death [of] the child and complaint of the mother have both been charged to my account, and I have been asked if the 'loss of one child, &c &c, was not enough to satisfy me'. This & other severe expressions have been used even by those whom I esteem.[1] Then, again, my predilictions are for a quiet life. I love the Bakwains, and believe the affection is reciprocal (we never had a disagreement), and I should prefer to attend to the instruction of my own children to sending them away from me. There is also the consideration that, as you cannot very well realize the distances I have to travel before I reach the field, I may appear more as a traveller than a missionary.

On the other hand, I am conscious that, though there is much impurity in my motives, they are in the main for the glory of Him to whom I have dedicated my all. I never anticipated fame from the discovery of the Lake. I cared very little about it. But the sight of the Tamunakle, and the report of other large rivers beyond, all densely populated, awakened many and enthusiastic feelings. The loss, or rather removal, of the child was a sore trial to me. It was the first death in our family; but was just as likely to happen had we remained at home, and we have now one of our number in Heaven.

Providence has not favoured our settlement at Kolobeng. The necessaries of life cannot be raised there by either ourselves or people. The Kolobeng has dried up, and it is absolutely necessary that the people remove somewhere else. I cannot attach one particle of blame to them for moving up the river. But then the important question comes before me, am I to build again for them? If there had been abundance of food for the Bakwains at Kolobeng, they would not have removed, and I should have remained with them. But the want of food has compelled them to remove a few miles off, and, as there is just as little probability of their obtaining a subsistence there, it would be labour in vain for me to build another house. In all probability they will be compelled to move again. The Bakwains promised fairly, and I by no means give up the hope that they will recieve the gospel; but they have been so pinched by hunger and badgered by the Boers they could not or rather they had too good an excuse for not attending to instruction.

Then, again, when we consider the multitudes which in the Providence of God have been brought to light in the country of Sebitoane,

---

[1] The quotation is from a reproachful letter written to D. L. by Mrs Moffat, and copied by him into *Private J.* (q.v., pp. 70–1).

the probability that in our efforts to evangelize we shall put a stop to the slave trade in a large region, and by means of the highway into the North which we have discovered bring unknown nations under the sympathies of the Christian world, if I were to choose my lot it would be to reduce this new language, translate the Bible into it, and be the means of forming a small church. Let this be accomplished, I think I could then lie down and die contented.

Two years' absence will be necessary. Kuruman is unsuitable as a residence for my family. It is too near. The reports made & circulated by the natives would render my wife miserable. She is again threatened by symptoms of paralysis, but now they extend down the whole side even to the toes. Frequent pregnancies will in all probability aggravate the complaint.[1] And as the children must go home for education, I believe it would be the best policy for her to take them to England herself. This step would give me time for the important service referred to above, and the voyage would probably restore her to her former strength. Nothing but a strong conviction that the step will tend to the glory of Christ would make me orphanize my children. Even now my bowels yearn over them. They will forget me. But I hope that when the day of trial comes I shall not be found a more sorry soldier than those who serve an earthly sovreign.

Should you not feel yourselves justified in incurring the expense of their support in England, I shall feel called upon to renounce the hope of carrying the gospel into that country, and labour among those who live in a more healthy country, viz. the Bakwains. But stay, I am not sure. So powerfully convinced am I that it is the will of the Lord I should, I will go, no matter who opposes. But from you I expect nothing but encouragement. I know you wish as ardently as I can that all the world may be filled with the glory of God. I feel relieved when I lay the whole case before you.

As it is probable some alterations will take place in our Colonial missions, could a stout young man from one of the older stations not be spared to take the burden of printing off Mr Ashton's hands, and allow him to occupy a new station, say at the Bamangwato? This tribe is very numerous. I counted 900 huts in passing, and there are two considerable villages close by. There are at least 6,000 souls in the locality. Numbers of these are Makalaka who have fled from the tyranny of

---

[1] D. L. does not mention that his wife had very recently (15 September) given birth to another child (named William Oswell), which was the reason for his remaining several weeks on the banks of the Botletle (*Private J.*, pp. 68–9; *Fam. Letters*, ii, p. 139).

Mosilikatse. Should they ever return to their own country, they would carry the knowledge of Christ with them. The Bamangwato have the custom of spreading themselves through the whole Bakalihari country and living for months among that people. We found a number of them among the Bushmen at Shobo's place. It seems a most desirable point for diffusing the knowledge of the Gospel. It is a healthy country too, and if taken up would form a link between me and the world, untill we have found a path down to the coast. The proposal is somewhat selfish, but I have often thought that large mass of people had claims on our sympathy. Mr Ashton would be immediately useful in consequence of knowing the language, and any young missionary could be immediately useful at Kuruman in consequence of the printing being easy of acquisition. Sekhomi the chief has a bad name, but scarcely deserves it. He has always behaved to me with extreme kindness. Mr Ashton might be persuaded to go if the persuasion came from you.

I feel the more anxious for a connecting link, because the bretheren who have advanced some way into the Interior do not feel it their duty to take any notice of us, except in the way of disapprobation. Indeed, I fear it will become manifest in the day of final account that ungodly insinuations, freely launched out against Sechele when his conduct was irreproachable, have proved a hindrance to the gospel of Christ.[1]

Bamangwato, 14th November

I beg leave to acknowledge the receipt of your letter dated 1st March '51, and thank you unfeignedly for the encouragement it affords to proceed in the path to which I concieved I was called by Providence. It affords me no ordinary satisfaction to find that you entertain the same views as actual observation and comparison of the claims of the Southern & Northern regions have led me to adopt.

The map sent was not intended for you. The large sprawling things put down as rivers were for the eyes of natives, who on being questioned understand a great sea-serpent looking thing better than an ordinary drawn river. The Sesheke is however a magnificent river. I think we are under rather than over the mark in calling it 500 yards broad. I shall write the Royal Geographical Society before I reach Kolobeng.[2] I shall acknowledge Captain Steele's present too.

I wish you had proposed the Dictionary of Sitcuana sooner. I col-

[1] D. L. maintained that Sechele's backsliding was due, at least partly, to 'the railing accusations of Mr Inglis' (see below, p. 230, and *Fam. Letters*, ii, p. 181).

[2] The letter, addressed to Steele, was published (with a few interspersed extracts from the present one) in *JRGS*, 1852, pp. 163–73. It gives many additional details about the journey, country, and people.

lected some materials for such a work many years ago, but, not being aware whether I should be able to procure funds for the printing of it, other objects engrossed my attention & induced me to lay it aside. If I should be prevented from entering the new region I shall recommence it with pleasure. If honoured to commence a work on the Zambesi, the new language will engross all my energies. But you will hear from me again on this point.

I have been advised of £20 paid by Sir Culling Earldly Earldly[1] to my account, and return thanks. I ordered £10 worth of books from Mr Snow, & requested him to apply to you for the money. Will you be kind enough to request Mr Snow to send me out this year's ('51) 'British Banner',[2] bound in cloth, and continue to send ½ yearly volumes of the same along with the missionary publications?

[End of letter cut away, probably for autograph]

[1] Sir Culling Eardley Eardley (1805–63), 'religious philanthropist' (*D.N.B.*), Treasurer of the LMS 1844–63. The £20 was a contribution 'towards the expenses of Dr. Livingston's proposed visit to the Lake Ngami' (*Report*, 1851, p. ix).

[2] A nonconformist weekly, published in London since 1848, to which D. L. had contributed two articles (about the Boers) in 1849. Cf. *Private J.*, p. 298.

VI

INTERLUDE AT THE CAPE

35. To ARTHUR TIDMAN
17 March 1852

[LMS 60. Received 8 May 1852. Previous publication: Campbell, pp. 90, 134–7 (incomplete); Chamberlin, pp. 164–8 (incomplete)]

Cape Town
17th March 1852[1]

My dear Sir,

The following statement was penned with the intention of transmitting it to our departed friend the Revd. J. J. Freeman.[2] He was intimately acquainted with our pecuniary circumstances in this country, and recommended me to draw £25 or £30 annually more than the usual salary to meet the extra expenses which our peculiar position involves, and as Mrs Livingstone[3] & family would come into his department while in England a full statement for his information & guidance seemed necessary.

It is scarcely worth while again to refer you to the peculiar obstacles which must be overcome before we can plant the gospel in the densely populated country drained by the Zambesi. The swampy boggy nature of a region more than 200 miles in breadth, the tsetse, the death of Sebitoane, the deep rivers, and the fever, prevented our proceeding at once to a part of the salubrity of which we could entertain a hope. The impropriety of removing the people from the only defences against the annual forays of the Matibele, and the fact that Sebitoane's people (who were composed of Basutos, Bamangwato, Bakwain, & other tribes) have nearly all fallen victims to the fever, led me to the conclusion that separation from my family had become absolutely necessary, for though I may be justified in risking my own life in the service of our

---

[1] After spending three weeks at Kuruman, which they left in the middle of January, D. L. and his family had reached Cape Town on 16 March (*Private J.*, pp. 79, 80).

[2] Freeman had died of rheumatic fever on 8.ix.51 (*Chronicle*, xv, 1851, p. 232). He was then Home Secretary of the LMS, hence the reference below to 'his department'.

[3] As Chamberlin mentions (p. 164, n. 2), 'This is the first example in this correspondence' of D. L.'s adding 'e' to his name.

Master I may not use the same freedom with the lives of my wife and children.

As much less expense will be incurred in procuring education for the children in England than there would be in Cape Town, the propriety of deciding for the former will appear evident. Their mother was affected by total loss of motion in the whole of the right side of the head & face, and has frequently been threatened by symptoms of paralysis in the whole of the right side and extremities; and, though now partially recovered, as the eldest of the children[1] is only six years of age it seems right, on account of both parent and children, that the expense of a voyage should be incurred. A residence in England of two or three years would prevent the frequent confinements which, notwithstanding the preaching of Dr Malthus & Miss Martineau,[2] periodically prevail and aggravate the complaint; and besides the probable establishment of her health, [and] the consolation of knowing that the children enjoyed a mother's care in passing from the extreme heat to which they have been exposed under many a bush in the wilderness to a cold & variable climate, time also will be given to me to form a Mission in some healthy locality in the Borotse country or beyond. I hope in that time, too, to be able to solve some interesting problems in relation to the slave trade, my full conviction being that this nefarious traffic will be abolished by the influence of Christian Missions, and that the London Missionary Society may hold as prominent a place as it did in the emancipation of the Hottentots.[3]

We have been six months in travelling from Sebitoane's country to the Cape, the whole of our stoppages not amounting to so many weeks. The weary way between either that country and the Kuruman, or the same country & the Cape, presents few inducements for me to trudge it over again after only a few months' sojourn there. If I am spared for two years I may be permitted to establish a Mission, and also find a way to the sea on either the East or West coast. If so far favoured by Him on whose Providence all depends, the long irksome land journey would be avoided & much time saved. The act of orphanizing my children, which

---

[1] Robert, born at Mabotsa early in January 1846 (*Fam. Letters*, i, p. 160); died 1865, of wounds received while fighting for the Federal Army in the American Civil War, and was buried 'in the great national cemetery of Gettysburg' (Blaikie, p. 340). For details of his history, cf. Seaver, *David Livingstone*, 1957, pp. 452–5.

[2] Thomas Robert Malthus (1766–1834) and Harriet Martineau (1802–76), writers *inter alia* on population problems.

[3] In 1828 the Government of Cape Colony had issued an Ordinance cancelling various restrictive laws hitherto applying to Hottentots and other coloured people, and placing them 'in all respects politically on a level with Europeans'; this measure was due very largely to the efforts of Dr Philip (Theal, *History*, v, pp. 502–3).

now becomes painfully near, will be like tearing out my bowels, for they will all forget me. But I feel it is a duty to Him who did much more for us than that. His command is, Go ye into all the world & preach the gospel to every creature. Forbid it, that we should ever consider the holding a commission from the King of Kings a sacrifice, so long as men esteem the same from an earthly sovereign[1] an honour.

I thought at one time that the family might proceed to Scotland at once, in order to be under the care of my parents, but they have been subjected to so much heat of late I believe the first winter must be spent in the South of England. The thermometer stood on the Zouga at 104° in the coolest part we could find in & under the waggon. Thomas had the fever three times in coming down that river. Agnes has since been ill from malaria inhaled on its banks. If I could support them in England I would not request an additional allowance for the purpose. I have no stock on hand, and though a Scotchman I have not yet availed myself of our lamented friend's suggestion, except in the way of over-drawing in order to defray extra expenses incurred in travelling.

With the exception of a few books & some clothing from home, every farthing of the salary has been spent economically in the prosecu-tion of my work. And besides the extra expenses, all of which some charge to the Society as 'travelling expenses', we have large losses in oxen by the 'tsetse'. Indeed, so far from having anything to meet the present emergency, but for the disinterested kindness of Mr Oswel we could not have come down to the Cape. He presented supplies for last year's journey worth £40, for that to Sebitoane upwards of £20, also a waggon worth £55. I recieved also from a chief a present of three elephant tusks worth £18. But one waggon was worn out, and I was obliged to purchase another for £80,[2] and for oxen to go to Sebitoane's I paid £47. New waggon sails £10. These are torn to tatters by each trip. I have paid off nearly all our cows to extra drivers, leaders, &c. Most of our oxen[3] are dead, and but for Mr O. presenting a number worth about £60 we could not have come down to the Cape.

In consequence of being obliged to hire fresh oxen[4] & other un-avoidable expenses, we have gnawed into the salary of 1853 a gap of £57. The whole of the present year's salary had been previously drawn for oxen, waggon repairs,[5] wages, &c &c. The expenses incurred in

---

[1] 'esteem the service of an earthly sovereign' (Campbell, p. 136).

[2] From C. A. Green (see above, p. 165). The wagon presented by Oswell had been acquired in 1846 (*Fam. Letters*, i, p. 182).

[3] 'Most of our own' (Chamberlin, p. 166).

[4] 'to have fresh oxen' (Chamberlin, p. 166).

[5] 'waggon & repairs' (Chamberlin, p. 166).

Cape Town will leave nothing remaining of the salary of 1853. The whole of the salary for 1852 was previously spent. I have now to crave your indulgence with respect to this overdrawing. I cannot possibly pay my people, and go back with supplies of meal,[1] tea, & coffee, unless I draw the salaries of '53 and '54. We have used no delicacies of any kind besides the above. I have been a teetotaller for 20 years. We think all the money drawn has been well spent when we could procure the articles we needed from Colesberg, though to the cost price we had to add land carriage for 500 miles.

It has been with very great reluctance I have been compelled to foredraw, and I should consider it a favour to be allowed time only to make it up. But the question will force itself on the mind, How is it that a Mission in the paltry village of Colesberg, already supplied with a Wesleyan & a Gospel Propagation Society's missionary and a Dutch Reformed minister, is allowed to draw on an average more than twice as much as a Mission 500 miles beyond the same market? This question stirs up our Scotch propensities amazingly, for we know that that Mission does not include $\frac{1}{25}$ part of the population of one of the Interior tribes. There is no itinerancy. There is not even the tear and wear of body involved in tying a few letters together for the bretheren beyond. We have to pay an agent both at Algoa Bay and at Colesberg to recieve all our letters & parcels. In the former place Mr Robson[2] informed me, eleven years ago, that he had given standing orders to the postwoman just to forward all missionary letters. The only benefit which has arisen through all these years in letters being addressed to his care has been an additional fourpence on each. But such thoughts I strive to drive from the mind.

I may, however, mention to you that Mr Moffat is suffering from an affection of the head, which I fear will eventually lay him aside. My opinion, expressed to him with sufficient earnestness, was that he ought to lay aside his translation and seek the re-establishment of his health in total relaxation on the sea coast, but I fear his finances, being in the same state as my own, has prevented compliance with my suggestions. Some of the knowing ones believe him to be rich, because he once recieved some money from the sale of his book, but that is all long since spent. And my private opinion, which I express to you in confidence, is that there is some probability of a valuable life being lost through the *injustice* of the London Missionary Society. Observe the word I use,

---

[1] 'meat' (Campbell, p. 137).

[2] Adam Robson (1794–1870), LMS missionary at Port Elizabeth since 1832 (*Register*, p. 24). D. L. had met him there in 1841, before proceeding to Kuruman.

'*injustice*'. Please to remember that I love the Society, and sympathize with the Executive in the difficulties which the stingy spirit out of doors throws in its way. But what but out & out injustice could induce you to charge the expense of the voyage of his son John[1] to his account, while the same item would have been put down to the general expenses of the Society had he been the son of Mr Christie[2] or Mr anyone else? A number of other items I know press heavily on his spirits. And we have published documents shewing that none of these would plague us if we took up our residence at the petty villages of Colesberg or Somerset[3] or Uitenhage or Bethelsdorp.[4] Who in England would believe that the average expenses of Bethelsdorp should be £224, of Colesberg £211, of Uitenhage £231, while the 'Apostle of the Bechuanas' draws on an average not much over £100?

My dear Dr Tidman, do look into this subject. Compare Colesberg & Kuruman, and if possible prevent the character of the Society being damaged by the knowledge of such inequality oozing out. The missionaries beyond the Colony who make triennial visits to Colesberg & Grahamstown must be distinguished from such as do not. The profit made by the plan[5] is equal to 9 months' pay, though an equal number of months are lost to the Society.

The expenses of outfit have been borne by a friend.[6] It amounted to £70. We were a queer looking set when we came to Cape Town. Clothes eleven years out of the fashion. We all needed being clad anew. The expenses of the voyage must be defrayed by you.

We shall write by next steamer and inform you by what ship Mrs L. and family will come. I return as soon as they are shipped.

Affectionately yours,
David Livingston

---

[1] John Smith Moffat (1835–1918) had sailed for England in March 1850 to attend school in Newcastle upon Tyne (*Fam. Letters*, ii, p. 82).

[2] George Christie (1802–70), LMS missionary at Hankey 1850–3; son-in-law of Dr Philip (*Register*, p. 30).

[3] Somerset East (32° 44′ S., 25° 35′ E.), an LMS mission station since 1841.

[4] About 9 miles N.W. of Port Elizabeth; an LMS station since 1802.

[5] 'by the place' (Chamberlin, p. 168).

[6] Oswell (cf. *Fam. Letters*, ii, p. 80, and below, p. 204).

36. To DAVID LIVINGSTON
14 April 1852

[LMS: Outgoing Letters, Africa, Box 7, pp. 468–70]

London
April 14th, 1852

Dear Brother,

We received in due course your several letters of April 30th 1851 from Boatlanama, & of the 1st & 17th Oct. ult. from the banks of the Zouga.

Through these interesting communications we have been put into possession of many important facts concerning the new & populous regions which you have been engaged in exploring, the course & related position of the numerous rivers that intersect the country, the habits & dispositions of the various tribes that dwell on their banks, the influence of climate, & other considerations bearing on the great practical question as to how far these discoveries are likely, in the good Providence of God, to open a way for the extension of Missionary effort.

Considering the repeated disappointments you have experienced in the attempt to establish a Mission among the Bakwain, we can feel little surprised that you should be desirous to direct your attention to other more promising localities, and altho' that consideration alone might not be sufficient to justify the measures proposed in your correspondence, yet, when we further bear in mind the severe trials that have recently overtaken our Missions in the regions beyond the Colony,[1] & the consequent derangement of the plans of many of our Missionary brethren, we cannot but foresee that the time may not be far distant when some of their number may be in a position to seek for other fields of enterprise. This view of the subject gives additional importance to any attempts that may be made to introduce the Gospel into the newly-explored regions.

The fact also that Sebitoane's country has already been visited by the Agents of that inhuman traffic which has so long been the curse & opprobrium of Western & Central Africa forms a most convincing

---

[1] The outbreak of the 'Eighth Kafir War' at the end of 1850 had been followed, *inter alia,* by the destruction of several mission stations, and also by the rebellion of many Hottentots on the Kat River Settlement; in consequence, some missionaries had been forced to flee from their posts (*Report,* 1851, pp. 15–16; 1852, pp. 13–15, 64–5).

5. J. J. FREEMAN

argument why the ground should be occupied without any avoidable delay by the Xtian. Missy. & the legitimate trader. We are happy to perceive that at present there is no disposition on the part of the Native tribes to encourage the slave trader, & we feel persuaded that the influence of the first Missionaries who may settle in the country would soon prevail to put it down, if not by exposing its atrocity at least by convincing the Natives that it would be greatly to their advantage to give the preference to the lawful trader.

We have given our best consideration to your proposal to send Mrs Livingston & your children to this country for a season, in order that you may be left at entire liberty for the space of say two years to prosecute your investigations in the regions that have been laid open to you. We deeply sympathise with you in the prospect of so extended a separation from those you love, but as the sacrifice seems to be an indispensable condition to the accomplishment of your object, & as a sea voyage seems to offer the most likely means for reestablishing Mrs L.'s health, we cannot but acquiesce in the propriety of your decision, & under the circumstances of the case we shall be happy to relieve you from the expenses connected with the voyage of your family to this country.

But with reference to the important ends contemplated in the present enterprise, with a view to ascertain the practical facilities offered in these new regions for Missionary operations on a more or less extensive scale, we have arrived at the decided conclusion that for many reasons it would be highly inexpedient that you should attempt the enterprise *alone*, and in this judgment you will doubtless heartily concur. We have accordingly Resolved:

That, in the judgment of the Board, it is indispensable that Dr. Livingston should be accompanied by a suitable coadjutor, if possible a Missionary, in his proposed journey into the interior of S. Africa, and they therefore earnestly recommend him to adopt measures in concert with his brethren of the Bechuana Mission for that purpose.

Mr Ashton, as you have yourself suggested, would in our opinion be a most suitable person to unite with you in the undertaking,[1] provided he could be disengaged for so long a period from his labours in the press, which in the present advanced state of Scripture revision by Mr Moffat might present an obstacle not easy to be overcome. This is a point we must therefore necessarily leave to be decided by yourself & the Brethren on a deliberate view of all the circumstances of the case; & in the earnest hope that in all your plans for giving effect to this important

[1] D. L. had in fact merely suggested that Ashton should establish a mission station among the BaNgwato (see above, p. 190).

enterprise you may be guided by the wisdom that cometh from above, & that the issue may be such as to redound to the Divine glory & to promote the great objects of Christian philanthropy by introducing the Gospel & its attendant blessings among the thousands of the African race yet in darkness and degradation,

I remain, Dear Brother,

Yours very truly,

Arthur Tidman

Forn. Secy., London Missionary Society

We have sent extracts from your correspondence to the Geog[raphica]l Soc[iet]y, & shall be happy to furnish that Socy. with fresh information as it comes to hand; but, in order to give additional attractions to your reports, we would suggest that you keep a regular journal recording any remarkable events, notices of the manners & customs of the different tribes, the natural history of the country, & other topics, which, as the result of observation at the time, are more likely to prove of permanent interest & value than the more vague & general impressions conveyed in a hastily written letter.

37. To ARTHUR TIDMAN
26 April 1852

[LMS 63. Received 7 July 1852. Previous publication: Chamberlin, pp. 168-170 (first three paragraphs)]

Cape Town

26th April 1852

My dear Sir,

The chief object of this letter is to advise you of the departure of Mrs Livingston and four children on board the 'Trafalgar', Captain D. Robertson, bound for London. She sailed on the 23d currt., and as this goes by the Royal Mail Steamer which will sail on the first of May you will in all probability recieve this before Mrs Livingston's arrival.[1]

In thus committing my family to your care, I may state that nothing but the fullest convictions of duty would have led me to adopt this step, but having already addressed you twice on this subject, and by full and explicit statements endeavoured to furnish data on which to form your

---

[1] She reached England on 23 June (see below, p. 206, and *Chronicle*, xvi, (Aug.) 1852, p. 185). This suggests that D. L.'s letter may have missed the mail steamer of 1 May, since it was not received in London until 7 July.

own judgement, I feel the less inclined to advert to the subject again. Your silence, however, makes me fear that my letters may have miscarried, and I shall add that our children have claims on those by whom *we* are sent.

It is well known that the laws of God avenge themselves on those by whom they are contemned. They resemble two-edged swords when caught by the blades. The emigrant Boers, who dispise the law of benevolence enuntiated in the declaration that God hath made of one blood all the nations of the Earth, are themselves becoming as degraded as the natives whom they despise. A slave population everywhere works the ruin and degradation of the free class which employs it. Tyranny and every other form of vice reproduce themselves, and the moral contagion spreads like leaven[1] by means of the children. It is but just that such contagion should infect those who fear not the vengeance of the divine laws or of Him who is their author. But missionaries expose their children to a contamination which they have had no hand in producing. We expose them and ourselves for a time, in order to elevate those sad captives of sin and Satan who are the victims of the degradation of ages. None of those who complain about missionaries sending their children home ever descend to this. And again, as Mr James in his 'Young Men from Home'[2] forcibly shews, a greater misfortune cannot befall a youth than to be cast into the world entirely without a home. In regard to even the vestige of a home my children are absolutely vagabonds. 'When shall we return to Kolobeng? When to Kuruman?' '*Never*. The mark of Cain is on your foreheads. Your father is a missionary.' Our children ought to have both the sympathies and prayers of those at whose bidding we become strangers for life.

I intend to leave during the course of the next week.[3] I need scarcely again advert to the plans which in consequence of what I believe to be the direct leadings of Providence I have been led to form. In passing to the distant region to which I feel called, I shall have to mourn over the defection of Sechele, now more apparent than ever. By letters which I have recieved since I have come to Cape Town, I learn that Sechele has plundered an Englishman whom he believed to have killed one of his people. I have little doubt but such is the fact, the Englishman being a person of immoral character, and the companion of the missing native declares that the Englishman inflicted injuries sufficient to terminate

---

[1] 'like leaves' (Chamberlin, p. 169).
[2] *The Young Man from Home*, 2nd ed., London 1840; by John Angell James (1785–1859), minister at Carr's Lane Chapel, Birmingham (*D.N.B.*).
[3] In fact, he did not leave until 8 June (*Private J.*, p. 84).

life & then left him.[1] Two companions of this same man (Moyle) have perished in suspicious circumstances.[2] One of them, named Dolman, perished near the Kolobeng, but being in the way to Cape Town at the time of his death I can give no particulars.

The plunder of Moyle by Sechele is quite unjustifiable, and as I stated before I believe Sechele is an apostate. He cannot be referred to as a trophy of grace. But never did man bid fairer for years to enter into the Kingdom of Heaven than he. You will see no success in that region so long as Inglis and Edwards are your missionaries. It would be absurd to expect the Divine blessing. I am sorry to write so, but it is the truth, and truth which ought to be known by the Directors. I do not wish to be or appear censorious, but, were I now placed in the most solemn circumstances, my past experience of the vicinity of these men would lead me to declare that it is a mere waste of life to labour near them. Eight years' experience has only strengthened the conviction that our Society would be incalculably more useful were there a safety valve by which such characters might be let off.

Believe me,
affectionately yours,
David Livingston

38. To ARTHUR TIDMAN
26 April 1852

[LMS 62. Received 7 July 1852. Previous publication: Chamberlin, p. 170 (first half of third paragraph)]

Cape Town
26th April 1852

My dear Sir,
I had the pleasure of recieving the day before yesterday your letter

---

[1] For further details, cf. *Fam. Letters*, ii, pp. 174–5. D. L.'s informant was Moffat.

[2] 'I should not be the least surprised though Moyle is found to be the murderer of both Robinson and Dolman' (*Fam. Letters*, ii, p. 175: 2.iv.52 Moffat). Henry J, Moyle had been to Lake Ngami in 1850 with a 'trader and hunter' named Robinson. who was later reported to have been killed by a crocodile in the Botletle River. In 1851 Moyle again visited the interior, accompanied by a young traveller and artist, Alfred Dolman (1827–51), who died on the way back, allegedly after eating poisonous wild berries, though the circumstances strongly suggested murder (cf. *Fam. Letters*, ii, pp. 136–7, 175, for further details and references to sources).

dated 14th April last,[1] and felt much gratified to find, before my departure, that you still evince the same friendly interest in my welfare and usefulness as heretofore.

I have to acknowledge with gratitude your kind suggestion respecting a companion in my proposed two years' sojourn. It manifests a kind concern for my safety and comfort. The Revd. W. Thompson takes the same view of the case as you do. But, though I fully appreciate your motives, I must say that you might as well recommend the Lieutenant-Governor as Mr Ashton. He will not go, unless forced to it by some agency more potent than moral suasion. I know his sentiments are, in reference to the whole project of introducing the gospel into a country where fever prevails, that it is a mere tempting of Providence. Even when Mr Freeman proposed in Committee[2] that he should remove only eighty miles from Kuruman, he flatly refused by saying, 'It would be taking Mrs Ashton to her grave'. If you could prevail on him to take up a halfway position, say with either the Bamangwato, Banwaketse, or Bakwains, that is as much as may be expected of him. If you fail, no one else will succeed in moving him from the Kuruman. With respect to the printing, it is, like all amateur works, extremely expensive when not executed by the trade. It would be quicker and better and cheaper done if sent to England by post than it is at present, with a missionary's salary and energies devoted to it. Our friend Mr Thompson thought of Mr Ross, but he cannot speak the language so well as to be understood by any except such as have been accustomed through a long course of years to European modes of thought and foreign idioms, and in addition to this the infirmities of his temper would spoil everything.[3] No one suitable for the undertaking has presented himself to my mind except Mr Moffat, and he is fastened to Kuruman by his work of translation.

Independantly of this, I consider that when in the habit of constantly looking to the Divine hand for guidance in all our movements, when no one possessed of a small measure of suitability and willingness makes his appearance we ought to conclude to go alone. I am not given to

[1] Since at that time the voyage between England and Cape Town normally took from one to two months, it is highly probable that D. L. misdated his own letter, and that '26th April' should perhaps read '26th May'. In another, also dated '26th April', he writes to Moffat: 'I have got no letter from the Directors' (*Fam. Letters*, ii, p. 181). In the LMS letter-book, Tidman's letter of 14.iv.52 is immediately preceded by one of the same date to Thompson, who acknowledged its receipt on 29.v.52 (and who on 1.v.52 had acknowledged another dated 14.iii.52).

[2] At a meeting held during Freeman's visit to Kuruman early in December 1849. D. L. was not present. (Freeman, *Tour*, p. 259.)

[3] D. L. greatly despised Ross, who had quarrelled with him during their voyage together from England (cf. *Fam. Letters*, i, pp. 124, 167–9, 175–6).

despondency or lowness of spirits. I enjoy a perpetual flow of good spirits. I felt more perplexity in reference to parting with my family and about my pecuniary affairs, and concerning which I lately wrote you, than I ever did in my life before. Had Mr Oswel not presented us with about £170 since we came here, I should have been in a fix. He clothed Mrs L. and family in a style we never anticipated. This I state in confidence to you. It would offend him to make it public. But it makes me comparatively easy in mind, and I am fully convinced that I am in the path of duty. The prevalence of the African fever makes me ponder over the subject of death, but after reviewing the whole subject I ask what I am good for if I cannot trust God to manage that, so that his glory will be promoted whether I live or die. I have, too, an abundance of work in prospect, and I hope you will pray for me that I may be kept pure and uncontaminated by the heathen, and that the great aim of preaching peace and good will may be constantly before my mind.

I cannot promise to keep a journal.[1] I am astonished you do not give a single hint as to whether you recieved a map or not.

I feel much gratified by your assurance that you will take care of my family in England. Mrs L. was much improved in health by our short stay here, and I hope will be much benifitted by the voyage, but I shall feel obliged if you procure the advice of Dr Bennett or some other eminent medical man (Mr Solly[2] perhaps) in reference to a return of the paralysis. The whole right side of the face was perfectly motionless and drawn to the opposite side, and pains along the whole side & extremities ever since may indicate deep-seated disease.

Believe me,
affectionately yours,
David Livingston

39. To WILLIAM THOMPSON
9 June 1852

[LMS 64. Previous publication: Chamberlin, pp. 170–1 (postscript omitted)]

[1] See above, p. 200. The *Letter of Instructions* issued to every LMS missionary stipulated, *inter alia*: 'We desire that you will keep a regular journal of all your proceedings, and of all events of interest, relative to your undertaking, that come under your observation' (p. 42).

[2] Samuel Solly (1805–71), surgeon at St Thomas's Hospital, London; 'a good clinical teacher and operator' (*D.N.B.*).

Paarl[1]
9th June 1852

My dear Sir,

I reached this yesterday evening without falling into mischief once, although I had no one to take care of me! Have remained with Mr Barker[2] through the day, and gave an address in the evening, which shews how very firmly I can hold to my resolutions of not speaking again till I got back to my own country.[3] But I am done with it now till I come to Griqua Town, and I can easily refuse Mr Hughs.[4] Don't despise my weakness: 'Ye that are strong, &c &c.' I found Mr Barker must sell his horse, and that the hire of horses up [to] the waggon[5] would amount to £3. I resolved to buy it, and now I can proceed without an attendant. I go tomorrow morning (Thursday), and will reach it on Saturday. You will recieve a bill of £12 from Mr Barker in the ordinary way (as salary).

It is just possible that George[6] may not be gone when this comes to hand. If so, will you tell him to bring a breed of large Malay fowls with him for Sebituané.[7] I forgot them till my own waggon went, and then again when George was getting ready. But if he has gone do not trouble yourself, as we can pick up a pair or two of some kind among the Boers.

I am sure you must be glad to get rid of me and my bothering intrusions, which were always about my own affairs. Accept of my hearty and most sincere thanks for your multifarious kind offices and good wishes. May God reward you. I hope a sense of gratitude for your disinterested friendship will never be effaced from my heart. Many thanks

---

[1] A village 36 miles E.N.E. of Cape Town (which, as already noted, D. L. had left on 8 June).

[2] George Barker (1789–1861), LMS missionary at Paarl 1839–56 (*Register*, p. 11).

[3] Although D. L.'s uvula had been 'cut off' at Cape Town, he still became 'quite hoarse' when delivering long addresses, and after one unfortunate attempt in Thompson's church wrote to Moffat (26.iv.52): 'I shall certainly not speak in public again anywhere South of the Chobe' (*Fam. Letters*, ii, pp. 177–8).

[4] The irrigation scheme at Backhouse (p. 123 n.) having proved impracticable, Hughes had returned to Griquatown.

[5] 'the hire of horses and the waggon' (Chamberlin, p. 171).

[6] George Fleming, a coloured West Indian living in Cape Town, who had been one of Oswell's servants on the journeys to L. Ngami (1849) and Sebetwane's country (1851). It had been arranged that he would now accompany D. L. and trade among the MaKololo with goods supplied to him by Mr H. E. Rutherfoord. He is frequently mentioned in *Private J.* and *Fam. Letters*; cf. also *Oswell*, esp. ii, p. 3.

[7] D. L. had promised to bring the MaKololo 'an iron pot next time we come into the country, also a larger breed of fowls & a larger breed of sheep & goats' (*Private J.*, p. 49).

to Miss Thompson[1] for her kind attentions to a poor forlorn widower from the Sesheke, and love to all the children.

Believe me yours very affectionately,
David Livingston

I have delivered the soiled linen to Mr Read[2] in the basket, and just remember that I have forgot to ask George for the armlets, &c, which you requested me to do. I recollected nothing more of the matter till this moment, and it is too late now. I must just bring you down some myself. He would ask outrageously for them, so you had better not apply to either him or his son-in-law. George asked £2.10.0 from Mr Rutherfoord junior for three or four assegais & something else, the whole being worth about 2/6.

It rains heavily here this morning (Thursday), but I hope it will clear up at noon. If so, I shall proceed. Mr Read goes a little way with me. He says, tell Mr Thompson to take care & not get into the clutches of Sir John Wylde.[3]   D. L.

40. To DAVID LIVINGSTON
14 July 1852

[LMS: Outgoing Letters, Africa, Box 7, pp. 491–3]

London
July 14th, 1852

Dear Brother,

Your communications of the 19th March and 26th April (two letters) came to hand in due course, and, tho' you will have left Cape Town long ere this, we are anxious that no time should be lost in relieving your suspense in regard to some important topics to which they refer.

Mrs Livingston and children, as you will have already heard, arrived safely in this country about the 23rd ult., and it will be a great satisfaction to you to learn that your dear wife's health has already undergone

---

[1] Thompson's sister (and, presumably, housekeeper, as he was then a widower).

[2] James Read, jun. (1811–94), LMS missionary at the Kat River Settlement, whom D. L. had met in Cape Town (*Fam. Letters*, ii, pp. 168, 172). He was now paying a visit to Paarl before returning to his own station (Thompson to Tidman, 2.vii.52).

[3] Chief Justice of the Cape Colony since 1834; b. 1781, d. 1859. His conduct while presiding over the trial of Andries Botha, a Kat River Hottentot accused of high treason (see below, p. 212), made D. L. term him 'an infamous hypocrite' (*Private J.*, p. 82).

a decided improvement, and that a good hope may be entertained of her complete recovery. She has since proceeded to Scotland.

I have the pleasure to state that, with a view to relieve your anxieties and from a considerate regard to Mrs Livingston's comfort, the Board have made an allowance at the rate of £120 per annum towards the support of herself and children during her stay in this country, and we shall be happy to do all in our power to promote the object of her visit and to manifest our sympathy in her behalf.

The views you express in a former letter, as to the desirableness of your being accompanied, on a journey involving such important results, by one of the Missionary brethren, remain unchanged, and we trust that you will take all practicable measures to [secure][1] such a companion. But should all efforts prove unavailing, it only remains for us to commend you, with all earnestness and affection, to the gracious Providence of God, in the hope that he will shield you from evil, direct and enlighten your steps, and crown your enterprise with the signal tokens of his favor and blessing.

The statements contained in your letter of March, in relation to the large extra expenditure incurred by your former journies, have necessarily occasioned us some concern and perplexity. But in appreciating the motives which have led you to forego the comforts of domestic life and the quiet routine of a Missionary station, in order to open up wider fields for the access of the Gospel, we are not unmindful of the fact that enterprises of this nature cannot be achieved without a corresponding outlay. The Directors have taken the state of your account, now overdrawn a rather considerable amount, into their kind and considerate attention, and, in the full persuasion that the extra expenditure has been absolutely unavoidable, and incurred moreover in the service of the Society, they are resolved to place the sum of £150 to the credit of your account.

The Directors have further given their best consideration to your painful representation of Mr Moffat's health, and we are now writing to urge him to lay aside all his engagements and undertake, at the Society's expense, a journey to the coast, or any other measure he may prefer, with a view to his deriving benefit from the change.[2]

[1] Word too faint to be legible.
[2] The Directors' letter (also dated 14.vii.52) was acknowledged by Moffat on 22 November. Although very grateful for the kind offer made to him, he regretted that for various reasons he could not at present leave Kuruman, the most important being the recent Boer aggression against the BaKwena and other tribes (J. S. Moffat, *Lives*, pp. 291–3).

There are some few topics touched upon in your recent correspondence, introduced in connection with Mr Moffat's case, which cannot with propriety be overlooked, especially as, by implication at least, they seem to involve a charge against the Directors of mismanagement and partiality in their administration. We have, in the first place, to regret the tone in which you have animadverted upon two of the Missionary brethren, Messrs. Inglis and Edwards. Ex parte representations of this nature, while involving a breach of charity, are little calculated to promote the cause of truth and equity. We have long been aware of the unhappy divisions existing between these brethren and yourself and Mr Moffat, but it cannot reasonably be expected that a case involving an accumulation of statements and counter-statements could be summarily disposed of at the suggestion of an individual, himself one of the parties concerned. Secondly, with regard to the alleged inequalities in the allowances to missionaries, we could show that some of your statements are not correct; and, with regard to others of them, it should be borne in mind that a Missionary looking at an object from an isolated point of view is very liable to misinterpret the measures of the Directors when applied in a wide case. We are, however, aware that there are circumstances connected with some of the smaller Missionary settlements which demand attention, and, so far as it may be deemed necessary, we shall seek to supply the proper remedy.

I may add, in closing, that we have now written to your excellent friend Mr Oswell, expressing, in general but strong terms, the high sense entertained by the Board of the valuable services he had rendered you in your previous journies.[1]

With every assurance of our fraternal regard, and of our prayerful sympathy on your behalf,

I remain, Dear Brother,
Yours very truly,
[Arthur Tidman]
Forn. Secy., L. M. S.

41. To WILLIAM THOMPSON
20(?) July 1852

[LMS 65. Previous publication: Chamberlin, pp. 171–4 (incomplete)]

[1] The letter, dated 10.vii.52, is published (incompletely) in *Oswell*, ii, pp. 5–6.

Scheit Fontein[1]

[undated]

My dear Sir,

Herein you will recieve the fulmination of the Commandant Potgeiter, who I believe has gone to a tribunal at which nothing but truth will be told.[2] It is a copy sent from the Committee by the then Secretary, Mr Ashton. The answer which they sent me at the same time is, I find, not by me, but it must be at Kolobeng, and as soon as I can lay hands upon it I shall forward it.

A reperusal of the document brought some circumstances to my mind which had nearly vanished from my memory. One was that when the Bakwains heard of the intentions of the Boers to molest me, they instantly called a Peecho and resolved unanimously to defend their missionary with their blood. On my objecting to their exposing their lives on my account, they replied it was on their own account, for whatever was done to me was done to them. They intended to mislead the Boers into a strong ambuscade if they found out by any means that they were approaching, and a simultaneous attack was to follow by both guns & assegais. If they should come upon us at unawares, the whole tribe was to rush to our house and defend us with their lives. Had Potgeiter come he would have met with a very different reception from any he ever had before. The tribes he has attacked never could do him or his party on horseback any harm. His fighting has been a series of cold-blooded murders. In his blood-thirstiness he has poured out drink-offerings to the Devil. [With] what a terrible surprise such men must look upon their prowess in the still shades of Hades. No false pretences there of 'making peace among the natives', and no Predikants to baptize them into the belief that they are Christians and no mistake, and then laud them in the '*Zoud African*'.[3]

I am however preaching to you instead of writing a letter. Well, when I saw the Bakwains were determined to doctor the Boers, I thought it right to send my family out of the way. Mrs L. was in child-bed, but much preferred going westward with the Bakwain women to

---

[1] Skietfontein (now the town of Carnarvon, 30° 59′ S., 22° 08′ E.), about 360 miles from Cape Town. The distance, and the reference below to slow travel, suggest that D. L. did not get there until about 20 July (since he reached Griquatown, almost 200 miles farther, on 15 August).

[2] Potgieter had died in December 1852 (C. Potgieter and N. H. Theunissen, *Kommandant-Generaal Hendrik Potgieter*, 1938, p. 261). The 'fulmination' was his letter of January 1849 to the District Committee, demanding D. L.'s recall (cf. above, p. 128). It was addressed to Ross, though Ashton had been elected as Secretary for that year (Minutes, 1848).

[3] *De Zuid Afrikaan*, a bi-weekly newspaper published in Cape Town since 1830.

going to Kuruman. The Kurumanites pressed upon us the propriety of sending the family out there,[1] and I did so about four months after the threats of the Boers had vanished into thin air. A short time after they left for Kuruman I departed for the Lake the first time. I remember, too, that the imputation of having run away nettled me more than all the rest. I wrote on the paper in pencil the words you see, & left the letter in a conspicuous situation at Kolobeng in case they should come when I was absent at the Lake. I distroyed about 350 letters before going, and many of these I regret, but felt unwilling anything should fall into their hands of which they could make any bad use.

I am here in the house of Mr Alheit[2] of Skeit Fontein, and may inform you how we have succeeded hitherto. We have come but slowly. My oxen were lean, but quite fresh. I used them only, and by buying some and exchanging others, as they became tired, for fresh ones, giving about 10/- on each for the extra flesh of the new ones, I succeeded pretty well. I shall soon be at the River,[3] and thence will get on well. The oxen I have now are in good condition & will carry me thither quickly. The waggon, however, is enormously heavy.[4] This loading is one of those things I shall do but once in my life. We had to pass through a bad defile, and hired a span from a Boer to take us through. He took us into it, but his large fat oxen could not move it farther. I inspanned our meagre beasts, and they walked out with it at once. The Boer then left us in disgust, and when we had got fairly through wanted payment, but this I declined. I shall feel glad when I deliver the articles to their owners. The woodwork of the wheels cracks from the enormous strain. There, now, take a lesson by my folly.

Of George I have seen nothing, though I have travelled so slowly. I gave him two men, so as they do not make their appearance he must be on his way after us, either by the road we have come by or some other. We shall be sure to meet at Kuruman.

I have been quite busy all the way with the Dictionary.[5] I did not know I had so many words in my head as I have put down, but every

---

[1] See above, p. 130, where D. L. writes that he had sent his family to Kuruman 'for the sake of refreshment', and below, p. 316, where he says they went 'in order to be out of the way of a threatened attack of the Boers'. The 'Kurumanites' were presumably his parents-in-law (the Moffats).

[2] Rev. Christoph W. Alheit, of the Rhenish Missionary Society; stationed at Skietfontein since 1847.

[3] The Orange River (see below, p. 214).

[4] 'I mean to put at least 2,000 lbs on the waggon. The iron axles will bear it' (2.iv.52 Moffat: *Fam. Letters*, ii, p. 174).

[5] See above, pp. 168, 192. The Grey Collection, S. A. Public Library, Cape Town, possesses the MS. of D. L.'s *Dictionary of the Sichuana Language*, 4to, pp.

time I sit down there is no end of them. They are hooked together by strange associations. I have not begun anything else. The waggon is most inconvenient for writing. I can write only on my side, and must doff & trek on my 'inexpressibles' only when lying flat on my back. I must be getting old & ill-natured now, for the constrained positions of my waggon life rather makes me crusty than gentle. The longer one lives the more one learns is, however, true.

I have been reading the tour of the Bishop.[1] He is quite an angel compared to me. Don't you see the effects of the Puseyite partial belief in salvation by works? He is quite in earnest, no doubt of it, he and the Archdeacon tramping it on foot. Well done, my hearties. If I had £800 or even £400 a year travelling expenses, as you my Lord and your venerableness the Archdeacon have, I would not be so self-denying. No, not I. I would sport good oxen in my waggon and good horses in my cart, and should now be somewhere beyond your Lordship's diocese, perhaps sitting at supper with the Bishop of Kuruman, aye with the Apostle of the Bechuanas.

You will have observed a great deal of ignorance apparent in his Lordship's notes, and a great deal understood or rather presumed in the readers for whom it is intended. See the Preface: you are expected to believe that he passed through unknown regions,[2] and even where he seems to have been without a path you find him looking for Mr Harding's spoor,[3] and mention is made of Captain Gardner,[4] but none of a body of troops which went through the same parts with a large

263, 'of which pp. 1–211 and 247–259 contain a Sehlapi [Tlhaping]-English Dictionary, arranged in the usual alphabetical order, according to the imperative forms of the verbs, and the full forms of the nouns, with their derivative prefixes' (W. H. I. Bleek, *The Library of . . . Sir George Grey*, vol. I, part I, 1858, p. 186).

[1] *A Journal of the Bishop's Visitation Tour through the Cape Colony, in 1850* [by Robert Gray, 1809–72, Anglican Bishop of Cape Town since 1847], London 1851. For part of his tour the Bishop was accompanied by Rev. N. J. Merriman, Archdeacon of Grahamstown.

[2] The statement actually made there was as follows: 'In the course of this extensive Visitation, which occupied the Bishop from Easter to Christmas, his Lordship travelled on foot, or in his wagon, through large tracts in which no vehicle had been seen before, and of which no description has been published.'

[3] The Bishop was then travelling overland from Natal through the Transkei to Grahamstown: '. . . our only help in finding our way has been what we suppose to be the track of Mr. Harding's wagons, when he came, a few weeks since, this way' (*Visitation Tour*, p. 90). Walter Harding, crown prosecutor of Natal, had been sent at the head of an expedition to demand payment of compensation, for cattle theft, from the Mpondo chief Faku (Theal, *History*, vii, pp. 238–9). He travelled 'with three ox-wagons' (*Visitation Tour*, p. 79).

[4] Alan Francis Gardiner (1794–1851), previously a naval officer, had visited Natal in 1835 and 1837 in order to attempt the establishment of Christian missions among the Zulu. The Bishop says of him merely: 'It was in this neighbourhood . . .

number of waggons. The earnestness with which he works is, however, very pleasant, and almost excuses the ignorance, the sour looks at the Independants, the grinning with watering teeth at the Dutch Predikants' salaries, the political partizanship, and inocent gloating over two simpletons, daughters of a (London) missionary.[1] He feels not all the while that he makes the best part of his book by imitating the Independant way of doing things. And as for the missionary's daughters, bless his heart, we could give him a couple of missionaries themselves, yes a couple three times told, and be no losers either.

I have nothing to tell you about the Boers or any one else. Have heard nothing about the Caffre war since I left, nor of Botha.[2] The Boers are certainly the remnants of the Lost Tribes of Israel. They speak of nothing but pounds, shillings, dollars, guilders,[3] sheep, & oxen. Their whole souls seem absorbed by this world's goods. Their talk is just exactly what you overhear in the Jews of London. I shall be glad when I hear something else.

Mr Alheit is a fine friendly man. He does not believe in baptismal regeneration, as do some of his bretheren. At least I believe so, for when I said that the Bishop liked him because of holding similar views on baptism he laughed and said, 'But we don't all believe in that doctrine'.[4] He seems a great admirer of Luther. He has been successful here. Has 80 communicants, but is plagued by the surrounding Boers badgering his people. Intends to remove to the Orange River with his people, but the present war prevents his getting the necessary permission from Government.

Please present kind regards to your sister, Ralph, Jessie, and my worthy friend Willie.[5] May God bless you all and help you, who are in

that Captain Gardiner, some few years since, was reduced to live upon sugar for some days' (*op. cit.*, p. 92).

[1] At Burghersdorp (Cape Colony) the Bishop 'had five candidates for confirmation, with whom I spent a couple of hours. Two of them were daughters of a former London Society Missionary' (*op. cit.*, p. 160).

[2] Andries Botha, field-cornet of the Kat River Settlement, had recently been condemned to death by Sir John Wylde on a charge of taking a leading part in the Hottentot rebellion (see above, p. 198 n., and *Private J.*, p. 82, where fuller details are given).

[3] The rix-dollar and guilder were old forms of currency, worth respectively 1s. 6d. and 6d.

[4] The Bishop does not mention Alheit, and went nowhere near his station. D. L.'s comment was presumably inspired by the statement: 'The Missionaries of the Berlin Society are, I believe, all strict Lutherans. They adhere to the Augsburg Confession, and to the Lutheran views of the sacraments. They complained to me of the very unsound views generally taught by English dissenting missionaries, with reference to the sacrament of Baptism' (*op cit.*, p. 20).

[5] Thompson's children.

the forefront of the strife, to be valiant for the truth & righteousness. I lost my horse about a week ago, a great affliction. He ran away. A trader called Bredencamp going back may find him, and if he writes I shall know how to do with the beast. He was an excellent traveller, but like many other travellers became disgusted with the way & went back. Malatsi, my man,[1] spent a week in search of him.

Believe me ever yours,
David Livingston

[1] A Kwena tribesman who had accompanied D. L. to Cape Town as a servant; one of 'the best . . . men I ever travelled with' (*Fam. Letters*, ii, pp. 183, 249). He subsequently (1859–60) went to the MaKololo with the ill-fated missionary party under Helmore, of which he was the first member to die.

VII

THE SACK OF KOLOBENG

42. To WILLIAM THOMPSON
6 September 1852

[LMS 66. Previous publication: Chamberlin, pp. 174–8 (incomplete)]

Kuruman
6th September 1852

My dear Sir,

Having by means of a sound constitution survived a tedious drawl[1] through the Colony, I crossed the Orange River at Priestcar,[2] a spot which has been selected for a mission station by Mr Alheit of Scheit Fontein. The enormous weight on my waggon soon after that told on one of the wheels, and down came the elegant Dutch vehicle, the African coach and ten, on to its marrow bones. Mr Hughs kindly lent a wheel, and by the assistance of himself and some of my old patients I managed to crawl to this place about 10 days ago. I was sometimes vexed with myself for having loaded up so much, but when I reach[ed] the places where I could offload it gave me sincere pleasure to hand the goods to the owners. I was disposed to blame myself most when we had to offload at the bottom of acclivities and carry the boxes up ourselves. I am now detained here getting my wheel mended.

I had written another letter to you and mentioned a number of conjectures respecting George, but his arrival at Kuruman today renders my surmisings as valuable as conjectures usually are. I could not understand what should have prevented him coming up to me on the way, and after waiting here a week I began to suspect he had got into mischief by going to Beaufort.[3] He has been at more expense than I have, and I had to spend upwards of £50 in the way. We shall now help him on. I waited for him as soon as I got a spot which possessed forage, but when he did not turn out I concluded he must have taken another road. I came here ten days before him.

---

[1] 'a tedious travel' (Chamberlin, p. 174).

[2] Prieska (29° 40′ S., 22° 45′ E.), on the south bank of the Orange River; about 115 miles from Carnarvon (Skietfontein) and 80 from Griquatown.

[3] Beaufort West (32° 21′ S., 22° 35′ E.), on an alternative, and older, route from Cape Colony to Griquatown.

6. SECHELE IN 1863

Now that I can calmly look back to my sojourn among the natives who live in a hollow under Table Mountain, and who dailly and nightly inhale effluvia known only to the initiated in the mysteries of sanitary reform, I do remember them with feelings of compassion. Poor creatures, living in a state of utter respectability, exchanging their how-d'ye-do's, their noddings, curtsyings, and ministerial breakfasts, and all the while to carnivori, the cannibals, I may say, of the Law & State & Puseyite Church, ready to spring upon them and devour them. They are obliged to live & walk as circumspectly as elephants among well-covered pitfalls. I do pity you from my heart. I could not breathe freely till I got over the Orange River.

Well, that is a fine letter from his Riverence Calderwood.[1] I look upon it with mingled feelings of scorn and shame. With scorn, when I think of an English professor of Christianity so unutterably mean as to join in the hue and cry against a poor Hottentot, and so dead to the shame of infamy as to confess at the same time that it has been his practice to act the part of a common informer, a salaried Government spy. I blush up to the ears when I read his confession (after spending years in the service of our Society) that he does not know the language sufficiently well to know exactly the statement of a native without an interpreter. Is it not disgraceful to find the gospel of Christ proclaimed in a *patois* called 'school Caffre'? We must not lose sight of this confession. It is good that he makes it, though that and other statements ought to cover him with lasting infamy. A man who could write as he has done will do more. This is not his last letter, nor his last stab at the cause of truth & righteousness.

You see how the Government officials feel towards the defence of Botha. In Scotland counsel is provided for the most depraved criminals at the expense of the state. This Reverend Commissioner would have us believe that such defence 'tends to break down important moral distinctions',[2] that its tendency is to cause the whole of Scottish society to be suspected, for we have criminals there out of every class. From Commissioners who can play the fool for £600 per annum, with the Bible in one hand & the sambok in the other, Good Lord deliver us.

The copies of Mr Read's letters have not reached any of the mission-

---

[1] Henry Calderwood (b. 1809), LMS missionary in Kaffraria 1838–46, then accepted Government office as Commissioner to the Ngqika ('Gaika') tribe, subsequently (Dec. 1847) appointed Civil Commissioner and Resident Magistrate of Victoria East. The letter referred to, expressing belief in Botha's guilt, was published in the *Cape Town Mail*, 15 June 1852.

[2] 'important social distinctions' (Chamberlin, p. 176).

aries up here. The Reports all did.[1] I have made arrangement for the delivery of your letters. Have recieved two notes from you. Mr Moffat's head is still affected. Nothing he has tried has the least effect on it. The translation goes on briskly notwithstanding.

Edwards has left his station, and the people of Mabotsa have come over to Sechele. The Boers are reported by an individual who came here two days ago to be encamped at Mabotsa.[2] They contemplate rooting out Sechele, and wait only till two or three of their party return from the Lake. They fear if an attack is made now that Sechele's people fleeing Northwards would meet their friends, and of course treat them as they now hope to do the Bakwains. They may find it more difficult to subdue Sechele than they dream of. But their plan is to secure the whole country to themselves, and prevent traders and travellers from going beyond them. One of Dr Robertson's converts,[3] called Chief-Commandant Pretorious, was feasted the other day not far from Boomplaats, where the battle was fought. They drunk the memory of Major Hogg in solemn silence,[4] but forgot the memory of the brave men who [were] butchered at Boomplaats by this same Pretorius. Is it right, or is it not, for the Bakwains to make the country too hot for this man's party after he strikes the first blow? I shall be there soon, and must give an opinion on the point. What would you advise? If it is right for Hottentot levies to fight against the Caffres,[5] it

---

[1] Read's letters, in defence of LMS policy, were published in the *S.A. Commercial Advertiser* (May–Sept., 1851) and reprinted as a pamphlet (1852) entitled *The Kat River Settlement in 1851*, to which Thompson also contributed. The 'Reports' were presumably copies of the annual *Report of the [LMS] Missions in South Africa*, edited by Thompson and published in Cape Town.

[2] Mosielele, the chief at Mabotsa, had refused to comply with further Boer demands for free labour. The local commandant (Scholtz) thereupon advised Edwards and his family 'to leave the station for safety', and they accordingly took refuge with Inglis at Mathebe (17 August). Shortly afterwards a Boer commando attacked Mabotsa, and then proceeded against Sechele, to whom Mosielele and his principal followers had fled a few days before (Edwards, in *S.A. Miss. Report*, 1852, pp. 39–41).

[3] Rev. William Robertson (1822–79), of Swellendam, was a member of the D.R.C. deputation to the Transvaal Boers in 1848 (see above, p. 128).

[4] In November 1851 the British Government had sent two commissioners, William S. Hogge and Charles Mostyn Owen, to deal with political problems in the Orange River Sovereignty. One outcome of their mission was the Sand River Convention (January 1852), which recognized the independence of the Boers in the Transvaal. Hogge died suddenly in Bloemfontein on 9 June. In July Pretorius, no longer a 'wanted man', visited the town, and was received by Owen and other officials 'with every mark of honour' (Theal, *History*, vii, pp. 324–33). For the battle of Boomplaats, see above, p. 129.

[5] During the 'Eighth Kafir War' (1850–3), the Government forces included special levies of coloured men ('Hottentots'), many of whom were drawn from mission stations (*Report*, 1852, p. 14, and *Fam. Letters*, ii, p. 170).

is right for Caffres & Bakwains to fight against the enemies of their country. I doubt if it is right to fight at all.

Mr Ross has gone to see his people again at Tauns.[1] He came along with me from Griqua Town as far as Daniel's Kuil.[2] He will return by way of Kuruman. The Directors have not written any of the brethren for a long time. Major Hogg will have some idea now as to whether the reports he circulated anent a certain person were true or false.[3] We shall all soon be hushed in the still & peaceful Hades. All this bother & bluster & blarney will recieve a quietus before many years, in as far as the present actors are concerned. What a hush takes place as the shades of death close around one. God grant that when we have finished our work we may be hushed to eternal rest on Abraham's bosom.

Kind love to your sister, Ralph, & Jessie. I won't mention Willie, because he did not come to help me. I tried your plan on one ox, and he became a beauty & so tame. All the Boers wanted to exchange him &, poor fellow, he was drowned in the Orange River. Three fell into a muddy place on a Saturday evening. We all worked the whole night trying to get them out of the sloughy bank, and as the morning dawned the finest of the whole lot expired. You may guess how eagerly we toiled when I mention that when daylight appeared I thought [it] was only about 12 o'clock.

I have not yet begun to write, but have not lost sight of the project. I have not been idle. A correct and lucid analysis of the language engages my attention and has taken up all my spare time.[4] I have devoted a whole evening to you. Your notes were good, but very short. You will some day write a longer, I hope. Poor Botha. The sentence is terrible. It is worse than death.[5] Poor fellow. The wicked shall not always triumph.

By same post I send a letter for my brother containing Sandillah's

---

[1] Because of inter-tribal disturbances, in June 1851, Ross had abandoned his station at Mamusa and gone with his family to Griquatown; shortly afterwards, the BaTlhaping at Mamusa had themselves moved back to Taung (*Report*, 1852, p. 67).

[2] A Griqua settlement at 28° 11′ S., 23° 33′ E., roughly midway between Griquatown and Kuruman.

[3] The implication seems to be that he had said something slanderous about D. L., possibly in regard to 'gun-running'.

[4] This was the first draft, dated 'August 1852', of *Analysis of the Language of the Bechuanas* (privately printed, 1858); cf. *Fam. Letters*, ii, p. 95.

[5] Botha's death sentence (see above, p. 212) 'has since been commuted to hard labour on the roads for life' (*Private J.*, p. 82). He was set free at the end of 1855, on condition that he did not return to Kat River (Thompson to Tidman, 8.xii.55).

speech to Renton,[1] to be printed in America. All we learn of the Caffre war[2] is one-sided. We must hear both sides. It is well Sandillah speaks out so nobly. Bringing out converts to assist the English is infamous. We must either preach passive resistance, or fighting for one's own countrymen.

D. Livingston

20th. You will see by Mr Moffat's to you the doings of Dr Robertson's dearly beloved bretheren.[3] I mourn over my books & medicines, instruments. Please say nothing about my losses, or some good Samaritan will forthwith send me odd numbers of the Evangelical Mag., the pictures extracted, 'Alleine's Alarm' without the title page, an odd volume Charnock's sermons,[4] &c.

Two parties of Boers are gone Sebitoané-wards. They will be cut off by Sechele's people. One of these parties would plunder me if they met me, so I think it will be well to wait here till they are out of my way, or killed. It is trying to wait, but God's good Providence has detained me so long just to prevent me falling into the very midst of the strife & losing everything.

I had a fine medical library, and many good works on general subjects. The former was my pride, & a great comfort. I have got lightened, and will move so much more easily now. You will hear of my Bakwains yet, they are not broken-spirited Hottentots. That attack sealed many Boers' doom.

Many thanks for the Psalter & other books. Doubly precious now. I send Sandillah's speech to be printed in America. Please notice if it comes to you. Also two letters for Mrs L.

[1] Sandile was one of the leading Xhosa ('Caffre') chiefs fighting against the Cape Colony, and Henry John Renton was a Scottish clergyman who had visited S. Africa in 1850–1 to inspect the stations of the Glasgow Missionary Society. The contents of the 'speech' are briefly summarized in *Private J.*, p. 83; it dealt, *inter alia*, with the employment of native converts 'to bear arms against their own countrymen'.

[2] 'the Caffre here' (Chamberlin, p. 177).

[3] In that letter (20.ix.52) Moffat described the Boer attack on the BaKwena at Dimawe (30 August), and the sack of D. L.'s premises at Kolobeng. For D. L.'s own account of the same date, written to his wife, see *Fam. Letters*, ii, pp. 184–6.

[4] *The Evangelical Magazine and Missionary Chronicle*, published monthly in London since 1793; Joseph Alleine (1634–68), *An Alarme to Unconverted Sinners* (first published 1672, and often reprinted). Stephen Charnock (1628–80) was the author of many theological works, also often reprinted, including *Discourses on the Knowledge of God*.

43. To WILLIAM THOMPSON
30 September 1852

[LMS 68. Previous publication: Campbell, p. 142 (brief extract); Chamberlin, pp. 178–81 (incomplete)]

Kuruman
30th September 1852

My dear Sir,

Enclosed you will percieve a letter which I have ventured to address to the Lieutenant-Governor. I have endeavoured to give a plain outline of the facts and merely hinted at the probable consequences, and now if the Government goes on heedlessly the blame will rest on its own shoulders. I enclose it to you, because I understand you are expected to be our go-between in all matters pertaining to the Government. The reason which I feel the chief one in my mind for troubling you is that you may exercise your judgement on it, whether it ought to be delivered at all.[1]

From it and Mr Moffat's letter you will have a pretty clear idea of the doings of Dr Robertson's converts, and may fancy that reverend sinner[2] turning up the white of his eyes and saying to them at the Communion table, 'Eat, O friends! Drink, yea drink abundantly, O beloved.' They went the whole hog — attended church on Sunday, hearing Mebaloe preach, and then made the parson flee for his life on Monday. He ran the gauntlet, some of them calling out, when they saw him with clothes on, 'Here is the chief', & then the bullets whistled over, behind & before him. He seems to have become terrified, ran through the midst of the Boers, & so fast his feet were dreadfully bruized. He has lost all he had, viz. 27 head of cattle & his furniture, &c. His house was burned by the *Christians*. He it was who stood by me when bitten by the lion, & got bit himself. He has been with me ever since I came into the country, but I fear this will be a settler for him. He is now on his way out here. Some fine young men whom I knew and loved have fallen. My heart is sore when I think of them. Sechele had two bullets through his hat, & a third through his coat sleeve. The Boers have lost one of their principal men. I don't know his name.

---

[1] The letter was duly delivered. Its text (from a copy made in Thompson's office) is published in Campbell, *Livingstone*, 1929, pp. 145–8.

[2] This derogatory phrase, and others like it (e.g., 'the reverend slanderer'), were inspired partly by the fact that Robertson had retailed to Robert Moffat, jun., and others, the charge of gun-running made against D. L. by the Boers ('The Story of the Black Pot', LMS 69; cf. below, p. 286).

The chief with whom Inglis lives is heart & soul with the Boers.[1] He ought to leave. He has informed Solomon that he is going to the Cape in order to send his wife and children to England, not of course in imitation of me, & Mrs Edwards sends her children to Walthamstow school.[2] If you ask the opinion of the Directors, you will find they would like Inglis to come home too, and there would be little doubt but that he would remain there.[3]

You may wonder what will be the end of all this, and you may perhaps wonder still more if I venture to say that I see nothing in it all unfavourable to the progress of the kingdom of Christ. There is evidently a process in operation in the whole of South Africa, and there soon will appear another wonderful development of His Providence who is wonderful in counsel & excellent in working. In every district of the country the process tends the same way. We 'poor renegades from the anvil and loom' long insisted that the Hottentots had souls, and our statements were looked upon as the blarney of silly enthusiasm. A few hundreds of them, however, take it into their monkey heads to rebel, and they actually kick the ossa coccyges of our dragoons and minié rifle men. No wonder that great was the wrath of the Govt. officials. Hottentot rebellion! What next? We may expect our cats to have a strike, 'cause missus don't give us the silver forks to eat with'. If we had hinted at a Hottentot rebellion I believe they would have believed that a cow could handle a musket as well as they. The rebellion is however a great fact, and the condemnation of Botha has sown seed which will yet vegetate. But I am away from my text. Everywhere there is a strong feeling of independance springing up. The English as a nation have lost character & honour.

The distruction of my property is a fortunate thing for me. There is not a native in the country but knows now for certain on whose side I

---

[1] Moilwê, chief 1845(?)–75 of the BaHurutshe at Dinokana (Mathebe), had furnished the Boers with oxen, corn, and 'fifty men', on their recent expedition against the BaKgatla and Sechele (Ross, in *S.A. Miss. Report*, 1852, p. 45).

[2] A boarding-school for the daughters of evangelical missionaries; founded 1838, and located in Marsh Street, Walthamstow, at that time 'a charming village, five miles from London' (Elsie Pike and Constance E. Curryer, *The Story of Walthamstow Hall*, 1938, pp. 17, 19, 31).

[3] Because they had protested against the enslavement of native children captured from the BaKwena and BaKgatla, Inglis and Edwards were expelled from the Transvaal by the Boers in November. Inglis then went to Philippolis, but soon afterwards left with his family for England. On arrival (May 1854) he severed his connection with the LMS, subsequently settling as a minister at Ayr in Canada. Edwards also went to Philippolis, but in 1856 moved to Port Elizabeth, where he died in 1876, having retired from the Society's service in 1874 'on account of age and infirmity' (*Register*, pp. 24, 56).

am. The Boers in plundering my house often expressed great regret that they had not got a hold of me. 'But we shall yet catch him', said they. How good God's Providence is to me. I was detained in Cape Town till I quite fretted, and then again in the way up. But now I can plainly see that had I got my own way I should have been in the very thick of the fight, for I always intended to spend a fortnight or so with the Bakwains.

I grieve over the losses they have sustained, but there is another point of view in which the matter may [be] considered. The majority of the Bakwains have heard the gospel repeatedly, but have not recieved it. They treated me uniformly with respect, but when Sechele professed faith in Christ they persecuted him bitterly. The Bakhatla have not only long refused to listen even, but treated Mr Edwards with great disrespect. Nearly £1,000 has been spent on them in vain. Indeed, their professed principles were to get all out of the missionary they could, but never recieve his message. The same may be said of the Bahurutse. And though the two stations are broken up, it is no cause for sorrow. The Bakwains, I am informed, attended both school & church better after I left for the Cape than for a long time previously; average of the school 80. Sechele's children are out here living with Mrs Moffat. They are well behaved. The son resembles his father in manners. They give much less trouble than was expected.[1] I think the seed sown will yet spring up among the Bakwains, though I may not live to see it.

I am at present prevented from leaving for my own country by two parties of Boers, who are now in the North and are to be cut off. If I attempted to save them they would very probably rob me in return, so must stand their chance. Sechele sends a message to me to wait a little yet, so though it is trying to wait when free & all ready for work I must submit.

I have just been drawn away from my writing by the chief Mahura. He is here on a visit. A great rogue. He made a remark worth noting: 'Sebube and Paul and you were taken out of the way of being killed. If either of you had been there you would certainly have been in the midst of the affair & been killed. God helped you by sending you out of the way.' Sebube & Paul are gone North. Sebube is a very brave fellow, native teacher to the Wanketse. He has lost all. Though Mahura is a heathen he has imbibed some Christian knowledge.

I have been thinking that I might draw £12 for Mebaloe. I have

---

[1] Sechele had in March sent his children to Kuruman to be educated there under Moffat's care (*Chronicle*, 1853, p. 64). The son, Sebele, was his heir, and duly succeeded him as chief of the BaKwena (1892–1911).

drawn nothing for some time for either him or Paul, our operations having been interrupted, but as it is a matter of business I shall write you if I do. No word from my better half yet.

Will you be kind enough to acquaint Mr Rutherfoord with any of the particulars of our hindrance which may interest him, also George's wife if you happen to see her.

Excuse this long ramble. My mind is troubled by the affections[1] of others. Poor people, when will they learn wisdom?

Believe me, yours of course,
D. Livingston

44. To WILLIAM THOMPSON
12 October 1852

[LMS 71. Previous publication: Campbell, pp. 107–8 (paragraphs 8–10, incomplete); Chamberlin, pp. 181–4 (paragraphs 8 onwards, incomplete)]

Kuruman
12th October 1852

My dear Sir,

Enclosed you will recieve two documents, which I doubt not will interest you and may be of use to you in your forthcoming work, 'History of the Cape Colony during the last ten years'. Put down my name as a subscriber for five copies. In the mean time, however, you may publish Viljoen's letter in the Mail or Advertizer.[2] It is pretty fair from one who has been an extensive dealer in gunpowder among the natives, and who, I have no doubt, had a load of the same article then in his waggon for sale. This is the same individual, too, who bought several boys at the Lake in 1851. I shall copy one of Sechele's letters for you before I close this, and if you thought proper you might send it on to the Directors.[3]

[1] 'afflictions' (Chamberlin, p. 181).

[2] Jan Willem Viljoen, 1822(?)–1904, a famous hunter often mentioned in contemporary works of travel, was field-cornet of Marico district. In that capacity he had written on 11.vi.52 to a Griqua named Adam Januarie, directing and empowering him to inspect all wagons going into the interior of Bechuanaland, and to confiscate any arms and ammunition carried without the requisite magistrate's permit. (D. L. saw the letter, a copy of which he enclosed to Thompson.) *The Cape Town Mail* and *The South African Commercial Advertiser* were newspapers published in Cape Town since 1841 and 1824 respectively.

[3] The letter, written by Sechele to Moffat and received at the beginning of October, described the Boer attack on the BaKwena. A translation (slightly abbreviated) was published in *Chronicle*, xvii, (February) 1853, p. 34. The original Tswana text (together with a complete translation) is given in *Private J.*, pp. 85–90.

I have sent a copy of Sechele's letter and also one of Viljoen's to the British Resident, Mr Green,[1] and a letter explanatory of the documents as violations of the provisions of the treaty of the Commissioners.[2] It is somewhat in the same strain as that sent through you to the Lieutenant-Governor, which I hope you recieved, but I conclude in the following manner: 'In the hope that the communication of these facts may lead to the cessation of the violation of the provisions, &c, of the treaty, *and compensation for losses sustained by such violation*, I am, &c &c, D. L.' Now I have not the smallest expectation of any compensation, but I thought I ought to make the losses known to the proper authorities, so that they may have no excuse if they pay no attention to them. And as the British Resident has two brothers now on a trading expedition to Sebitoane's country,[3] and they having lost considerable property in the plundering of my house and burning of Sechele's town — their relays of cattle, too, were taken away — all which property is believed to belong to the British Resident himself, it is not unlikely but that he may claim compensation, and should he get it I may come in for a share. At any rate it will look better for him to make a noise about my property than about his brothers', alias his own.

The Boers are on the watch for his brothers and Webb,[4] &c, who are in the country beyond the Bamangwato. Indeed, we heard by some hunters who came two days ago that the Boers are waiting for the English gentlemen somewhere between the Bamangwato and the Zouga, with laudable intention of plundering them. I don't want the English gentlemen to be killed, but I am inclined to pray that they may be stripped to the buffs and come out like those bashful blades who were told to tarry at Jericho.[5] I am quite glad they have lost a good deal at Kolobeng. I am only afraid they don't get insulted enough to make

[1] Henry Green, Resident of the Orange River Sovereignty July 1852–March 1854.

[2] The Sand River Convention (see above, p. 216 n.), signed on behalf of the British Government by Hogge and Owen. The provisions violated by the Boers, according to D. L., were: (4) 'that no slavery is or shall be permitted or practised in the country to the North of the Vaal River by the Emigrant Farmers', and (5) that 'mutual facilities and liberty shall be afforded to traders and travellers on both sides of the Vaal River' (*P.P. England 1854*, XLIII, p. 526).

[3] They were Charles Alexander Green (see above, p. 165) and Frederick J. Green. The latter subsequently became a well-known venturer into the interior (cf. the biographical sketch by E. C. Tabler in *Africana Notes and News*, xi, 1954, pp. 35–42).

[4] William Frederick Webb (1829–99), an army officer who was then in Bechuanaland on a shooting expedition. For his association with D. L., who in 1864–5 lived at his home in England, see *Livingstone and Newstead*, 1912, by Alice Z. Fraser (Webb's daughter).

[5] 2 Sam. 10: 5; 1 Chr. 19: 5.

them speak out when they come to the Colony. I, being one of the 'rebel maakers',[1] and a fanatic withal, the only comfort that will be bestowed on me will be, 'sarved him right'. But if some of the Devil's children be hustled, then we shall have a decentish boohoo.

I added a private note to the British Resident, giving the news so far as we have heard them of his brothers, their losses, the success of their trading at Sebituane's, and the probable plunder of all they have got, &c, making the picture quite plain. He won't need spectacles to see the Boers hauling out the big tusks out of his brothers' waggon, will he? And if he says nothing sharp to the Boer Republic, it will be because Mr Commissioner Owen lays an embargo on everything likely to disturb his bantling.

So, the mighty fuss about punishing Kreli has turned out a windbag. Well done, Kreli![2] And you, ye Fingoes, remember Botha. Verbum sat. sap. The world is becoming worse, I fear. The Pope at home, and Sandillah & General Uithaalder abroad. What next? Will you come to the dinner to Uithaalder?[3] Of course he will get a dinner as well as Pretorius.

The Peit Scholtz who was feasted at Natal with Pretorius was the Commandant at the Kolobeng![4] He did not bury all the dead of his own party. And they are all now dreadfully exasperated at me. They say I taught Sechele to shoot Boers, and they will have my head yet. As I have still a little use for my head, I am on the look out here, watching to see the path clear ahead. And what, think you, is the drama in front? A party of Boers waiting beyond the Bamangwato to plunder & perhaps kill a few Englishmen, and at the same time two parties of natives on the look out to kill them. It will be a wonder if a Boer escapes. When the path is clear, then I shall have [a] run for it.

All is peace beyond. Some Griqua hunters have approached the outposts of Mosilikatse, and he sends a message to Mr Moffat: 'Why don't you come and see me? Be sure and come, and bring a chair for me. All

---

[1] D. L. is using the Dutch word for 'makers'.

[2] Chief, 1835–92, of the AmaGcaleka, one of the Xhosa tribes fighting against the Colonists. By the time that peace was concluded with him (Feb. 1853), his tribe had suffered heavy losses of cattle, and he himself had to pay a substantial fine (Theal, *History*, vii, pp. 106, 109, 112, 113),

[3] Willem Uithaalder, leader of the rebel Hottentots. A reward of £500 had been offered for his capture, but he escaped beyond the border, where he lived until his death in 1865 (Theal, *op. cit.*, pp. 103, 113, 115).

[4] Pieter Ernest Scholtz, commandant of Marico district, led the Boer expedition against Sechele because Pretorius was ill. The two had visited Natal in May 1852, when Pretorius was given a public dinner by the inhabitants of Durban (for a detailed account of which see W. C. Holden, *History of the Colony of Natal*, 1855, pp. 151–8).

you told me (about the Boers) & fighting & killing is true.' He wants to make peace with the Griquas, &c. O, how I wish I were away in my own country, swampy & boggy though it be.

The reasons which make me doubt whether I ought to draw anything for Mebaloe are the following; and as you are fond[1] [of such things] you may take it as part of the history of the Bakwain Mission. I mentioned to you that, after three years' consistent conduct and profession of faith in Christ, I baptized Sechele on the first Sabbath of October 1848. In March or April 1849 it was discovered that he had had connection with one of his former wives, whom, in consequence of having a young child and no parents, he had found impossible to send away with the others. He at once confessed his sin, and added as an excuse that, having been accustomed to her, he had not at the time felt as if he were sinning by going to another man's wife. He professed much penitence, entreating me not to cast him off, 'as he hoped to stand along with me before the throne of Jesus'. I cut him off from fellowship, and as he entreated to be allowed to remain as a *spectator* only at the ordinance, and I felt that I must not count him as an enemy, I acceded to his request. He sat back from the spot where the few believers communicated on two or three occasions which occurred subsequently to his fall, and, his manner being no ways changed from what it had been previously, I indulged the hope that if he continued to walk uprightly for two or three years we might again recieve him.

Immediately after his fall I wrote to the Directors about it, knowing that they would sympathize with me in my sorrow, and I mentioned to them subsequently the fact of his walking consistently. I thought this was sufficient unless I had restored him again. But as soon as I heard of his conduct in the case of Mr Moyle, as it seemed widely different from consistency I wrote to the Directors a detailed account of the circumstances, and stated that I now considered him an entire backslider, though not an apostate.[2] I was the more careful to give the facts of his case because they had in some speeches made reference to his conversion, and some who did not, of course, know what I had written thought that I must still be holding up Sechele to the Board as a convert.

Well, eight or ten months after Sechele was cut off a worse affair came to light amongst the young people belonging to the families of the two native teachers Mebaloe & Paul, viz. excessive impurity,[3] and

[1] Last word on page, hence the suggested addition.
[2] But see above, p. 202: 'The plunder of Moyle by Sechele is quite unjustifiable, and as I stated before I believe Sechele is an apostate.'
[3] Described more fully in *Fam. Letters*, ii, pp. 27, 31.

when I began to make enquiry I found out that the teachers must have known of it and kept me in ignorance. This is a peculiarity among Bechuana believers. They never will make known the sins of their fellow believers, and when anything comes to light then they quietly remark, 'O, we knew all about it long ago'. The wives of the teachers, too, had been using enchantments. I felt very much vexed to think I had been administering the ordinance to them as consistent believers, and the whole town knowing all the while what their conduct had been. Their number being only seven I cut the whole off, having had no ordinance at all since. None of them ever asked why they were kept so. They seemed determined to act as if they had never been guilty, or as if they believed that I knew nothing about it. Paul's family being notoriously bad, I requested him to leave, but he did not go. Mebaloe however confessed to me, before I went to the Cape, that they had done great harm to the cause. 'In fact', said he, 'we have spoiled the teaching at Kolobeng.' The Boers now have cleared out the whole of them. I did not pay them anything from the time I discovered their inconsistency, but Mebaloe having confessed his sin, and also carried on the school up to the time of the Boers' attack, I may perhaps without impropriety draw a year's salary for him. I have not yet, however, made up my mind.

There are always two sides to a story. Well, the other side is this. Ashton loquitur: 'Livingston cut off the whole of the believers at Kolobeng because he had not moral courage to cut off Sechele'; and he recieves the delinquints into Kuruman church without asking a note of demission according to the universal custom of the churches here. Then, again, he proposed to Mr Moffat to write a joint letter to the Directors denouncing my falsehood 'in holding up Sechele to the Directors as a convert, all the while knowing that he is an apostate'. Mr M. of course declined this. Now I am in a fix. If I haul him up for his remarks, it will be another quarrel such as took place nine years ago,[1] when Edwards and Inglis took it into their heads to say I quarrelled with them, and which quarrel, the Directors tell me now,[2] still exists. If I let him alone and say nothing, then he will be sure that his remark about my want of moral courage is correct. Shall I brave the row, or the imputation? I feel inclined to do the latter, as requiring more courage than the former. This will be 'Jouk[3] & let the jaw gang by'.

---

[1] As the quarrel had occurred in 1845 (see above, p. 65), 'nine' should presumably read 'seven'.

[2] See above, p. 208.

[3] Duck.

But I am giving you letters equal in length to the Times Newspaper, and you give me ½ sheets. Take care, my friend. Old John Wylde is nothing to me if I open out on you. Tell me some of your trials, omitting the Brit. Quar. one,[1] and how you manage to overcome. It is something to overcome oneself. I would not mention names above, but to put down a blank would not be treating you with any confidence, and I cannot help believing that you possess a great deal more prudence than I ever did or ever will get hold of.

In proof of want of prudence, I intend to begin tomorrow another spell for the British Quarterly on the Caffre war. It is high time that we speak out. We must pitch into them. It is infamous to see our Cape Government scraping and bowing to the Mobocracy of that cesspool called Graham's Town.[2]

I have sketched out a grammar, but done nothing else except collecting words and making notes (a very few on natural history). When I think of it, it grows on me and seems a work of a life time, and I suspect mine will not be a long one. I cannot get over the idea that complaining of one's ailments is old-wifish, yet a pain in my chest I never felt before, when I exert myself to speak as loudly as I used to do in preaching, warns me that my days are few. In preaching in Sichuana, which I do occasionally, I feel at home, & speak much more loudly and quickly than when gasping for words as much as for breath & voice in Union Chapel.[3] Will you present my kind remembrances to Dr Abercrombie,[4] and ask him what he would recommend for a pain apparently confined to the middle & upper lobes of the left lung? I feel it only when I preach loudly. It continues half a day afterwards. I use sponging the whole body, the chest in particular, with cold water, but have not much inclination to use medicines unless recommended by a judicious old practitioner as he. The throat, I am sorry to say, is not so much benefitted

---

[1] D. L. had contributed to *The British Quarterly Review*, xiv, no.27, August 1851, pp. 106–13, an unsigned article highly critical of LMS institutions in Cape Colony. Thompson prepared a rejoinder, but 'told me he would not have written as he did had he known or suspected the author to be a missionary' (*Fam. Letters*, ii, p. 170).

[2] 'The Grahamstown people are bitter beyond measure against missionaries. They have supplied the Caffres with guns and ammunition, and always want a war, because they can sell everything to the military at enormous prices. A war enriches them. They hate the missionaries who befriend the natives' (29.ix.51 Watt; cf. *Fam. Letters*, ii, p. 153).

[3] Thompson's church, in Church Square, Cape Town. D. L. had spoken there on 25.iv.52. 'I felt dreadfully at a loss for words in English, while ideas came up in barrowfuls. I became quite hoarse in about ten minutes after I began' (*Fam. Letters*, ii, pp. 177–8).

[4] James Abercrombie (1797–1870), a prominent Cape Town surgeon, who had operated on D. L.'s uvula (*Fam. Letters*, ii, pp. 169, 177–8).

as I expected. There is no symptom of any disease whatever in the lung. I feel nóthing but the pain & a feeling of weakness.

Yet, that you may not think me entirely destitute of prudence, I may mention that I have remained here more than a month after my wheel was repaired, waiting till the Boers have got out of my way. They intend, it is reported, as soon as they hear of my passing to send a party on horseback after me, and if I will not come back they must kill me. I intend to lighten the waggons of as much food as possible, and everything else except bare necessaries, and then we shall have a run. I shall travel mostly at night, keep well to the West, and if I get back to Sekhomi's he will take care that they don't bring me back. (O diabolos, you work hard for your own.) I feel a little ashamed at lingering here, now that I have no incumbrance, but what can be expected since I have become a worshipper of the goddess prudence?

Tell Ralph that the miserable white poney is become fat again & carries me about finely. He would not know it now.

15th. Have just heard that the Boers have stripped Mosheu the Koranna of everything. See Mr Moffat's book for an account of Mosheu.[1] The Boers are reported to be quarrelling among themselves; the widows of those killed at Sechele's won't recieve their share of the plunder, and curse Pretorious bitterly because he pretended to be sick while he sent their husbands on commando. Last Sunday I preached 3 times, and did not feel the pain I have had for some time, so you need not think anything more about it. Ludorf is at Motito, having fled from his people.[2] They too are flying. Philipolis Griquas are said to be stabbing each other, through brandy of course. I shall write to Directors by next opportunity.

Ever yours, of course,
D. Livingston

45. To ARTHUR TIDMAN
2 November 1852

[LMS 72. Previous publication: *Chronicle*, vol. xvii, (April) 1853, pp. 65–6 (edited extracts); Chamberlin, pp. 184–9 (incomplete)]

[1] *Miss. Labours*, pp. 592–605 passim. 'Mosheu' (Massau) was chief of the Taaibosch tribe of Korana Hottentots, then living at Mamusa.

[2] Joseph D. M. Ludorf was a Wesleyan missionary working among the BaRolongboorraTshidi at Lotlhakane (near Mafeking). The people having abandoned their village because menaced by the Boers, he was now on his way to Bloemfontein with his family, and passed through Kuruman at the beginning of November (*Private J.*, p. 93).

Kuruman
2d November 1852

Dear Sir,

With feelings of unfeigned gratitude I acknowledge your letter of July last, containing information respecting the safe arrival of Mrs Livingston and family in England; and I hereby tender my fervent thanks to the Directors for the various arrangements by which my mind is relieved from anxiety, and I am constrained to dedicate anew my whole being to the service of our Lord and Master.

I have special reason for gratitude in the kind consideration shewn towards the case of Mr Moffat. Every variety of treatment which we have either seen, heard, or read of, has been tried, but hitherto without the smallest effect on the complaint. Sudden pressure on one side of the head having been observed to make some little difference in the constant loud ringing sound within, I recommended iodine, on the supposition that the symptoms might have been caused by hypertrophy of one of the cerebral membranes, but there is not as yet the slightest benefit from its employment. The thorough manner in which he applies himself to the translation involves a large amount of mental toil. Incessant attempts to make the Sichuana harmonize with the Hebrew render the undertaking nearly the same as learning the latter language and translating too. The various uses of each Hebrew word are ascertained, and uniformity in the use of the Sichuana attempted. Assistance in this is drawn from the Dutch, German, French, & English translations, and also from a number of commentaries. Complete cessation from this severe toil is almost the only means which remain to be tried for his recovery, and the fact that Mrs Livingston began to amend as soon as she came within the influence of the sea air makes me think favourably of a visit to the coast. Mr Moffat's own inclination, if he could tear himself away from translation, would perhaps lead him to visit his old friend Mosilekatse, that chief having lately sent him a pressing invitation.[1] It is gratifying for us to know that all excuse on the ground of want of means is now removed, and whatever the ultimate issue of the disease may be, there will [be no] cause for complaint.

I am sorry to find that my remarks on the relative expenditure in the Colony and countries beyond have appeared to imply a charge of maladministration on the part of the Directors. Those remarks were

---

[1] Through some Griqua traders who had visited the outposts of the MaTebele (Hughes, in *S.A. Miss. Report*, 1852, p. 30). Moffat did in fact visit Moselekatse, for the third time, in 1854, 'primarily for reasons of health' (*Matabele Journals*, i, pp. 139–382).

founded on data published in the Colony, shewing the average expenditure for a series of years; and though it is quite true that 'a missionary looking to an object from an isolated point of view is very liable to misinterpret the measures of the Directors when applied in a wide scale', it is not quite so obvious that the relative or numerical value of these data can be affected by our mode of viewing them. Having full reliance on the purity of motive which influences and controuls the general administration of the Directors, I imagined that their attention might be drawn to certain inequalities, without impugning their integrity; and even now, if we push aside for a little the very laudable touchiness on the subject of management, my remarks may be viewed as implying no more than want of faith in their omniscience.

In pages 42–43 of the printed 'Letter of Instructions' I am enjoined to present, from time to time, statements respecting 'the circumstances and necessities of the ajacent country, and of the course of events and opinions bearing on the interests of Christianity.'[1] I have refrained from the performance of this duty during the last eight years. I have been deterred from furnishing information, concerning events which were notorious to the whole Bechuana country as hindering the gospel of Christ, by the fear that my judgement might be biassed by the 'difference' to which you refer. During those eight years of silence on my part, it was notorious that the Bakhatla had repeatedly by public proclamation rejected the gospel. Not one individual of the tribe was permitted to attend either school or church, and consequently £800 of the Society's funds were spent on two or three families who had come to Mabotsa for the sake of better gardens. Mr Inglis spent one of his first four years in formally holding school for Mr Edwards with the children of these highly favoured families. The contemptuous treatment of Sebubi, the native teacher among the Wanketse, by Mr Edwards, the railing accusations of Mr Inglis against Sechele during the period of the consistent walk and conversation of that chief — on these events, & opinions founded on these events, I refrained from remark. There is no reference to them in my letters during the last seven years.

But when winding up my connection with that part of the country,

---

[1] 'In addition to the extracts from your journal, and regular half yearly letters, we request that you will transmit from time to time documents prepared with greater care, and embracing a wider range of subject. It is our desire that these communications comprise not only an account of the extent and peculiarities of your station, and the most striking occurrences connected with your own labours, but a statement of the circumstances and necessities of the adjacent country, the course of events and opinions among the people, bearing on the interests of christianity; a retrospect of the progress already made, and view of the prospects opening up before you' (*Letter of Instructions*, p. 43).

it seemed natural and proper to obey the positive injunctions of the Directors and give a general view of the causes of the failure of the Mission in the Kolobeng district. Between this view, and a quarrel which took place eight years ago, a connection is instantly established, and Mr Moffat is lugged into it too. As he was not engaged in that quarrel, I begin to suspect that the *'connection'* was suggested by some member of the South African Committee who had been seven years out of office. I can scarcely believe that the Directors are totally oblivious of the fact that, for the sake of peace, I yielded up a splendid station and good prospects for a new people and a locality which did not afford the promise of the necessaries of life, and yielded it up too though cooly informed by Mr Edwards 'that had he known of my desires he would have waived the whole quarrel'. I was convinced that I could not work in connection with him afterwards, and did what ministers in England do, viz. maintain perfect silence. Had I done what some better men do to Dr Campbell, evince my hostility by a perpetual stroke,[1] there would have been some ground on which discernment of motive might tread. But having carried out my desires to carry the gospel to another tribe, irrespective of Mr Edwards's furious attacks on my character in order to secure Mabotsa to himself, I am almost as much startled at the exhumation of the old quarrel as if I had met a resurrectionist. I feel sorry that any of my remarks have conveyed a charge so different from what I intended, and beg leave to withdraw whatever may after the above explanation appear offensive.

I reached Kuruman about three months ago. I was longer on the way from Cape Town that the distance required, and all the other hindrances which occurred were at last crowned by the complete breaking down of a wheel near this place. As soon as this was ready I prepared to leave, but the news of the horrid deeds of the Boers arrived, and I then percieved that a kind Providence had been detaining me that I might not fall into the hands of the marauders. Had I been able to travel as quickly as my desires dictated, I should have been at Kolobeng at the very time of the attack, and as the Commandant repeatedly expressed sorrow at not having caught [me], and also his determination to cut off my head, I feel certain that they would at least have taken all the property I now have, and rendered my present enterprise abortive.

[1] John Campbell (1794–1867) was editor of *The Christian Witness* (official organ of the Congregational Union) and other periodicals, including *The British Banner*. His outspoken criticisms of 'any deviation from what he held to be evangelical orthodoxy' created much resentment, and 'on more than one occasion the Union found itself dragged into hot debates over the management of its official publications' (R. W. Dale, *History of English Congregationalism*, 1907, p. 721).

They are much exasperated against me because Sechele cut off about thirty of their number,[1] and resolutely refuses to block up the path to the North for Englishmen. They have attacked and dispersed eight tribes since I came into the country, and though great numbers of the natives have fallen, not a drop of Boerish blood has been spilled. The Wanketse and Bakhatla followed the usual course of tribes in that quarter: they fled without attempting to strike a blow on those who were wantonly killing them. But Sechele fought a whole day; therefore, say the Boers, 'that horrid doctor must have taught them to fight'. It is remarkable that those who evinced most inclination to learn to read have shewn the most bravery, and the leading opponents of the gospel found their hearts melting with fear as soon as the Boers approached. Mebaloe, the native teacher, remained till the commencement of the firing, and then left. When the commando approached, the Bakwains, seeing the advantage of attacking before the camp was formed, were eager to begin, but Mebaloe's advice to avoid striking the first blow was listened to, and thence arose all the subsequent success of the Boers.

The particulars, so far as we could ascertain them from eye-witnesses, were transmitted to Mr Thompson for publication. I forwarded a statement of my losses through the violation of the treaty to the Lieut.-Governor by the same hands, and also a similar statement to the British Resident, H. Green, Esqre, at Bloemfontein. I have little hope of any redress from the Colonial Government, but thought it right to let our wrongs be known to those in authority, and as the British Resident has brothers engaged in the trade of the new country, I entertain the hope he will exert himself to prevent the way being blocked up by these ignorant savages. It is necessary to distinguish between the Colonial farmers of Dutch extraction who are usually called Boers, and those in the Interior, of the same name, whose independance has been lately acknowledged by the Government. The latter are the dregs of the Colonial population, and if we do not bear in mind the general belief they entertain that black people are soulless, it is difficult to believe the records of their barbarity and callousness in shedding the blood of the coloured people.

I can declare most positively that the Bakwains have given no offence to these Boers during the last eight years, and the only reason they

---

[1] Sechele wrote to Moffat (see above, p. 222) that 28 Boers had been killed in the attack on Dimawê (*Private J.*, p. 89). Pretorius, in a letter to Henry Green (23.ix.52), mentions only 3 killed and 6 wounded (*P.P. England 1852-3*, LXVI, p. 752). Cf. *Fam. Letters*, ii, p. 185.

themselves could urge for attacking them were that Sechele refused to become their vassal and prevent English traders and others from passing him towards the countries beyond.[1] I have not the smallest wish to screen Sechele from blame. The Bakwains, Wanketse, and Bakhatla, have wilfully rejected the gospel, and have brought on themselves the just judgements of God by their unbelief; but the head and front of Sechele's offending, in the estimation of the Boers, is neither more nor [less] than refusal to obey their repeated demands to shut up the Interior from English enterprise. They are determined to secure all the ivory now brought from the Lake region to themselves. The plea of preventing the English from dealing in arms and ammunition among the natives is a mere subterfuge, as it is notorious they deal largely in these articles themselves.

Their determination makes me more resolved than ever to open up a new way to the Interior, and the experience of that kind providence, which prevented me falling into the hands of those who would have at least sadly crippled my efforts, encourages me to hope that God graciously intends to make some further use of me. I have recieved friendly assurances of welcome from the principal men of the Makololo, by means of native traders who have lately returned from that country; and though the present delay is the more difficult to endure, inasmuch as it is consuming the time in which I am unencumbered, it may be that I am thus prevented from falling a victim to the fever.

The losses we have sustained amount to upwards of £300. We shall move the more lightly now that we can put all our goods into one waggon. Cannot say I take joyfully the spoiling of my goods. If they had made any use of my books and medicines I could have forgiven them, but tearing, smashing, and burning them was beyond measure galling.

The notice taken of Mr Oswel by the Directors has been highly gratifying to my feelings. By a letter from Mrs L., I find that he is still anxious to befriend us.

I am, Dear Sir, yours affectionately,
David Livingston

Nov. 12th. I am preparing to start for the North during this week, or the beginning of the week following.

[1] According to Pretorius (*loc. cit.*), the main reason for the attack was Sechele's 'repeated threats and intimidating conduct' towards the inhabitants of Marico district. The BaKwena themselves say it was due to Sechele's refusal to surrender Mosielele (Schapera, *Ditirafalô*, pp. 51–2).

46. To WILLIAM THOMPSON
24 November 1852

[LMS 73. Previous publication: Chamberlin, pp. 189–92]

Kuruman
November 24th 1852,

My dear Mr Thompson,

Am sorry to say I am still here in durance vile, but matters are in a fair state now for effecting my escape. I could not get drivers, people were all so afraid of going Northward. I have made arrangements with two Hottentots, and think I shall be off positively before the next moon. The delays which have occurred have prevented me falling into Boerish hands, so I am thankful, and indulge the hope that God has still some little work for me to do. The belief that my hindrances from the Cape off to the Kuruman are providential makes me submit with a good grace.

Fine fellows you Cape worthies are. Mr Fairbairn[1] tells his contemporaries that the connection of the Dutch Church with the State is very slender, and you believe it, of course. They get £200 per annum, and the State appoints the ministers, or has all the patronage in its hands. Our connection with the Society is half as slight again, for we only get £100. He of course knows what sort of people he is speaking to. Humph. Sir George C[athcart][2] tells the Caffres that they may recieve the Gaika warriors into their houses. Receipt of stolen goods is no crime in his eyes. It's 'for any sake take them away, I can't beat them'.[3] Boohoo, O thou mighty man of valour. That's 'extermination', 'driving over the Kei',[4] 'unconditional submission', 'complete subjugation', and £500 for Uithaalder's head too. I intend to offer £5,000 for the Lion's Head[5] which looks down at Church Square, said Lion's head to be delivered at Lattakoo, and I give you the first offer. What unutterable

---

[1] John Fairbairn (1794–1864), of Cape Town, editor and proprietor of the *S.A. Commercial Advertiser.*

[2] Lieut.-Gen. the Hon. George Cathcart (1794–1854), Governor of Cape Colony, and commander-in-chief in S. Africa, March 1852–May 1854; K.C.B., 1853; 'crushed the Kaffirs and Basutos' (*D.N.B.*).

[3] 'I can't bear them' (Chamberlin, p. 189).

[4] The Kei River, eastern boundary of British Kaffraria (annexed to Cape Colony in 1847).

[5] A prominent peak immediately to the right of Table Mountain (as seen from Table Bay).

meaness this Sir George Gibbet Cathcart[1] can be guilty of, & a
Scotchman too. Did I not tell you we Scotchmen are a bad set?

I don't understand your question about responsibility. The Superintendant will get all the blame of everything bad if he allows the Committees to do wrong.[2] I think the Directors will do so. In Africa we all
blame each other, and we are blamed by everybody else. Make them all
Independant, that's my advice.

D. Livingston

I have sent a paper on the Caffre war to the B. Quart.[3] If this is
blabbed by the Dr I shall not write any more for him.[4]

P.S.[5] By this post I send 10 letters addressed to your care, and post
paid as far as Cape Town. There is no use in attempting to pay beyond
that. You must open an account against me and put down postage,
forage, and all other monies expended on my behalf. I enclose a letter to
Mr Macgibbon of the Botanic Gardens,[6] and if you can spare time to
glance over it you may oblige me in one of your walks next winter by
putting him in remembrance.

Macgibbon's letter contains seeds. 2 of the above-named letters are
for yourself. I say 'put down all monies, &c'. What hypocrisy! If
honest I would say, you may either put it down or not, I see no prospect
of ever paying you. If I live to come back to Cape Town, I shall get a
share of Mr Holl's parlour in the house by the Jetty,[7] or a lodging in
the Union Workhouse. Please request Mr Pococke to get a supply of

---

[1] 'Sir George Gilbert Cathcart' (Chamberlin, p. 190). Cf. below, p. 237: 'It
would be unspeakably pleasing to Sir George to hang us all on one gibbet'. Cf. also
Travels, pp. 106, 107: 'The lamented Sir George Cathcart . . . an able and sagacious
governor . . . of whom it is impossible to speak without respect.'

[2] Thompson had sent to all LMS missionaries in S. Africa a printed circular of
queries (dated 30.ix.52), in which he asked, *inter alia*: 'In the event of any real
or supposed interest of our Society being overlooked, or for the want of prompt
action being sacrificed, upon whom do you consider would the responsibility
rest?'

[3] Blaikie, p. 128, quotes a letter (dated 3.x.53) indicating that D. L. had sent 'the
Caffre War paper' to his friend D. G. Watt, who was to arrange if possible for its
publication. The attempt was apparently unsuccessful.

[4] Presumably Dr Robert Vaughan (1795–1868), editor of *The British Quarterly
Review* 1845–65 (*D.N.B.*). For his 'blabbing', see below, p. 254 n.

[5] This postscript, written on a separate and smaller piece of paper marked
'Business', is filed in the same jacket (LMS 74) as Letter 47. The contents clearly
show that it was meant for Thompson, and I have followed Chamberlin in making
it part of the present letter, though it is undated.

[6] James McGibbon, Head Gardener of the Botanic Gardens, Cape Town (*C.G.H.
Almanac*, 1852, p. 159).

[7] Possibly Edward Holl, a tailor in Burg Street, Cape Town (*C.G.H. Almanac*,
1852, Cape Town Directory); but I have not discovered what connection, if any, he
had with D. L.

vaccine virus from the Institution for me.[1] I forgot it. If you are acquainted with the officer, he will do it better & send it post free.

I shall probably draw £12 for Mebaloe. This is all the business I have to transact or trouble you with.

One of the letters is for America through Captain Holmes,[2] & you will perhaps be good enough to present my kind remembrance to him. As the post is not going for an hour or two, I may have time to write another letter, which will be eleven to your care.

47. To ARTHUR TIDMAN
12 December 1852

[LMS 74. London postmark: 18 MR 1853. Previous publication: Campbell, pp. 141–2 (part of first paragraph)]

Kuruman
12 December 1852

Dear Sir,

Enclosed you will recieve a letter to Sir John Pakington, H.M. Secretary for the Colonies.[3] I wrote to the Lieutenant-Governor Darling[4] an account of the attack of the Boers on Kolobeng, and sent also a similar letter to H. Green, the British Resident, with the addition of a claim for compensation, my property having been destroyed in the violation of a treaty. I scarcely expect any compensation, but thought the more noise we made the less likely would they be to do the same thing over again. But the more I become acquainted with the present Governor Sir George Cathcart's feelings, the less hope I have of the least favour being shewn to anything in the shape of either missionary or Hottentots. Indeed, it would be unspeakably pleasing to Sir George

---

[1] John Thomas Pocock was head of a firm of 'chemists and druggists' in Cape Town, a deacon of Union Chapel, and on the committee of the Cape Town Auxiliary of the LMS (*C.G.H. Almanac*, 1852, p. 146, and Directory). The 'Institution' is presumably the Vaccine Institution at Cape Town, from which 'Vaccine Virus is transmitted, free to all parts of the Colony, on application being made to the Secretary' (*ibid.*, p. 137).

[2] Gideon Skull Holmes, U.S. consul at Cape Town (in succession to Chase); a committee member of the Cape Town Auxiliary (*C.G.H. Almanac*, 1852, p. 146 and Directory).

[3] Sir John Somerset Pakington (1799–1880), created Baron Hampton in 1874, was 'Secretary for war and colonies under Lord Derby in 1852' (*D.N.B.*). D. L.'s letter to him was published in *P.P. England 1852–3*, LXVI, pp. 803–4.

[4] Charles Henry Darling (1809–70), Lieutenant-Governor of Cape Colony 1852–1854.

to hang us all on one gibbet. He will never forgive the Hottentots, for completely foiling him in war, nor us missionaries, because our belief that Hottentots have souls has turned out, in connection with the name of this mighty man of valour, true all the world over. Such being the case, I mustered courage to write to his master, Sir John Pakington. I think I have good cause for complaint, but whether I have done it in a proper manner, and whether it ought to be presented at all, I leave entirely to your decision.

A Mr Codrington, a gentleman of large landed property in Wiltshire,[1] lost a good deal of property at Kolobeng. He had gone down the Limpopo on a hunting expedition, and when he returned his cattle and goods were gone. As he has Parliamentary influence, he will make some noise about the affair. He goes home to England now. Only one half of his cattle were taken, and the other half were by some mistake left behind. Sechele sent them out to Mr Moffat, and though an attempt was made by the person who had them in charge to steal them, the people here pursued them, overtook the thievish Englishman (a Mr Simpson),[2] fined him, and the price of the missing cattle and such as remained are in custody here for the owner. It is pleasant to see the people making efforts to promote justice, and perhaps it is not always wrong even to fight for their country. Rains have fallen, and I have nearly succeeded in getting a complement of men. I fully intend starting from this on the 14th currt.

I advised you of £10 for books from Mr MacLehose,[3] and another £10 for clothing from Mr Drummond, neither of which sums, though deducted from my salary, have yet been drawn. They will be applied for soon. I gave Mebaloe £10 in consideration of his losses at Kolobeng, and because he had kept school and other services and remained at his work up to the commencement of the firing. He is now at Kuruman.

Believe me yours affectionately,
David Livingston

---

[1] Captain William Codrington, of Wroughton, near Swindon; he was a shooting companion of Webb, whose sister he subsequently married (Fraser, *Livingstone and Newstead*, p. 8).

[2] J. Simpson, a trader, then on his way back from an expedition to the MaKololo, in the course of which all his oxen had died of tsetse bite (*Fam. Letters*, ii, p. 196; *Private J.*, p. 95).

[3] James MacLehose, bookseller and publisher, Glasgow; a friend and correspondent of D. L. On 14.i.53 D. L. wrote to Mrs L.: 'Ask MacLehose to send my account. Don't forget to tell MacLehose to draw the ten pounds which I advised of. It has been deducted from my salary, for I wrote to the Directors about it from Boatlanama' (*Fam. Letters*, ii, 202). But in his letter to the Directors (see above, p. 172), he had in fact said nothing about MacLehose.

I have written during my sojourn here an Analysis of the Sechuana. It may be accepted by the Asiatic Journal.[1] If published some months hence, you will see I have some important topics in view in it.

13th December. I leave this tomorrow afternoon.

D. L.

[1] D. L. sent the MS. to his friend Watt, for submission to the *Asiatic Journal*; it was, however, not published there (see *Private J.*, p. 95).

VIII

RETURN TO THE MAKOLOLO

48. To WILLIAM THOMPSON
17 September 1853

[LMS 76. Received 17 March 1854. Previous publication: Campbell, pp. 124, 126 (two paragraphs); Chamberlin, pp. 190–1, 192, 198–202 (incomplete)]

Sekeletu's Town,[1]
17th September 1853

My dear Man,

Your letters are 'necessarily brief', so you say, and I am bound to believe the Right Reverend Father William Capeton, seeing he hath recieved two students from Hankey into his ghostly care.[2] Ah, mine are necessarily long, long winded or flatulent, as a follower of Esculapius expresseth it. The reason whereof lieth in an immense sheet of paper[3] which must be filled, for Nature abhorreth a vacuum, and want of time to shorten them.

The Directors and you are wonderful men. The former decline to write concerning certain minutes of Committee, though informed that no meeting will take place till such writing has been recieved,[4] and they at same time cooly tell me that they hope I shall derive counsel, assistance, &c &c, from the Committee of which no meeting can take place. Then you, if I recollect aright, twitted me about our Committee being defunct, and yet presume the matter of a companion will come before it. But who will go? I am gone. No matter, my companion can follow. The Directors requested Ashton to leave the Kuruman and settle with a tribe, as I had done. He refused. Subsequently Mr Freeman proposed

---

[1] Dinyanti, which D. L. had reached from Kuruman on 23 May. He then explored the Zambesi valley (see below), and on his return (15 September) found that two European traders had brought mail for him (*Fam. Letters*, ii, p. 214; *Private J.*, p. 234). Sekeletu was Sebetwane's son, and had recently become chief of the Ma-Kololo, on the abdication of his sister Mma-Motsisane. He died in 1863.

[2] Hankey, about 50 miles N.N.W. of Port Elizabeth, was an LMS training institution. Two of its European missionary students had gone to Cape Town 'to see more of general society than Hankey affords' and for further study under Thompson's direction (Thompson to Tidman, 6.ix.52, 24.i.53).

[3] The page measures 15.7 × 10 inches.

[4] The District Committee had not met since December 1849 (*Fam. Letters*, ii, p. 165).

in Committee held at Kuruman that Ashton should go to Borigelong. He refused by saying, 'It would be like taking Mrs Ashton to her grave'. 'Then you must take the entire charge of the printing press' (Mr Moffat had till then done the press work), 'and leave Mr M. to devote his entire time to translation'. This, you will percieve, settled him at Kuruman. Mr Moffat is the only man willing to go, but would it be advisable for him to do so? No, certainly. But here I am, after my 8th attack of fever, the last very severe, being accompanied with large discharges of blood. It has made me quite thin, but as I am becoming old and skinney per process of time that does not matter much. I never laid by, but vertigo from exhaustion compelled me to give up some of my sedentary work.

By the way, it now glances accross my mind that the daguerrotype portraits entrusted to Mrs De Smit had not in November last been delivered.[1] I blame myself severely for entrusting them to a young man through his mother. She of course, good woman, wished to oblige, but what thousands of gracious mothers have striven to make their sons appear obliging, every one else understanding it as merely efforts to make silk purses out of sow's ears. Though too much given to jesting tonight, I am really very sorry for the loss I fear Mrs L. has sustained. She feels it very keenly, and I cannot repair the loss.[2]

Please retain the medal in Cape Town till you hear from me.[3] It is not likely I shall ever come your way again. Here one of your questions holds up its phiz at me: 'Unless you discover a good way to the sea, either to the East or West, how are we in future to send men to the region of the Lake or to the parts beyond? For Lobale?' '*In future*'. The dear man! How many has he sent in time past? 'Unless you discover a good', &c. An indifferent one will do for those who have any pluck in them; and for those who have none, the old overland route may be safely recommended, for they will discover some important & very large field of labour a long way south of the Orange River, in which they will be associated with a Wesleyan, a Church of England clergyman, a Dutch Predicant, and a Government schoolmaster, each

[1] These were portraits taken while D. L. and his family were in Cape Town. Mrs de Smidt (as it should be written) I cannot identify; the Cape Town Directories for this period list several families of that name.

[2] In the LMS archives there are two portraits of D. L. taken at Cape Town in April 1852 (one is reproduced as the frontispiece of this volume), which suggests that the 'loss' may have been repaired. They were presented to the LMS in 1947 from the estate of Mrs Isabella Henson, a grand-daughter of Moffat.

[3] This was the silver medal awarded to D. L. in 1852 by the Geographical Society of Paris, for the discovery of Lake Ngami. 'Mr Thompson informs me it is in his possession' (22.ix.53 Frédoux: *Fam. Letters*, ii, p. 222).

of whom considers the 10 shanties and 8 shopkeeper's houses as his 'sphere of labour', involving the most excrutiating responsibility.

I was delayed long at Kuruman by the Boers and want of people, for all feared to go North; but having got over these difficulties we made very good progress, till we came into Lat. 19° 16' South. There all my people were knocked down by fever except one Bakwain lad.[1] I managed the hospital, and he the oxen, and by God's mercy none were cut off. When we were able to move Northwards, the poor Bakwain lad took it too. I had to drive and cut a path too, for keeping more to the Eastward in order to avoid the tsetse we travelled through a densely wooded country, in which the axe was in constant operation. But for two Bushmen who managed the loose oxen and otherwise assisted, we could not have moved. Some were still so weak we had to lift them out and into the waggon.

When we came near the Chobe, the ajacent country was flooded for 15 miles out. Vallies appeared like large deep rivers, with hippopotami in them. We tried long in vain to get a ford through one large river called Sanshureh.[2] Our Bushmen decamped too. So I took a small pontoon, kindly presented by Messrs Webb and Codrington, and the strongest of my weak crew, crossed the Sanshureh, ½ a mile wide, and went North to find the Chobe & people. We waded among reed and high grass for three days, trying to obtain a passage in to the Chobe through the dense masses of reed &c which line its banks. On the fourth day we attained our object, launched the pontoon, and after passing along about 20 miles we reached a Makololo village. In their figurative language they said I 'had come down upon them as if I had dropped out of a cloud, yet I came riding on the back of a hippopotamus'. A rumour had reached the Makololo previously, and two parties had been sent out in search of us. All our difficulties were now at an end. Canoes were soon sent down by the chief, our waggons &c were transported accross the country & river, & after proceeding North, in order to avoid the flooded lands on the other side, we turned S.W. & reached the town.

Our reception was far more flattering than I could have anticipated. The chief, just over 18 years of age, said he rejoiced to obtain another father instead of Sebitoane, and repeated[ly] requested me to name whatever I wished, and he would shew his affection by giving it — cattle, ivory, &c &c; and he seemed distressed when I refused to name

---

[1] The incidents mentioned here and in the next paragraph are described much more fully in *Private J.*, pp. 103–36.

[2] A flood channel or 'arm' of the Chobe. D. L. says he struck it at *c.* 18° 04' S., 24° 06' E. (*Travels*, p. 174).

anything. He is not equal in appearance or abilities to his father, but there is nothing weak or childish in his conduct or conversation, and several executions which have taken place on account of conspiracy shew that he is not destitute of Sebitoane's energy. He is afraid to learn to read at present, 'lest it should change his heart and make him content with one wife', as in the case of Sechele. I like a frank objection. One cannot get hold on a 'Ya, Mynheer'. They are too oily.

I have just returned from a nine weeks' tour through the country in search of a suitable location for a Mission.[1] Went up the Borotse River or, as it is universally called by the Makalaka[2] (the aboriginal inhabitants, the black race of whom I spoke), the Leeamby or 'The River'. [We] reached the confluence of the Loeti with its light-coloured water, also that of the Leeba or Lonta. Londa is the proper name, because it comes from Londa, the capital of a large state. The confluence of the Londa and Leeamby is in 14° 11′ South.[3] This is a point of great importance for the Leeamby turns thence away to the East N. East. The Londa [is] about 150 yards wide, the Leeamby 250 beyond it. The Londa, coming from the N. & by W. or N.N.W., is, I dream, yet to form part of our way West. Conveyance by water is of great importance. With 6 paddlers we went 44 miles of Latitude in one day of 10½ hours, and taking into account the windings of the river, and our course being what sailors term a 2½ point one, the actual distance must have been upwards of 50 geographical miles. The river is one of very great beauty & breadth. It is often more than a mile broad, with islands 3 or four miles long in it. These are covered with sylvan vegetation, the rounded masses of which seem to recline on the bosom of the water. The tsetse spoils the most beautiful and healthful spots.

I must reserve details, but after a laborious search have not found a spot I could pronounce salubrious. We must brave the fever. It is God, not the Devil, that rules our destiny. Surely we may when slave traders do. I met Arabs from Zanguebar, subjects of the Imaum of Muscat, who could write readily, and Portuguese from the farthest trading station inland on the West. The latter, probably through the influence of the Chevalier Du Pratt's letter and passport,[4] shewed me every

---

[1] See *Private J.*, pp. 181–234, for a detailed account.

[2] 'The general name' applied by the MaKololo 'to all the black race on the rivers', perhaps because they were as dark-skinned as the true MaKalaka of N.E. Bechuanaland (*Private J.*, p. 146).

[3] As used here, 'Leeamby' is the Kabompo, and 'Londa' or 'Leeba' the Zambesi above its confluence with that river (cf. *Private J.*, p. 219). The 'Loeti' is the Lungwebungu, which joins the Zambesi from the N.W. at *c.* 14° 19′ S.

[4] Alfredo Duprat (1816–81) was the Portuguese consul at Cape Town; his 'passports' are mentioned in *Private J.*, p. 81.

civility. An intrigue with an under-chief who had pretensions to the chieftainship enabled the latter to drive a brisk trade in slaves in the northern half of the Makololo country. Nothing was done here to encourage them to call again. A stockade was erected in the Borotse country, a flagstaff for the Portuguese banner set up, [and] a small cannon given to the pretender, who, it is supposed, gave authority for the prosecution of the slave trade contrary to the orders of the chief. The conduct on the part of the merchant was very silly, for no sooner was the intrigue known than the chief conspirators were cut off and their bodies tumbled into the river. On my remonstrating against bloodshed, the answer given was, 'We are still Boers, we are not yet taught'. They would have expelled the slave merchant too, but refrained on my representing that their doing so might injure me in the West, and their departure is to take place soon.

I go Westward as soon as the rains commence. I have preached in many spots where the name of Christ was never heard before. This is matter for gratitude. Hope the gospel will yet be established in these savage lands. I travelled in a company of 160 in 33 canoes. From the chief downwards all strove to shew kindness. Nine weeks' intimate intercourse, hearing their conversation, anecdotes, quarrelling, roaring, dancing, singing, and murdering, have imparted a greater disgust at heathenism than I ever had before, and, on comparison with Southern tribes, a firm belief that missionaries effect a great deal more than they are aware of, even when there are no conversions.

I am sorry you cannot be furnished with a correct sketch of the country which I have seen. I have used the last bit of tracing paper for the Directors. 2 letters for America per Captain Holmes, a packet for Dr Tidman, 4 English & one Canadian letter.

Please inform your sister that the fish and bracelets were punctually delivered to Mamochisane, who expressed herself pleased with the gift.[1] She gave over the chieftainship to her brother, and that, too, gracefully. She had no taste for ruling, preferring to be married and rear a family. She seems a very affectionate mother, sending every now & then during our interview to see if her child were awake, and hurrying off to it quicker than ladies in this part usually do when informed that she was

[1] The passages beginning with this sentence are written on a much smaller sheet of notepaper (c. 8½ × 5½ inches), which is filed in LMS 73 together with Letter 46, written on paper of the same size and colour. Chamberlin (pp. 190–1) accordingly prints them as part of that letter. But the context indicates that they are much later (D. L. met Mma-Motsisane on 9.viii.53, cf. *Private J.*, p. 202), and the facetious reference below to 'William Capeton' suggests that they really belong here (cf. the opening sentence of this letter).

roasted or only prepared for roasting. They made a little song about it

As I don't wish to be guilty of plagiarism I have to ask your permission to adopt the following flourish which though similar is not identical with yours.

David Zambezi
his mark +

Not for every one's eye of course

Unto the Right Reverend & Venerable William Capeton with greeting (scoticé)

needed. The fish was an object of great attraction among the Borotse. Many disputes took place as to its genus, and, the scales being removed, whether it were roasted or only prepared for roasting. They made a little song about it.[1]

As I don't wish to be guilty of plaguarism, I have to ask your permission to adopt the following flourish (not for every one's eye of course), which though similar is not identical with yours [see facsimile].

Unto the Right Reverend & Venerable William
Capeton with *greeting* (Scoticé).

We have a new claimant[2] for the discovery of the Lake, viz. Mr Wilson,[3] a trader who *asked and obtained* permission from me to accompany us as such. Oswel & Murray were not pleased with me for giving permission. His opinion was never on any occasion asked, never spoke a word in any emergency, paid nothing to the guides, was fed and otherwise assisted, and got a fine load of ivory for next to nothing. Yet some of his friends, in order to detract as much as may be from my honours, set up his claims as the *true discoverer* of the Lake. He, it seems, says we should all have turned back but for him. Now the question of turning was never mooted except by Sekhomi's messenger. My answer was, 'They must put me in my grave first'. Mr Oswel asked what I had said, and when I told him he replied, 'I am very glad to hear *you* say so'. Murray may have spoken to Wilson about turning, but the idea never entered my head, I know. On the single word 'turn' hang all Mr Wilson's claims. I perhaps ought to give him the medal on such serious grounds. But turn we didn't, so to us belongs the discovery.

The information I have given is scantier than I should like you to have got, but time is awanting.

Farewell, dear brother.

I heartily approve of your conduct in the case of Sechele.[4] He enter-

---

[1] The words are given in *Private J.*, p. 128, preceded by the remark: 'The burden of the song was a fish made of pottery, sent by Miss Thompson to the daughter of Sebitane'.

[2] 'a new claim out' (Campbell, p. 126; Chamberlin, p. 190).

[3] 'Mr Williams' (Campbell, loc. cit.). In *Travels*, p. 190, D. L. mentions 'a notice in one of the Cape Town papers' that Wilson 'was the true discoverer of the Lake!' I have not located that 'notice'; it was apparently written by another trader, named Campbell (cf. *Fam. Letters*, ii, pp. 239-40).

[4] Sechele had visited Cape Town in April–June 1853, hoping to be sent to England, at the expense of the LMS (since he was 'here without money'), so that he might appeal in person to Queen Victoria for redress against the Boers. Thompson, unwilling 'to do anything that might commit the Society to expense and responsibility', refused to pay for his passage, but raised a loan of £60 to defray the cost of his journey back to Bechuanaland (Thompson to Tidman, 9.iv.53, 21.iv.53, 21.vi.53).

tained the project for many years, but always recieved my decided veto on it. Again and again have I said, 'Your duty lies among your own countrymen, and not to be stared at as a wild beast, or as the children of strange towns do to me'. When I met him at Kuruman,[1] he had made up his mind to go with others. All I could say was, 'You need not think of the Governor, he is gone to punish Moshesh.'[2] 'But I will go to the Queen.' Could say nothing about her, and as he appeared to be going at the expense of others did not feel at liberty to object farther than by telling him the difficulty I had in getting ammunition.[3] He was perfectly aware of my sentiments about going to England. I have always been opposed to exhibiting real or supposed converts prize-cattle fashion. Whatever he may be now, I have not the shade of the shadow of a doubt that during the $2\frac{3}{4}$ years before his admission he was sincere & most consistent. If those who blame you want him now, let them come down with the dust & send for him.

49. To ARTHUR TIDMAN
24 September 1853

[LMS 77. Received 17 March 1854. Previous publication: Campbell, pp. 158–60 (portions of first two paragraphs); Chamberlin, pp. 202–10 (in full)]

Town of Sekeletu, Linyanti
24th September 1853

My dear Sir,

When the obstacles which caused our detention at Kuruman were removed, we passed quickly towards the country of Sebituane, untill within one degree of latitude from this town. All the people were then suddenly laid prostrate by fever, except one lad and myself. This caused a further loss of time, but through the goodness of God all recovered.

The paragraph beginning with this sentence is written on a slip of paper, 7.7 × 3.9 inches, filed in LMS 74 with Letter 47. Chamberlin prints it as part of Letter 46, but it clearly belongs either here, or with Letter 50, since D. L. could not have heard earlier from Thompson about 'your conduct in the case of Sechele'.

[1] D. L. had left Kuruman on 14 December 1852, met Sechele (*en route* to Cape Town) at Motito on the 19th, accompanied him back to Kuruman, and then set out again for the North (*Private J.*, pp. 95–6).

[2] Chief of the Basuto, 1820(?)–70; attacked by British troops under Cathcart, in December 1852, because of continuous cattle-lifting by his people from European farmers in the Orange River Sovereignty (Theal, *History*, vii, pp. 333–43).

[3] While at Cape Town, D. L. had applied to the Government authorities for the requisite permit to take ammunition beyond the borders of the Colony. His request was ultimately granted, in full, but only after a vexatious delay (cf. *Private J.*, p. 81; *Fam. Letters*, ii, p. 179; *Travels*, p. 106).

On reaching this, the southern capital of the Makololo, we were recieved with all the demonstrations of welcome which they are accustomed to bestow on their chiefs. The idea seemed universal that with a
missionary some great indefinite good[1] had arrived. Many expected to
be elevated at once to a condition equal to that of the Bakwains and
inhabitants of Kuruman, of which they had recieved very exaggerated
accounts; others imagined that they would very soon be transformed
into civilized men, possessing the clothing, horses, arms, waggons, &c,
of Europeans. 'Jesus had not loved their forefathers, hence their present
degradation. He had loved the white men, and given them all the wonderful things they now possess. And as I had come to teach them to
pray to Jesus, and to pray for them, their wants would soon be all supplied.' A very great deal was expected too from medicines and my
liberality in giving things I have not in my possession. Patient industry,
and perseverance in learning, were never thought of.

The chief, not yet nineteen years of age, frequently pressed me to
name something I wished, so that he might by presenting it shew his
affection and, I suspected,[2] induce me forthwith to commence the work
of metamorphosis by means of enchantments. But when I steadily
refused to mention any object I desired more than to secure their
temporal and spiritual welfare by means of the gospel, he seemed to test
my sincerity by presenting 4 small and 8 large elephants' tusks. I had
not an opportunity of refusing them, as they were brought and laid
down by the waggon during my absence; and then the chief came and
begged me so earnestly to accept them, I felt at a loss how to act. In
other circumstances I should have felt no hesitation in appropriating
them to defray expenses incurred entirely on account of his people. But
as it was, though I had no direct evidence that the chief's object was
such as I have described, the mere suspicion led me, when departing
for[3] the Borotse country, to request him to leave orders that if any
traders came my ivory must be used as well as his own. By this means
no offence was given, which might have been the case had I at once
sent them back.

Some months were spent here, for though I soon proposed to examine
the country in order to discover a suitable locality for a Mission,
Sekeletu objected, first that he had not yet had a satisfactory look at me,
he must see me longer, then he could not think of allowing me to go
alone, he must accompany me and see that no evil befel me. This re-

---

[1] 'definite good' (Campbell, p. 158).
[2] 'I expected' (Campbell, p. 159).
[3] 'departing from' (Chamberlin, p. 203).

quired considerable preparation, during which I offered to teach the people to read. Long and profound were the deliberations over this. They are never in a hurry in Africa. And reading seems so supernatural, it cannot be explained to those who know nothing of letters. At last the chief told me that he was 'afraid that learning to read might change his heart, and make him content with one wife only, as in the case of Sechele'. It was in vain to urge that the altered state of mind contemplated would be as voluntary as the present: no underhand means would be employed to convert, all the means employed being open teaching; there is no compulsion, the truth is taught respecting God's will, and the belief or unbelief of the instructed is left as an affair between their Judge and themselves. It was just as I have felt in my early years, in contemplating that everlasting preaching, praying & singing prolonged into Heaven. Quite failing to realize the altered state of mind which produces a relish for such service, it seemed as if celestial joys might be endured, rather than be consigned to the other quarter.

As I was then subjected to repeated attacks of the fever, I did not press the subject long. But when we returned from the Borotse, an experiment of which I have reason to be satisfied was set on foot. Sekeletu's father-in-law and step-father were appointed to learn to read, in order that their experience may serve as a beacon to others. Though the plan exhibits the extreme of African caution, they applied themselves so vigorously they and several others mastered the alphabet perfectly in one day. But teaching to read being less my object in this journey than preaching the gospel of peace, while endeavouring to discover a salubrious locality for a Mission, I shall proceed to relate our visit to the Borotse country.

Two sketches are enclosed, one long and large, or just[1] as I put it down as we went along, the other small, reduced to the Latitudes & Longitudes according to observations taken as opportunities occurred. The large is sent in order that you may see several remarks which my pen is not fine enough to insert in the reduced scale, and in order that if necessary a more correct reduction may be made.

We embarked on the river, called everywhere Leeambye, at the village of Sekhosi,[2] our fleet consisting of 33 canoes, and our company of about 160 men. From the bend at Katima-molelo[3] up to the com-

---

[1] 'is just' (Chamberlin, p. 205). Those maps are not in the LMS archives.

[2] In *Travels*, p. 208, 'Sekhosi' (Sikosi) is identified as a Subiya headman living at 17° 29′ S., 24° 33′ E. The official *Gazetteer of Geographical Names in the Barotseland Protectorate* (Lusaka, 1959) lists two villages of that name, at 17° 23′ S., 24° 12′ E., and 17° 26′ S., 24° 27′ E., respectively (p. 136).

[3] Katima Mulilo, 17° 28′ S., 24° 14′ E. (*Gazetteer*, p. 32).

mencement of the Borotse valley, the country is covered by forest and tsetse. The country otherwise seemed well adapted for a residence. Many villages of Banyeti, a poor but industrious people, are situated on both banks.[1] They are expert as hunters of hippopotami & other animals; they cultivate grain too, extensively. At the bend above named commences the rocky bottom which forms cataracts and rapids all the way up to the Borotse. The river is of very great beauty and breadth. In the Northern confines of Latitude 16° the high banks seem to leave the river and stretch away to the N.N.E. and N.N.W. untill between twenty and thirty miles apart. The intervening space is the Borotse country, and is annually inundated as Lower Egypt is by the Nile.

The valley is covered with coarse succulent grasses, which are the pasturage of large herds of cattle during a portion of the year. There are many villages of Makololo in the valley. I have not put down all that I visited, and many were seen in the distance. But there are no large towns. The reasons are, the mounds on which alone towns and villages are built are all small, and the people require to be separate, on account of being rich in cattle. Nariele[2] does not contain 1,000 inhabitants. The ridges are thickly strewed with villages. The people, Banyeti and Barotse, are not rich in cattle, but they require to live apart on account of cultivating large gardens of sugar cane, sweet potato, manioc, yams, millet, maize, &c &c. The exhalations which arise from a valley 20 miles broad and about 100 long produce fever, which is very fatal even among natives. It prevails most virulently when the waters of inundation are retiring.

We went North till we came to the junction of the Leeba or Londa with the main stream Leeambye, in 14° 11' South Lat., and found the country presenting the same characteristics as I have described. On returning towards Nariele I went to the Eastern ridge, in order to examine that and see the establishment of a merchant from the farthest inland station of the Portuguese opposite Benguela.[3] A stockade had been erected, and a flagstaff for the Portuguese banner planted. The houses of the merchant and some bastards were in the West African style. The owner,[4] whom I had previously seen at Linyanti, was absent,

---

[1] These people 'inhabit the south-eastern portion of the Barotse valley, and are found around the Gonye Falls' (F. S. Arnot, *Garenganze*, 2nd ed., 1889, p. 67 n.).

[2] Naliele, 'the chief town of the Makololo' (*Private J.*, p. 202). Its situation is given in *Travels*, p. 685, as 15° 24' 17" S., 23° 5' 54" E., and in *Gazetteer*, p. 101, as 15° 22' S., 23° 01' E.

[3] A port on the coast of Angola, at 12° 34' S., 13° 24' E.

[4] Antonio da Silva Pôrto (1817–90), a famous figure in the history of Angola. There is much about him and his doings in *Private J*.

but his servants did their utmost to shew me kindness. When my boat-men prepared my bed outside, they insisted on my occupying their master's couch, and I never felt so grateful in my life for a warm shelter, for I was in the cold stages of one of the intermittents which continue to plague one after the fever. I thought of going Westward in company with this merchant, but the sight of gangs of poor wretches in chains at the stockade induced me to resolve to proceed alone.

I have not, I am sorry to confess, discovered a healthy locality. The whole of the country of Sebituane is unhealthy. The current of the river is rapid as far as we went, and shewed we must have been on an elevated table-land, yet the inundations cause the fever to prevail very extensively. I am at a loss what to do, but will not give up the case as hopeless. Shame upon us, if we are to be outdone by slave traders. I met Arabs from Zanguebar, subjects of the Imaum of Muscat, who had been quite accross the continent. They wrote Arabic readily in my note book,[1] and boldly avowed that Mahomet was the greatest of all the prophets. In pursuance of a nobler object than theirs, I have determined to try and fulfil the second part of my enterprise, viz. to open up a way to the coast. I give the West the preference, because it is nearer.

If my calculations are right, the Longitudes of the map of last year are all wrong; the waggon stand, for instance, instead of being in 26° is 23° 48' or 50'. I have repeated the calculation of Lunar distances again and again, and always with the same result. But I do not wish this error published untill I hear from the Astronomer at the Cape, to whom I have submitted the observations and also some occultations by which to test them.[2] But for the destruction of my celestial map by the Boers, I might have determined the Longitude by occultations alone, they being much more to be depended on than the common method of Lunar distances. If then I am right, we are nearer the West than the East coast. Nariele is in 23° East, and the confluence of the Leeba or Londa not much more. I have not had time to work out the Longitude of that point, but the river (Leeba) comes from the capital of a powerful state, whose chief is reported to be friendly to foreigners. If I am permitted to return by this chieftain, it will be water carriage for perhaps ⅔ds of the way. And should a Mission be established there in time it will be all the better.

I intend to try for Loanda[3] because, though farther, many English

---

[1] The inscription is reproduced in *Private J.*, p. 227.

[2] Maclear's comments on D. L.'s observations were published in *JRGS*, 1854, pp. 301–6.

[3] Luanda, 8° 50' S., 13° 15' E., on the Atlantic coast; the capital of Angola.

live there. I go on horseback, waggon travelling being reported impossible on account of forests and numerous rivers. The Portuguese are carried in hammocks slung on poles. Two slaves carry a man. It does not look well. The Portuguese maps are all constructed from native reports, so no dependance can be placed on them. Many tribes inhabit the country, all more or less accustomed to the visits of strangers. The greatest difficulty I apprehend is that of making our objects understood. Their languages bear a close affinity to the Borotse dialect, but this I was compelled to give up reducing.

I never had a touch of the fever till my employment became sedentary here. I have had eight attacks since. The last, when going North of Nariele, was very severe, being accompanied with large loss of florid blood. It thinned me much. But on no occasion did I lay by. Fits of vertigo, probably from exhaustion, troubled me for some time; everything seemed to rush to the left, and I had to lay hold on something to prevent a fall. These induced me to give up collecting Borotse words and other materials for a dictionary. Though still thin, the intermittents have left, and I am only waiting for the rains to commence to start for the West. They begin next month.

It will be seen that Mrs L. had better not come to the Cape to meet me at the time appointed. If I reach Loanda in February, I must return with the people again, and will be here instead of at the Cape. The time unavoidably lost by Boers and fever renders a little extension of my furlough necessary. Then, if the Directors sanction a permanent station, or any other form of labour for this miserable interior, some other mode of travelling in from the West must be arranged. A few kind words to Mrs L. from you will, I think, make her willing to prolong her stay in Scotland.

Although the prospect seems dark for the Interior, it may not be quite so gloomy as I have drawn it. The natives describe the mortality as very great, and that attacks of fever are excessively frequent & severe. I have given you their ideas. But my own, except at times, are not so sombre. I tried native remedies in some of the attacks to which I was subjected, in order to discover if they had any valuable means of cure, but after being stewed in vapour baths, and smoked over fires of green plants in hot potsherds, &c &c, I find that our own medicines are more efficacious and safer. I have not lost a single patient by fever. And if I had been able [to] regulate my diet, &c, I should not have been subjected to so many attacks. As it was, we were frequently compelled to eat on the principle of laying in a stock for the next day, my own people being too weak to go with me, and the Makololo cook only in the evenings when travelling. Then if I left the canoe in order to visit a village, there are so many branches of the river intersecting the valley everywhere I was always wet up to the middle. I fear to give you either a too encouraging or discouraging report. I am afraid to incur the responsibility of inducing you to regard the case as hopeless. The American missionaries report the Gaboon station[1] as not warranting the long-established belief that Europeans could not live there, and my firm conviction is that even the Interior of Africa merits a fair trial. Such with the help of God and your sanction I am determined to give it.

The slave trade was prohibited here, and a large party of Mambari, who were here endeavouring in vain to renew it, fled precipitately as soon as they heard that I had crossed the Chobe. The Makololo remonstrated with them, but they asserted that I would take all their goods from them because they dealt in slaves. A Portuguese came from the West, but he, finding no market, remained only three days and returned.[2] It was different in the Borotse or Northern division of the country. Another Portuguese merchant came thither, and by means of an under-chief who had some pretensions to the chieftainship obtained free access to all the Banyeti, Batoka and Bashukulompo villages East of the Leeambye. Then the stockade, which gave great offence to the Makololo, was erected without the knowledge or permission of the chief. They would have commenced hostilities at once, in order to drive the whole slave-trading party out of the country, but a variety of considerations induced me to intercede for them, and by that intercession they will be allowed to depart in peace.

Probably decieved by the assurances of the disaffected under-chief,[3] they seem to have had no idea of the risk they were running. But when the conspirator came down with the intention of cutting off Sekeletu, he was instantly seized and killed. His father and several others were cut off in the most cold-blooded manner, and when I remonstrated against the shedding of human blood the counsellors quietly remarked, 'You see we are still Boers, we are not yet taught'. But for this unfortunate affair, no trading in slaves would have been allowed. In this they have the precedent of the former chief of the Borotse, who refused to grant the Mambari permission to visit his country as slave traders. A

[1] Gabon, in equatorial West Africa, where American missionaries had been at work since 1842 (Groves, *Christianity in Africa*, ii, p. 67).

[2] Cf. *Private J.*, pp. 176–9. His name was Caetano José Ferreira.

[3] Named Mphephe, he was 'a nephew of Sebitoane's', and governor of the Barotse valley. The story of his conspiracy and its fatal ending is told more fully in *Fam. Letters*, ii, pp. 219–20, and *Private J.*, pp. 181–4, 210–11, 232–3.

cannon of small calibre was found in the possession [of the] under-chief mentioned.

The country in the direction of Mosioatunya has high mountains, and the Batoka country is a high table-land without trees except along the rivers. Healthy spots might be found in both of these, but in neither did I feel it duty to travel, because the vicinity of Mosilikatse renders it impossible for Makololo or any other tribe to reside there. A change may yet be effected among the Matibele which would change the present aspect of affairs.

Believe me, Dear Sir,
Yours affectionately,
David Livingston

50. To WILLIAM THOMPSON
11 October 1853

[LMS 78. Received 17 March 1854. Previous publication: Chamberlin, pp. 212–15 (almost complete)]

11th October 1853
Linyanti

My dear Man,

I sent you a few days ago a long letter per a Mr Francis Thompson,[1] who came up as far as the Chobe in company with a trader, Mr Chapman;[2] and since I sent off the packet I find I have had time to transcribe the enclosed paper, which I have taken the liberty to believe you will not object to read. It contains the marrow of a much longer one carefully written for the same destination, but it was penned in our way here,[3] and though it contains a much fuller view than this, many points are now out of date, and will be much more so before reaching Dr Vaughan.[4] I had given up the idea of sending it at all, till the idea of

[1] A young Yorkshireman who had emigrated to S. Africa in 1850; killed by native rebels in Griqualand West, 1878 (cf. *Matabele Thompson*, ed. Nancy Rouillard, Johannesburg 1953, pp. 8, 9, 22).

[2] James Chapman (1831–72), author of *Travels in the Interior of South Africa*, 2 vols., 1868. In vol. i, pp. 161–81, he describes his visit to the Chobe with Thompson (late August to early October), and mentions (p. 167) that he 'had brought up some boxes and parcels' for D. L., to whom he makes several other references. The two did not actually meet, being some distance apart, but communicated through native messengers.

[3] Cf. *Private J.*, p. 100: 'February 5. Finish a paper on Trans-Vaal Boers and slavery, for Quarterly'. This paper, apparently rejected by the *British Quarterly*, was published (posthumously) in the second (1881) edition of Blaikie, pp. 490–511.

[4] Editor of *The British Quarterly Review* (see p. 235 n.).

an abbreviation struck my mind, and now I fear that the haste evident in its composition & writing will render it unfit for the pages of a Review. However, I send it, and my object in enclosing it to you is to request you to note any passages you may see to be out of date by the time you get it, and signify the same to the Dr. Is this too much to ask? Well, I shall not send you the next, but will just tell you it is much better than this. Indeed, if it were not my own child I would say it is a very good one. So good I may perhaps keep it to myself altogether. It is on Missions: the privelege of being allowed to engage in them, their future, &c &c.[1] I wrote it in the weary way accross the desert, and if it never does aught else it has comforted my own mind.

The second paper about which I told you, and which Mr Cameron said would be published, will not trouble you.[2] I meant it to be a continuation of the same subject, believing the one would not be complete without the other. This, it seems, is not admissable in a Review. Much of the article will be otherwise employed, and as doing good was my object I am quite satisfied. I think I have the same object in the present article. It is a misfortune to be so far from proof sheets; one could make the composition so much more smooth and perhaps telling. If I ever send that I have by me at present, it will be my last.

As I am on the subject of literature, I may say you are a very fine editor. The only letter of any pretensions in your Report has, 'What is the *result* of these *effects*?', and about ½ a dozen 'Admittings' spanned into one trektow of a sentence like African oxen. You will shelter yourself by saying you promised to give the manuscript to the printer.[3] Ah, very well.

Your friend Anderson[4] has reached the Lake. This will be a useful path for traders to the Lake. But all our Southern coast, viz. of Sebitu-

---

[1] Published (incompletely) in Blaikie, pp. 475–81.

[2] It was apparently a sequel to the paper on missionary policy already published in the *British Quarterly* (see above, p. 227). D. L. had sent it to Watt from Cape Town in March 1852. James Cameron of Cape Town, a builder, was secretary of the local LMS Auxiliary (*C.G.H. Almanac*, 1852, p. 146 and Directory); he had a son, studying in England, who 'I believe gets information as to the papers, and sends out word to his father . . . all about them before they are published. This is scarcely Review fashion, and will I fear diminish their moral influence. The father is rather a talkative Scotchman' (x.52 Watt).

[3] The reference is to a report by Daniel Helm on 'Zuurbrak, or Caledon Institution', published in *S.A. Miss. Report*, 1852, pp. 55–8; the passages criticized by D. L are on pp. 55 and 57. (Thompson, who edited the *Report*, states on p. iv that 'The Reports of the respective Stations are printed as furnished by the brethren who sign them.') A 'trektow' is the tow-rope of a wagon.

[4] Charles John Andersson (1827–67), author of *Lake Ngami* (1856) and several other works; the first European to reach the Lake from the West (July 1852).

ane's country, is infested by tsetse, except one small strip, and a better path than to Walwich Bay[1] must be made. I have lost eight oxen by my people allowing the cattle to wander once. I find the watch given me by the Geo. Soc.[2] an excellent one, and have corrected several errors in Longitude by its means, but send my observations to Mr Maclear for verification before publishing them. It is probable the Lake is wrong, as we never attempted or could attempt to establish its Longitude. We never had watches worth anything.

You very kindly say you fear for the result of my going in here alone. I hope I am in the way of duty. My own conviction that such is the case has never wavered. I am doing something for God. Have preached the gospel in many a spot where the name of Christ has never been heard, and would work still more in the way of reducing the Borotse language if I had not suffered severely from fever. Exhaustion produced vertigo, causing me, if I looked suddenly up, almost to lose consciousness. This made me give up some of my sedentary work. But I hope God will accept of what I can do. The temperature in the shade is about 100° Fahr. during the day, & often 90° at 9 o'clock at night. But a merry heart doeth good like a medicine. If I allowed my mind to dwell constantly on the miserable degradation, wickedness, & sad prospects of the people here, I might become melancholy and soon die. But we have a fair world, and all the wonderful works of our father in it, and I believe we ought to allow our minds to dwell on the beautiful more than on the evil. I am never low spirited. It might be different if I had a crusty companion. I have experience in the matter. And my thoughts never turn with any longing except for my family. I think we are immortal till our work is done, not on the platform only but on the pestilential plains of the glorious Leeambye.

Remember me to Miss Thompson & the young ones. I think this goes by Walwich Bay. If the packet should reach you by this route, a small bag of seeds for the Botanic Garden accompanies it.[3] They were collected in the way here. I contemplate going to Loanda as soon as the rains begin. They moderate the temperature. The dry dust with which the winds are now loaded produces fever. Your letters are miserably short.

David Livingston

---

[1] Walvis Bay, 22° 59′ S., 14° 31′ E., on the coast of South West Africa.

[2] See above, p. 170.

[3] Cf. *Private J.*, p. 237: '6th October. Send off my parcel with a bag of seeds.' They were taken to the south by Chapman, who, however, went not via Walvis Bay but by the usual overland route to Kuruman, which he reached on 11 Feb. 1854 (*Travels in S. Africa*, i, p. 213).

In my other paper I give a hint to Mr John Pears or Pearson, who wrote a letter in the British Banner.[1] 'A number of church members, proceeding to the funeral of a friend in the vicinity of Cradock,[2] observed the footprints of eight Bechuanas, who had travelled about 600 miles in search of employment a few years before, and were now returning home with the fruits of their honest industry. After the funeral these Christians armed themselves, and in the belief that these Bechuanas were Caffres followed their trail, found them sitting quietly behind some bushes, and shot down seven of them unchallenged & unresisting. The eighth was taken prisoner, & it was then found they were peaceable labourers. This bloody affair was published in the papers, & no more notice taken of it. These Boers pass uncensured to the table of the Lord. They eat & wipe their mouths & say, we have done no wickedness. Can the Revd. John Pears give us any further information on this subject?' We suppose these people were Bakwains, many of them having gone to work in that direction and never returned. Their wives are still waiting for them. This would have been out of date now.

I have left a page for your remarks in Dr Vaughan's note. Although intended for Colonists, I cannot permit its publication in the Colony. It is utterly useless to speak to them except through the press of Europe.

The gentleman who takes this, Mr Chapman, goes by Walwich Bay, and will deliver the letters to you without the expense of postage through the Colony. He has not been successful in trade. Various causes prevented. The seeds will be delivered either to you or to the Botanic Garden.

This is the 17th October. Rain made an attempt to begin last night. Will you send Hoffmeyr's letter to my old lodgings?[3]

51. To ARTHUR TIDMAN
8 November 1853

[LMS 79. Received 4 July 1854. Previous publication: Campbell, p. 160 (second paragraph); Chamberlin, pp. 215–17 (incomplete)]

[1] Rev. John Pears, minister of the Dutch Reformed Church at Somerset East (Cape Colony), had published in *The British Banner*, 1852, pp. 459–60, a very long letter defending the native policy of 'the Colonists and Dutch Church'.

[2] A village in eastern Cape Colony, at 32° 10' S., 25° 37' E. The passage in quotation marks was written by D. L., not Pears.

[3] While at Cape Town in 1852, D. L. had lived in a house hired from a member (whom I have been unable to identify more precisely) of the well-known Hofmeyr family (*Fam. Letters*, ii, p. 168). In *Private J.*, p. 237, he mentions writing to Hofmeyr, among others, at the beginning of October.

Linyanti
8th November 1853

Dear Sir,

By a letter dated September last I informed you of my intention to proceed Westward in order to open up a way to the coast. I was then waiting for rains, and as these have now commenced I leave this on the 10th currt. I have altered my mind with respect to the route which I intend to try. We sent men to the Westward in order to examine if there is any strip of country free of tsetse in that direction. Their report was unfavourable. I then resolved to go on the trail of the Mambari, but the slave merchant signalized his departure by seizing two men and a woman as slaves. The Makololo assembled immediately, and compelled him to unchain the captives.[1] This affair made me alter my resolution again, for if I followed his footsteps the different tribes through which we have to pass would naturally believe me to be of the same clan. Indeed, knowing what my precursors had done I should not feel very respectable to myself. I therefore intend going up the river Leeambye to the point at which we turned in August, and then ascend the Leeba to the people called Balonda[2] and proceed Westward by land. The chief has lent me his own canoe, and as I was unable to take a horse to the Borotse country, on account of the tsetse at this season biting by night as well as by day, Sekeletu placed four riding oxen at my service. These are now in that country, so I hope to get on. I go in the canoe from this down the Chobe[3] to its confluence, then up the Leeambye and Leeba till we reach the falls reported to exist on that river. The canoe will be sent back, and we must do the best we can beyond.

I leave in company with Borotse people alone. The people we brought from Kuruman have been rendered useless by fever, so I send them back.[4] I am again through God's mercy and kindness quite recovered from the effects of that disease. I think I am getting rid of intermittent too, and, if spared, will impart some knowledge of Christ to many who never before heard his blessed name. There are many and very large tribes in the direction in which we go. All are sitting in darkness and the shadow of death. I hope God will in mercy permit me to establish

---

[1] Cf. *Private J.*, p. 277. The 'slave merchant' was Silva Pôrto.

[2] BaLunda. 'The Lunda, Luena, and related peoples together occupy most of the eastern half of Portuguese Angola and smaller areas in the north-western districts of Northern Rhodesia and in Katanga Province of the Belgian Congo' (Merran McCulloch, *The Southern Lunda*, 1951, p. 1).

[3] 'down to Chobe' (Chamberlin, p. 216).

[4] The main reason for their being sent back was their misconduct, described at length in *Fam. Letters*, ii, pp. 231–4, 236–7, 238–42.

the gospel somewhere in this region, and that I may live to see the double influence of the spirit of commerce and Christianity[1] employed to stay the bitter fountain of African misery.

In the sketch enclosed in my last I neglected to mention that the ridges noted therein only shew the commencement of lands not usually inundated. There are very large tracts of country beyond these, which are annually flooded either wholly or partially. The Leeambye is not the only source of the waters of inundation. The reports of intelligent

natives lead me to believe that the Bashukulompo or Maninché river, the Loeti, the Kabompo, the Makoma, and Leeambye, are all branches (of one river), leaving and returning to the parent stream in a remarkably level country.

This ideal sketch [see facsimile] will perhaps enable you to understand my meaning. The dotted lines at the top may be the situation of an immense river, or of very numerous branches each pouring out vast quantities of water. You will percieve also that the country is peculiar, and will require a modification perhaps of our plan of operation therein. In no other country is there such a large surface of land annually inundated as in this.

[1] 'the double influence of commerce and Christianity' (Campbell, p. 160).

My letter of September contained three enclosures for Mrs Livingston. It contained full information respecting the visit to the Borotse. This opportunity of transmitting letters was unexpected,[1] but though I had written fully before I thought it well to let you know of the alteration of my plans, and that I am on the point of starting.

I am,

affectionately yours,

David Livingston

P.S. As Sesheké is only about 7 days on foot from the Maninché, and the falls of Mosioatunya may be avoided by sailing down that river into the Zambesi, this may be a good path down to the East Coast. I mention this in case of my being cut off.

D. L.

---

[1] They were sent with the coloured trader George Fleming, who was also escorting back D. L.'s servants (*Fam. Letters*, ii, pp. 236, 237, 241).

IX

TO LUANDA AND BACK

52. To WILLIAM THOMPSON
14 May 1854

[LMS 82. Previous publication: Chamberlin, pp. 217–23 (virtually complete)]

Calimba
14th May 1854[1]

My dear Sir,

I am not far from Loanda, and as I shall have very little time to spend in writing there, because my purse is light and followers numerous and hungry, I give you a few particulars now.

We have had a most tedious journey from the land of the Leeambye. We went up the Leeba 40 or 50 miles, then left the canoes, and went forward on oxback to the first chief of the Balonda, called Kabompo or Shinté.[2] He highly approved our object in opening up a way for commerce into his country, and shewed his sincerity by giving us guides and sending orders to all his people in the route to supply us with food. This kindness hindered our progress, for every village must have time to prepare meal &c for us. But the rains hindered us much more. Never did I endure such drenchings, and all the streams being swollen we had to ford many, the water flowing on the rustic bridges waist deep. Others we crossed by sticking to the oxen the best we could, and a few we made a regular swim of. My Borotse, for with them alone I travelled, did not know I could swim, and the first broad stream we came to excited their fears on my account. 'Now hold on fast by the tail, don't let go'. I intended to follow the injunction, but tail and all went so deep I thought it better to strike out alone for the bank, and just as I reached it I was greatly gratified to see a universal rush had been made for my

---

[1] In *Travels*, p. 383, D. L. states that he spent 14 May at 'Cabinda' (not 'Calimba'). According to *MS. Journal*, p. 233, 'Cabinda' was roughly midway between Ambaca and Golungo Alto, and one hour's distance (*c.* 3 miles) west of Zanga [9° 10′ S., 15° 01′ E.].

[2] Ishindi, commonly written 'Shinde', is the official name assumed on accession by the chief of the Luvale group of BaLunda in Balovale district, N.W. Rhodesia (McCulloch, *The Southern Lunda*, p. 26). D. L., who describes 'Kabompo; or, as he likes best to be called, Shinte' as 'the greatest Balonda chief in this part of the country', reached his village on 16 January (*Travels*, pp. 273, 289).

rescue. Their clothes were all floating down the stream, and two of them reached me breathless with the exertion they had made. If we could march, I got on very well. I don't care much for fatigue, but when compelled to stand still by pouring rains, then fever laid hold with his strong fangs on my inner man, and lying in a little gipsey tent with everything damp or wet was sore against the grain.

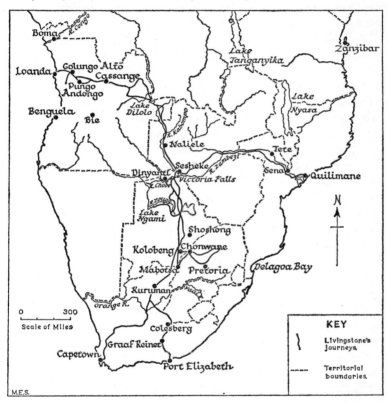

Frequent and most severe attacks of intermittent made me miserably weak, but I never lay by for that, and we managed to make occasional progress, through a population & country to which I can offer you no comparison in the South. We came to a village every few miles, some-times passed 10 in a day. These were civil. How could they be other-wise? The fellows were living in a Mahometan paradise. We often entered a village, and when sitting on oxback could only see the tops of the huts in a wilderness of weeds. By & bye the villagers emerged from their lairs, men & women each smoking a long pipe and followed by crowds of children. Very little exertion is required to procure the staff

261

of life, which in these parts is the manioc. A part of the forest is cleared of brushwood, and fires made round the larger trees leave them standing dead. Cuttings of the manioc are inserted in the ground and the earth drawn up around them. Maize, beans, earth nuts, &c, are planted between, and here we have a supply of food for years. The climate is so good, they are either planting or reaping the whole year round. All the different grains, roots, &c, may be seen at one time in every stage of growth.

Indeed, the country generally is fertile in the extreme, and very beautiful. It is flat, but lies in ridges or waves. The ridge of each wave is covered with dense dank forest, and the trough a pleasant valley containing either a bog or stream in its centre. The Boerish Eden, Magaliesberg,[1] will bear no comparison to this land for fertility and beauty. The forest trees shoot up to an enormous height as straight as arrows, and all being covered with white moss shew the humidity of the climate would require no irrigation for English wheat. Through some of these forests we could scarcely move on oxback. Swinging climbing plants of from an inch to three or four in diameter abound, and when drizzling rain makes the darkness of the forest darker we were often caught (*more* Absalom). The ox when you attempt to stop him rushes on the faster, and down comes the rider on the crown of his head. Mine, a most perverse beast, often went out of the way or narrow winding path on purpose, and always tried to administer an effective kick to shew how he would act if he had the upper hand.

The country to the West of that which we travelled through is called Lobale, and was impassable, the water standing on its plains waist deep. We had sometimes to make a divergence from our path in order to avoid such, and two or three times passed over plains 12 or 15 miles broad about 6 inches deep. Other plains presented the appearance of large rivers flowing fast towards the rivers, and must be the sources of the annual inundations of the Borotse, &c. The water is always clear, because rains fall on a dense mat of grass only. The southern part of the Lobale is well peopled, but the plains, being at other than the rainy season destitute of streams, have but a small population. The East is all densely populated, and pass by the name Balonda. They are idolators. Near every village an idol is seen, a block of wood with a rough human head carved on it, or a lion made of clay and two shells for eyes, standing in a little shed. The people, when unsuccessful in any enterprise, or

---

[1] The modern district of Rustenburg (Transvaal): 'the soil is rich, fruit is plentiful and large quantities of citrus, tobacco and cotton are grown' (*Guide to Southern Africa*, ed. A. Gordon-Brown, 1959, p. 596).

sick, beat a drum before them all night, and they are otherwise very superstitious. They would not eat with us, nor in our sight, though they took meat from us and eat it at home. When I saw their numbers, and thought of the vast multitudes there are in this land all living without God and without hope, I often sat down with feelings of dispair. When will they be supplied with the gospel of Christ?

As we approached the Portuguese settlements, the people became worse & worse, and at last instead of gifts of food we were offered knocks on the head. The Chiboque,[1] for instance, are most outrageous blackgaurds. We came to them as quiet as Quakers, and were spending Sunday on Peace Society principles when a whole tribe surrounded us fully armed with guns, arrows, spears, and short swords. They were all vociferating and brandishing their weapons simultaneously. I sat down and asked the chief to do the same, and then, demanding silence, requested to know what was the matter. Our crime consisted in one of our men, when spitting, allowing a small drop of the saliva to fall on one of them. I replied, if the chief could seriously say such was a crime I was willing to pay a fine. (On such frivolous pretexts we had often to pay enormous fines.) He accepted one, but his warriors rejected it and demanded one thing after another, untill by demanding one of our number to be sold as a slave we saw their intention was regular plunder, and armed ourselves for the worst. They feared my arms alone. Indeed, we were as a company unprepared for fighting, but armed as we were not a man of chief or counsellors would have escaped the first onset. We determined to let them shed the first drop of blood, and sat looking at them in all their heathenish shouting. This resolute bearing made them more reasonable, so they accepted an ox, and gave us two or three pounds of the flesh to shew they were of a generous disposition after all.[2]

We were often so treated, and at last no passage allowed past a town or village without paying for it. I paid away nearly all I had — oxen for provisions & riding, clothes, razors, spoons, &c.[3] Then we all got angry, chafed in mind and hungry, and replied angrily to their demands. Sometimes I was furious and would have fought, but my companions were more pacific, stripping themselves of their ornaments & paying for passage. At other times they were on the bloody key and I was quakerish, and we rose up by night and passed our enemies, expecting

---

[1] BaChokwe, a Lunda group living mainly between the Kasai and Kwilu Rivers (eastern Angola).

[2] This incident, which occurred on 5 March, is described more fully in *Travels*, pp. 339–43.

[3] 'Oxen for provisions, and riding clothes, razors, spoons, &c' (Chamberlin, p. 220).

an assault in every thicket and glen we came to. And, after all, I thank God sincerely in that he prevented us from shedding human blood.

When we reached the Quango,[1] I had made up my mind to part with my bedding for a passage, but we were prevented by a small tribe from approaching the ferry. I could not pay both tribe and ferry with what I had remaining, and there they laughed at us, with their teeth filed to a point, and hair elaborately plaited & ornamented. 'You must just go back the way you came', 'if you cannot pay us you will see what we can do', &c &c. Ah! you Caffres have been spoiled by missionaries, I suppose. The Reads have been among you exciting you to rebellion, that they have. Here a young Portuguese sergeant appeared, & enabled us to get over the Quango without more trouble. Our difficulties were ended.

All we have met in the Portuguese territory have been civil, and Sergt. Cypriano de Abreu began the hospitality which we have everywhere recieved from the Portuguese. We arrived at Cassange[2] naked and famished. There they clothed and fed us. May God reward them. At Ambaca I found the Commandant[3] an enlightened friend of Africa*, one who has written, spoken, and suffered, in her behalf, and his sentiments are in unison with those of many in the upper ranks in Portugal. I have on the whole been agreably disappointed in the Portuguese. They are extremely polite and hospitable, and all lament the state of supineness into which their nation has sunk.

(* I have since found out he is so only in profession. One cannot rely on the most plausible speeches of even Governors. They are excessively corrupt. D. L.)[4]

Loanda, 14th Augst.

I reached this city on the 31st of May, and was glad to tumble into bed as soon as I arrived, knocked up, and no mistake, by fever and diarrhoea. The first house I called at was that of Edmund Gabriel, Esqre, Her Majesty's Commissioner for the suppression of the slave

---

[1] The Cuango, which D. L. reached on 4 April in 'lat. 9° 53′ S., long. 18° 37′ E.' and describes as 'the boundary of the Portuguese claims to territory on the west, (*Travels*, p. 364; and, for the incident at the ferry, pp. 364–6).

[2] Cassanza, 'the farthest inland station of the Portuguese in Western Africa'; located, according to D. L., at 9° 37′ 30″ S., 17° 49′ E. (and on modern maps at 9° 40′ S., 17° 40′ E.). He got there on 13 April. (*Travels*, pp. 368, 375.)

[3] His name was Arsenio de Carpo (*Travels*, p. 382). D. L. reached Ambaca (9° 16′ S., 15° 12′ E.) on or very soon after 2 May (*MS. Journal*, p. 189).

[4] This note was added in the margin, evidently at the same time as the second part of the letter.

trade;[1] and a most disinterested, generous friend he has proved himself to be. He is the only Englishman in this city, and it contains a population of 11,000 souls. I recovered partially, then had a relapse, & nearly marched off from the land of the living. I have now, however, by God's mercy got round again, and will start on my return on the 20th currt.

The officers of our cruizers have been very kind, and the Portuguese authorities too. The Bishop of Angola[2] is the acting Governor. He recieved us very kindly, and assured my men of his protection. Sends a present to Sekeletu, consisting of 2 coats, ornamented with lace, & a horse. There are no bibles here. The prosperity of the city depended on the slave trade, and as that is virtually suppressed they have no hope of gaining filthy lucre except by the revolution of the English, or such other blessing as the devil might bestow. The province is fruitful in the extreme, and of rare beauty. Two crops of all sorts of fruits per year. Coffee, the best I ever tasted, grows & yields in 3 years, if they would only stick the plants in the soil; sugar, pine apples, everything in fact. But the Portuguese actually buy all their flour & bread from the Yankees, instead of growing wheat themselves. The coffee trees were chiefly planted by the old missionaries, and their churches are all in ruins. But most of the Portuguese of mixed blood can both read & write. They teach each other. How I long for a few Bibles.

But it is questionable whether I shall return this way. I intend going down the Zambesi to Quilimane[3] rather than this way. So many rivers & thickets prevent me attempting this way with the waggon — they have no roads here. And tomorrow is a grand festival in commemoration of having driven the Dutch out of the country. The Dutch began to make a canal to lead water to the city.[4] It has never been completed, and all drinkable water has to be carried from the Bengo, 8 or 9 miles distant.[5] The harbour, once a splendid one, is now filling up. Indeed, ships cannot now anchor within a mile of the city, & all look on & take the world easy. The trade is in the hands of the Yankees. No English

[1] b. 1821; entered Royal Navy 1842; in 1845 was appointed arbitrator in the mixed British and Portuguese Commission established at Luanda under the Lisbon treaty (July 1842) for the suppression of the slave trade; acting Commissioner 1856 —; full Commissioner 1859—; d. December 1862 (*Foreign Office List*, 1864, p. 165).

[2] 'The Right Reverend Joaquim Moreira Reis' (*Travels*, p. 390); bishop of Angola 1849–56 (*Grande Enciclopédia*, xvii, p. 873).

[3] Quelimane, 17° 53′ S., 36° 51′ E., a Portuguese settlement on the coast of Moçambique.

[4] Luanda was in Dutch hands 1641–8. The 'unfinished canal', from the R. Cuanza (south of Luanda), is mentioned in *Travels*, p. 395.

[5] The Bengo enters the sea a little to the N.E. of Luanda.

house has established itself. This arose from Loanda getting a bad name some years ago.

George I left at the town of Sekeletu. I wished him to leave as soon as possible after I left. He leans on me. This won't do at all. The Portuguese give ten times as much for ivory as English traders.

Kind salutations to your sister & all the family. I have not got a single line from any one, though I wrote you all by a trader called Chapman, who was accompanied by one Thompson from Natal.

Ever affectionately yours,
David Livingston

53. To ARTHUR TIDMAN
4 July 1854

[LMS 84. Received (in Foreign Office) 15 September 1854]

St Paul de Loanda
4th July 1854

Sir,

At the request of Mr Livingston, I beg to inform you that he arrived at this place on the 31st May last, labouring, I regret to say, under an attack of fever and diorrhoea which, being succeeded by a relapse, has reduced him so far as to prevent him for the present from reporting to you the particulars of his journey from the Zambeze, whence he last had the honor of addressing you in November 1853.

Sekeletu supplied Mr Livingston with 27 men and a sufficient number of oxen to enable him to prosecute his journey to this Coast. The party then proceeded northwards a considerable distance up the River Leeba, until they came into the country of the Balonda, where they left their canoes and went forward on ox-back. This country is of immense extent, and extremely populous. The inhabitants are all idolators, the figure of a lion formed of clay, or the representation of a human head carved upon a pole, being seen at almost every village. The people, however, though extremely superstitious, manifested the greatest kindness to the party, and the chiefs not only highly approved of the object Mr Livingston had in view, but even aided him to the extent of their ability. They found this to be the character of the natives until they came to the vicinity of the Portuguese settlements, where it changes for the worst, payment for passage being demanded by most of the tribes, and exorbitant fines levied for the most trivial and imaginary crimes. Sometimes a whole tribe surrounded the party and threatened to murder them if their demands were not satisfied. Mr Livingston, not being provided with goods to meet these unexpected extortions, was obliged to part with the cattle intended to serve him and his party as food and a means of conveyance, and even to dispose of a great portion of his wearing apparel and the cloths and ornaments of his party.

Having at last reached the River Quango, determined to part even with his bed clothes to obtain a passage, he was delighted at meeting with a Portuguese settler, by whose authority he succeeded in crossing on payment of a reasonable fare, and three days afterwards he reached the town of Cassange, in Latitude 9° 37′ 30″ South and Longitude 23° 43′ East,[1] where all difficulties with the natives ceased.

Through the whole of this journey they had almost incessant heavy rains, and rarely did 24 hours pass without the party being completely drenched. The country is extremely fertile and abounds in beautiful streams, which at that time were swollen into considerable rivers, even those rustic bridges which they did use being considerably submerged, and some rivers they had to swim. These operations much retarded their progress. The country being so flooded, and the path[s] they followed being those generally adopted by the natives, through dense forests of gigantic trees bound together by a wonderful variety of creeping plants, it was impossible to judge whether a waggon could be taken through it.

Mr Livingston requests me to add that, although still extremely weak, he is now convalescent, and he hopes by the next opportunity to have the pleasure of communicating with you himself.

> I have the honor to remain,
> Sir,
> Your obedient servant,
> Edm. Gabriel

---

[1] In *MS. Journal*, p. 183, the longitude is given as 17° 43′ E. (from calculations made on 20–21.iv.54); in *Travels*, p. 375, it is corrected to 17° 49′ E.

54. To ARTHUR TIDMAN
14 January 1855

[LMS 86. Previous publication: *Chronicle*, vol. xix, (October) 1855, pp. 217–219 (edited extracts); Chamberlin, pp. 227–32 (incomplete)]

Cassange, Angola
West Africa
14th January 1855[1]

Dear Sir,

As soon as I was sufficiently recovered from the severe indisposition which kept me prostrate for a long time after my arrival at Loanda, I wrote you a full account of the journey concerning which you have probably recieved information from other sources. I regretted you had not recieved the earliest intelligence directly from my own hand, and that regret was increased on learning a few days ago at Pungo Andongo that all my letters & maps had been lost in the wreck of the 'Forerunner' off Madeira.[2]

Having left the river Zambesi or Leeambye in Lat. 14° 11′ South and Long. 23° 40′ East, we ascended the Leeba untill we had the country of Lobale on our left and Londa on our right. We then left the canoes and travelled N.N.W. on ox-back till we reached the Latitude of this place, viz. 9° 37′. Thence proceeding Westwards, we at last reached Loanda.

In passing through a part of Londa we found the people exceedingly kind, and generally anxious that we should succeed in opening up a new road to the coast. They belong to the negro race, and are more superstitious than any of the Southern tribes. They would not eat with us, and near every village we observed an idol, consisting either of a clay figure of a lion or alligator, or a block of wood on which a human face was rudely carved. In cases of sickness, or of failure in any pursuit, offerings of food are presented and drums beat before them during whole nights. The Balonda invariably go armed with short broadswords, large bows and arrows, and guns, and seem to possess but little sense of security in their own country. Cases of kidnapping of children occurred while we were passing, and these, with persons who flee from

---

[1] Leaving Luanda on 20 September 1854 (*Travels*, p. 397), and making a slight detour to the north, D. L. reached Cassange again on 18 January, and from there despatched the present letter on the 25th; on the 14th, the date he gives above, he was at Tala Mugongo (*MS. Journal*, pp. 315, 317).

[2] D. L. reached Pungo Andongo (9° 44′ S., 15° 35′ E.) on 11 December 1854, and left on 1 January (*MS. Journal*, pp. 301, 313; *Travels*, p. 428). The *Forerunner* had been wrecked on 25 October, and he received the news on 23 December (*MS. Journal*, p. 310; *Fam. Letters*, ii, p. 266).

one chieftain to another, are generally sold to half-blood Portuguese who visit the country as slave dealers. The country appeared to contain a large population, and it abounds in the necessaries of life. The soil is fertile, and the climate admits of the crops appearing in all the different stages all the year round.

The time of our visit was unfortunately the season of the heavy rains, which appear to follow the course of the sun in his progress North. Our experience can scarcely be considered a fair criterion of what may occur during the rest of the year. Perpetual drenchings, a hot sun (the temperature never under 84° in the shade) quickly drying our clothing, and frequently sleeping in damp beds, prevented my forming a reliable idea of the salubrity of the climate. My companions, all native Zambesians, had nearly as much sickness as myself, intermittent fever being the complaint from which we all suffered most. The country, however, is elevated, and abounding in flowing streams is moreover of great fertility and beauty. The time spent in the way was also longer than may be required at other seasons, because we had to halt early in the afternoons in order to allow the men to build little huts for shelter during the night. The dense tangled forests, however, presented an insurmountable obstacle to travelling in waggons. But the plains on our West may not be similarly obstructed.

When we came into the vicinity of the Portuguese settlements, the tribes treated us rather scurvily. Some levied heavy fines on the most frivolous pretences, others demanded payment for leave to pass at all. I parted with everything I could dispense with, and my men gave all their ornaments & most of their clothes either for food, fines, or ferries. But when we explained that we had nothing we could part with besides, it did not in the least appease the violence of the mobs which surrounded us — we must pay either a man, an ox, or a gun, and were looked upon as interlopers wishing to cheat them out of their dues. At last, on reaching the river Quango, by the generous assistance of a young Portuguese sergeant of militia we entered the territory of Portugal, and recieved the kindest treatment from all classes all the way to Loanda.

In that city I arrived nearly knocked up, and suffering from fever & dysentery. Edmund Gabriel, Esqre, Her Majesty's Commissioner for the suppression of the slave trade, and the only Englishman I know in the city, most generously recieved me and my 27 companions into his house. I shall never forget the delicious pleasure of tumbling into his bed after sleeping six months on the ground, nor the unwearied attention and kindness through a long sickness which Mr G. invariably shewed. May God reward him.

My companions were struck with awe at the sight of a city, and more especially when taken on board H.M. ships of war. The kindness of the officers of the cruizers removed the last vestige of fear from their minds, for, finding them to be all my countrymen, they saw the fallacy of the declarations of the negroes, of every village we came to West of Cassange, 'that the white man was taking them to the sea, and would sell them all to be taken on board ship, fattened, and eaten'. They were afterwards engaged in discharging coals from a ship for wages, and will marvel to the end of their lives at the prodigious quantity of 'stones that burn' one ship could contain. They previously imagined their own little canoes on the Zambesi the best vessels, and themselves the most expert sailors, in the world.

His Excellency the Bishop of Angola, then the acting Governor of the Province, recieved my companions with great kindness, and assured them of his protection and friendship, as well as desire to promote commercial intercourse with the country of Sekeletu. He also sent a present of a horse and handsome dress for that chief, and shewed very great attention to myself in my sickness. The merchants, too, of Loanda took the opportunity of our return to send presents to Sekeletu; and as they give much more for the produce of his country than can be or is done by merchants from the Cape Colony, it is to be hoped that intercourse with either Cassange or Loanda will promote the civilization of the Interior.

I return, because I feel that the work to which I set myself is only half accomplished. The way out to the Eastern coast may be less difficult than I have found that to the West. If I succeed, we shall at least have a choice. I intend, God helping me, to go down the Zambesi or Leeambye to Quilimane. May, in order to avoid the Falls of Mosioatunya and the rapid & rocky river above that part, go accross from Sesheké to the Maninche-Loenge, or river of the Bashukulompo, and then descend it to the Zambesi. If I cannot succeed, I shall return to Loanda, and thence embark for England. I expected letters at Loanda, and feel much disappointed at recieving none. I asked my friends to write to that place, and now suppose they believed I should never reach it. I shall feel obliged if you send a letter to Quilimane. I know not whether I shall reach it. I mean to try. Enclosed in this is a letter for my family.

Business. My companions, decidedly the best I ever travelled with, were given by Sekeletu for my assistance without any idea of remuneration. As wages are a most effectual means of breaking up the feudal system and that form of domestic slavery which prevails throughout Africa, I resolved to give them each a small payment in goods. For this purpose I drew on you for £50 by a bill in favour of Mr Gabriel, dated 19th June 1854. It was sent to his agents, Mrss Woodhead & Co., No. 1 James St., London. Finding subsequently the balance of that sum insufficient for the supply of goods necessary for the return journey, viz. to purchase food, reward our friends who shewed kindness, and conciliate our enemies, who verily were 'no better than they should be', I afterwards drew £25 in the same way. The bill was dated 16th August 1854. This second bill may have gone down in the Forerunner. I hope the above may meet your approbation.

Another matter, for troubling you with which I beg to apologize. As it may appear very unbusinesslike to refer to transactions without positive dates, I can only plead the destruction of my papers by the Boers at Kolobeng. Having recieved, according to order, periodicals from James Maclehose, bookseller in Buchanan St., Glasgow, I requested him to send his account in, to the best of my recollection, 1851; and, when I recieved it, immediately transmitted a bill in the usual form to Mr MacLehose, and at the same time advised you that the sum (£20) might be deducted from my salary. I heard nothing more of the above referred to bill, nor had Mr Thompson any notice of it in 1852. But believing you had paid the amount to Mr MacLehose, I caused it and two other bills to be deducted from my last account current with the Society when in Cape Town (1852). When on my way to the Zambesi in the end of the same year, a letter from Mrs L. informed me that Mr MacLehose had told her he had not recieved the bill of which I speak. Now, as I am quite certain the bill for £20 was sent to Mr MacLehose's address, I wish to ascertain whether it was paid to him. If, as I suspect, the bill and letters were lost, I shall feel obliged if you pay Mr MacLehose £20, as that sum was deducted from my salary when the account was last made up in Cape Town.

Another sum of £20 was deducted at the same time, under the same impression, viz. that a bill in part payment for clothing had been recieved by a merchant and presented to you for payment, and that, though your advice of the same had not yet (in 1852) come to Mr Thompson, it would come before I returned from my present journey. I have learned from Mrs L. that I owe something to the same party. I do not know the present address of this merchant, but it is probably known to Mrs L., and you will favour me by allowing her the above sum or any part of it to liquidate the debt, as it is positively deducted from the salary.

A sum of £10 was deducted also in favour of Mr Snow, but in his case the date was 1852. I hope he has applied for his money.

In the case of [the] first two bills of £20 each, I have had fears that they may have been lost, and therefore trouble you before I leave the world of mails and correspondence.[1]

Private. I have been remarkably well treated by the Portuguese. The Government did everything in its power to facilitate my progress through the Province, and this, I have reason to believe, was according to the wishes of the Government of Portugal. I carry a letter from the Bishop of Angola, the head of the provisional government, to all the commandants and governors of districts and forts, to furnish me with everything requisite, and that I should incur no expense whatever in their territory. These gentlemen, however, had already treated me, on the 'voluntary system', with so much politeness and hospitality I had not the face to present the letter of authority. Concerning this courtesy, for which I feel abundantly thankful, I may remark that the Portuguese in Africa have a good character for polite hospitality. But I came amongst them in a peculiar manner — I came out from behind them. It would, I suspect, be a different story if a missionary had come to Loanda and wished to go in from thence.

I visited several of the 'extinct convents' or, as we should say, deserted missionary stations. The churches are standing in some instances, and would require but little to put them into good repair. South American fruit trees grow in the neat gardens which the missionaries laid out. The bedsteads stand in the dormitories as they left them, and the big chests in which the bretheren stowed their grub. But there were no books, nor any inscriptions on the graves which would enable one to learn something of the dust which sleeps beneath. But, turning to the people, we soon recognize their memorials in the great numbers who can both read and write. There are very few of the people of Ambaca who cannot use the pen, and the sight is not uncommon in that district of a black man sitting in the evening with a fire-stick in one hand and a pen in the other, writing in a beautiful hand a petition to a commandant. I looked upon these relics of former times with peculiar interest, because if the labours of the Jesuit missionaries who were expelled by the

---

[1] '26th Jany. 1855. Sent off by the mail yesterday morning letters for Dr Tidman, Mrs L., with requests furnish again bills for bookseller which seem to have been lost, viz. £20 to MacLehose, £20 to Mrs L. for Drummond, and £10 for Snow. Also another copy for Mr Gabriel for a bill of £25, 16 August, which is probably lost' (*MS. Journal*, p. 317). A pencil note (not by D. L.) on the margin of the present letter indicates that Snow's bill was paid on 24.ix.1852; those in favour of Gabriel and MacLehose are referred to in Tidman's reply (see below, p. 277); of Drummond's there is no mention.

Marquis of Pombal[1] have so much permanence, surely those of Protestants who leave the living word behind them will be no less abiding.

I was informed by a canon of the church, whom I lately met in Pungo Andongo, and who had recently returned from a visit to Portugal as conductor of the Prince of Congo, that in the Congoese territory there are no fewer than twelve churches, and not a single priest. This gentleman was a wooly-headed black, yet a dignitary of the church, universally respected for his virtues, and has had an order conferred on him by the King of Portugal.[2] We English feel very complacent with ourselves when we compare our way of treating people of colour with that of the Americans, but the Portuguese would stare as much as I did to see (as in the case of Botha) a judge treating with levity a case of life and death, and a brandy bottle on the bench beside him in full view of the court.[3] The insalubrity of the country is the cause why there are so few priests in Angola. Intermittent fever is excessively prevalent, and it usually produces enlargement of the spleen, which sooner or later ends fatally.

Among the benefits conferred on the country by the missionaries may be mentioned coffee. A few Mocha seeds were planted, and it has now extended itself over the whole country. The Portuguese are now in a state of transition from illicit to licit commerce. The former being effectually repressed by our cruizers, they turn enthusiastically to coffee, plantations of which are dailly discovered in the forests and only require to be cleaned to yield as good quality of fruit as can be found in the world. A few months ago it was discovered near Cassange, 300 miles inland.

I cannot send you a map, and this is not so full an account as I wished to send.

I am,
affectionately yours,
David Livingston

[1] Under the influence of the Marquis de Pombal (1699–1782), secretary of state for foreign affairs, the Jesuit order had been banished from Portuguese territory in 1759.

[2] Cf. *Travels*, p. 426. D. L. met this 'gentleman of colour' on 30 December 1854 (*MS. Journal*, p. 313).

[3] 'At last a bottle of wine was brought in. Sir John Wylde took several swills, pretending he was so much fatigued he needed it, [and] pursed up his mouth after each glass as if he did not like it' (*Private J.*, p. 82).

55. To ARTHUR TIDMAN
10 February 1855

[LMS 87]

Cassange
10th Feby., 1855

Dear Sir,

It affords me much pleasure to be able to repair in some measure the loss caused by the wreck of the 'Forerunner', by means of the enclosed maps of the Province of Angola and that portion of the country of Lunda through which we passed.[1]

You will thereby be able to appreciate some of the obstacles presented by wood and water to the formation of a path such as we have been accustomed to use. Only the larger streams, or such as we found large, are inserted in the Lunda portion. But ajacent to all these, and in many other parts, there are large dense forests. And if we take the barriers presented by bogs, rivers, and thickets, into consideration, it looks as if it would be a waste of life to attempt single-handed to worm a way for a ponderous Cape waggon.

The actual distance is not great between the northern parts of Sekeletu's country and this, the commercial capital of the Interior, where European supplies may be obtained and mails pass to the coast twice or three times every month. And if some of our strong young misisonaries would view the limited spheres in which they spend their lives in comparison with that presented in ... to good account.[2] At present I think it best, before working farther in this direction, to secure a choice by examination of the way down to the other coast. I leave this on the 13th currt.[3]

If, looking at the map, you may wonder why Little Fish Bay[4] or Benguella was not attempted, being so much nearer than Angola,[5] the reason was the presence of the tsetse on our Western borders.

[Signature cut away]

Letters for Dr Tidman and Mrs L. were sent on 23d ult.[6]

[1] 'While here [at Cassange], I reproduced the last of my lost papers and maps' (*Travels*, p. 435); 'I am busy copying the map for the Society and others' (10.ii.55: *MS. Journal*, p. 330). The copies mentioned above are now in the LMS archives (LMS 87); others were sent to Maclear, Murchison, and Charles L. (*MS. Journal*, pp. 331, 332).

[2] About three lines (say 15 words) cut away (together with signature on back).

[3] 'We left Cassange on the 16th' (*MS. Journal*, p. 332).

[4] Moçâmedes, 15° 10′ S., 12° 10′ E., on the coast of Angola.

[5] D. L. means the modern province of Luanda.

[6] Added on margin of first page. In *MS. Journal*, p. 317, the date is given as 25 January.

56. To DAVID LIVINGSTON
24 August 1855

[LMS: Outgoing Letters, Africa, Box 8, pp. 362–7. Previous publication: Campbell, pp. 232–3 (paragraph seven); Seaver, pp. 269–70 (paragraph seven and postscript)]

London

August 24*th*, 1855

Dear Brother,

In the absence of any reliable information as to where a letter might be likely to overtake you on your route, we have delayed writing longer than we could have desired; but, in common with a large circle of friends and well-wishers, we have continued to cherish the liveliest interest in your enterprise, not unmingled with solicitude as to your personal safety.

I have now the pleasure of replying to your several communications under date Sekeletu 24th September, Linyanti 8th Novr. 1853, St. Paul de Loanda 4th July 1854, and Cassange 14th January ult., the last mentioned having come to hand only within these few days; but we have, as you are aware, to deplore the loss of the valuable packet despatched by the 'Forerunner'. We received also a most obliging communication from your kind friend Mr Gabriel, of St Paul de Loanda, in which that gentleman described the suffering state in which you arrived at that place, and gave also some particulars of your journey.[1]

The exposure to heavy rains and excessive heat, by which you and your native Zambesian attendants were invalided on passing through the country, in all probability laid the foundation of the more severe and protracted illness from which you suffered on reaching the Coast, and grateful indeed must have been the hospitalities accorded to you by Mr Gabriel. While it would appear that from several of the native tribes on your route you received marked attention and assistance, others of them, bordering on the Portuguese settlements, seemed to conspire to throw every obstacle in your way. Undaunted however by this repulsive treatment, and the perils and hardships incidental to such a journey, you were enabled to press onwards until, through the superintending care of Divine Providence, you had accomplished one of the main objects of your enterprise, by opening a high road from the interior to the shores of the Atlantic. We were happy to find that not only from

[1] Apparently a reference to Letter 53, included among those acknowledged above. No letter of that date (4.vii.54) was received from D. L. himself, who was then too ill to write.

Her Majesty's Commissioner, but also from the Portuguese authorities and others on the Western Coast, you received all the attention and aid that kind feeling and apparent sympathy in your plans could dictate.

With a view to extend your researches in the opposite direction, you now propose to follow the course of the Zambesi or the Leeambye, in the hope of being able to find an outlet to the Eastern Coast or, failing that attempt, to retrace your steps to Loanda; your ultimate object, in either event, being to take your passage to England. Your announced design of crossing the Continent from West to East, by which you will have to traverse unknown regions and be cast upon the tender mercies of savage men, seems to be an enterprise bolder and more hazardous than any you have hitherto undertaken; but, as anything in the way of friendly counsel or dissuasion would now be fruitless, we can only indulge the earnest hope that the same gracious Hand, which has hitherto guided and sustained you in so many perils, may conduct you in safety to Quilimane, the spot indicated in your letter as the Ultima Thule of your projected land journey.

In deciding to proceed to England, you have doubtless been influenced by reasons which are likely to have due weight with the Directors. The immediate interests will be injured by your absence from the field of missionary labour. The objects pursued by your exploratory tours have, to a certain extent, been most successfully accomplished, so that as respects any future plans of operation it may be desirable that, while proceeding to join Mrs Livingston in this country, you should also have the opportunity of meeting the Directors, who, with many other friends, will be most happy to tender their congratulations on the results achieved by your indefatigable labor in the cause of philanthropy and science.

Of the value attached by the Royal Geographical Society to your discoveries, it has afforded a renewed proof in awarding to you the Queen's Gold Medal, which I had the pleasure to receive on your behalf from the hands of its President, Lord Ellesmere, at its Annual Meeting in May last;[1] while the University of Glasgow has also testified its approbation of your services in extending the range of human knowledge by conferring upon you an honorary degree.[2]

The Directors, while yielding to none in their appreciation of the

---

[1] This meeting, at which it was announced that D. L. had been awarded the Patron's Gold Medal for 1854, is described in *JRGS*, 1855, pp. lxxvi–lxxvii, and *Chronicle*, xix, (Sept.) 1855, pp. 188–90. Francis Egerton (1800–57), first Earl of Ellesmere, 'statesman and poet' (*D.N.B.*), was President of the R.G.S. 1853–5.

[2] At a meeting of the University's Senatus Academicus on 15 December 1854; the degree was that of LL.D. (*Chronicle*, xix, (Feb.) 1855, pp. 36–7).

objects upon which, for some years past, your energies have been concentrated, or in admiration of the zeal, intrepidity, and success, with which they have been carried out, are nevertheless restricted in their power of aiding plans connected only remotely with the spread of the Gospel. Of the important bearing of your researches upon the interests, not only of science, but of general humanity, we have the most entire confidence; and we would also cherish the hope and belief that they will ultimately tend to the diffusion of Christian truth among the populous but yet uncivilised tribes inhabiting the districts to which you have obtained access. But your reports make it sufficiently obvious that the nature of the country, the insalubrity of the climate, the prevalence of poisonous insects, and other adverse influences, constitute a very serious array of obstacles to missionary effort; and even were there a reasonable prospect of these being surmounted — and we by no means assume they are insurmountable — yet, in that event, the financial circumstances of the Society are not such as to afford any ground of hope that it would be in a position, within any definite period, to enter upon untried, remote, and difficult, fields of labour.[1] In view of these circumstances we should, independently of the pleasure of seeing you amongst us, regard your visit to England as affording a most favorable opportunity for conferring with you fully on your future plans.

In relation to the points of business to which you invite our attention, I have to state that your bill dated 19th June 1854, for £50 in favour of Mr Gabriel, was duly accepted on the 7th Sept., and that under date 16 August, same year, for £20 (not £25 as stated in your letter) was accepted on the 3rd April ulto. The bill of £20 which you mention having forwarded to Mr Maclehose has not been presented. But the state of your account with Mr M. will perhaps be best understood by our giving you the following extract of a note received from him, bearing date, Glasgow, March 23rd 1855:

'Mrs Livingston called upon me some time ago, and requested me to forward to you our account against Dr Livingston. This I now do, and you will see there is a balance due to me of £1.7.10. You will observe that, of the entire account of £45.8.10, the Dr has only sent me £10.

---

[1] In July 1855 the Directors had issued a special appeal to meet an accumulated deficit of £13,000. 'The present amount of debt is a serious hindrance to the Society's operations, and, instead of sending forth more labourers to reap the fields already white unto the harvest, the Directors will be unable, unless the heavy burden is removed, to sustain those already engaged in this service ... It would be to the Directors an occasion of the deepest regret, were they brought under the necessity of recalling a single Missionary, or of diminishing any branch of their Missionary labours' (*Chronicle*, xix, pp. 146–7).

But the Rev. John McRobert[1] has paid me £34.1.0 on a/c of some native teacher or school for missionaries, I am not sure which, but Dr Livingston knows, and this £34.1.0 he, I believe, pays to some parties on the spot. Mr McRobert, I know, wrote to Dr Livingston about part of this sum (£12 I believe), so there is yet £22.1.0 of which I fear he has not yet heard from me, but he has heard I think from Mr McRobert. The regular way no doubt should have been to have paid this money to the Mission House, and to let Dr Livingston pay me himself. At the same time, we feel it to be unnecessary trouble and expense to send the money to Africa (through the Missionary Society) and to have it returned to pay me.'

You will accordingly have simply to pay over the sum of £34.1.0, mentioned in Mr Maclehose's note, to the proper parties in Africa, and to give us credit for the £1.7.10 which we have paid to Mr M.

In compliance with your suggestions, we address this letter to you at Quilimane, and a duplicate will be forwarded to Loanda; and, in the earnest hope that the good providence of God will, in due time, conduct you in safety to the shores of your native country, I have the pleasure to subscribe myself,

Dear Brother,
Yours very truly,
[Arthur Tidman],
For. Secy. of the Lon: Missy. Society

P.S. I have the pleasure to report that Mrs Livingston, whom I have seen within these few days, is, together with your children, in good health, but she is, of course, looking forward with no little anxiety to the termination of your long and perilous journey, and your reunion with your family.

57. To WILLIAM THOMPSON
13 September 1855

[LMS 88. Previous publication: Chamberlin, pp. 233–6 (incomplete)]

Linyanti
13th Septr 1855[2]

My dear Mr Thompson,

We have had an unexpected opportunity of sending letters back to

---

[1] Congregational minister at Cambuslang 1838–46. His wife had been collector of the money sent to D. L. for the support of Mebalwe (see above, p. 102).

[2] D. L. and his companions had reached Dinyanti on 11 September (*MS. Journal*, p. 499).

7. WILLIAM THOMPSON

Angola, but the time afforded has been so short I have sent a few notes only. This will follow the Arab who left this morning,[1] and I hope will reach you some time or other and let you know I am not unmindful of my friends, though separated from them by a precious big lump of this which the philosophers call 'our *little* planet'! I have scarcely had time to peruse my letters, which we found had lain on an island in the Leeambye, close to falls of Mosioatunya, a whole year.[2] Such a rush of thoughts and trembling emotions when I opened letters from my family you may imagine if you can, taking it into consideration that I have been without information for nearly three years. Thank God I had no reason to sorrow. I requested my friends to write to Loanda, but though detained there for many months by sickness I never got a line; and I suppose their respectful silence may be translated into a rebuke for imagining that I should ever reach that port. 'You think more highly of yourself than you ought to think'. Well, I must try and be thankful even for that.

I commence the descent of the river for Quilimane at the beginning of October. The path we have already opened up has many advantages. The Portuguese post comes 3 times a month to Cassange, 300 miles inland, and goods are considerably cheaper than in the Cape Colony. I mean such as missionaries require: coffee, tea, sugar, cloth,[3] &c. Labour is extremely cheap in Angola, & anything manufactured by the natives is got for a trifle. I bought a pair of Wellington boots at Pungo Andongo, more than 100 miles from the sea, for five shillings and eight pence English money, and that was exactly the price given to natives by a merchant of the place for *one pound* of ivory. This is more than the slimmest Boer would get in Cape Town. The difference in prices was explained by the Americans giving larger prices than the English. They have all the Loanda trade in their hands. The advantage to the natives is, out of sight, greater than in the Colony. Take Cassange and any spot 300 miles inland from the southern coasts of S. Africa, a native will get from five to seven times more in the North than in the South for his ivory.

The trade of the Portuguese might have been pushed much farther, but, as I saw the other day in a history of Angola, a law was made prohibiting white traders from going into the Interior, because in almost every case in which war was necessary to punish the natives for the

---

[1] The Zanzibar slaver Ben-Habib (*MS. Journal*, p. 507), whom D. L. in later years met again in East Africa.

[2] Cf. *Fam. Letters*, ii, pp. 260, 267–8; *Travels*, pp. 499–500.

[3] 'clothes' (Chamberlin, p. 233).

murder of white men, investigation shewed that the white and not the black man was the aggressor. Black men 'não calçada'[1] might be sent with goods, but no white man go himself under a severe penalty. And this law continued in force during successive governments. I think it is still in force, for when I was coming through Cassange lately the Commandant sent an order to all the traders (abour 40) along the River Quango & other places in the vicinity to return to the village, and on their refusal the matter was remitted to the Governor of Loanda.

There is no restriction on trade except what is implied in the above. It goes briskly from both coasts. Arabs and Portuguese are met with everywhere. The latter are like our Griquas, namely half blood, and it is curious they have been found in the course of a few generations to become black again. The Portuguese marry black women, there being very few white ladies in the country, and, unlike our immaculate Transvaal congregation, never disown their children. I made enquiry, and found one person only whose children might answer, like Topsy,[2] 'Never had any father nor nothing'. Persons of colour of respectability sit at the tables of the richest without, as far as I could observe, any distinction on account of race. And I met a canon of the church who was as black as a Caffre, with short wooly hair, thick lips, &c. He is greatly respected, and the gentleman with whom I was living had known him as having acted with uniform propriety in his high office for 28 years. He had just returned from accompanying the Prince of Congo to Portugal, and the King had decorated him with one of the orders of merit as a token of approbation.

I found the Portuguese exceedingly hospitable, not to me alone but to all traders whom we met either going or returning. They are certainly equal in this respect to the Dutch of former times, and to their descendants of the present day as I found them in the Western districts, not yet soured by the frequent visits of blackgaurd scoffing Englishmen.

The black races in the vicinity of the Portuguese settlements are immeasurably worse than the Southern tribes among which I have had experience. From the Casai to the Orange River I should say to every traveller or trader: Behave like a gentleman, and you will be treated as

---

[1] Unshod. 'The privelege of wearing boots is conferred on certain [men] by their native chiefs. They then, though quite black, call themselves "white men", they then speak of the unbooted as "that black", though they themselves may only a few days before have given a consideration for liberty to put their feet in knightly attire themselves' (*MS. Journal*, p. 252).

[2] D. L. had ordered a copy of Mrs Stowe's *Uncle Tom's Cabin* from the bookseller John Snow in January 1853 (12.i.53 Snow).

such; play the monkey, be impudent, and try to cheat, and you will get 'monkey's allowance'. The greater wickedness of the tribes North of the Casai admits of easy explanation,[1] but you must be content with my assertion only, for the moment. When I can find time I shall let you into it. Rest assured it has not been caused by the ruffian zendelings[2] of the Independants' Society.

I was the first missionary they ever saw, and we were attacked four times by them. Plunder was their object. Once *we beat them* off by simply sitting and looking at them, after telling them they must strike the first blow. They were well supplied with guns, and sometimes presented them at us. Another tribe began by plundering the goods carried by those of our party in the rear. Firing and shouting ensued when we went back to them, and the chief, being busy loading,[3] un-expectedly found a revolver within a foot of his stomach, and hostilities were quickly brought to a close without any one being hurt on either side. On several other occasions we were considerably bothered, and it appeared as if we must fire. But in addition to a strong aversion to shedding human blood, I had the schoolboy feeling of 'strike your match' wonderfully strong. I wished, if I must turn 'soger', I had a parcel of Russians or Velschoons[4] in opposition, and not these poor ig-norant savages. At present I firmly believe that we might go back with-out a tithe of the molestation we experienced, and two or three harmless visits would render the path as safe as a Colonial one.

It is not likely I shall ever go South again except by sea. My waggon stands as safe here as it would do in Mr Hoffmeyer's garden. Nothing was touched during our two years' absence. It is simply useless except as a house. Canoes are the means of conveyance. The Leeambye & Chobe rose unusually high this year, and people went in canoes in nearly a straight line from Linyanti to Sesheke, about 130 miles. I don't know where we shall settle, except that it must be to the North of this. The country is finer there. We never carried water, but passed two or three good streams each day all the way to Loanda. The natives are all armed with guns and swords, and they have finished the game. The only fault of the new path is, it admits of conveyance by human labour alone. The forests and boggy rivers present insurmountable obstacles to waggons. There is another path to the East coast, which crosses at a

---

[1] See below, p. 297.

[2] The Dutch word for 'missionaries'.

[3] 'busy leading' (Chamberlin, p. 235).

[4] Afrikaans *velskoen*, shoe made of untanned hide; obviously intended here as a synonym for 'Boers'. The reference to Russians was evidently inspired by the Crimean War, then in its second year.

certain point a Lake (Tanganyeñka) 3 days broad. From the information I possess,[1] it would be easier to go that than the way down the Zambesi, but like the path we have already opened it does not admit of waggons. Clearly, then, the path of duty is that I leave the discovery of another Lake to somebody else, and try to get water carriage to the coast by going down the Leeambye.

A glance at a paper of '53 shews that it is 'believed' the proper treatment of the Caffres involves delivering over the whole of the Bechuanas & Griquas to the power of the Boers beyond the Vaal River. It is unfortunate for both parties, and especially for the Boers; for if they were guilty of no fewer than eight murderous attacks, during my residence in the country, on tribes which in no instance ever attacked them, while fearing the English Govt., irresponsibility may now lead them to greater degrees of guilt. I never saw or conversed with them without feeling the deepest commiseration and distressing sorrow. Poor old Potgeiter and Pretorius are gone to the presence of the all wise and merciful saviour.[2] I wish they had not forbid us to preach unto the gentiles that they might be saved.

My companions, all Zambesians, behaved remarkably well. The Governor sent a present of a general's dress finely ornamented with gold lace, a sash, cocked hat, & sword (a horse which died), and the merchants two bales of different kinds of cloth, beads, &c &c, and two donkies. *They* are not affected by the bite of tsetse. Preparations are making for returning with a great quantity of ivory.

Your policy to the Bechuanas and Griquas shews minds enlightened by the full jet of the oxyhydrogen light of modern civilization (free trade). What a mercy it is the new Constitution[3] won't get the credit of inventing measures for effectually driving your northern trade into new channels.[4] Will you get another pound of ivory from the north bank of the Chobe? If any one thinks so, he had better get some idea of the trade carried on by Mambari, bastard Portuguese, and Arabs from both coasts and from parts which I need not mention. If I had my will, I would prefer English traders to the others, because they, unlike my Transvaal friends, purchase no slaves. The Arabs, bastard Portuguese, & Mambari, purchase chiefly for domestic purposes, and in this respect

---

[1] Obtained from Ben-Habib (*MS. Journal*, pp. 500–1).

[2] Potgieter had died in December 1852, and Pretorius in July 1853.

[3] The Cape Colony had been granted responsible government, under a new constitution, in 1853.

[4] 'The policy of Government in stopping ammunition from Griquas and Bechuanas will effectually drive commerce into other channels' (*MS. Journal*, p. 507: 25.ix.55).

resemble the marauders who carried off my school children.[1] But they never interfere with our trying to teach the way of Salvation. I shall never forget the rage into which poor old Potgeiter got when in the mildest terms I told him, if he prevented me from teaching the tribe Bahukeng by means of old Paul, the guilt would be his. He stuttered, and at last called another to answer me.[2] The Lord preserve us from blood guiltiness.

The Arabs pray in the mornings. They say Jesus was a very good prophet, but Mahomet was far greater & better. They strike up great friendships with me wherever we meet, calling me 'father', &c, and telling the people how much we hate the slave trade in which they are engaged.

I am very well pleased to see you have lifted up your voice against certain iniquities, though I have not yet read the pamphlets.[3] Onward, my man. There are lots of good men and true in the Colony who sympathize with what is righteous and just. It is unfortunate that they have been often spoken of as one and the same with the worst portion of the Transvaal body. The sentiments & conduct are as different as those of the English settlers in Australia are to the Ticket-of-leave gentry.

With kind salutations to Captain Holmes and your family,

I am very affectionately yours,

David Livingston

A disjointed sentence in your note, about being satisfied with our position in the church, seems to point to something not right in my last. I don't remember it, & certainly never intended aught but civility.

[1] Among the captives taken by the Boers after attacking the BaKwena in 1852 were many children; D. L. himself recorded the names of 124 (*Fam. Letters*, ii, p. 200).

[2] Cf. *Fam. Letters*, ii, p. 9; *Private J.*, p. 302. The 'Bahukeng' (BaFokeng) were Mokgatle's tribe (see above, p. 95).

[3] Thompson had recently published several pamphlets on S. African affairs, including, for example, one entitled *A Word in Behalf of the Down-Trodden in South Africa* (reprinted from the *S.A. Commercial Advertiser*, Feb.–March 1854). Another is referred to in the following Letter.

X

MISSIONARY PROSPECTS

58. To WILLIAM THOMPSON
27 September 1855

[LMS 89. Previous publication: Chamberlin, pp. 236–40 (incomplete)]

Linyanti
27th September 1855

My dear Mr Thompson,

I have just learned that my Arabian post-office man is detained at Sesheke by the sickness of one of his party, so I am glad of the opportunity to write a little appendix to that hurried note of the 13th. I particularly wish to express my sympathy in the bereavement you have been called on to suffer in the departure of your most excellent father-in-law.[1] I hear of it only now, and as I have always, since my attendance on his theological lectures and ministry, regarded him with very great affection, I think of his removal with unfeigned sorrow. May God grant us grace to follow in his footsteps. Unquestionably he served God in his day and generation with rare abilities and unswerving devotion, through good & through bad report. When such are removed we feel somewhat nearer to the grave. There seems to be nothing now between it and us. May we live in Christ and for the prosperity of his great cause, and recieve the welcome 'Well done', as we have every reason to believe our much lamented friend has done. I shall always revere his memory.

I believe I did not refer very pointedly to what may be called missionary prospects in this region. And the reason is, I feel perplexed on one point, viz. the insalubrity of the climate. It is no obstacle to myself personally. I think no London Society's 'zendeling' worth his salt would bolt at that. Even though we have no law against cowardice (vide the 2d Art. of the Bushman commando, mighty men of valour),[2] most of

---

[1] Thompson's deceased wife had been the daughter of Dr Ralph Wardlaw (p. 116), who died on 17 December 1853. D. L. had attended his lectures at Glasgow University in 1836–8.

[2] In his pamphlet *The Down-Trodden in South Africa* (see p. 283), Thompson had included two highly critical letters about a raid made in Jan. 1854 by 30 Boers in the O.F.S. on a band of Bushmen, 19 of whom were killed, including women and children. The '2d Art.' refers to the second letter, which likens the massacre to the shooting down of game.

our fellows must feel in the same way. And my better half would go as readily as any one. But I am not clear on exposing my little ones without their own intelligent self-dedication.

As far as opportunity goes, there is no lack. There are tribes and villages without number to the North and East of this, and all would be proud of the presence of a white man. I know of no hindrance to missionary operations in any part of the country North of the Zambesi and towards the centre of the continent. And every day we hear of commerce extending its ramifications in all directions. Only think of the way this letter goes — by an Arab from Zanzibar who takes charge of a party of Makololo with ivory for Loanda. When they return my late companions will be ready to start again, so one relay will always be abroad on business. Before my trip the Makololo never visited another tribe except to plunder. They have not given this trade up yet, for two forays were made during my absence.[1] (Not being in the country I did not lend my pot. What a mercy. The 'ill report' won't be retailed in Government House again.[2]) But the remedy for that and every evil is being applied. The blessed word of the living God has been preached, though in much weakness, and the prayers of God's people are ascending as incense before the throne of the Hope of Israel. And the time is coming, the set time, when all nations shall call Him blessed.

I have been guilty of some innocent wonderment in seeing it stated, in terms lugubrious enough, that the Bakwains, Bakhatla, and Bahurutse, &c, were not a whit better for all our labours, nay much worse.[3] I followed the rule invariably of making no enquiries respecting the labours or conduct of other missionaries among *natives*, and therefore can say nothing about Bahurutse or Bakhatla. But about the Bakwains the verdict would, I most sincerely think, require reconsideration. During the whole of our sojourn there we strove so to conduct ourselves as that there should be no cause of offence except concerning the law of our God. I feel humbly and heartily thankful to our Heavenly Father for enabling us to effect this. It is a point of vital importance in estimating what has been effected among a people. So when we left we

---

[1] Cf. *Fam. Letters*, ii, p. 264; *Travels*, pp. 502–3. One 'foray' was against the BaTawana at L. Ngami, the other against 'a chief living far to the N.E.'

[2] Sechele, on setting out to attack Kgakge (see p. 90), had borrowed from D. L. 'a black-metal pot to cook with'. Rumour subsequently converted the pot into a cannon. 'The colonial government was also gravely informed that the story was true' [viz., that D. L. had lent Sechele a cannon]; 'and I came to be looked upon as a most suspicious character in consequence' (*Travels*, pp. 35–8 *passim*). Cf. below, p. 286.

[3] D. L. says elsewhere that this statement was made, in writing, by Edwards and Inglis (*Fam. Letters*, ii, pp. 272–3).

had not one single enemy in the whole tribe. (If it were necessary for me to seek a 'character', I would confidently refer to the Bakwains for it.) And even when the waggon was inspanned on our departure for Sebituane's country, Sechele and his principal men tried to persuade me to remove to the (afterwards) scene of the massacre of his people, offering to build a house and church free of expence. I need not refer to my reasons for refusing (I am perfectly satisfied as to their validity), except that the principal one was determined hostility to the requirements of the gospel, unmixed with any hostility to ourselves.

Some may think this hostility to the gospel evidence of deterioration from their state of heathenism. I believe it to be a most important step in advance from that state, for though they refuse to bow in humility to the Divine law, the truths they have imbibed exert a most salutary influence on their morals. (Sechele asked the Boers on commando not to fight on Sunday. The former beat the Bakwains hollow in lying & meanness, and it would be an insult to compare the honesty of the Bakwains with the dishonesty of the Boers.[1]) I know this to be a fact, a plain palpable fact. And if any one doubts it, as he cannot compare what the Bakwains were with what they are, let a comparison be made between the Makololo and Bakwains. Why, in coming from Makolo[lo] & meeting with them and some of the people near Kuruman, who still hate the gospel as much as the Bakwains, I used to feel I had entered civilized life. I don't wonder at it. The word of the living God has been brought in contact with their hearts & minds. This word has life and power. Few human souls can withstand its force, and no hatred, however deep, can quench its power. I bless God from the bottom of my heart for allowing me to sow the good seed among the Bakwains. Their present posture is a terrible one if they continue so to the end, but though they do so it is God's will the offer should be made, though thousands both white and black make a bad use of it. You will probably live longer than I shall.[2] Remember seed was sown among the people of Sechele.

I thank you for publishing the 'Pot' defence. I have not seen the remarks of Scholz, or whoever it was that wrote in a defamatory way against me.[3] I bear the poor wretched Boers in the Interior no malice.

---

[1] These two sentences were added in the margin. Like all other derogatory references to Boers in this letter, they are omitted by Chamberlin.

[2] D. L. died in 1873, Thompson (who was two years older) in 1889.

[3] In the *Cape Town Mail*, 19 and 23 April, 1853, appeared a very long letter on 'The Transvaal Boers and Sechele', by 'Jno. Kotze', which alleged, *inter alia*, that D. L. had supplied Sechele with 'firearms and ammunition'. Thompson in reply published there (26 April) an edited version of a MS. left with him by D. L. in

I never did, but I pitied their ignorance and wickedness. Although I were a Boer myself I could not help saying, as they do, that in *morality* they are decidedly inferior to the Bakwains, and considerably worse indeed than the heathen who have had no advantages. I think it is not usual for Editors of newspapers to publish defamatory remarks against persons whom they know cannot, for months or as in my case years, have an opportunity of answering them. They would not in England publish the like against officers in an Ar[c]tic expedition, would they? But you have got a new constitution now, and Mr Buchanan[1] has crept under the wing of a likelier hen. Requiescat in pace.

I have got only one scrap from you, but it accompanied the celestial map & pamphlets. Go on & fear nothing, my friend. O, Oh! What a shame to spring on the poor bishop, the first and only bishop, and box his ears so unmercifully.[2]

Believe me very affectionately yours,
David Livingstone

I get no letters from my wife. Cannot account for it no way. Hope she has not come to the Cape. But you will take care of her, no doubt.

Excuse thin nasty Yankee paper. I have nought else.

May I beg you to give the Directors notice of my welfare at this date. I cannot write them now.

Wretched Yankee paper this. All else is expended. Assuredly they need rags.

59. To ARTHUR TIDMAN

12 October 1855

[LMS 91. Previous publication: *Chronicle*, vol. xx, (September) 1856, pp 191–9 (edited extracts); Chamberlin, pp. 240–55 (incomplete)]

Linyanti on the River Chobe,
12th October 1855

Dear Sir,

The excessive heat and dust which prevail previous to the com-

1852, entitled 'The Story of the Black Pot, alias The Story of selling the gun'. In this D. L. wrote: 'If you can prove that I either *lent* or *sold* or *gave* a gun or anything else but a *black pot* and a handful of salt to Secheli, I shall willingly leave the country.'

[1] William Buchanan, proprietor and editor of *The Cape Town Mail* (which in July 1853 was amalgamated with the *S.A. Commercial Advertiser*).

[2] Under the title 'Speak Gently; or The Anglican Bishop of Cape Town — His Letter and His Book', Thompson had reprinted in pamphlet form letters contributed to the *S.A. Commercial Advertiser* (Jan. 1854), in which he commented scathingly on the Bishop's *Visitation Tour* (1850). The comments were inspired by a recent pastoral letter (to Grahamstown) absolving the frontier colonists 'from any injustice or aggression' towards the native tribes.

mencement of the rainy season have prevented my departure from the town of Sekeletu, as I intended, at the beginning of this month, in order to descend the Leeambye or Zambesi. And though often seized with sore longing for the end of this pilgrimage,[1] the certainty that the present weather would soon lay me up with fever, at a distance from friends, almost reconciles the mind to the delay. As I now possess considerable knowledge of the region to which I have devoted some years of toil, I will employ my present comparative leizure in penning a sort of report,[2] which may enable you to form a clear idea of Intertropical Africa as a missionary field.

It may be advantageous to take a glance at the physical features of the country first, in order to be able to appreciate the nature of the obstacles which will [have to] be surmounted by those whom God may honour to introduce Christianity into this large section of the heathen world. The remarks made for this purpose must be understood as applying exclusively to the country between 18° and 10° South Latitude, and situated towards the centre of the continent. The region thus indicated may be described as an extensive plain, intersected in every direction by large rivers with their departing and re-entering branches. They bear on their bosoms volumes of water such as are totally unknown in the South, and never dry up, as the Orange and most [other] African rivers do. They appear as possessing two beds, one of inundation, and another cut out exactly like the Clyde above Bothwell Bridge.[3] They overflow annually during the rainy season in the North, & then the beds of inundation (the haughs or holms) are all flooded, though, as in the Borotse valley, they may be more than 20 miles broad. The main body of the water still flows in the now very deep low-water bed, but the rivers look more like chains of lakes than streams. The country between this and Sesheke was during the present year nearly all under water. The parts which remained dry are only a few feet above the general level, and canoes went regularly from Linyanti to Sesheke, the distance being in a straight line more than 120 miles. It was an unusually wet year, and the plains are not yet free from large patches of stagnant foul-smelling water, though we expect the rains of another season to begin during the present month.

The inundation, if I may judge from my own observation, is by no

---

[1] I have borrowed this phrase for the title of the following chapter.

[2] In the National Archives of Rhodesia (photostat copy, LMS 18.A), there is a preliminary draft of this 'report', also dated 12.x.55. As it occasionally clarifies obscurities in the final text, it will be cited below where relevant, as *Draft*.

[3] 'one of inundation, and the other cut out in that which may be called the bed of low water' (*Draft*).

means partial. The exceptions are where outcropping rocks form high banks, and there we have rapids and cataracts, which impede navigation and have probably always been the barriers to inland trade. When the supply of water from the North diminishes, the rivers are confined to the low-water channels, and even at their lowest are deep enough to prevent invasion by enemies who cannot swim or manage canoes. Numerous lakes of considerable size are left on the lately flooded meadows by the retiring rivers, and these are either fringed with reeds, or covered with mat rushes, papyrus plants, the Egyptian arum, the lotus, and other water-loving plants. They are always drying up, but never dry ere the next wet season begins.

The country over which the rivers never rise is rarely[1] 200 feet higher than the holms. More frequently it is under 100 feet. In many parts there are plains so level, the rain water stands for months together 6 or 8 inches deep. We waded accross some upwards of twenty miles broad, and fish, otters, and water tortoises, appeared in numbers and quite at home among the grass, bushes, & trees.

These peculiarities result in a great measure from the form of that part of the continent to which our attention is directed. It appears to be of a basin or trough form. The hollow is much more elevated certainly than the sea, but it is considerably depressed in reference to two longitudinal ridges or fringes on its Eastern and Western sides. I was led to the recognition of this fact by contemplating the Lotembua[2] running in two and nearly opposite directions. Parting at the Lake Dilolo,[3] the Northern portion is discharged into the Casai, and thence into the Atlantic by the Congo. The Southern half disembogues into the Leeba, and thence into the Indian Ocean by the Zambesi. The boiling point of water shewed this takes place at the highest part of the basin. It is a sort of partition in it, and both North and South of it all the feeders of the great draining rivers flow from both Eastern and Western ridges towards the centre of the continent.

The general direction of the ranges of hills, and the stratification of the rocks dipping down towards a central basin now much filled up by eruptive rocks, I had noticed many years ago; and information recieved from Arabs, of two large shallow lakes within the Eastern ridge, make[s] me wonder I did not recognize what seems so self-evident now. I advance the view to you now with the less diffidence inasmuch as I have just ascertained, by the perusal of a speech of Sir R. Murchison before

---

[1] 'nearly' (Chamberlin, p. 241).
[2] Lutembo, a headwater stream of the Zambesi.
[3] In lat. 11° 33' S., long. 22° 05' E.

the R. Geogr. Soc.,[1] that he promulgated the same idea so long ago as 1852. I cannot imagine how he recieved the information; but, from his eminent scientific attainments, it is certain to be from a reliable source, and as I reached the conclusion from independant but very jog-trot observation, the view of that gentleman is surely correct.

I may have dwelt too long on the foregoing topic, but you will at once percieve it has a most important bearing on our prospects. The great humidity produced by quick evaporation from such a vast expanse of water and marsh, the exhuberant vegetation caused by fervid heat and a perfect flood of light in a rich moist soil, and the prodigious amount of decaying vegetable matter annually exposed after the inundations to the fervid rays of the torrid sun, with a flat surface often covered with forest, and little wind except at one season of the year, all combine to render the climate far from salubrious for any portion of the human family.

I really do not desire to deepen those dark colours in which the climate of certain parts of Africa have been pourtrayed. But in dealing, even prospectively, with that sacred thing human life, it is necessary to be conscientiously explicit. Take the experience of the Makololo, who are composed of Basutas, Bakwains, and the Bamangwato. They came from a dry climate, than which there are few more salubrious in the world. They have not been 20 years in this quarter, but, so great has been the mortality among the men, the tribe presents all the appearance of being destined at no distant day to extinction. I have heard Sebituane (Sebitane his own people call him), and many others, complain of the numbers of children who have been cut off by fever. (It is necessary to qualify their experience a little in view of the general practice of smoking the Cannabis sativa, which in the form of hachshisch is nearly as injurious as opium among the Turks.) The women are less fruitful than formerly, and ascribe the difference to the excessive operation of a natural phenomenon (menstruation) produced by the climate. This may explain why they are generally less subject to fever than the men. The Barotse, Batoka, Bashubea, &c, who belong to the true negro race, now constitute the body of the tribe. Those who can boast of being pure Makololo are considered the aristocracy, & are a mere handful. The negroes differ from the Bechuanas in being very prolific. Every village we entered in the North swarmed with children. This

---

[1] Sir Roderick Impey Murchison (1792–1871), geologist, was president of the R.G.S. 1851–3. The 'idea' referred to was expounded by him in his presidential address in May 1852 (cf. *JRGS*, 1852, pp. cxxii–cxxiv), a copy of which he sent to D. L., whose reactions to it are given more fully in *Travels*, pp. 474–5, 500.

perhaps explains why, notwithstanding all their wars, kidnapping, slave selling, and mortality by fever, they are such an imperishable race. I supposed the mortality to be considerable among them, because many with whom we formed acquaintanceship in going North were in their graves when we returned, but we saw many aged men too.

Having given the dark side of the picture first, the impression may have been produced that it can have no other. Before deciding, let me try and give the brighter phase as fairly. No one seeing the country around Linyanti or Sesheke could form an idea of what it becomes farther North. The southern portion is the least desirable of the whole, for when we go beyond the Borotse the land gradually becomes more lovely, untill in Londa (Lunda) we reach an exceedingly well-watered fruitful country. It is flat, but the luxuriant loveliness of many a spot will remain in my imagination for ever. As for the interior of Angola, if Eden sent up so quickly such a rush of rank vegetation our progenitor must have found sufficient occupation in dressing it. The very thing to be dreaded, you think. (The great moisture does not appear so undesirable after one has been pining, as we did, under a sky of brass, untill we almost believed the Prince of the power of the air had too much of his own way there.)[1] The miasmata from such luxuriance must be terrible. It rises from the decay of a hundred thousand organisms, every one of which is beautiful. But the London Directors surely have not been such unprofitable hearers of sanitary sermons as to forget that they inhale perenially effluvia, miasmata, poison, from millions of things, almost every one of which is too horrible to name.

The fever is certainly the great bugbear of this field. But it must ever be borne in mind that it is the only one. There are few other diseases. No consumption, nor scrofula, nor madness. (3 cases of mania, one of puerpural insanity, & one of senile dementia, in 15 years, do not require notice in a general statement.) Measles and smallpox paid a passing visit some twenty years ago. (Singularly enough, inoculation was employed in the latter disease.) I have seen but one well marked case of hydrocephalus, three of epilepsy, but none of cholera, cancer, or hydrophobia or delirium tremens, and many other diseases common in England.

'Silent friends' et id genus omne would here have light purses. The paucity of complaints renders people less gullible than with you. A person is very rarely suspected of malingering, and though all have the most implicit faith in medicine, homoeopathy never alters nor alleviates

---

[1] Added in the margin.

a single symptom. Indeed, odyle,[1] table turning, popular mesmerism, are all the accomplishments of high civilization. The only exception is where a state of extacy, allied to hypnotism, is produced by violent action of the voluntary muscles, the individual pretending to the prophetic afflatus. The application or even threatened application of that which is recommended for the backs of children and fools produces instantaneous return to propriety.

The most common diseases are inflammations of different organs, but neither these nor fever should form a barrier to missionary enterprise. I imagine they will not, for those minded to engage therein have never yet stipulated for a field in which death has absolutely no darts in his quiver. I hope I am not estimating the prospect of subjection to frequent attacks of fever too lightly, for should missionaries who are educated and sent out at great expense be cut off, as soon as they enter on their labours, by causes which might have been foreseen and avoided, great losses would be sustained by both the church and world.

But can any unfavourable inference be drawn from my personal experience in respect of fever? I believe decidedly not. It is true I suffered severe attacks of the disease no fewer than twenty-seven times in the space of $2\frac{1}{2}$ years. But it will readily be confessed that sleeping month after month with only a little grass and a horsecloth between me and the ground emitting so much moisture, dew is deposited so quickly on the glass roof of the artificial horizon if placed on a box, and within it if placed on the trough on the ground, it is extremely difficult to observe the stars; exposure in comparative inaction to the hot sun by day, in a temp[eratur]e generally upwards of 90° in the shade (my poor ox 'Sinbad' would never allow 'the old man of the sea' to hold an umbrella!); drenching showers, often making me deposit the watch in the arm pit; the lower extremities wetted regularly two or three times every day by crossing marshy streams; and food in the half journey North and half passage South purely native (with the exception of fine Angola sugarless coffee), and that is composed of that article which is sold in England as the lesser bird seed, manioc roots, and meal, all of which contain so very much starch the eyes become affected, as in the case of animals fed on pure gluten or amylaceous matter only (no ulcer was actually formed, but this I attribute to being occasionally able to procure a fowl and some maize) — these constitute rather a pitiful hygiene, and few who follow will have to endure the like.[2]

---

[1] 'Power assumed to pervade nature & account for magnetism, crystallization, chemical action, mesmerism, etc.' (*Concise Oxford Dictionary*).

[2] In *Draft*, this very long and clumsy sentence is worded thus: 'It will readily be

These privations, I beg you to observe, are not mentioned as if I considered them in the light of *sacrifices*. I think the word ought never to be mentioned in reference to anything we can do for Him who, though he was rich, yet for our sakes became poor. But I supposed you could not well appreciate my experience at its true, or rather no, value unless I stated the drawbacks to fair treatment of the animal economy I came into collision with. No unfavourable opinion, surely, can be formed from mine, as to what the experience of one less exposed to the vicissitudes of the weather and change of diet might be.

I beg that in the event of publication the parts marked by a line on the margin may be suppressed.[1] Unless I mentioned privately the foregoing circumstances, it might be supposed I was speaking too lightly of a disease which has inspired so much terror.

The fever may be said to commence at the latitude of Lake Ngami (20° South), and extends to the equator or beyond it. But from 8° South Lat. it generally assumes the intermittent or least fatal form. (I would speak in a different tone if I believed this to be the West Africa remittent. That terrible disease seems to baffle all remedial means. I believe it occasionally becomes epidemic in the country mentioned. I have seen a few mild cases. Yet, in the intervals, we have a more salubrious field than the Church, Baptist, Americans, & United Presbyterian, missionaries.)[2] The sequelae of this are enlargement of the spleen and great emaciation, which after a considerable period end fatally. Abundant warning is always given to seek cure by change of climate, and we have not far to go, for a few degrees of Southing introduces [one] into the dry pure air of the desert, and every step in that direction is made in the very remarkably healthy tract termed the Interior of Southern Africa. I have had the complaint in its severest forms, and when checked by exposure during its course vomiting of large quantities of blood ensued, yet I am aware of no organic affection as the result. Indeed, I am as well now as ever I was in my life. The greatest in-

believed that sleeping on the damp ground month after month; exposure in comparative inaction by day to the hot sun (always above 90° in the shade, and my ox would never allow me to hold an umbrella); drenching showers, & lower extremities wet two or three times every day; food, during the journey north, the latter half of the journey south, with the exception of sugarless coffee purely native, viz. of manioc roots or meal, which contains so much starch the eyes become affected as in the case of animals fed on amyliae or glutenalone, and occasionally birdseed, meal, & a fowl — these constitute more pitiful hygiene than missionaries who follow will have to endure.'

[1] The 'parts' so marked are the two preceding paragraphs. Substantial portions were nevertheless included in the extracts published in *Chronicle*, 1856 (p. 193).

[2] Added in margin.

convenience I was subjected to was being less energetic or quite useless for long periods as a missionary.

One cause of the great mortality which prevails at certain times, and particularly at the period of drying up of the inundation, is the want of prompt though not heroic treatment. Neither doctors nor patients hurry themselves. Though his services may not have been asked till danger appears, the medical man must throw his dice[1] first, and spend hours of talking over that. Then, if it is late in the afternoon, he will go and dig the roots tomorrow, and even then stirs not till the sun is well up. The treatment, when once fairly in operation, is undoubtedly that best adapted to overcome the disease, for they set themselves assiduously to induce profuse and long continued action of the skin. By a combination of this with simultaneous but gentle stimulation of the internal organs, which as well as the skin have ceased excretion, I have found no difficulty in relieving and ultimately curing every case submitted to my care. My company of 27 persons were often attacked (two of them being jaundiced appeared as if affected by something of the West African remittent), but all were brought home in good health. With an equal number of Europeans it might have been otherwise.

But I apprehend no great mortality among missionaries, men of education and prudence who can, if they will, adopt proper hygienic precautions. Excuse me if I remind you this is more than the natives of London can effect, though liable to three if not four forms of fever. Their bread will never be whitened by bone dust, alum, or sulphate of copper. The detestable adulterations of which you are the victims are here unknown.

And even though it may still be thought a disease sufficiently menacing, the terrible ravages it committed among the Northern or Independant Boers, in a sweep it made a few years ago round the Cashan mountains,[2] shew it is not to be regarded as an unmitigated evil. Radama called a complaint of the same nature one of his best generals.[3] Neither English nor French soldiers could be hounded on to a Caffre war in Madagascar for the especial benefit of 'Frontier settlers'.

It may appear ludicrous to look even askance to a fever for protec-

[1] Divining-bones.

[2] The name used by some early travellers for the range of hills now known as Magaliesberg (cf. *Fam. Letters*, ii, p. 129). The 'sweep' referred to was early in 1852 (Edwards, in *S.A. Miss. Report*, 1852, p. 38).

[3] Radama I (b. 1791) was king (1810–28) of the Hovas in Madagascar, where the LMS had started work in 1818. He was friendly to the English, and seized several French settlements on the island (*Larousse du XXe Siècle*, v, p. 903).

8. ARTHUR TIDMAN

tion. I bear with the loss of my entire property, plundered as the very first act of the independant existence of the Transvaal Boers, with very great composure, for it would have cost me a world of time and trouble to have brought it here. But it is bitter to be told, by the Boers who heard him, that Her Majesty's Commissioner said 'they might do as they liked with the missionaries',[1] and then to have the additional insult of the Cape Governor that 'if we go into the Interior it must be at our own risk'.[2] If so, and it never yet has been at anything else, why appoint a consul at Bloemfontein for which England must pay a handsome salary? Such gratuitous insults to loyalty, and confessions of imbecility, from Commissioners and Governors, were never dreamed of in America, though they can go great lengths in some disreputable directions. We will not become disloyal, though. On we intend to go, as heretofore, at our own risk.

We have enlarged considerably the boundaries of British commerce, and have conveyed an impression to thousands of Africans of British justice and honour. Witness Sechele's faith in the character of Queen Victoria, on the strength of which he travelled from the vicinity of the Tropic to Cape Town, more than a thousand miles, certain, if he could only get near enough to tell her, his case would be attended to. And certainly it would have been, for hundreds of his children reduced to hopeless slavery, in direct violation of the treaty, is nowhere else looked upon by British statesmen with indifference. At Kuruman I dissuaded him from the attempt to go to London. 'Will the Queen not listen to my story?' I could not say, Nay. Well, English officers just returning from fighting with Basutas, his own family and friends, with that love of fair play which distinguishes them generously contributed upwards of £60 to defray his expenses to England.

Let our rulers be entreated, by all that is good, to forbear allowing such noble-minded men being employed (as the Russians against Magyars) in crushing men who have for years shewn a devotion to their chiefs only equalled, not surpassed, by that of the Scottish Highlanders to the Pretender. A Caffre war presents no elements of honour, and it is impossible for any one who loves the English soldier not to view with alarm the persevering efforts to get up another in Natal.[3] Some mem-

---

[1] In his letter to Pakington (p. 236), D. L. says this remark was made by 'Mr. Commissioner Owen'.

[2] Cathcart's comment on D. L.'s claim for compensation was that the 'losses and inconveniences he has sustained . . . do not amount to more than the ordinary occurrences incidental to a state of war, or to which those who live in remote regions of South Africa beyond Her Majesty's dominions must be frequently liable' (*P.P. England 1852–3*, LXVI, p. 750).

[3] 'to get up another Natal' (Chamberlin, p. 248).

bers of a Commission sitting there lately[1] unblushingly advocate compulsory labour, others removal of 100,000 Caffres by 8,000 whites; and this, too, though the Recorder of the district[2] declares that history does not present an instance in which so great security for life and property has been enjoyed. The killing modesty of the Colony bravodoes becomes evident when you see the men who say, 'I would drive the 100,000 over the border by force', 'I would make a law to compell them to give their young men to us to labour', described by another of the examined as 'generally men who came to the country in search of employment themselves'. They cannot now dig, but to beg for enrichment by a Caffre war they are not ashamed.

In regard to the people inhabiting this large and populous territory, it is difficult in the absence of all numerical data to present a very precise idea. The tribes are large, but divided into a great number of villages. So thickly were these dotted over the country that, in travelling in a straight line in which we could rarely see more than a mile on each side, we often passed ten or twelve hamlets in a single day. Occasionally, however, we marched 10 miles without seeing any. In no part of the South I have visited is such a population seen. Angola contains 600,000 souls, and Londa seemed more populous and of larger extent than it. The Cape Colony, with 200,000 souls, possesses some hundreds of missionaries and other Christian instructors and schoolmasters, but it will bear no comparison with Londa as a missionary field. The Makololo territory has several tribes — Batōka, Barotse, Bashubea, Banyeti, Matlotlora,[3] &c — and there is no impediment to immediate occupation by missionaries. And to such as aspire to the honour of being messengers of mercy to the actual heathen, there is no more inviting [prospect][4] in South Africa.

I am not to be understood as meaning that any of these people are anxious for the gospel. They are quite unlike the intelligent, enquiring race in the Punjaub, or the vivaceous islanders of the Pacific. But there is not such callous indifference to religious truth as I have seen, nor yet that opposition which betokens progress in knowledge. But there is a large population, and we are sure, if the word of life is faithfully preached, in process of time many will believe.

I repeat again that I know of no impediment to immediate efforts for

---

[1] The Natal Native Affairs Commission, appointed in September 1852, 'to investigate and report upon the best measures to be adopted with a view to the future government of the natives' (Theal, *History*, vii, p. 237).

[2] Henry Cloete (1792–1859), Recorder of Natal 1845–55.

[3] Either a nickname (unidentified) or, just possibly, a corruption of BaTotela.

[4] Missing word supplied from *Draft*.

their instruction. Every headman and chief in the country would be proud of the visit or residence of a white man. There is security generally for life and property. I left by mistake a pontoon in a village of Londa, and found it safe 18 months afterwards. Some parcels sent by Mr Moffat, by means of Matibele, lay a whole year on an island in the Zambesi near Mosioatunya. It is true it was believed that they contained medicine which might bewitch, but regular rogues are seldom scared by such preventatives.

The Balonda are a friendly industrious race, and thousands of the Balobale find an asylum among them from the slave-dealing propensities of their chiefs. They seem to possess a more vivid conviction of their relation to the unseen world than any of the Southern tribes. In the deep dark forests near their villages we always met with idols and places of prayer. The latter are spots about four feet broad and forty long, kept carefully clear of vegetation and fallen leaves. They resemble garden walks branching off from the common footpath, and have two or three partitions accross them of split sticks or grass, and generally terminate at a tree. Here in the still darkness of the forest night the worshipper, either male or female, comes alone and prays to the gods (Barimo) or spirits of departed relatives, and when an answer to the petition seems granted, meal or other food is sprinkled on the spot as a thankoffering.

The Balonda extend to 7° South Lat., and their paramount chief is always named Matiamvo.[1] There are many subordinate chiefs, all nearly independant. The Balobale possess the same character, but are more warlike, yet no prudent white man would be in the least danger among them.

It seems proper to refer to the Chiboque, Bashinje, and Bangala,[2] who treated us more scurvily than any 1 had previously met with in Africa. And in estimating their activities, it will be but fair to concieve ourselves as placed in their circumstances. They have often been visited by slave dealers of colour, and the nature of the country precluding the use of vehicles the merchants are always obliged to hire 40 or 50 carriers, whose clannish feelings are all on the side of the tribes mentioned. In any difficulty they are ready to save themselves by abandoning their employer. On arriving at any village, they tell how much he has been mulcted at those already passed. The chief sees he has but one man

[1] Mwata Yamvo, hereditary title of the ruler of the BaLunda in S.W. Katanga, from whose kingdom the other Lunda tribes are offshoots (McCulloch, *The Southern Lunda*, pp. 11–14).

[2] BaChokwe, BaShinji, and BaMbangala, of eastern Angola.

and a few personal slaves with whom to deal, and regulates his demands accordingly, and the merchant, feeling his ackward position as well as [being] desirous to curry favour in order to induce him to part with his people, his sole source of importance, generally accedes to every demand. Real Portuguese would not submit to the imposition, but the men of colour they employ always do, and justify the squandering of their employer's property on the ground that resistance would place in jeopardy the whole in going and a great part in returning, for nothing is easier in a densely wooded country than to abstract chainful after chainful of slaves, or kidnap straggling carriers in the rear.

The tribes have by this process imbibed the idea that they have as undoubted a right to these fines as our good bishops have to theirs. Could it therefore be otherwise than utterly disgusting to get the impudent answer from 28 Chartists, who had only five guns, 'We won't pay for treading on the earth of God, our common father?' They were indignant to behold an unblushing attempt to defraud the revenue, and uttered shouts of most patriotic disgust. Could we have done less? Sometimes they levelled their guns at us, and it seemed as if we must fight to prevent entire plunder and reduction to slavery. A quiet arrangement by which chief and councillors were quite within range of the spearmen, and our assertion that we were neither slave-dealers nor soldiers & would fight only after they had struck the first blow.[1] It would have been dangerous to fire without killing, for one being defenceless till the piece is reloaded, the enemy is encouraged by seeing a good chance before this can be effected.

These were trying times, the more especially as I had no prediliction towards ending my carreer as a 'soger'. But it cannot be said they acted unreasonably. Indeed, considering their circumstances and entire ignorance of our previous good conduct, unreasonableness cannot be said to be a more obstinate hereditary complaint in Africa than in Ireland. I thank God we did them no harm, and no one need fear vengeance on our account. A few more visits on the same principle would render them as safe as all other tribes, concerning which it may confidently [be] stated that if one behaves as a gentleman he will invariably be treated as such. Contrary conduct will give rise to remarks and treatment of scorn.

Reference has been made to the Barotse, Batōka, &c, as of the true negro race which occupies the Interior of the continent. By their sub-

[1] In *Draft*, this incomplete sentence and its predecessor are worded thus: 'Sometimes [they] levelled their guns at us, and it seemed as if we must fight to prevent entire plunder and reduction to slavery, but we were always careful to make them understand that we were neither slave-dealers nor soldiers, and would only fight after they had made a beginning.'

jection to the Makololo they have acquired considerable knowledge of the Sichuana language. We have thus a very important field open in a tongue into which the whole of the sacred scriptures will, it is hoped, soon be translated. And the time necessary for learning and reducing the negro language may not be so barren as is usually the case. The Barotse, Batoka, Balonda, and Ambonda, dialects (or language spoken by the Angolese), with those spoken in Luba & beyond, as also those of people on the East coast, are all undoubtedly cognate with the Bechuana tongue and Caffre.[1] The very considerable number of words exactly alike, or only slightly varied in their inflexions, can only be explained on that hypothesis, for there has been no intercourse between those tribes, at least for centuries past. Each of the negro tribes readily learns the language of the others. The Bechuanas, however, often fail to acquire that of the negroes, though living among them. Yet my companions acquired it in Angola as readily as I could a smattering of Portuguese, and failed entirely in the latter. Fever prevented my learning more of the Balonda than the interpreter of a late Cape Governor had of Sitchuana, when he cooly told his employer that a language, into which the Pentateuch is fully and idiomatically expressed in a very great number fewer words than it is in the Septuagint Greek or verbose English, was not capable of certain remarks made by a Basuta chief.[2]

The influence of the sacred scriptures in the true negro language[3] will be immense. If we call the actual amount of conversion the direct results of missions, and the wide diffusion of better principles the indirect, I have no hesitation in asserting that the latter are of infinite more importance than the former. I do not undervalue the importance of the conversion and salvation of the most abject creature that breathes. It is of overwhelming worth to him personally. But, viewing our work of wide sowing of the good seed relatively to the harvest which will be reaped when all our heads are low, there can I think be no comparison.

It seems necessary, in pointing out a large new field and counselling its immediate occupation, that I should advert to this subject, for we have been amused once and again of late with the *discovery* that concentration of missionary agency is what is needed, and not that sowing

---

[1] They all belong to the family of languages now known as Bantu (the name given them in 1862 by Dr W. H. I. Bleek).

[2] Cathcart stated in a despatch to Pakington (21.vii.52) that he had received a letter in English from Moshesh, 'containing expressions which I understand are not capable of being rendered in the Basuto language' (*P.P. England 1852–3*, LXVI, p. 734); this, he added in another despatch, to the British Resident in Bloemfontein (2.ix.52), 'I have ascertained from my interpreter' (enclosure in Thompson to Tidman, 5.ii.53). Cf. *Travels*, pp. 114–15.

[3] 'in the three negro languages' (Chamberlin, p. 252).

beside all waters which led you to send Morison and Milne to be lost among 300,000,000 idolators,[1] and the Church Missionary Society to look to the Antipodes & Patagonia & East Africa, with the full knowledge that charity begins at home. The question involves various elements which I have not the means of solving. I therefore speak with diffidence, though any report within my reach during the last ten or twelve years seems to say, '*the more concentration the less success*', i.e., if you increase missionaries so that they bear a proportion of more than one to 2,000 or 3,000 of the population, in ten years the proportion of communicants will be very much less per man employed than if the proportion had been one to 20,000 of the people. I refer to Africa alone, and, as it has been held forth as an example of the good effects of concentration, it is singular, if you glance at the numbers of communicants & numbers of missionaries, the one is in inverse ratio to the other, though it is believed that there is not much difference in the standards of admission.

Time is more essential than concentration. Let the seed be sown, and there is no more doubt of its vitality and germination than there is of the general spring & harvest in the course of nature. Although I have not the most distant hope that we shall ever approach to anything like converting or 'conversions to order', the subject merits attention, inasmuch as it may be elicited that there has been a great deal more done both directly and indirectly in India than men believe. Will it be out of place to recommend the subject to our friend Mr Mullens of Calcutta?[2]

It might be premature to contemplate the probability of any results from the circulation of the edition of the Testament which was furnished to Park.[3] But the circumstances are somewhat similar, seeing all the Arabs I have met with are able to read and write. We may accomplish that which he was not permitted to do. It will at all events be working in the right direction. Schemers though we may be, there is this difference between us and the worldly wise: while they seem annoyed with our fanaticism, we are really glad to see their schemes, whether of prison or sanitary reform, Niger expeditions or soup kitchens,

[1] Robert Morrison (1782–1834) and William Milne (1785–1822), sent to China by the LMS in 1807 and 1812 respectively (*Register*, pp. 7, 10).

[2] Joseph Mullens (1820–79), LMS missionary in Calcutta 1844–65 (*Register*, p. 57). In *Report*, 1852, p. 25, statistics about LMS activities in India are quoted from a pamphlet he had written; D. L. refers to them in *MS. Journal*, p. 517 (7.x.55), and discusses 'concentration' there on pp. 515–17.

[3] 'If I am permitted to enter on this large and interesting field, I shall get copies of the Arabic Testament, of the edition furnished to Mungo Park, and distribute them among the Arabs' (*MS. Journal*, p. 505: 23.ix.55). Mungo Park (1771–1806) explored the course of the Niger R. in W. Africa 1795–9, 1805–6 (*D.N.B.*).

and wish they would make another attempt at the commercial aspect of this field.

The Africans are all deeply embued with the spirit of trade. We found great difficulty in getting past many villages. Every artifice was employed to detain us that we might purchase our suppers from them, and having finished all the game they are entirely dependant on English calico for clothing. It is retailed to them by inches. A small piece will purchase a slave. If they had the opportunity of a market, they could raise on their rich soil abundance of cotton and zingoba beans for oil. I cannot say they were lazy, though they did seem to take the world easy. Their hair was elaborately curled. Many of their villages were models of neatness, and so were their gardens & huts. Many were inveterate musicians, and made one remember how much of our Anglo-Saxon energy is expended in dress & in the howling of pianos.

The men who went with me to Loanda did so in order to open up a path for commerce, and without any hope of payment from me. Though compelled to part with their hard won earnings in that city for food on our way home, I never heard a murmer. The report they gave of the expedition both in public and private, and very kind expression[s] towards myself, were sufficiently flattering. A fresh party was dispatched with ivory under the guidance of an Arab from Zanzibar, and two days only given for preparation.[1] And when they return, or even sooner, my companions are to start again. That their private opinions are in accordance with their public professions I have evidence in the number of volunteers who offer themselves to go to the East with me, knowing I have not wherewith to purchase food even. And they are not an enthusiastic race either. There is not the least probability of any mere adventurer attaining much influence among them.

If the movement now begun is not checked by some untoward event, the slave trade will certainly come to a natural termination in this quarter. Our cruizers have rendered slaves of so little value now on the coast, the Mambari purchase for domestic use alone, and they can still buy in some of the Batōka tribes only on account of the very high value put upon small pieces of clothing. They could not come for slaves alone; but the Makololo, feeling the value of the ivory which enables the Mambari to make the trip, have resolved to purchase it all. Commerce has the effect of speedily letting the tribes see their mutual dependance. It breaks up the sullen isolation of heathenism. It is so far good. But Christianity alone reaches the very centre of the wants of Africa and of

---

[1] 'A fresh party was dispatched with ivory, in company with an Arab from Zanzibar, two days after our arrival' (Draft).

the world. The Arabs or Moors are great in commerce, but few will say they are as amiable as the uncivilized negroes in consequence. You will see I appreciate the effects of commerce much, but those of Christianity much more.

Theoretically, I would pronounce the country about the forks of the Leeba and Leeambye or Kabompo and river of the Bashukulompo as a most desirable central point for the spread of civilization and Christianity. And, unfortunately, I must mar my report by saying I feel a difficulty as to taking my children there, without their own intelligent self-dedication. I can speak for my wife and my self only. We will go whoever remains behind.

Affectionately yours,
David Livingstone

60. To ARTHUR TIDMAN
2 March 1856

[LMS 93. Received 28 July 1856. Previous publication: *Chronicle*, vol. xx, (September) 1856, p. 196 (edited extracts); Chamberlin, pp. 257–8 (in full)]

Tette or Nyungwé
on the river Zambesi, Africa
2d March 1856

My dear Sir,

Having by the mercy of God reached the farthest inland station of the Portuguese this morning,[1] I gladly avail myself of an opportunity to Quillimane to advise you (and Mrs L. by the enclosed note) that I am thus far on my way down the river. It will be gratifying for you to hear that I have been able to follow without swerving from my original plan of 'opening a way to the sea, on either the East or West coast, from a healthy locality in the Interior of the continent'. Not untill two months ago was I aware of the existence of any salubrious point, though I now recollect a reference made thereto by Sebituane; but I followed out the other points with the persuasion I was doing good, if only by leading commerce towards breaking up the old sullen isolation of heathenism. And now I can announce not only a shorter path for our use, but, if not eggregiously mistaken, a decidedly healthy locality. By this fine river, flowing through a fine fertile country, we have water conveyance to with[in] 1° or 2° of the Makololo, the only impediments

---

[1] D. L., with 114 of Sekeletu's men, had left Dinyanti for the East Coast on 3 November 1855 (*Travels*, pp. 515, 526).

I know of being one or two rapids, not cataracts, and the people in some parts who are robbers. I have come thus far with but little loss, and as we are trying to civilize those whom the worldly wise would call by no better name, and be content to pay well for getting them shot, we may risk a little without fear of bankruptcy.

The Portuguese have been amazingly kind. Here they are no less so than in Angola; and much of it is owing, I believe, to my public-spirited friend Alfredo Duprat, Esquire, at Cape Town, and to the Right Reverend Bishop of Angola. The kind interest which many of my countrymen have shewn in my work makes me feel deeply grateful, and somewhat ashamed withal at having done so little to deserve it. Many would have done much more than I could effect, and done it better. This is true on the one hand, but one may take the comfort of believing that there is a pretty large sprinkling of clever people who would not have done so much. I am not so elated in having performed what has not, to my knowledge, been done before in traversing the continent, because the end of the geographical feat is but the beginning of the missionary enterprise. May God grant me life to do some more good to this poor Africa.

I have a report written for you, but it requires copying. I rest a few days here, because I have been on foot through a very rough stoney country; oxen all dead by tsetse, and too poor to buy a canoe. With one, I could have been here a month ago. In excellent health. No fever all the way from Linyanti.

Affectionately yours,
David Livingstone

61. To WILLIAM THOMPSON
2 March 1856

[LMS 94. Previous publication: Chamberlin, pp. 255–6 (virtually complete, except for the addendum on 'Business')]

Tette or Nyungwe,
on River Zambesi, East Africa
2d March 1856

My dear Sir,

Reached this, the farthest inland station at present occupied by the Portuguese, early this morning, and though I feel pretty well tired out from marching through a rough stoney bushey country without path for the last week or so, it gives me much pleasure to be again able to address those whom I left some years ago in the world. When we came to the Zambesi below the Falls, or rather near its confluence with the Kafue or Bashukulompo River, we found ourselves among tsetse, which soon settled all the oxen. The usual mode of travelling is by canoe, and the thick jungle and hills all along on both banks of the river make travelling on foot very tedious. Had I been a little richer and had purchased a canoe, I should have been here six weeks ago. But I am in perfect health, and when rested will probably be ready to forgive my ancestors for always acting on the principle of, 'Man wants but little here below, nor wants that little long'.

The Portuguese are as kind here as they were in Angola, and that is saying a great deal. Somehow or other I had imbibed a sort of prejudice against them, probably from their obstinate persistence in the slave trade. But actual intercourse has fully convinced me that we are liable to form a very wrong opinion of the majority from the contumaceous acts of the few. I believe I am a good deal indebted to Mr Duprat for his kind recommendations. I have not met with a single instance of incivility among them, and many of them are men of intelligence with whom it is refreshing to pass an hour. It is utterly unlike the everlasting 'myn vaagen, myn Uithaalder, paarde, myn moi dick vrouw',[1] &c &c.

I cannot give you any very precise information in this note. I believe our prospects are pretty fair, though there will always be enough of danger in the enterprise in these parts to make none but men of pluck engage in it. I think we have water carriage all the way by this fine river to within 1° or 2° of the Makololo. Near the coast the fever prevails more than it does inland untill you get into the great valley. Then here, and below this, there is danger of being robbed. But on the whole I am not disposed to think our prospects dark. Having once been robbed by a congregation of Christian murderers, one is not so timorous of the heathen.

After resting a few days I intend going down the river to Quilimane.

Believe me ever yours affectionately,

David Livingston

I enclose the Directors' letter to you. It would be a mercy to them to have it copied. It was so hot the ink would not stick. Yet some of it is for them only.[2]

---

[1] Cape Dutch (Afrikaans) for: 'my wagon, my Uithaalder, horses, my nice fat wife'. In *Private J.*, p. 84, D. L. cites these and a few similar expressions as representing the only topics of Boer conversation. Cf. also above, p. 212.

[2] The letter referred to here is No. 59, mentioned in No. 60 as 'a report' needing to be copied. 'I read with very great interest the letter to your address, but as the [mail steamer] was to sail that afternoon . . . I immediately posted it, without waiting to take a copy as Dr L. had requested me to do' (Thompson to Tidman, 8.vi.56).

Business.[1] *Business.* I drew while at Loanda two bills on Dr Tidman through Mr Gabriel's agent, the Messrs Woodhead and Co., 1 James St., Adelphi, London, = one bill £50, dated June 1854, and another, dated 16th August 1854, for £20 or £25, I believe the former.

I had, previous to going to Loanda, given a bill to Mr Moffat for £30, and have the impression one of £10 was sent to my brother, Charles L., of Plympton,[2] for books to that amount which he sent. If not noted by you, it is unsent, and you will oblige me by sending that sum, as part of the salary from the L. M. S. I have forgotten my notes at the waggon.

Will you oblige me by forwarding a correct statement of my account with the Society to England? making a note of two bills in my last account, 1852, one to Mr Maclehose & another to Mr Drummond, said to be undrawn, though I have not taken up the amount on account of believing they had been applied for. Mr M. told Mrs L. he had not drawn his. I desired her to examine the accounts in London to see if this were true, but not having heard more of it must settle the affair myself.

Excuse the want of paper, which compells me to write on this scrap.

D. Livingston

2d July. I find the bill has not been drawn by MacLehose; but that of £20 remains as it was in my last account, 1852, the money having been paid in liquidation of my account with MacLehose, & no advice sent of the receipt.   D. L.

---

[1] Beginning here, the MS. consists of a loose sheet of paper, filed separately as LMS 90. The reference to notes having been forgotten at the wagon suggests that it was written after D. L. had left Dinyanti for the East Coast, and the postscript was obviously added after he had received, at Quelimane, Tidman's letter of 24.viii.55. I place it here purely for convenience, though, as indicated by the date of Thompson's letter cited in the preceding note, it must have been sent separately and received much later. It is, on the other hand, certainly earlier than any of the remaining letters to Thompson.

[2] In November 1854, while at Golungo Alto, D. L. wrote to Charles L. at 'Plympton, near Boston, Massachusetts, United States' (*Fam. Letters,* ii, p. 250). For Moffat's bill, see *ibid.,* ii, p. 233 (letter dated 1.xi.53).

62. To ARTHUR TIDMAN
23 May 1856

[Draft.[1] National Archives of Rhodesia and Nyasaland; photostat copy, LMS 20.A]

Quilimane, East Africa
23d May 1856

My dear Sir,

In coming Eastwards from the country of the Makololo we cross a ridge or broad belt of elevated land, which seems well adapted by its salubrity for the residence of European missionaries. It is about 2° of Longitude broad, and of unknown length. There is but little forest except on the hills, & the landscape consists of open undulating lawns covered with short herbage, such as poets and natives call a pastoral country. Its greatest defect is the want of flowing fountains, but that is compensated by the absence of marsh and fever. The general name it bears is the Batōka country,[2] and the ruins of large towns met with everywhere shew it was lately densely peopled by the tribes of that name. They are not exterminated, but war has driven them to the hills which fringe the Zambesi and others situated to the East and North. The Makololo, who occupy their present position solely on account of the protection which the deep reedy rivers of the great valley affords them from their enemies, the people of Mosilikatse, have a strong desire to reoccupy this fine tract of country: and as it is comparatively near the East coast of Africa by this noble Zambesi, and affords a prospect of that invaluable blessing, health, while labouring to disseminate the knowledge of Christ's holy gospel, I wish to communicate freely my hopes and fears respecting this desirable opening.

Our first efforts would necessarily be among the Makololo, the composition of which tribe you already know, because they are extremely friendly, and every white man would enjoy perfect security for life and property among them. They are situated on the borders of the true negro family, upon which it is impossible as Christians to look without feelings of the tenderest interest. The numbers of true negroes in the

---

[1] Although never sent, the receipt of Tidman's letter of 24.viii.55 evidently having led D. L. to substitute No. 63, this letter is included here because it embodies his considered views on the possibility of founding a mission station in Central Africa. As some of the contents show, it was certainly drafted after his arrival at Quelimane (20 May), though possibly not as early as the date given at the head. He had left Tete on 22 April.

[2] Now known as the Batoka Plateau (N. Rhodesia).

Interior of the continent are very large, but no estimate can be formed, for no one can tell how far they extend. Their language is unquestionably cognate with the Sichuana and Caffre, and their superstitions — the mere wreck of a primitive faith floating down the stream of time — are everywhere identical.

All seem to possess a strong tendency to religious worship, and a remarkably vivid impression of the continued existence of departed souls. One of them, seeing my men almost overcome by weakness and hunger in killing an elephant, ran to a companion for something to make an offering. He had nothing but snuff, but he poured that out at the root of a tree and prayed to his ancestors for success. When I came up I was informed of the meritorious action, 'as those people with whom you are travelling do not know how to pray'.[1] When we spoke to any of them of God, as the hearer of prayer through Jesus Christ, they always listened with most respectful attention, though they have been accustomed to address departed relatives only. The Supreme Being, as among the Bayeiye on the Zouga, is called Reza and Molungo = the Morimo of the Bechuanas, & Nyampi of the Barotse. He is believed to be the former and governor of all things. The souls of ancestors being, except in cases of witchcraft & lightning, the only authors of evil, their anger is often deprecated by offerings of food. The crime of witchcraft is punished with great severity, and ascertained by the ordeal, the entire number of the accused attesting their innocence, during the drinking of the infusion employed, by holding up their hands to heaven.

The power of their chiefs is by no means absolute, and their laws of succession such as to prevent the tyranny of a grasping unscrupulous father from being perpetuated in the person of his son. The most powerful states which have arisen among them have never attained a high degree of civilization, because destitute of literature. The names sovreign, emperor, &c, which have been applied to Matiamvo, Cazembe, Monomotapa, &c &c, are inappropriate, as these 'potentates' have each less power than our own Sandilla in Caffreland.[2]

They are all fond of agriculture and trade. The women are treated with great consideration, and I believe they generally deserve it. In this opinion I am not influenced by prejudice in favour of the negro race. Not a single improper or impudent expression from a black

---

[1] This incident, which occurred on 14.ii.56, is described more fully in *Travels*, pp. 607–8.

[2] Kazembe is the hereditary title of the ruler of the eastern BaLunda (Luapula valley), and 'Monomotapa' (MweneMutapa) was similarly the title borne by every successive ruler of the VaKaranga in S. Rhodesia. For Sandile and Mwato Yamvo, see above, pp. 218, 297.

woman ever met my ear during a residence of fifteen years among Bechuanas.[1] I should not have been able to say the same had I been a missionary in London. A white man of good 'common sense' may expect kind and civil treatment throughout the Interior till he comes upon the borders of what we call civilization. The natives sometimes even quietly put up with wrong. I knew an instance, in which the eccentricities of a European were manfully borne with on the ground that 'such vapouring conduct shewed him to be insane'!

I mention these points, because I believe they aptly characterize that race which forms the grand nucleus of the population of Africa. I am not to be understood as speaking of them as a people without guile. If they were already good, they would have no need of our labours. But this is the race which more than any other has suffered from the unscrupulous rapacity of the white man. And though it has been a nation scattered and peeled and trodden down for ages, they are so imperishable — they dwell in the presence of all their bretheren — slavery cannot extinguish nor can the white man's diseases decimate them. They really seem preserved for purposes of mercy as much as God's ancient people, the Jews. We did not wipe out all our obligation when we paid twenty millions.[2] We have still a debt of gratitude to Jesus on our own account besides, and there is no greater privilege on earth than, after having had our own chains broken off, to go forth to proclaim liberty to the captives, the opening of the prison to them that are bound.

This river presents an excellent highway into the Interior. In the event of Sekeletu removing to the Kafue or Bashukulompo River, which is six or eight days from Sesheke, we could come or send down canoes to Tete for supplies. Six weeks or two months for going and returning would be sufficient. This in time would be a safe route, but it would always be expensive, in consequence of all European goods coming from Europe by way of Bombay to Mosambique, and to the latter only during the monsoons. There would be no difficulty in coming down to Quilimane, for there is no impediment to canoe navigation except a small cataract about 20 miles above Tete; but the force of the current is such that, though we came from Tete to Senna[3] in five days, it would have taken twenty to ascend again. And the delta of Quilimane

---

[1] Substituted in MS. for 'them', presumably under the influence of the preceding 'fifteen'.

[2] On the abolition of slavery in the British colonies (1833), Parliament had voted £20,000,000 for the payment of compensation to the owners.

[3] Sena, 17° 30′ S., 35° 03′ E., a Portuguese settlement on the Zambesi; roughly midway between Tete and Quelimane. D. L. got there from Tete on 27 April, and left for Quelimane on 11 May (*Travels*, pp. 658, 663).

is very unhealthy. I got very severe tertian fever as soon as we entered it, and am not yet recovered.

The branch called the river of Quilimane can scarcely be named as an arm of the Zambesi. It is not more than three or four yards wide at its point of departure, while there is a mile of water rolling past to Luabo[1] and other ports. It was not so formerly, but the rivulet of Quilimane being filled up for 12 or 15 miles, land carriage is there necessary. We are thus compelled to adopt the most tedious mode of conveyance where the presence of the fever indicates the quickest. The bar of Quilimane, too, is so bad every vessel which enters is in danger of shipwreck. A Hamburgh vessel was lost a short time ago,[2] and on my arrival I learned to my bitter sorrow that eight of the crew of H.M. Brigantine Dart, including the commander and two officers, were lost on the same bar when coming in to pick me up.[3] This has embittered all my joy in reaching Quilimane. I feel as if it would have been easier to have died for them, than to bear the thought of them all cut off from the joys of life on my account.

The state of the population on the river is such as to warrant apprehension in view of ascending it with my family. By the witchery of the slave trade, the attention of Europeans and others was entirely withdrawn from every other source of wealth. Coffee, cotton, sugar, oil, wheat, iron, and even gold, were abandoned for the delusive gains of a trade which rarely enriches, and when that was rendered, by the activity of our cruizers, much more dangerous than gambling for gold, stagnation and decay succeeded. War with the native tribes followed, and, as these were led by men of Portuguese and Asiatic extraction, the commerce of the river was greatly damaged and many of the merchants ruined. The tribes have not been conquered, and this induces most of the independant natives to treat the Portuguese with less respect than formerly. Some of the true Caffre or Zulu family proceed so far as to levy heavy tribute on the inhabitants of Senna, and no merchant can proceed up the river from Tete without paying fines to the chieftains situated there. We experienced considerable difficulty as we approached the Portuguese possessions on this account, for we had no goods where-

---

[1] Immediately above the Zambesi delta, at 18° 30′ S., 36° 10′ E.

[2] 'A Hamburgh bark, the Carmelite, was stranded on the bar, and sold' (MS. Journal, p. 831). D. L. heard this while at Sena.

[3] This must have been about the end of April. The Dart had called at Quelimane in March, picked up the letters D. L. had sent from Tete, and then went on to Moçambique for provisions 'and promised to return again soon' (MS. Journal, p. 836). She left Quelimane for the Cape on 2 May (Thompson to Tidman, 8.vi.56). D. L. heard the news of the accident on reaching Quelimane (MS. Journal, p. 841).

with to pay, though while farther inland we were treated well everywhere. I mention this difficulty, though I have no doubt but that with the influence of God's spirit on the hearts of the heathen it may be surmounted.

By the very great and disinterested kindness of Major T. A. A. Secard,[1] the Governor of Tete, I was enabled to recover from the fatigues of part of the journey by remaining with him till the healthy season began in Quilimane. He also generously furnished food for my numerous retinue, and most of them have obtained employment besides. I regret I could not bring them to the sea. The sight of ships and commerce has such a good effect on their minds, for when they see such examples of our superiority they readily admit that the bible has something in it, for those who read it and bow down before the unseen God *are no fools*'. But Quilimane, like even the most fertile spots in Africa, is subject to periodical famines, because native grain never keeps more than one year. Many thousands perished from hunger during the past season, and the unsettled state of the river rendering it necessary for us to have a lieutenant and gaurd of soldiers for safety, I brought only a few of my companions, and the dearth of provisions renders it necessary for them to return at once to Tete. By this you will percieve that my residence in England must be very short. Too short, I fear, to allow of my being cured of disease of the spleen and kidneys, which has shewn itself in the fevers of the delta. I had not a single symptom of them after the journey to Angola. The sea voyage may, however, set me right.

Reverting again to the fact with which I commenced this letter, I most fervently thank God that I have such news to communicate; for if the gospel be proclaimed to the immense population in the regions beyond, and missionary operations conducted with the same general wisdom and purity which have been exhibited for the last thirty years in the South, it is impossible to estimate the blessings which will thereby descend on Central Africa. The present seems a fair opening into the vast Interior, and one which I earnestly hope will not be neglected by the Christian Church.

My experience leads me to believe that, in so far as life and property are concerned, the field is a safe one. Indeed, no idea can be formed of the state of the central parts from the exterior fringe of illiberal Moors, Boers, and other semi-savages. I never entertained any suspicions of foul play while among pure negroes, and was with one or two excep-

---

[1] Tito Augusto d'Araujo Sicard (*Travels*, p. 628). D. L. met him again on returning to the Zambesi in 1858, and had further occasion to be grateful to him (*The Zambesi and its Tributaries*, 1865, pp. 44–5).

tions always treated politely. Indeed, so thoroughly civil were the more central tribes, I began to think that the statements privately made to certain travellers, of machinations against their lives, were only cunning ruses concocted by the parties from the previously expressed suspicions of the travellers themselves. A missionary of ordinary prudence and tact would certainly secure respect, and, though the negroes be at present much wedded to their superstitions, the blessings of civilization and peace which we convey would before long secure us a good name among all, and the benignant touch of God's Holy Spirit would fill their dark hearts with the light and love of the gospel.

It seems, too, such a Providential opening for South African missionaries. They have been so abundantly blessed in their past labours that it can be truly said of even the stations farthest North, 'Now, heathenism, properly so called, no longer prevails at our principal stations; and a casual observer could not now distinguish between the members of our churches and those who make no profession of religion, beyond merely attending its outward means' (See Report of the Cape Town Auxiliary for 1854, page 55).[1] With the feelings which past success inspires for the still further spread of the glorious gospel, it must have been extremely mortifying to be hemmed in by Boers, who in hindering the gospel of Christ truly know not what they do. Some, however, will very properly prefer the pastoral relation and entire support by their people. But there are no doubt others who, retaining the desire in full force which made them leave their native land to preach the gospel where Christ's name is not known, will hail with joy an opening by which they may still follow the vocation of missionaries to the heathen. If I am not over sanguine in my hope of changes produced by the natural operation of Independant principles, and others which seem called for because heathenism no longer prevails at our principal stations, much may be effected in the new region without any additional outlay on the part of the Society.

It being absolutely necessary to get through this delta during either April, May, June, or July, on account of its well known insalubrity, and also because I have a number of Sekeletu's people waiting for me at Tete, my stay in England must be extremely short. I mention this in order that you may have as much of the short space as possible for any arrangements it may be desirable to make.

I am at present waiting for a passage either to the Cape or to Bombay,

---

[1] The quotation is from a report about Kuruman, written by Ashton (14.i.55) and published in *S.A. Miss. Report, 1854*, pp. 55–7. D. L. presumably found the *Report* among the mail left for him at Quelimane by the *Dart*.

and will transmit this by the readiest conveyance to England. Should it come to hand before myself, you will much oblige me by forwarding the enclosed note to Mrs Livingstone, and giving her directions where she may find quiet lodgings in the outskirts of London. Excuse the trouble and

Believe me, Ever affectionately yours,
David Livingstone

XI

THE END OF THE PILGRIMAGE

63. To ARTHUR TIDMAN
23 May 1856

[National Archives of Rhodesia and Nyasaland. Previous publication: Blaikie, pp. 483–7 (in full)]

Quilimane
23d May 1856

Dear Sir,

Having by the good Providence of our Heavenly Father reached this village on the 20th currt., I was pleased to find a silence of more than four years broken by your letter of the 24th August 1855.[1] I found also that H.M.'s Brigantine Dart had called at this port several times in order to offer me a passage homewards, but on the last occasion in which this most friendly act was performed her commander, with an officer of marines and five seamen, were unfortunately lost on the very dangerous bar at the mouth of the Quilimane River. This sad event threw a cold shade over all the joy I might otherwise have experienced on reaching the Eastern Coast. I felt as if it would have been easier for me to have died for them than to bear the thought of so many being cut off from all the joys of life in generously attempting to render me a service.

As there is no regular means of proceeding from this to the Cape, I remain here in the hope of meeting another cruizer, which the kindness of Commodore Trotter[2] has led me to expect, in preference to going by a small Arab or Portuguese trading vessel to some point on the 'overland route to India'. And though I may possibly reach you as soon

---

[1] The obvious implication is that the letter was awaiting him at Quelimane. But in *MS. Journal*, p. 840, he explicitly states that on reaching Quelimane (20 May) he 'found some letters, but none from my family . . . nor the Directors'; and in Letter 64 he informs Thompson that he received Tidman's letter 'a short time before the arrival of the Frolic'. That ship was at Quelimane early in July (see p. 317). I assume, therefore, that he both heard from and answered Tidman not earlier than about the middle of June. The date given at the head may either be a slip of the pen for '23 June' or, possibly, was copied carelessly from the date on (the unsent) No. 62, which he may have consulted before writing.

[2] Henry Dundas Trotter (1802–59), commodore of the Cape of Good Hope 1854–7 (*D.N.B.*).

313

as a letter, it appears advisable to state in writing my thoughts respecting one or two very important points in your communication.

Accompanied by many kind expressions of approbation, which I highly value on account of having emanated from a body of men whose sole object in undertaking the responsibility and labour of the Direction must have been a sincere desire to promote the interests of the kingdom of our Lord among the Heathen, I find the intimation that the Directors are restricted in their power of aiding plans connected only remotely with the spread of the gospel. And it is added also that even though certain very formidable obstacles should prove surmountable, 'the financial circumstances of the Society are not such as to afford any ground of hope that it would be, within any definite period, in a position to enter upon untried, remote, and difficult, fields of labour'.

If I am not mistaken, these statements imply a resolution on the part of the gentlemen now in the Direction to devote the decreasing income of the Society committed to their charge to parts of the world of easy access, and in which the missionaries may devote their entire time and energies to the dissemination of the truths of the gospel with reasonable hopes of speedy success. This, there can be no doubt, evinces a sincere desire to perform their duty faithfully to their constituents, to the Heathen, and to our Lord and Master. Yet, while still retaining that full conviction of the purity of their motives which no measure adopted during the sixteen years of my connection with the Society has for a moment disturbed, I feel constrained to view 'the untried, remote, and difficult fields', to which I humbly yet firmly believe God has directed my steps, with a resolution widely different from that which their words imply. As our aims and purposes will now appear in some degree divergent — on their part from a sort of paralysis caused by financial decay, and on mine from the simple continuance of an old determination to devote my life and my all to the service of Christ in whatever way he may lead me in Intertropical Africa — it seems natural, while yet without the remotest idea of support from another source, to give some of the reasons for differing with those with whom I have hitherto been so happily connected.

It remains vividly on my memory that some twenty years ago, while musing how I might spend my life so as best to promote the glory of the Lord Jesus, I came to the conclusion that from the cumulative nature of gospel influence the outskirts even of the Empire of China presented the most inviting field for evangelical effort in the world. I was also much averse to being connected with any Society, having a strong desire to serve Christ in circumstances which would free my service from all professional aspect. But the solicitation of friends in whose judgement I had confidence led to my offers of service to the London Missionary Society. The 'Opium War' was then adduced as a reason why that remote, difficult, and untried, field of labour should stand in abeyance before the Interior of Africa, to which, in opposition to my own judgement, I was advised to proceed. I did not, however, go with any sort of reluctance, for I had great respect for the honoured men by whom the advice was given, and unbounded confidence in the special Providence of Him who has said, 'Commit thy way unto the Lord, &c. In all thy ways acknowledge him, and he shall direct thy steps.' I was contented with the way in which I had been led, and happy in the prospect of being made instrumental in winning some souls to Christ.

The Directors wished me to endeavour to carry the gospel to the tribes North of the Kuruman. Having remained at that station sufficient time only to recruit my oxen, I proceeded in the direction indicated, and while learning the language I visited the Bakhatla, Bakwains, Bangwaketze, and Bamangwato tribes, in order to select a suitable locality for a mission, in the hope of succeeding in making a second Kuruman or central station, which would, by God's blessing, influence a large circumference. I chose Mabotsa, and no one who has seen that country since has said the choice was injudicious. The late Revd. Dr Philip alone was opposed to this plan, on account of solicitude for my safety, 'because Mosilikatze was behind the Cashan mountains thirsting for the blood of the first white man who should fall into his hands, and no man would in his sober senses build his house on the crater of a volcano'.[1] Having removed to the Bakwains of Sechele, I spent some of the happiest years of my life in missionary labour, and was favoured in witnessing a gratifying measure of success in the spread of the knowledge of the gospel. The good seed was widely sown, and is not lost. It will yet bear fruit, though I may not live to see it. In the pursuit of my plan I tried to plant among the tribes around by means of native teachers & itineracies. We have heard again and again of a 'preparatory work going on' in India, but whoever heard of such in Africa? A village of 600 or 800 may have one or even two missionaries, with schoolmasters and schoolmistresses, and the nearest population, fifty or one hundred miles off, cannot feel their influence. Believers will not, in many cases, go beyond the circle of their own friends & acquaintances.

I was happy in having two worthy men of colour to aid me in diffusing a knowledge of Christ among the Eastern tribes, but the Boers forbid

---

[1] 'It is said the late Dr Philip, when these Missions were forming, said that it was like building under a volcano' (Inglis to Tidman, 16.x.52).

us to preach unto the gentiles that they might be saved. My attention was turned to Sebituane by Sechele at the very time this happened, but I had no intention of leaving the Bakwains. Droughts succeeded, and these, with perpetual threats and annoyances from the Boers, so completely distracted the mind of the tribe that our operations were almost suspended. It is well known that food for the mind has but little savour for starving stomachs. The famine, and the unmistakeable determination of the Boers to enslave my people, at last made me look to the North seriously. There was no precipitancy. Letters went to and from India respecting my project before resolving to leave,[1] and I went at last after being obliged to send my family to Kuruman in order to be out of the way of a threatened attack of the Boers.[2] When we reached Lake Ngami, about which so much has been said, I immediately asked for guides to take me to Sebituane, because to form a settlement in which the gospel might be planted was the great object for which I had come. Guides were refused, and the Bayeiye were prevented from ferrying me accross the Zouga. I made a raft, but after working in the water for hours it would not carry me. (I have always been thankful, since I knew how alligators abound there, that I was not then killed by one.) Next year affairs were not improved at Kolobeng, and while attempting the North again fever drove us back. In both that and the following year I took my family with me, in order to obviate the loss of time which returning for them would occasion. The Boers subsequently, by relieving me of all my goods, freed me from the labour of returning to Kolobeng at all.

Of the circumstances attending our arrival at Sebituane's, and the project of opening up a path to the coast, you are already so fully aware, from having examined and awarded your approbation, I need scarcely allude to it. Double the time has been expended to that which I anticipated, but as it chiefly arose from sickness the loss of time was unavoidable. The same cause produced interruptions in preaching the gospel — as would have been the case had I been indisposed anywhere else.

The foregoing short notices of all the plans which I can bring to my recollection since my arrival in Africa lead me to the question, which of the plans is it that the Directors particularize when they say they are restricted in their power of aiding plans only remotely connected with the spread of the gospel? It cannot be the last surely, for I had their

---

[1] 'I communicated my intention to an African traveller, Colonel Steele, the aide-de-camp to the Marquis of Tweedale, at Madras, and he made it known to . . . Major Vardon and Mr. Oswell' (*Travels*, p. 46).

[2] But cf. above, p. 130.

express approval before leaving Cape Town, and they yield to none in admiration of the zeal with which it has been executed. Then which is it?

As it cannot be meant to apply in the way of want of funds deciding the suspension of operations which would make the connection remote enough with the spread of the gospel by us, I am at a loss to understand the phraseology, and therefore trust that the difficulty may be explained. The difficulties are mentioned in no captious spirit, though from being at a loss as to the precise meaning of the terms I may appear to be querulous. I am not conscious of any diminution of the respect and affection with which I have always addressed you.

I am yours,
affectionately,
David Livingston

64. To WILLIAM THOMPSON
8 August 1856

[LMS 100. Previous publication: Chamberlin, pp. 258–62 (almost complete)]

At sea
H.M. Brig Frolic
8th August 1856[1]

My dear Friend,

I could not have been more surprised by your own personal appearance at Quilimane than I was by that of George Fleming on the 10th ult., and when I witnessed all the kind preparations you had made for my comfort in travel it appeared like a scene we see in dreaming.[2] I had begun to fancy my letters contained an order forthwith to return whence I had come. On perusal, however, I found that I am somewhat to blame, in not stating explicitly my intention to go from Tette to Quilimane soon after the dispatch of my letters, and thence proceed to

---

[1] D. L. had left Quelimane on 12 July (*Travels*, p. 682).

[2] D. L.'s letters from Tete were received at Cape Town, through the *Dart*, at the end of May. 'In none of the letters was there any reference as to what his future plans were likely to be.' Rutherfoord therefore suggested to Thompson that Fleming should be hired to go to Quelimane with supplies and with instructions to 'proceed in quest of' D. L. if he had not yet reached that port. The naval authorities at the Cape gave Fleming a passage in the *Frolic*, which left Simonstown on 8 June (Thompson to Tidman, 8.vi.56). 'As the village [Quelimane] is twelve miles from the bar, and the weather was rough, she was at anchor ten days before we knew of her presence, about seven miles from the entrance to the port' (*Travels*, p. 681).

England. I had mentioned my plans so often I unfortunately took it for granted that all my friends knew them perfectly, and when the Tett[e] packet left I intended to proceed down the river in a few days afterwards. Indeed, I fully expected to overtake it at Quilimane, but my good friend Major T. A. d'A. Sicard, the Commandant of Tette, generously advised me to remain untill the beginning of the healthy season in the delta, viz. April.

I was not without need of rest, for our cattle having all been killed by tsetse I had a severe spell of trudging on foot, and had become tired and thin enough. My men got food from the worthy Major, and employment in carrying wood, & in canoe work also. About 16 came down with me to Senna. Eight returned thence to Tette, and eight came to Quilimane, but were glad to go back too, for there was a famine in the land which cut off thousands. My head man, named Sekwebu, I have taken with me — a sensible worthy heathen, but for whose tact and knowledge of the Zambesi language I might not have been here today.[1] The rest, about 110, are to remain at Tette till I return to take them to their own land again.

Such was my plan; but a short time before the arrival of the Frolic I got a letter from the Directors, by way of Mosambique, in which I am told that 'they are restricted in their power of aiding plans connected only remotely with the spread of the gospel'. And they add that, even though certain obstacles (fever, tsetse, &c) should prove surmountable, 'the financial circumstances of the Society are not such as to afford any ground of hope that it would be in a position within any definite period to undertake untried, remote, and difficult, fields of labour'. I had imagined in my simplicity that both my preaching, conversation, and travel, were as nearly connected with the spread of the gospel as the Boers would allow them to be. The plan of opening up a path from either the East or West coast for the teeming population of the Interior was submitted to their judgement, and secured their formal approbation. I have been seven times in peril of my life from savage men while laboriously and without swerving pursuing that plan, and never doubted but that I was in the path of duty. Indeed, so clearly did I percieve that I was performing good service to the cause of Christ, I wrote to my brother that I would perish rather than fail in my enterprise. I shall not

---

[1] 'Sekwebu had been captured by the Matabele when a little boy, and the tribe in which he was a captive, had migrated to the country near Tete; he had travelled along both banks of the Zambesi several times, and was intimately acquainted with the dialects spoken there. I found him to be a person of great prudence and sound judgment' (*Travels*, p. 513). In *MS. Journal*, p. 547, he is called a 'Letibele' (sing. of MaTebele).

boast of what I have done, but the wonderful mercies I have recieved will constrain me to follow out the work in spite of the veto of the Board. If it is according to the will of God, means will be provided from other quarters.

I recieved all the articles sent in charge of Captain Peyton[1] and George Fleming, as noted in the lists which accompanied them. Some, as the clothing for myself, bedding, stockings, &c, were most welcome, and did not come certainly before they were needed. Some woolen articles, and others which would spoil by keeping, I directed to be sold, and others, as the desk and work-box, I left at Quilimane for future use. The money, viz. fifty sovreigns and 500 Spanish dollars, I took with me.[2] I have some debts against me up the river for clothing &c, of which, though my kind friends there refused to give a formal account, I consider myself bound to repay by bringing articles which I know they require. As I could not settle my affairs at once, I leave it for a future time. About 18 tusks belonging to Sekeletu are left also in charge of Colonel Galdino José Nunes,[3] in whose house I lived at Quilimane, with orders to sell them in case of my death and remit the proceeds to Sekeletu. The money from you I reserve for oceanic use. The dollars are said to be worth 4/2 or 4/1 only at the Mauritius, though you gave, I hear, 4/6 for them. Rather than part with them at such a loss I shall, if not needed as passage money, keep them for the Zambesi again. I suppose all goes down to my account with the Society. I prefer the overland passage to that by the Cape, because I have a chance of a free passage from one of the companies, P. O. O.[4] I believe, and none from the common vessels which pass your way. I wish to come back without any delay in England.

I was happy to see Ralph's name among those who recieved prizes at the College. Hope he will profit largely by the mental discipline he now enjoys, and become fit to serve our great Creator in his day and generation.[5] How are the other two little Hottentots, Jessie & Willie? If they

---

[1] Lumley Woodyear Peyton, (acting) commander of the *Frolic*, a 16 gun sloop stationed at Simonstown, Cape of Good Hope (*Navy List*, April 1856, pp. 46, 152).

[2] The *Frolic* 'brought abundant supplies for all my need; and 150 *l.* to pay my passage home, from my kind friend Mr. Thompson ... The Admiral at the Cape kindly sent an offer of a passage to the Mauritius, which I thankfully accepted' (*Travels*, p. 681).

[3] 'One of the best men in the country' (*Travels*, p. 672).

[4] Peninsular and Oriental, and Orient, Steam Navigation Company.

[5] Ralph Wardlaw Thompson (1842–1916), Thompson's eldest son, was then a student at the South African College, Cape Town; he subsequently became Foreign Secretary of the LMS, 1881–1914 (B. Mathews, *Dr. Ralph Wardlaw Thompson*, 1917, p. 11, 15, 46 ff.).

lag behind Ralph, and I am obliged to write about them in a book, I shall give them Boer names, as having no Wardlaw blood in them. 'My dear wife', you say; and I knew not you had one.[1] Of course I fell into a quandary as to who had taken charge of you, if she had a long nose or red hair, or squinted, but I was obliged at last to recieve the compliments with thanks, though only from as yet an abstract idea.

12th August.

We came into Port Luis,[2] Mauritius, this afternoon. A lovely island it seems, but not nearly so fertile looking as the banks of the Zambesi (inland). I cannot, of course, give any notice of my future, but may tomorrow. I intend to live on board Frolic till I sail homewards, for I had a little touch of my African fever yesterday, & the purer the air the better. I shall visit Mr Lebrun[3] when I can, & see his Malagassi. At St Augustine's Bay[4] we saw many of them. They resemble closely the better classes of Makololo, and many words in their tongue shew them to be true negroes. The French are causing them to emigrate to Bourbon[5] by promise of wages & facilities for returning. It seems all fair and above board work, for they had an official of the French Govt. aboard to see that none but free men were taken.

Respecting George Fleming, I suppose it will be best to settle with him in Cape Town, for besides not having more money than I may need, supposing I get not a free passage, the agreement[6] does not specify what was to be given, supposing he was required to do no more than has happened. Here he has able seaman's pay as Captain's servant. He serves me too. He came to Quilimane with another man of colour, who left us at St Augustine's Bay. He would have found no difficulty in going to Tete, as it is all fair sailing, though against the stream. Whatever you think proper to give, please put it to my account. I have full confidence in your discretion. I only feel sorry that my not noticing my plans in the Tette packet should have caused you so much anxiety and perplexity.

[1] Thompson's first wife, a daughter of Dr Ralph Wardlaw, had died in 1849 (*Register*, p. 38). In June 1853 he married again, his new wife being a Miss Tunstall, in charge of an LMS school in Cape Town (Thompson to Tidman, 20.viii.53).

[2] Port Louis, 20° 10′ S., 57° 30′ E., the capital of Mauritius.

[3] Jean Joseph Lebrun (1789–1865), LMS missionary in Mauritius 1814–33, LMS agent there 1841–65 (*Dict. of Mauritian Biography*, p. 212; *Register*, p. 10). His 'Malagassi' were mostly emancipated slaves, but included Christian refugees from Madagascar, which the LMS had been forced to abandon (1836).

[4] St Augustin (Madagascar), 23° 31′ S., 43° 46′ E.

[5] The island of Réunion, 400 miles S.E. of Madagascar.

[6] Between Thompson and Fleming, dated Cape Town 3.vi.56, and specifying the terms of the latter's engagement (LMS 98).

I send letters for the Kuruman along with this. Sekwebu's mind seems affected by the marvels he sees. The steamer which took us into the port was a terrible apparition to him. All are very kind to him. One who went to Loanda became insane also, but recovered in a few days, as I hope Sekwebu will.[1]

Remember me kindly to Captain Holmes, and thank him for a letter of recommendation he kindly sent for Mr Azevedo.[2] That gentleman was not at Quilimane, but I met him three days beyond, near his estate, and with his well known benevolence he lent me a covered boat, which was extremely acceptable to me suffering from a raging fever.

Is your sister married too?

Ever affectionately yours,
David Livingstone

65. To ARTHUR TIDMAN
26 August 1856

[Original missing; copied from *Chronicle*, vol. xx, (November) 1856, p. 241]

Claremont, Mauritius
26th August 1856

My dear Sir,

I am happy to inform you that, by the favour of God, I am thus far on my way home. I came from Quilimane to this island in H.M. brig 'Frolic', Commander Peyton, from whom and his officers I received much kindness. Here I have enjoyed the hospitality of Major-General Hay,[3] and am fast recovering from an affection of the spleen left by fever caught in the Quilimane delta. I hope to embark next month for some point in the overland passage, that being a shorter way than by the Cape, and am

Affectionately yours,
David Livingston

---

[1] Shortly after this was written, Sekwebu, driven 'insane' by his rough experience of sea travel, committed suicide by drowning (17.viii.56 Moffat: *Fam. Letters*, ii, pp. 290–1; cf. *Travels*, pp. 682–3 and, for the other case mentioned, p. 409).

[2] 'A man who is well known by all who ever visited Kilimane, and who was presented with a gold chronometer watch by the Admiralty, for his attentions to English officers' (*Travels*, p. 671).

[3] Charles Murray Hay (1802–64), commander of the garrison in Mauritius 1855–1857 (*Dict. of Mauritian Biography*, pp. 586–7).

66. To WILLIAM THOMPSON
17 September 1856

[LMS 101. Previous publication: Chamberlin, pp. 262–4 (incomplete)]

Claremont, Maurituis
17th Septr. 1856

My dear Mr Thompson,

I have, as you will see by the date, remained here considerably longer than I intended, but having arrived with a severe affection of the spleen, a consequence of the fever in the Quilimane delta, and finding that this climate was proving curative, I have delayed my departure till the present time. I have been most kindly and hospitably entertained by Major-General Hay, and as his house is situated about five miles from Port Luis, and on an elevated spot with a cool climate, it has answered the end of completely curing me. I had but two returns of tertian, and the pain in the spleen is quite gone. I am ready to go back to Africa again, thanks to the Author of all our mercies, not forgetting the good kind-hearted man with whom I am living.

I have had another object in view besides health, viz. a wish to see the Commodore and thank him for his kindness.[1] I wished also to talk to him about Africa, as I intend to work still in that poor trodden-down country, even without the aid of our Society, if I can only get back again. I got a letter at Quilimane, the only one since I saw you last, and I am informed that 'the Directors are restricted in their power of aiding plans connected only remotely with the spread of the gospel', and also that even 'though certain obstacles (as fever, tsetse, &c) should prove surmountable, the financial circumstances of the Society are not such as to warrant the hope that it would be in a position within any definite period to undertake untried, remote, and difficult, fields of labour'. As these statements are embalmed in some flattering sentences of approbation respecting my late efforts in opening up the continent to the sympathies of the friends of Christianity, I suppose that it is intended to send me to to some of the tried, near, and easy, fields, where I may wax fat and kick like Jeshurun.[2]

As the proposition, to leave the untried remote and difficult fields of labour as they have been ever since our Saviour died for the poor sinners who inhabit them, involves my certain severance from the L. M. S.,

---

[1] As mentioned below, Commodore Trotter was 'expected daily' at Mauritius (p. 323).

[2] Deut. 32: 15.

and the attempt to support myself and return in the best way I can, I have given a certificate to George Fleming for the money, viz. 500 Spanish dollars and fifty sovreigns, which you sent, and which I told you in another letter I meant to retain for the homeward voyage. I go 'overland', because I have a hope of a free passage part of the way. If I am not successful in obtaining that, then there will be but little over.

I leave a waggon and about 18 oxen at Linyanti, another at Cape Town, which does not seem to have been repaired according to promise & will not sell for much.[1] I managed to get through all my clothing &c &c before I got to Quilimane, but have a sextant, chronometer watch, and double-barrelled gun, and about £50 of debts of honour to black men, so am not exactly in the position of the prodigal returning to his father, but am poorer considerably than when I landed in Africa some sixteen years ago. Yet I shall leave you without abuse of any sort. The Directors have always treated me well, and I shall always remember you all with affection.

I am sorry Fleming was engaged so firmly as in the agreement. I cannot get rid of it. He was entered as Captain's servant at Quilimane, and recieves about 1/6 a day (about £2 per month) for that, but says, 'that is nothing, he is engaged at £10 per month till he gets to the Cape',[2] and will insist on the fulfillment of the written agreement. I wished to make an arrangement with a Captain going to the Cape, whereby his services would be taken as part of his passage money, but he objects to this because 'they would make him do everything', i.e. in working the ship. I proposed to stipulate for personal service alone to the Captain, but he said, No, let the passage be paid, and no terms made respecting his service. The agreement specifies services to Captain Peyton, and that he is to be under my controul,[3] but he sticks to the £10 per month as the part most agreable to his ideas of the proper fulfillment of his duties. I would have sent him off at once on our arrival here, but the Commodore was expected daily, and Captain Peyton wished to take him to the Cape free of expense.

[1] In 1858 D. L. presented the Cape Town wagon (a gift from Oswell) to his brother-in-law J. S. Moffat (*The Matabele Mission*, ed. Wallis, 1945, p. 4).

[2] The agreement specified (clause 8) that Thompson would pay Fleming 'the sum of ten (£10) pounds sterling a month, reckoning from the 1st June 1856, and ten pounds for an outfit' (LMS 98).

[3] Clause 1 of the agreement reads: 'Mr Fleming undertakes to proceed to Quilimane in H.M. Sloop of War the "Frolic", and to render any assistance that may be in his power to the Commander during his stay on board that vessel, and to the Revd. Dr. Livingstone whenever and wherever he may find him, placing himself entirely under the direction of that gentleman to serve him an any capacity he may desire.'

It is unfortunate that Fleming was engaged at all, as he is a most unlikely person to go anywhere in the face of danger; but this you could not know, and I should probably have been as much mislead in respect to his travelling abilities as you, but for my intercourse with him in the way to Linyanti. He requires one on whom he can lean; deprived of that, he has no self-reliance whatever.

I am sorry, too, that my statements respecting going to England were not more specific, thereby causing you much anxiety on my account. I thank you heartily and sincerely for all the trouble you put yourself to, and pray that God may abundantly reward you.

Affectionately yours,
David Livingston

I enclose a certificate in the way of business. The lists are left at Quilimane. I took a part of the articles for immediate use.

28th. Put George Fleming on board the Irene today, & paid £10 for his passage.

[Enclosure]

Claremont, Mauritius
17th Septr. 1856

I do hereby certify that I recieved from the Revd. William Thompson, as agent for the London Missionary Society, the sum of five hundred (500) Spanish dollars and fifty (50) sovreigns, while I was at the village of Quilimane, and also goods as clothing for myself, beads, writing materials, &c, to the value of (as per accounts left at Quilimane).

(Signed) David Livingston.

I have paid £10 for his (Fleming's) passage to the Cape.

D. L.

67. To WILLIAM THOMPSON
31 October 1856

[LMS 103. Previous publication: Chamberlin, pp. 264–5]

On board S. S. England
31st Octr. 1856

My dear Mr Thompson,

Having left the Mauritius on the 22d, we now find ourselves within two days of Galle,[1] and as we may find the steamer for Aden about to

---

[1] A port on the S.W. coast of Ceylon.

leave as we enter that port, I prepare a note to let you know of my progress thus far. I believe I let you know, by a letter per George Fleming, that I had by my sojourn at Mauritius got completely over an affection of the spleen, entailed on me by frequent attacks of fever. This happy result was owing, by God's blessing, to the salubrity of Claremont, the residence of Major-General Hay, whose hospitality I shall ever remember with gratitude. I saw but little of Mr Le Brun, but hear he has been very useful in Mauritius and is deservedly respected. I saw less of his sons.[1] One lately went to Seychelles with his wife, who is consumptive. The Bishop has gone thither also, in the Frolic, but for religious purposes.[2]

As I was five miles from town, I did not form many acquaintances, and have for a long time been longing most ardently for reunion with my family. As for the future, I can say nothing. I shall let you know how I shall act when I have seen my way clear myself.

If you are writing to Kuruman, I shall feel obliged by your mentioning that I am so far well and on my way home. Also, if George Fleming is near you, say (as he cannot write or read what is written) that he must look after ten shillings, which he directed a man of the Frolic called Muno, or some such name, to recieve and pay to Mrs Wright[3] for my washing. Muno recieved the money as directed, but told Mrs W. that George owed it to him, and I had to pay Mrs W. another ten shillings instead. Muno is a coloured man, and George will know him by this if I have mistaken the name. My peacoat which you sent from the Cape is gone, & a new blanket is substituted by an old one, which served me all the way from Loanda and was given to the poor fellow who drowned himself. Another is taken away, which I prized as that thrown over me by Sekeletu during a terrible storm.[4] I don't know whether these things have been stolen or not in the Frolic. The parcel does not seem to have been touched. But about the money there can be no doubt, & George can manage that when the Frolic comes to the Cape.

Believe me,
affectionately yours,
David Livingston

[1] John J., and Peter, both of whom were then also LMS missionaries in Mauritius. John's wife died in August 1857 (*Register*, pp. 58, 63-4).
[2] This refers to Vincent William Ryan (1816-88), Bishop of Mauritius 1854-67; he had left for the Seychelles on 11 October on a 'visitation tour' (*D.N.B.*; Ryan, *Mauritius and Madagascar*, 1864, p. 42).
[3] Not identified.
[4] This incident (described in *Travels*, p. 516) occurred early in November 1855, on the way from Dinyanti to Sesheke (which D. L. left for the East Coast on the 13th).

Misfortunes don't come alone. My sextant got smashed by George putting it to the tiller below. He had packed it without [my (?)] knowing. Tell Mr Maclear my misfortune.

3rd Novr. Found the Nubia ready to sail for Suez at Galle yesterday. Will sail today at 4 o'clock.[1]

[1] From Galle, D. L. sailed to Suez; thence he travelled overland to Alexandria, where he boarded the *Candia*; at Tunis he changed to the *Elbeji*, for Marseilles, then went by rail across France, landed at Dover, and ultimately reached London on 9 December (*Fam. Letters*, ii, pp. 293–4).

LIST OF MAIN REFERENCES

THE following list does not include all works cited in the footnotes, but only those bearing directly on Livingstone, the L.M.S., and southern Africa.

MANUSCRIPT SOURCES

(A) D. LIVINGSTONE: Journal 1853–6 (owned by Dr H. F. Wilson, St Fillans, Perthshire)

(B) D. LIVINGSTONE: Letters to H. Drummond (LMS archives), R. Hayward (Livingstone Memorial, Blantyre), J. MacLehose (National Library of Scotland, Edinburgh), A. Murray (Union Archives, Pretoria), T. Prentice (Rhodes-Livingstone Museum, Livingstone), B. Pyne (National Library, Edinburgh), D. G. Watt (LMS archives, Rhodes-Livingstone Museum [13.ii.48], Livingstone Memorial [18.viii.50])

(C) Letters to Directors and Officers of the L.M.S. from W. Ashton, R. Edwards, J. J. Freeman, W. Inglis, R. Moffat, A. H. Potgieter, W. Thompson (LMS archives)

(D) Minutes of Meetings of the Griqua and Bechuana District Committee, 1844–8 annually (LMS archives)

PUBLISHED WORKS

AGAR-HAMILTON, J. A. I. *The Native Policy of the Voortrekkers*. Cape Town, 1928

BLAIKIE, W. G. *The Personal Life of David Livingstone*. London, 1880

BREUTZ, P. L. *The Tribes of Marico District*. Pretoria, 1953

British Parliamentary Papers. *Further Correspondence re State of the Orange River Territory* (1852–3, LXVI.1646; 1854, XLIII.1758)

CAMPBELL, J. *Travels in South Africa*. London, 1815

Travels in South Africa . . . Second Journey. 2 vols. London, 1822

CAMPBELL, R. J. *Livingstone*. London, 1929

Cape of Good Hope Almanac and Annual Register for 1852. Cape Town, 1851

CHAMBERLIN, D. (ed.) *Some Letters from Livingstone 1840–1872*. London, 1940

CHAPMAN, J. *Travels in the Interior of South Africa*. 2 vols. London, 1868

CUMMING, R. G. *Five Years of a Hunter's Life in the Far Interior of South Africa*. 2 vols. London, 1850

DEBENHAM, F. *The Way to Ilala: David Livingstone's Pilgrimage*. London, 1955

DOKE, C. M. *Bantu: Modern Grammatical, Phonetical, and Lexicographical Studies*. London, 1945

ELLENBERGER, D. F. *History of the Basuto, Ancient and Modern*. London, 1912

FRASER, ALICE Z. *Livingstone and Newstead*. London, 1913

FREEMAN, J. J. *A Tour in South Africa.* London, 1851

GLUCKMAN, M. 'The Lozi of Barotseland in North-Western Rhodesia', pp. 1–93 of *Seven Tribes of British Central Africa* (ed. E. Colson and M. Gluckman). London, 1951

GROVES, C. P. *The Planting of Christianity in Africa. Vol. II: 1840–1878.* London, 1954

JALLA, A. *Litaba za Sicaba za Ma-Lozi.* 3rd ed. Sefula, 1934

JOUSSE, T. *La Mission Française au Sud de l'Afrique.* 2 vols. Paris, 1889

KIRBY, P. R. (ed.) *The Diary of Dr. Andrew Smith .. 1834–1836.* 2 vols. Cape Town, 1939, 1940

LANGUAGE, F. J. 'Herkoms en Geskiedenis van die Tlhaping', *African Studies*, vol. i (1942), pp. 115–33

LE ROUX, S. D. *Pioneers and Sportsmen of South Africa 1760–1890.* Salisbury (S. Rhodesia), 1939

LIVINGSTONE, D. (Unsigned) Article on L.M.S. Institutions in the Cape Colony, *Brit. Quarterly Rev.*, vol. xiv (1851), pp. 106–13

Missionary Travels and Researches in South Africa. London, 1857

Family Letters 1841–1856, ed. I. Schapera. 2 vols. London, 1959

and C. *Narrative of an Expedition to the Zambesi and its Tributaries.* London, 1865

See CHAMBERLIN, MONK, SCHAPERA, WALLIS

LONDON MISSIONARY SOCIETY. *A Register of Missionaries, Deputations, etc., from 1796 to 1923.* Fourth ed., by J. Sibree. London, 1923

Letter of Instructions, &c. [n.d.]

Report of the Missions in South Africa ... in connection with the London Missionary Society. Cape Town, 1850–55. [Annually; ed. W. Thompson]

The Missionary Magazine and Chronicle, vols. iv–xxi (1840–57)

*The Report of the Directors to the .. General Meeting.... * Annually, 1840–57, [etc.]

LOVETT, R. *The History of the London Missionary Society, 1795–1895.* 2 vols. London, 1899

MCCULLOCH, MERRAN. *The Southern Lunda and Related Peoples.* London, 1951

MACKENZIE, J. *Ten Years North of the Orange River.* Edinburgh, 1871

Austral Africa: losing it or ruling it. 2 vols. London, 1887

MARAIS, J. S. *The Cape Coloured People 1652–1937.* London, 1939

METHUEN, H. H. *Life in the Wilderness; or, Wanderings in South Africa.* 2nd ed. London, 1848. (1st ed., 1846)

MILLER, O. B. *The Woody Plants of the Bechuanaland Protectorate.* Kirstenbosch, 1952. (Reprinted from *Journal of South African Botany*, vol. xviii)

MOFFAT, J. S. *The Lives of Robert and Mary Moffat.* London, 1885

MOFFAT, R. *Missionary Labours and Scenes in Southern Africa.* London, 1842

See SCHAPERA, WALLIS

LIST OF MAIN REFERENCES

MONK, W. (ed.) *Dr. Livingstone's Cambridge Lectures*. 2nd ed. Cambridge, 1860 (1st ed., 1858)

OSWELL, W. E. *William Cotton Oswell*. 2 vols. London, 1900

SCHAPERA, I. 'Short History of the BaNgwaketse', *African Studies*, vol. i (1942), pp. 1–26

'Notes on the History of the Kaa', *Ibid.*, vol. iv (1945), pp. 109–21

The Ethnic Composition of Tswana Tribes. London, 1952

The Tswana. London, 1953

SCHAPERA, I. (ed.) *Ditirafalô tsa Merafe ya BaTswana*. Lovedale, 1940

Apprenticeship at Kuruman . . . Journals and letters of Robert and Mary Moffat 1820–1828. London, 1951

Livingstone's Private Journals 1851–1853. London, 1960

SEAVER, G. *David Livingstone: his Life and Letters*. London, 1957

SMITH, A. *See* KIRBY

SMITH, E. W. *Great Lion of Bechuanaland: the Life and Times of Roger Price, Missionary*. London, 1951

THEAL, G. M. *History of South Africa*, vols. V–VII. New ed., London, 1926–7

WALLIS, J. P. R. (ed.) *The Matabele Journals of Robert Moffat 1829–1860*. 2 vols. London, 1945

The Zambesi Expedition of David Livingstone 1858 to 1863. 2 vols. London, 1956

WELLINGTON, J. H. *Southern Africa: a geographical study*. 2 vols. Cambridge, 1955

WILLIAMS, A. F. *Some Dreams Come True*. Cape Town, [1948]

INDEX